The Notorious Sir John Hill

The Notorious Sir John Hill

The Man Destroyed by Ambition in the Era of Celebrity

George Rousseau

LEHIGH UNIVERSITY PRESS
Bethlehem

Published by Lehigh University Press
Co-published with The Rowman & Littlefield Publishing Group, Inc.
4501 Forbes Boulevard, Suite 200, Lanham, Maryland 20706
www.rowman.com

10 Thornbury Road, Plymouth PL6 7PP, United Kingdom

British Library Cataloguing in Publication Information Available

Library of Congress Cataloging-in-Publication Data

Rousseau, G. S. (George Sebastian)
The notorious Sir John Hill : the man destroyed by ambition in the era of celebrity / George Rousseau.
p. cm.
"Co-published with the Rowman & Littlefield Publishing Group, Inc. "—T.p. verso.
Includes bibliographical references and index.
ISBN 978-1-61146-120-6 (cloth : alk. paper) — ISBN 978-1-61146-121-3 (electronic)
1. Hill, John, 1714?–1775. 2. Humanists—England—Biography. 3. England—Intellectual life—18th century. 4. Authors, English—18th century—Biography. 5. Botanists—Great Britain—Biography. I. Title.
CT788.H54R68 2012
942.07092—dc23
[B]

2012004926

∞™ The paper used in this publication meets the minimum requirements of American National Standard for Information Sciences—Permanence of Paper for Printed Library Materials, ANSI/NISO Z39.48-1992.

Printed in the United States of America

For John Francis Sturley, who kept saying that
John Hill's story should be told, and who is also a second son

Contents

Introduction

"Sir" John Hill (1714–1775) was one of Georgian England's most vilified men despite having contributed prolifically to its medicine, science, and literature. Born into a humble Northamptonshire family, the son of an impecunious God-fearing Anglican minister, he started out as an apothecary, went on to collect natural objects for the great Whig lords and became a botanist of distinction. But his scandalous behavior prevented his election to the Royal Society and entry to all other professions for which he was qualified. Today, we can understand his actions as the result of a personality disorder; then he was understood entirely in moral terms. When he saw the die cast he turned to journalism and publication, and strove maniacally to succeed without patronage. As a writer he was also cut down in ferocious "paper wars." Yet by the time he died, he had been knighted by the Swedish monarch and become a household name among scientists and writers throughout Britain and Europe. His life was a series of paradoxes without coherence, perhaps because he was above all a provocateur.

In time he would also become a filter for the century in which he lived: its personalities—great and small—as well as the broad canvas of its culture, and for this reason any biography necessarily stretches beyond the man himself to those whose profiles he illuminates. He typified the often-comic ardor of trying to make something of yourself without education and connections. By courting celebrities (Fielding, Johnson, Hogarth, Garrick, Sterne, Hans Sloane, Linnaeus, the major London printers and publishers) and crossing swords with England's institutions (the Royal Society, the British Museum, all the learned societies), he would also serve as a channel for future historians in search of them as well as the era's underbelly and cultural power brokers. He was not just "famous" or "infamous" so much as a conduit to the galleries of personalities with whom he interacted: botanists and naturalists, literati and dunces, patrons and underlings, the good and the great, and such colorful but still shadowy figures as William Stukeley (the advocate of Stonehenge), Emanuel Mendes da Costa (the Jewish embezzler and secretary of the Royal Society repeatedly jailed), the temperamental Earl of Bute (the dethroned prime minister then also known as the "Maecenas of Botany"), and many others. Without Hill it would be less apparent today what the stakes for fame had been like in eighteenth-century England, especially in metropolitan London.

The Notorious Sir John Hill is the first biography of this incongruous figure, set into the context of the developing celebrity culture of his era. George Rousseau draws upon letters, diaries, and dozens of anonymous tracts to recreate Hill's tortured life and the varieties of vilification his contemporaries heaped on him, as well as to pinpoint his ambition's psychological toll.

Acknowledgments

I could not have written this book without relying on its archival predecessor: *The Letters and Papers of Sir John Hill* (New York: AMS, 1982), which I compiled over two decades, and the huge Mendes da Costa archive in the British Library (*DAC*). More information has been amassed since publication of the former in 1982, and I hope most of the gaps in that collection have been spotted and corrected here. Future students will doubtlessly discover further lapses, but I alone remain responsible for the materials and interpretations presented in this book.

The material on which this first biography is based has also depended on many persons and libraries. The below list acknowledges the tip of an iceberg, and I regret that many of these figures are no longer alive to read my acknowledgment: Hugh Amory, Catherine Armet (Bute Archives), Nicholas Bennett (vice-chancellor and librarian, Lincoln Cathedral), Leila Brownfield, Richard Brummitt, Adam Budd (Edinburgh), E. J. Burford, the Marquess of Bute (Mount Stuart, Rothesay, Scotland), Ray Desmond (Kew Gardens Museum and History Project, London), Richard Dillon (Sutro Library, San Francisco), Karl Erikkssen (librarian of the Swedish Medical Academy, Stockholm), Susan Evans, Joseph Ewan, Victor Eyles, J. M. Farrar (County Record Office, Cambridge), Mordechai Feingold, Jane Flick, Kevin Fraser, Eric Freeman (Wellcome Library), Roger Hambridge, David Haycock, Blanche Henrey, Patricia Hernlund, Mary Hyde (Viscountess Eccles), David Johnson, Leslie Kerr (Society for the Encouragement of Arts, Manufactures and Commerce), Joseph Kiefer, Michael Kinch, John H. Langbein, J. Leo Lemay, Colin LeMessurier (genealogist), Richard Lutes, T. J. McCann, M. E. Novak, Hugh Ormsby-Lennon, Richard Palmer, Ronald Paulson, Roger Powell (genealogist), Roy Porter, James Reveal (botany, University of Maryland), Pat Rogers, Ronald

Rompkey, Lynn Sbiroli, Beverly Schneller, William Schupbach (Wellcome Trust Library), William Stearn, Joy Thomas (the Society of Barbers and Surgeons, London), Karina Williamson, Jennifer Willis, and Helmut Watzlawick. I thank all for their generosity and kindness.

Also, David Johnson and Peter Magnusson, who were research assistants working on Hill with me at Harvard in the early days, and, later on, Roger Hambridge and Leila Brownfield at UCLA; the late Roy Porter who continued to think Hill's story worth telling, and was even so puckish as to promote Hill's name among London publishers who ought to have interested themselves in a biography of this figure; the many librarians and staff members of the Bodleian Library, British Library, Bürgerbibliothek Bern in Switzerland, Bute Archives in Mount Stuart Scotland, William Andrews Clark Memorial Library, Houghton Library, Linnaean Society, UCLA Special Collections, and the Wellcome Trust Library.

I owe special debts to four of these scholars. David Haycock, Stukeley's biographer, toiled in many archives for the Hill-Stukeley relation before his own exemplary biography of Stukeley appeared, and clarified how important Stukeley had been for Hill. Beverly Schneller, one of our most learned students of mid-eighteenth-century print culture, helped me understand Hill's most important publisher, Mary Cooper. Maximillian E. Novak, my former colleague at UCLA for three decades, whose own biography of Defoe remains a model of scholarly biography at its pinnacle, shed light on Henry Baker, Defoe's son-in-law. Dr. Norland Berk, a New York–based psychiatrist, teased out Hill's "dark side" more proficiently than anyone I know and put flesh on his neuroses.

One name, the late Betty Rizzo's, stands solitary among the scholars. Sadly, she cannot read the fruits of her own labor on Hill. She plied me with primary Hillian materials for more than three decades, and until the time of her recent death continued to think it no less than *scandalous* that Hill, however infamous and notorious and prone to scandal himself, had been "written out." Just before she died, I promised her to persist and I wish she could see that her years of collecting have not been in vain.

I owe another kind of debt to my two editors in Bethlehem, Pennsylvania: Monica Najar and Paul Scott Gordon, who took on the biography in the first place; and to David Baker in Oxford, England, who prepared the illustrations for publication and dealt with many aspects of the digital preparation of the manuscript. And still another to Rosemary and Richard Briant who gave me the use of Rose Cottage, deep in the Black Mountains of Wales, over three summers where many of these chapters were drafted. But my greatest debt remains, as always, to my partner, John Frances Sturley, who sustained my effort beyond the call of filial duty.

Preface

Every generation raises up figures who defy the categories of explanation of their times. John Hill (1714–1775) was one, and no single label or prototype adequately explained him to his contemporaries, or unfolds his life for us today. Existing historical models can capture Hill the quack, Hill the apothecary, Hill the botanist, Hill the hack; Hill the adventurer, the man-about-town, the rascal, and so forth; but not the flesh-and-blood composite Hill who was the amalgam of these as he lived his life, day to day, year in and year out over six decades. This first biography aims to do that without recourse to any fixed paradigm presenting a coherent Hill.

Hill was incoherent: jagged at the edges, even by his own inconsistent standards, especially his character in relation to his system of values and the socioeconomic realities under which he functioned. If my approach appears eclectic it is because I have tried to identify the strands and organize them into patterns recognizable to readers today without falling into the mousetrap of consistency—the last thing I want to claim for Hill's life. But I have not sought to reduce him to "essential Hill" or know him in the novelist's sense. This is a first biography, not a novel, and I try not to tidy up his oddities, or court his replication, repetitiveness, and voluminosity.

Such a book might appear dispensable if Hill's life had not shed such unexpected light on the extraordinary interconnectedness of life and letters, especially the developing professions of science and medicine in mid-eighteenth-century England. Each of these disciplinary areas has been cultivated with great expertise in our time; but the mid-Georgian figures who actually straddled these borders and—more crucially—whose careers demonstrated the perils of seeking success in several fields, are few and far between.

A list can be compiled, especially of doctors as men of letters, where Hill must be included, but none will have been as notorious.

The Bodleian Library Catalogue in Oxford lists 264 titles for John Hill. The British Library in London lists even more, and several of the great American research libraries contain almost as many. Hill did not write all these works and several are later editions of earlier ones, yet his output was staggering by any measurement. Nevertheless, many more primary titles than this were needed, many in musty old libraries, to reconstruct his life.

Who was this man? Despite his galloping scribosis he was also a distinguished botanist. But this was just the start. He was also, alternatively, a villain, a rascal, a cheat, a fraud, a fake, a plagiarist, a provocateur, a wag, as well as arrogant, hypomaniacal, and naïve; yet endlessly and fascinatingly attuned to the eighteenth-century culture of celebrity that drove him to "the frenzy of renown," in Samuel Johnson's famous phrase. More than anything his career serves as a filter to illustrate what was at stake in Georgian England's mad quest for recognition. His career demonstrates, in miniature, aspects of the historical genealogy of our own cult of celebrity.

Hill was also overreachingly ambitious, uncannily intuitive, puzzlingly indefatigable, and sickeningly cowardly: extremes causing him to be universally vilified. It is hard to think of anyone else in mid-Georgian England who aroused more widespread contempt, and occasionally pity. His contradictions are legion, and the more I pondered his life and works the more I wanted to unravel his strange story. But Hill did not live in a void: no matter how ambitious or unrelenting, cunning or stealthful, he moved within Georgian society, and his strange relation to diverse, professional communities spurred me as forcefully as the man's exasperating contradictions. To locate him I had to explain how each—the man and his culture—interacted.

The writing of a first biography depends for its form on the biographer's notion of what biography is. I do not believe in so-called "definitive biography": the setting out of all the facts in what will piously become the "ultimate interpretation." I doubt that even scholarly readers want a "definitive biography" of such an unknown figure who has been written out of the record for two centuries. Others have challenged "definitive biography" for even major figures more diligently than I can here. Suffice it to say that my interest is the extraction of patterns capable of revealing the man's pulse, and how he was able, simultaneously, to court flux and live with uncertainty. He improvised his way to fame, floating between fixed roles and developing professions, often without understanding how he was refracting his times and serving as one its sharpest filters.

My experience in unraveling the motives "within the man" has resembled the voyage to a new country; not because I claim that Hill is unlike anyone else, or because my retrieval differs from prior reconstructions—there have been no extended narratives—but as the result of my experience of locating him. I have crisscrossed his life so many times, taking such different routes extending from the chronological and disciplinary to the psychological and sociological, that often I have thought I knew it well enough to sketch its boundaries. But no sooner was I persuaded of these markers, than I reminded myself I was telling someone's story for the *first* time—and trying to get it right.

Some readers may have preferred a linear narration of the "facts" (as if such facts could be served up without being interpreted and contested). Why not just present the known facts, they may ask, apart from other observations, including your own reasons for immersing yourself, with minimum interpretation?

Such a route was impossible for me. Not merely because biographical facts lend themselves to slippage but also because such an approach would have eliminated Hill-the-filter. And it is this last function that Hill, more than most of his contemporaries, offers for early Georgian society: that culture's strengths, weaknesses, and excesses—its dark underbelly. I have, additionally, been as "engrossed in the journey" as in "fixing the narrative" or "observing Hill-the-filter." This is no argument that the plain facts of his life are ancillary, unhelpful—not at all; just that I am the type of traveler who voyages out to discover patterns and personalities and reflect on the journey taken. I could not have served up this rapacious figure without locating myself within his cultural orbit.

Hill often refers to "the Town" in his letters and *Inspector* papers as "t'Town." I preserve his usage throughout this book for narrative purposes. The abbreviations used in the text are found before the start of the bibliography.

Illustrations

Anticipations

"The obscure sleep on the walls, slouching against each other as if they were too drowsy to stand upright. Their backs are flaking off; their titles often vanished. Why disturb their sleep? Why reopen those peaceful graves, the librarian seems to ask, peering over his spectacles, and resenting the duty, which indeed has become laborious, of retrieving from among those nameless tombstones Nos. 1763, 1080, and 606."

—Virginia Woolf, "The Lives of the Obscure,"
in *Collected Essays*, Hogarth Press, 1967, iv: 120

"What a curious thing is that undefinable flavour of personality—suggestion of physical quality, odour of the man in his unconscious and spontaneous self-determination, which attracts or repels people so powerfully, and is at the very root of love or dislike."

—John Addington Symonds, "On Manhood," 1878,
in *Collected Essays*, vol. 1: 335

"We live in a celebrity-obsessed culture, but until recently the history of celebrity has been little discussed."

—Tom Mole, *Romanticism and Celebrity Culture, 1750–1850*, 2009, preface

"Celebrity-worship and hero-worship should not be confused. Yet we confuse them every day, and by doing so we come dangerously close to depriving ourselves of all real models. We lose sight of the men and women who do not simply seem great because they are famous but are famous because they are great. We come closer and closer to degrading all fame into a sickening notoriety."

—Daniel J. Boorstin, "On Notoriety . . . ,"
in *The Decline of Radicalism*, 1969, p. 267

"It is, I believe, a very just observation, that men's ambition is, generally, proportional to their capacity."

—Samuel Johnson, *Life of Hermann Boerhaave* in *Coll. Works*, 1825, VI: 275

"Would you believe what I know is fact, that Dr Hill earned 15 guineas a week, by working for wholesale dealers?—he was at once employed on six voluminous works, of botany, husbandry, etc. published weekly. I am sorry to say this journeyman is one of the first men preferred in the new reign: he is made gardener of Kensington, [a] place worth £2000 a year. The King and Lord Bute have certainly both of them great propensity to the arts—but Dr. Hill, though undoubtedly not deficient in parts, has as little title to favour in this reign, as Gideon the stockjobber in the last. . . ."

—Horace Walpole to Henry Zouch, January 31, 1761

" . . . romantic fancy pours
The magazines of *Proteus* forth, and builds
Huge castles in the air."

—William Thompson, *Sickness*, 1746, III: 134, lines 436–38

"Q: Ambition or talent: which matters more to success? Rushdie: "No question but that it's talent. Ambition suggests a desire for great worldly success."

—Salman Rushdie, "The Inventory," *FT Magazine*, October 9, 2010

"There's no value in delivering historical accuracy . . . I mean—if it's going to be spiritually true, you have to connect it to the present. You read all the research and then you must forget it—you must write about the time we live in now."

—Adriano Shaplin on his play *The Tragedy of Thomas Hobbes*,
Financial Times, November 8, 2008, Life and Arts Section, p. 13

Late November 1766. Wind rustles through leaves scattered on the ground, blowing its chill through the dank seeds he sifts. From groin to knees he tingles, shivering, his nerves throbbing as if coated in icicles. Winter has arrived early this year, hastened his gouty condition. He has been deteriorating ever since summer warmth faded, but he has told no one, not even Henrietta, how bleak he is about the future. The nights draw in earlier now to remind him that he can no longer carry heavy plants about or walk without a stick. For weeks he has hobbled up the small Westbourne stream beyond the pest house toward the crossing (to the current-day Queensway), unable to walk beyond its westward curve toward Paddington Green.

He used to leap through the deer path. Now he has ceased courting his former curiosity as he did when sauntering to the west of his land, with its storehouses of specimens and seeds, toward Shaftesbury House, situated on the north side of the road, or further down the Bayswater turnpike toward the brick kiln on the south side, three minutes beyond the western edge of the palace gardens at Kensington.

Today he feels more decrepit than usual. He is not yet old, and he has only walked a few hundred yards through the parterres of the eastern palace gardens; those surrounding the large round pond—the "basin," as it is called here in Bayswater—strewn with the wild ducks and geese who gather to bask in the sun waiting to be fed. Earlier this morning he looked at himself in a glass: how wan he is, he ruminates, his taut face drawn inward, his tall limbs and ankles contracting, circulation failing. His interior monologue is grim: I am fifty-two, I am an old man.

A pair of dogs chases each other; a virile man on a horse is riding toward the West Country. He has come galloping down the Tyburn turnpike past the small jail and convent beside it making for the "Bayswatering hole," as everyone knows it here, but he is not coming to the "Doctor" to buy plants or seeds. The beeches and oaks on his land have grown to great height since he bought these fields seven years ago. His birchen strong-fence holds up to separate his small compound from the turnpike. A woman holding the arm of a young girl pulls her wrap close to her in the shrill wind. Winter snow will soon descend.

How quickly his life has dissipated, he thinks to himself. Eight years earlier, still in the pink of health and riding high, he had found this rural sanctuary three miles to the west of St. James to store his seeds and plants. He and Henrietta were then living in plush accommodations in St. James, and continued to reside there as the children matured and pushed their way toward adolescence. But then his patron, Lord Bute, fell from grace, his own luck turned, and this crippling disease appeared, leveling him to this. His finances no longer hold: he and Henrietta pay their rates in both residences and feed the children, but the carriage and six, the gold cane and gloves, the guests and late nights, all are gone, and under duress that chills his fingers as they write he works away at *The Vegetable System*. Fourteen volumes have appeared—twenty-six are planned; but his creditors are seeking recourse through the law and Henrietta—bless her, dear wife—cannot bail him out forever. His agents in North America continue to ply his seeds and panaceas but the profits are small. He has no stamina left to replace them with others, nor the tenacity to chide them. He bends down and writhes as the twilight zone descends on him.

Angelic Henrietta remains the saint she has been from the day he found her, caring for him in times like this to indulge his moods and sulks. But her patience is wearing and the fire needs more wood. A few days later, while strolling on the north edge of the palace gardens toward the Serpentine, torrential rain pours down, and he pulls his coat toward his neck for warmth and turns back. He is chilled to the bone, his toes on fire with inflammation. His memory throws up images of former years punctuated by scenes of success; memories of how his father Theophilus had told him as a boy he was preordained to prosper. If only his lordship—Bute—had not failed in office. His lordship, the former prime minister, had embodied all his hope but now he is fallen from grace, recalled, removed from office and flung into self-imposed exile, in flight to Mount Stuart in the wilds of the Western Isles and now, more recently, wandering like a leech-gatherer through the Swiss alps. John has not heard from his lordship for two years—each letter goes unanswered.

The blood in his veins flows slowly in this wind; his brain recalls how "life in town amidst the great and famous" spurred him—without that purpose he would have given up the ghost. Although cold now and wrapped by night in a rug, he can still hear the din of those greeting the well-known "Dr Hill of St James." He feels irrevocably tired; if his circumstances deteriorate further he will retreat forever, and endure his gout, watching his high beeches and oaks in solitude as they bend to the wind's nighttime roar.

He feels unbearably low, wonders how much time he has left. His own well-worn panaceas, the "great five," prove useless for his malady and despite Henrietta's love and care he wonders whether he will live long enough to finish *The Vegetable System*, see the girls grow up and marry. As he walks back to the house the rain pours down, chilling numb limbs and stiff toes, and the crisp, deadened leaves blow in symmetrical gusts. Can he carry on to Christmas—the first Christmas they have spent away from the salons of St. James and the smoky coffeehouses to the east?

February 1767. Little in his weary life delighted the "Great Cham of Literature," Samuel Johnson, more than being summoned by his sovereign to "a private conversation with His Majesty" in the library of the Queen's residence at Buckingham House and its large, overlaid rooms, thick carpets, and splendid collections of books.[1] His Majesty, George III, now approaching thirty years of age, had heard of the "Doctor's" visits to help choose the books for Queen Charlotte's library and expressed a desire to his librarian, Mr. Barnard, to be told when the good doctor would visit next; and Barnard, remembering his sovereign's request, seized the moment and whispered to Johnson that His Majesty had come into the building. Bringing the king by candlelight into the library on this gloomy winter afternoon, Barnard found Johnson warming himself by the fire—but the moment he saw his sovereign, he stood up and waited for a cue. The king was wonderfully easy and began to converse about the doctor's having recently visited Oxford and wished to know about their libraries and whether the "Cham" was writing any work of literature. They conversed in this way for some time, the king also inquiring what he thought of Bishop Warburton's learning and Lord Lyttelton's just published biography of Henry II.

Johnson, having answered these questions honestly and fairly, was taken aback when his sovereign carried on by asking him what he thought of "Dr Hill." Queen Charlotte had met the famed botanist at Kew—botany was her ruling passion. Perhaps she spurred her husband to pose the question or whetted his curiosity. The king, for his part, flashed back to Bute, thinking how his former favorite, his constant tutor not so long ago, had filled his ears to the point of bursting about Hill. Johnson replied that he thought Hill an "ingenious man but had no veracity" and then, immediately, followed on by describing how Hill had attached three or four microscopes together to enlarge the object he was observing. The king was amused and retorted that Hill would be found out in this untruth because "every one who can look through a microscope will be able to detect him." That was Hill.

The "Cham" recognized he had dispraised this public figure in the eyes of his sovereign and thought he had best say something positive, and quickly quipped that "Dr Hill was, notwithstanding, a very curious observer; and if he would have been contented to tell the world no more than he knew, he might have been a very considerable man, and needed not to have recourse to such mean expedients to raise his reputation." The king, done with his four questions, turned next to the newspapers and magazines of the day. Johnson walked away wondering why everyone, even his king, was talking about Dr. Hill: what had the good doctor done to make himself so notorious? He fudged more than the results of his microscope if the rumors reaching George III were any indication.

May 1965. I first heard about John Hill during a PhD viva at Princeton University. Graduate students were required to pass a viva called "Orals" before we could write a doctoral dissertation: an exam covering the whole era of one's specialization, whether Medieval, Renaissance, or later, as in my case, the Enlightenment. Before the "Orals" you sat a long written examination stretching over several days, but once finished, and without yet learning the results, we proceeded directly to this Great Terror called "Orals." The Examiner's Committee of three could ask any question within the chronological limits of your epoch. Jokes about the successes and failures of prior students abounded, and the accepted wisdom was that "it all depended on your examiners." Some demanded facts, others ideas, yet others the lives of authors and histories of theories. The well-prepared student was attuned to the species of question being asked and, if not, the slightest miscalculation—preparing facts instead of ideas, or ideas instead of lives—could lead to failure.

Having selected the Restoration and Eighteenth Century, then amalgamated into a single historical period for the purposes of examination, I knew I could expect two key examiners: the late American professors Louis Landa and Henry Knight—or "Bing" as we knew him—Bing Miller. Landa, the senior member, was a "no-nonsense facts man"; Miller also commanded an arsenal of facts but—according to the accepted wisdom—required more for a "pass." Every day I prepared "facts" and kept them handwritten on hundreds of flash cards in those years before PCs and the Internet. The further "inside word" about Landa, borne out by his erudite displays in graduate seminars, was that he could dwell on the most minute details: the names of cats and dogs (Gray's cats, Boswell's dogs); the costs of apples and oranges or how much an "orange lady" could have charged for one orange in 1710; or the full titles of primary works that had influenced a "primary author" like Defoe or Swift, for example, the complete titles of the works by Alexander Selkirk that influenced the composition of Defoe's *Robinson Crusoe*, or the complete title of George Cheyne's treatise about melancholy forming a backdrop to Richardson's *Tragedy of Clarissa Harlowe*.

So I memorized cats and dogs, apples and oranges, and even ascertained the cost in modern equivalence of growing a hothouse pineapple in the year when Tobias Smollett—one of the century's important novelists—presented this fruit for the first time in fiction, his *Adventures of Peregrine Pickle* (1750–1751). I was becoming a walking encyclopedia—a freak. I have since lost the flashcards and notebooks but the memory of their compilation remains, as does the balmy spring day of the viva. Air inert, flowers reaching high blossom on Princeton's gothic stone walls, wisteria in full flush in scented turrets, and the "memory freak" soon to be imprisoned by the examiners.

I answered questions about Locke's influence on literary authors, Defoe's familiarity with travel literature, and the proverbial questions about cats and dogs. Miller prompted me further for the "facts" of Fielding's reading, and Landa, in turn, zoomed in on Pope, on whom he remained as fixated as stargazers looking through the telescope Milton saw in Arceti. Then the viva turned amicable, we were laughing about "duncery," especially Pope's variety in *The Dunciad*, when Landa interjected with a further question about Pope's dogs. I knew about Pope's favorite dog "Bounce," but Landa requested genealogies: *all* the dogs, their names, etc. If only he had inquired about dunces.

I muddled through, but when Landa saw how vacant my face was growing he followed on with a new, unrelated question: "*Who was John Hill?*" *John Hill? John Hill who,* I wondered. I was dead in my tracks: at least Pope's dogs were familiar terrain but who was John Hill? I had not heard of him and froze up thinking I misheard Aaron Hill, the actor, about whom I could have spoken. Landa benightedly softened the blow: "he was a prolific writer," he limped in his deep, gentlemanly Texan drawl, "he went by the name of Sir John Hill, you will surely know about his literary relations with Henry Fielding and Laurence Sterne—no?" Bing Miller lighted up, a Falstaff having come into the state of final mirth, knowing very well who this chap was, as an expert textual editor of Fielding's works would; but I simpered in silence wondering how I could have missed out on someone so prominent and prolific.

I froze: must have appeared transfixed to the examiners, terror in my eyes, pleading ignorance, whispering "I do not know," and then apologized saying how deeply humiliated I was. Landa smiled as if he were to light up one of the many Havana cigars he smoked and declared the examination finished while I cringed: those flashcards and notebooks, those thousands of facts about cats and dogs and dunces, to end in this debacle. Would I step outside the room—this was the custom—and while outside the committee deliberates, then the chair calls you in and either congratulates you or breaks the news. The longer you waited the worse the outcome, indicating that the committee was divided or could not make up its mind. To me it seemed an eternity but then Landa opened the door.

"You have passed," he declared in sustained Texasese, "but the committee thinks you should apprise yourself about John Hill." His eyes twinkled in the way eyes can when under the kindly brow of an avuncular supervisor. Written in their sweet gaze seemed to be the word "immediately." I thanked him and the rest of the committee, disappeared, and proceeded directly in exhaustion to the reference section of Princeton's well-stocked Firestone Library where I located the "H" volume of the old *Dictionary of National Biography* only to find, to my amazement, Hill sitting in state sprawled over many columns: "John Hill, calling himself SIR JOHN, a member of the Swedish Order of Vasa, miscellaneous writer"[2] and apparently the author of over one hundred works. Or was it two hundred? I was too exhausted to count.

"Who *was* this man?" I remember yelping. The janitor swept the other way.

Christmas 2010. My decision to frame Hill as biographically "notorious" crystallized in 2007. Its competitors in psychological arrogance and naiveté, among other structural, framing categories, were persuasive but in the end less compelling. Since the Enlightenment "notoriety" has been a word applied to extremes of behavior, especially criminal, as in highwaymen, murderers, pirates, robbers, spies, and other types of malefactors. The word always suggested extreme limits wherein only the notorious dare tread. Some of the most "notorious" criminals in Hill's era were incarcerated in Newgate Prison, and by the second half of the eighteenth century interest awakened in dramatizing these opportunists—no routine criminals as in Gay's *Beggar's Opera*—as stage protagonists, as in Thomas Holcroft's *The School for Arrogance* (1791) that suggested the most "arrogant types" could now become dramatic subjects. American literary historian Katherine Kittredge studied some of these types as the "notorious lewd" among women, and demonstrated their transgressive aberrations among "hags, tarts, killers, and freaks."[3]

More recently, the annals of the notorious have retained their criminal dimension while superimposing the moral. If "Blackbeard" (Edward Teach, 1680–1718) was promoted in the American colonies just before Hill's lifetime as the "most notorious pirate" who ever lived, others' crimes were less visibly flagrant, and as time progressed the ranks of the notorious included those who were merely in the first line, as it were, rather than those who were criminally implicated. Among the Victorians, Daniel Douglas Home (1833–1886) was considered "notorious" for being "the first psychic,"[4] that is, the most extreme psychic ever; and playwright Arthur Pinero imagined his heroine Anna Ebbsmith as "notorious" in *The Notorious Mrs. Ebbsmith* (1895) for being first and foremost vehement in criticizing social conventions, especially marriage, and for advocating free love for everyone.

But in the eighteenth century the category began to include moral realms, as in the interior world of scribblers. Charles Price (Anon 1800) (1723–1786), a contemporary of Hill, commonly called "Old Patch," was imagined, for example, as a "most notorious character" for many crimes of which his forgeries were the most extreme. Sabbatai Zevi, (Anon 1708) who claimed to be the long awaited Jewish Messiah who founded the Sabbatean movement in England, was primarily conceptualized as "a notorious impostor" by his opponents for his cabalistic scribbling. The term was increasingly used of those who wrote, as when some adversary applied it to John Tutchin (1661–1707), the Whig pamphleteer who was often lumped with Daniel Defoe.[5] Here Tutchin is called "that notorious and bold scribbler the Observator," anticipating scribbler Hill "the Inspector." Tutchin's crime? Not merely insults against church and state, libel and slander, but scribbling too much. He was "notorious" for being such a rampant and constant scribbler. It is an indictment that will increasingly be hurled against hacks in the dunciadic world of Hill's formative years and a charge made against Hill at mid-century *ne plus ultra*, not only for his voluminosity but for scribbling about every subject known to man.

NOTES

1. G. B. Hill, vol. 2, 33–41, provides the text of Boswell's account and lists Boswell's sources, together with a reconstructed dialogue of the interview.
2. Its author was George Fisher Russell Barker (1848–1927), a London barrister who wrote dozens of entries in the old *DNB*.
3. Kittredge, 94.
4. Lamont, preface.
5. Anonymous, *An Account of the Birth, Education, Life and Conversation of That Notorious and Bold Scribbler the Observator* (1705).

I

1

The Mountebank's Road Out

In the fens of north Cambridgeshire, on the old dirt road from Peterborough to March, lies the peaceful village of Whittlesea. It is far from the Wash, its nearest body of water, and its hinterland is flat and wet. Foreign travelers could imagine themselves to have arrived at the end of the world, or even beneath it. The only nearby place betokening "civilization" is Spalding, about five miles away but lying over the border in neighboring Lincolnshire. Here gather the famous "Gentleman's Society," a select group too erudite for Anne Turner's kin, and in this corner of old England she would will to her second son John Hill—*our* John—the only land he ever inherited. He had few prospects in life, and she favored him among her children.

Whittlesea was positioned far from the glittering town houses of St. James and the posh quarters of the Savoy, which imperiously sat like some Venetian palace on the river Thames in Georgian London. Anne had never journeyed to London; Peterborough was her outpost, large enough to overwhelm her. She left her dowry house and small plot to John in a testament before her death as partial recompense for his niche as her "second son," in the knowledge that there would never be sufficient funds to educate him.[1] Peterborough lay only a few miles to the east of Whittlesea, a town where simple folk like the Turners went to shop for special occasions in the late seventeenth century, hear news and listen to entertainments, and it also boasted a "Society for Learning" although not so eminent as the illustrious "Gentlemen" in Spalding.[2] Precisely when Anne left Whittlesea is unclear, as are most other details of her life, but she seems to have met her future husband, Theophilus Hill, when she was eighteen, in 1705, and they married by license that year, on December 17, at the church of Ely Saint Mary, just months after Theophilus turned twenty-five and graduated from the University of Cambridge.

He was a mature groom, having already spent several years at Cambridge where he studied medicine. His nature was firmly fixed on charity and poverty. Greed—the greed of mankind—was his constant refrain. It was his war cry too against mankind, and he lost no opportunity to rehearse how greed had been the deadliest of the Seven Sins. It poisoned human relations and destroyed societies. This is why he was a *particular* type of Anglican: drawn less to the Church of England than to vows of poverty and rituals of stoic fortitude. Christmas was following on the heels of his marriage in just one week; besides, he was returning home to Rothwell, and his new curacy there would allow him leisure to read and forage in the nearby countryside for plants. It was wiser, he thought, to comb the woods and fields for their wealth than hoard purchased goods.

His heroes were Christian saints who had lamented the greed of the world and also understood why human greed and God's nature were one. John Ray, the great English botanical naturalist, had died a few weeks before Theophilus's wedding, having also generated a revolution in natural history. Gratias Ray, botanical science was now on a surer footing, and for Theophilus, who had a passion for collecting and classifying plants according to their medicinal value, Ray had been a ray (no pun) of sunshine—a hero whose *Wisdom of God Manifested in the Works of the Creation* (1691) he owned and whose catalogues of plants he coveted. If only Theophilus could have afforded to purchase one. He could not, but rested quiet in the knowledge that Ray had also been the kind of Christian he was. Or so Theophilus thought.

Wife in hand, carriage jolting along and weighed down with old, large wooden boxes, the couple returned to nearby Rothwell to set up as the village doctor and his good young lady. His failure to submit a thesis upon leaving Cambridge counted for little against him. He was the youngest son of the squire of Rothwell: Sir Edward Hill, whose family owned "mills, meadows, and closes," and a pedigree from Henry II.[3] Theophilus preferred pastoral Rothwell to the hubbub of Peterborough, twenty miles to the east over the Northamptonshire border, even though he had met his future wife Anne there.

The Hills were royalists who never abandoned their allegiance to the king during the Civil War. Sir Edward remembered the clash of factions during his childhood, even if they were less strident in Cambridgeshire than Oxfordshire. He had educated his sons, sent them to university and taught them to be proper gentlemen. Theophilus, born in 1680, was more pious than studious; admitted a "scholar" to St. Peter's College,[4] where he matriculated to read medicine and was awarded a degree (without thesis) in the summer of 1705. It was an *annus mirabilis* of sorts: graduation from Cambridge, the death of his father Edward, marriage to Anne, and removal to a curacy.

Theophilus was a holy man who placed medical learning and piety in the service of his almighty Anglican God, and would pass down these beliefs to his sons. But he also grew up in an atmosphere whose air breathed medicine's spiritual dimension: "sick states" bred "sick citizens," he used to say, and vice versa, as part of his incantation against greed. "Sick physical bodies" in "sick souls" sought in vain for salvation for lack of time to heal themselves before deliverance. England, he thought, lay in the jaws of a moral crisis; had to be "healed," as pressingly as the individual human soul. Soul was paramount for him, especially soul groping for salvation. Poised with fervor and priestly orthodox rhetoric, he communicated these beliefs to his sons.

During the first decade of his marriage, from 1705 to 1715, he focused on his family and clerical duties, especially his second son, John, born in 1714, as we shall see, who proved to be a problem. He was unlike his older brother, Theophilus Jr. (1706–1779), who was easygoing, predictable, and as pious as his father. John was moody and kept to himself. He was capable and bright but displayed bouts of shouting and irritability. Few brothers can have been so different, as made clear by their responses to the village. Rothwell then had a small church in the center of its village green dotted with smoking chimneys and sheep in the nearby fields. Despite Theophilus's deaconic duties at the much larger church in Peterborough, he preferred the peace and calm of miniscule Rothwell. He did not lament struggling in Rothwell to make ends meet. Father Edward's small legacy assisted the newly married couple, but even then £200 would not sustain them for very long;[5] and Theophilus was aware he could not educate both his sons at Cambridge as he and his six brothers had been.

Pere Theophilus had written his Cambridge dissertation on the topic of "the medicine of the soul": this much-discussed topic of Christian apologetics for which he was awarded the degree of "bachelor of medicine" in 1708, three years after leaving. Now he was a medical doctor as well as priest: his clientele grew, he read and prayed, and concurrently dreamed of the Enlightenment perfection of man through learning, stoicism, and the cultivation of curiosity throughout nature's domains. William Stukeley, another Cambridge man, visited him during the summer of 1708 when he was first titled "doctor of medicine," jotting in his diary that Theophilus was "a physician of note and eminence in Practice."[6] Stukeley would become a loyal family friend to the end of his own life.

Four years later, during the summer of 1712, Stukeley noted that Theophilus stayed awake all night to trace a satellite seen in France in 1686 by the illustrious Italian astronomer Giovanni Cassini.[7] By now, 1712, the Hills had two boys: Theophilus Jr. and John (not yet our John), born in 1706 and 1707, respectively.[8] A third, Christopher, was born in 1710, but both John and Christopher died in 1713 as children, their cause of death unknown, and

Anne was soon large with child again, bearing our John on November 17, 1714.[9] So came "our John" into the world, on a cold gray November day, at their small home in Rothwell, the younger of only two remaining boys.

It was an easy birth for this healthy, young mother and produced a robust child. Also around this time Theophilus became increasingly nonconformist, displaying a radical version of Christian stoicism. He published his ideas in 1720 as *Stoic Philosophy; or, The Praise of Poverty. A Poem,*[10] descanting against the growing cults of luxury then prevalent even in towns like Peterborough, let alone in the great capital to the south, where the recent South Sea Bubble pyramid had just exploded. Greed: it was greed now escalated to a national vice. His stoic philosophy claimed that hardship strengthened the character, prepared men for death and the eternal life, and enabled them to serve God in the way He deserved.

Theophilus Sr. was a type of "English Enlightenment" figure not uncommon in the early eighteenth century: pious, probing, searching for truth by system building, incapable of seduction by riches, optimistic about the perfectibility of man through adversity and endurance. This was no blind obeisance to miracles or salvation, although both attracted him. Besides, he was a "gentleman graduate" by dint of learning and piety; stoically courting poverty, as in the poem he wrote with that title, and was proud to be "poor" if he could be spiritually "rich." It is hard to know just how poor they were, but by 1715 they fed three children: Theophilus Jr., John (our John), and a daughter Anne, born in 1717 and named for her mother.

Theophilus Sr. had few friends apart from the already mentioned stalwart William Stukeley (1687–1765), the genial antiquarian and perpetual archaeologist who would later campaign to restore ancient Stonehenge.[11] Stukeley's family owned estates in the fens near Boston, and he practiced medicine there before returning to London in 1717. He and Theophilus had met in Cambridge, and Stukeley visited him in 1708 in Rothwell three years after Theophilus and Anne were married while raising their young family. Stukeley was then a medical student at Corpus Christi College and had made excursions that summer to neighboring physicians "of any Note & eminence in Practise."[12] Theophilus had been recommended, and Stukeley called on him one afternoon in a visit that would pay off many times: not merely when both men found themselves at the nearby Spalding Gentleman's Society, but through Theophilus's not-yet-born son John.

The two men differed in their investment in greed. Stukeley did not see it as the devil his friend did. He was an optimist, unlike Theophilus, and more inclined to think the perfection of man possible than man's necessary damnation through greed. Perhaps this is why Theophilus so rarely attended meetings in Spalding. True, the Spalding men corresponded more than they met, and they were indubitably an early prototype of the networks of correspondents visible in the fast-developing Republic of Letters. The great Isaac Newton himself was a member, as were the Gale brothers, sons of the Dean of York, as well as our young "Dr. Theophilus Hill," cleric and physician. Years later, when our John was riding high as the "Inspector" in the 1750s and terrorizing t'Town as an *enfant terrible*, he relied on Stukeley for memories of his childhood, as well as favors and moral support.

At home our John quarreled with his older brother during games and play, and may never have acquired what modern psychologists call "boundaries." The defect was significant for his adulthood: for his adult competitive drive and egomania. Later John would concede that he had displayed unnatural "competition" with his older brother, but otherwise his boyhood was noticeably solitary. Theophilus reared him according to his own Stoic dream about the virtue of poverty and the sin of excess;[13] drilling into him the belief that suffering was God given and unpredictable; its only appropriate response an unrelenting fortitude and resignation. Few days unfolded without Theophilus lamenting how the English were going to rack and ruin, corrupted by new wealth, and newly sunk in debt and debauchery. The capital—London—incarnated the New-Age vice. Despite its filthy temptations it was no place for his sons.

"Modern life" amounted to excruciating greed, he told his boys, especially John whom he was self-educating. This was the story, almost a litany, young John heard; an imaginative boy growing up in the rustic fields of Northamptonshire who was more attracted to the colorful, visiting charlatans and mountebanks than his father's moral tales; especially on fair days, with their trapezes and tinctures for this and that ailment, this far more than his father's pieties. But John also rejoiced when he and his father collected specimens and observed animals and insects. Eventually, he rebelled against his father's position. More attractive by far was the developing Georgian aspiration to high living and the consumption of goods through wealth. The disparity made him feel victimized by Theophilus Sr.'s piety and became its principal casualty. It would not erupt for several years, until John himself arrived in London and joined the ranks of—what Theophilus then routinely referred to as—the sinful "Sons of Satan."

Years later, as an adult man approaching forty, John recorded having been unusually "shy" during his boyhood;[14] perhaps too shy to abscond altogether from Rothwell or play with other children. He also remembered his jollity to animals. He felt tenderness for brute creatures of this world and sympathy for their habitat. He roamed the marshes to the east of Peterborough, and watched frogs and toads in their ponds; saw the "meer hennings" in the sunrise, wallowing in the water. His native countryside was empty, but he learned where the footpaths were. Here, close to plants and animals, often in the bogs, no competition lurked as it did with his older brother Theophilus Jr.

John's education at home was "systematic": Theophilus taught him Latin and Greek and how to "botanize."[15] There is no record of tutors coming to their house or John's having attended any school. He grew to be tall, thin, and angular (as are gouty types often in old age), a treelike stripling; and by the onset of puberty he was almost as tall as his father to whose small library he was glued: here "Dr. Hill" gave him first-class tutelage in the ancient languages. Theophilus Sr. owned a medical library of about thirty books, mostly texts from his medical days at Cambridge, and a larger collection of approximately one hundred theological and religious books. John mastered their Latin through application and by dint of linguistic flare. A library of some one hundred and thirty titles was large for such a modest family, and he had inherited many from Sir Edward.

For Theophilus, "science" was a runner-up to theology for its utility; especially the ability to distribute utility. "Science" amounted to medicine and natural history: each so capable of improving man's lot. But science was also the child of religion and morality, and gave to humans their dream of perfection of man. He worked hard to endorse a sense of "natural religion"—religion revealed in nature—and labored to show that religion is the pursuit of happiness by the practice of truth and reason. In this sense he stood apart from so many dissenters in the fen country; dissentient men and preachers who cut against the grain of the Church of England. Nor was the curate Theophilus a card-carrying deist, as were some of the scientific gentlemen he encountered in Peterborough and Spalding.

This was ample reason to spend time in the fields with John, while Theophilus Jr., who was taught in a village school, prepared for university entrance. God revealed himself, thought father Theophilus, through nature, just as philosopher William Wollaston had described in the *Religion of Nature Revealed* (1722), a book Theophilus owned and read many times aloud during John's youth. Theophilus's love of botany was enhanced by his reading of it, a practice useful for medicating and for nurturing. All this was perfectly clear to Theophilus, but it is less evident what young John thought of the education he was receiving. His adult pronouncements, recollected thirty years later in his *Inspector* columns, sprung more prominently from common sense—so preponderantly it is difficult to know what he made of his education at home and whether it concealed childhood demons.

The linguistic part of his education in Latin and Greek was more noteworthy, for without this secure grounding in the ancient languages he could never have amounted to much in the virtuous Republic of Letters. Theophilus spent much time with the lad, teaching him how to translate from the ancient languages. John had learned to read English early and displayed an uncanny affinity for turning a phrase. When not preoccupied reading his father's books, father and son roamed the local fields, collecting and classifying specimens, John basking in the attention given him now that his older brother was preparing to leave for Cambridge. He was happiest, he later recounted, when they gathered plants and wild flowers in the woods. John acknowledged this great debt later on—indeed his periodical literature has so many "indulgent fathers" that the stereotype seems to have become a region of his adult mind.[16] As he wrote in *Inspector* 6, he was the child "of the best and most indulgent father in the world."

When John was thirteen the family moved to Denham in Buckinghamshire, enabling Theophilus to assume the curacy of the larger parish there. Denham was the seat of his elderly cousin, Sir Roger Hill: a larger and more affluent parish than Rothwell and one holding advantages for the family. Cousin Roger was friendly and generous; he would welcome his cousins from the north, and this is what he did. It was not merely Denham's proximity to London that attracted Theophilus, and the notion of seeing old friends like Stukeley more routinely,[17] or the notion that it might give employment to both his sons and he would be nearby, but the lure of family. Several other Hills than Sir Roger also lived in the vicinity and could assist him while raising his young family.

He and Anne arrived by Christmas of 1727 and installed their family of four—wife and two children, one brother (John), and one sister (Anne)—in a small house near the vicarage in Denham Place early in the winter of 1728.[18] Sarah Hill, a cousin on Theophilus Sr.'s father's side, was living there at the time, a prosperous lady given to garden teas, and Thomas Stirpin was the rector of the church, a parish of approximately two hundred persons. By summer Sir Roger was seriously ailing and was dead on December 29, at eighty-six, to be followed to the grave a day later by his heir and eldest son Roger, only forty-four. One imagines what commotions and commiserations there must have been in these bleak days just after Christmas. The elders dead, their heirs too, the future looked uncertain and just one month later, in January 1730, Rector Stirpin himself died. Theophilus buried all of them, blessed the rest, and wondered what life would be like from now on in Denham Place, having lost three of his closest family and friends. But hope remained: the other Hill cousins were healthy—William and Sarah—and quickly warmed to Theophilus's family.[19]

Theophilus Jr. did not move with them. A few years earlier he had matriculated at Emmanuel College where he went to read theology.[20] Theophilus Sr. further smoothed his eldest son's way by the removal to Denham Parish while Theophilus Jr. filled his shoes in the canonry at Peterborough "reading Morning Prayer."[21] A year later, in 1728, Theophilus Jr. was ordained, before graduating, while his fourteen-year-old brother John gazed po-faced from the stands at home.

He "watched" more than his family, fascinated—as he was—by the strolling clowns and magicians who paraded at feasts, the charlatans and mountebanks gadding about on market day. They entranced him, and he could sit for hours, as he notes in his adult journalism,[22] his attention focused on their stunts. The furthest goal in his mind was moving up the clerical ladder, as older bother Theophilus Jr. was doing. Theophilus was eventually "licensed" and "instituted to a living" a mile or two north of Grantham, in Lincolnshire, and there, deep in England's right shoulder, remained for the rest of his long but dull life, which would lay in such stark contrast to his notorious brother's. He raised four children and ministered to his parish flock almost to the end of the century.

The two brothers were never close—John's resentment was too pronounced for that; and once Theophilus Jr. settled in remote Lincolnshire and John in London they rarely saw each other. Denham had virtues over Rothwell, yet placed no more farthings, it seems, into the family coffers, nor did Theophilus Sr. covet them. When it became evident around this time (1728) that there were no funds to send John to Cambridge—the obvious university in view of the family's educational pedigree there—our second son became increasingly unruly. His aptitude for languages and reading was enviable, but he also had a wild side: a streak that did not lend itself to tutorial taming, other than for his father, so it was agreed after much debate that he would apprentice himself to a London apothecary.

This was around 1729–1730, after the mentioned "Hill deaths" of 1728–1729, as they were known in Denham. Around this time, John ran away with a group of itinerant mountebanks he had watched; an unsurprising event given that for years he had been glued to their visitations—their quack demonstrations to the backdrop of hurdy-gurdies and fluted pipes—and secretly desired to become one of their band. The evidence is scant[23] but not its logic: someone with John's forming temperament, combining genuine ability with disappointment at his university prospects, was piqued by their nomadic lives. He had watched them ply nostrums, scribble pamphlets, extract teeth, and drum up street audiences: he could too on elevated wooden platforms. This time, however, he appears to have returned to Denham and the good graces of his parents.

Not for long. By 1730 he was off to London on the chaise from Denham with his small box of clothing and a few books. Apprentices then were usually indentured for five to six years and, according to Robert Crawford, the author of the most authoritative guidebook to "trades" in those decades, they were paid circa £10–12 per annum.[24] Crawford wrote specifically to help parents make their choice of master and geographical location, outlining the innate skills necessary for each trade, occupation, or profession, together with the probable costs of acquiring the competence to practice them and their likely monetary rewards afterward.

Who found young John a master, and who decided he should be apprenticed to an apothecary? The likeliest source is some member of Theophilus Sr.'s congregation in Denham. Most apprenticeships were then obtained by family or kin—an extended family—and between the contacts of his father and brother, young John would have had various possibilities. His apprenticeship to an apothecary is furthermore unsurprising: father and son had spent so much time together—learning languages and reading about natural history, collecting specimens in the fields, classifying and drying them—that this vocation was the likeliest for John.

But strapped fathers could not afford to apprentice their sons to London apothecaries, geographically the most highly sought-after place in the country. Somehow Theophilus Sr. found master "Edward Angier in the Strand, of St. Clement Danes," and perhaps father and son also visited his premises and witnessed his domestic surroundings, as well as checked out his reputation by doing a round at the local tavern or spin at the coffeehouse. This was in November 1731, when Hill was seventeen. Angier agreed to instruct John and care for his daily needs in accordance with guidelines set down by the Society of Apothecaries for £42 per annum, a large sum then.[25] But he died shortly after Hill's arrival. So Hill was taken to another apothecary on July 4, 1732. Coincidentally, Thomas Bearcroft also died, and it may have seemed to the novice Hill that his apprenticeship was bred in the spirit of an evil curse. Eventually, John was turned over to Robert Watson and remained with him until 1736, bringing the total time of his indenture to approximately four years; respectable for an apprentice except that young Hill did not become a freeman of the Society of Apothecaries, the guild successful apprentices joined.

Yet again Hill fled to the itinerant charlatans, identified with them, and became—like them—a would-be quack-scribbler-actor. This time the departure from Watson foreshadows the erratic behavior also besetting his later life. Some London apprentices were known to attach themselves to high-livers who corrupted them, but other apprentices learned to be discreet: sober and reasonably well behaved in the master's house, even if wild once out of the neighborhood. The proverbial apprentice would keep the tokens of high living far from his master's house, and live a checkered life beyond it. But no evidence exists that young Hill was homesick. He never regretted leaving home. Nor did he comment on his parents in any illuminating way, nor would he in adult life other than fleetingly and nostalgically about father Theophilus Sr. Thirty years later, when writing a treatise about managing children, he had an opportune moment to insert autobiographical remarks about his own childhood, but wrote nothing negative.[26] Fleetingly he glanced back at his parents without opprobrium. His childhood had not been unhappy outside the knowledge that he was a second son for whom there would be no resource to obtain a university education. This grated, of course. Yet he had his people, the mountebank-quacks. They were family too; he reveled in their theatricality and never returned to Denham.

But this was not the whole story. Periods of itinerancy also defined a type of adolescence; prepared him for the real world he would never have otherwise known had he remained within a provincial village like Denham. The John Hill we will see throughout this life had no idea of settling down as an adolescent, nor did he later. He could not have behaved as he did, so outlandishly and waggishly, had he not been a runaway. Even if his itinerant years are not documented, they must have endowed him with a reality principle about the external world he could not otherwise have acquired.

This was less a sense of what it meant to be a "charlatan-mountebank" than the spectacle the charlatans created, even when doubling up as charlatan-actors. The fanfare trumpeting their arrival into the village, the droning sounds of primitive instruments even if not hurdy-gurdies, the raising of the platform, and, eventually, the dressed-up and powdered protagonist-charlatan himself. In this school of life the young Hill learned everything about the drama of charlatanry but nothing about its relation to academic science or university medicine. Still less about its villainy or validity. What he knew was that this atmosphere and its cunning participants fired him up.

From the artful mountebank-quacks he also drew inspiration to make something of himself. He may not have seen, for example, the celebrated actor Joseph Haines moonlight from Drury Lane to appear as the medicine man "Giussepe Hanesio" in the provinces and at Bartholomew Fairs, but had watched other thespians like Haines who further instilled the idea of combined acting and peddling.[27] Nor would he have laid eyes on William Read, the illiterate tailor from Aberdeen who had been knighted in 1705 and became Queen Anne's "Oculist in Ordinary" after peddling his "Excellent *Styptic Water*" and "cutting off cancerated breasts" throughout England. "He has been a mountebank," Jonathan Swift complained to Stella in 1711, after Read had invited him to dinner: "He makes admirable punch, and treats you in gold vessels. . . . But I am engaged and won't go." In maturity Hill would also trot out the "gold vessels" in his velvet-feel accommodation in Westminster, but for now he had no need to cross over to the Continent to learn from charlatans like Josef Anton Stranitzky, the great Austrian actor, how to double as a tooth-drawer: most lowly of all tasks on the stage-itinerant; or follow Beppo Balsamo from the fetid gutters of Palermo to the satin salons of Paris, Moscow, and Vienna where, as Count Cagliostro, he dazzled polite society with his quacksalving prowess.

No one can be certain how he found his particular models for the itinerant quack. My version of his youth is that he located them on native soil—at home in and around London. They came in all forms and shapes: as astrologers, herbalists, peddlers, prophets, scribblers; charlatanism their common genus no matter what their species. Some had warmed their fingers in Grub Street too, as would Hill very shortly. Collectively they taught him how "to administer" and "vend" on the mountebank stage: his two demonstrable assets as he started out on his own voyage of discovery at just sixteen. His geographical whereabouts after leaving Watson are murky but not his activities: they were clear. He was approaching twenty, he had no formal education beyond this apprenticeship or money to hand, but he was deft, could act, and sell, and swiftly scribble lines about his medicaments. He was veritably a budding English quack.

At home in Denham, Theophilus Sr., now into in his fifties, had long since settled into his Buckinghamshire sinecure, and would live for almost another two decades, until 1746. His grave in Denham Churchyard was still visible when I inspected it in 1982. Both sons, Theophilus Jr. and John, loved him, and perhaps John the more poignantly, for he knew how much time his father had invested to educate him at home. Our Hill, for his part, had neither a good or bad childhood but an aborted one. By his teenage years he was an adult—of sorts. Hill never reflected on his childhood during adulthood. And a case can be made, as this life often does, that he never really grew up. But very early on he had acquired two skills, in reading and botanizing, and these were largely owing to the loving care of father Theophilus.

Figure 1.1. Tombstone of Theophilus Hill Sr. in Denham Churchyard, Buckinghamshire.

Photograph taken by George Rousseau (1982).
Reproduced by kind permission of Professor George Rousseau.

NOTES

1. No death certificate has been found but JH commented in various sources, including his *Inspector* papers of the early 1750s, that she died when he was still young.
2. Stukeley, MSS Eng. Misc. d. 719/3: 1732; Moore, chapters 3–4; H. J. Winter, 74–76; Dack, 5–8.
3. Cokayne, 3179.
4. The current college Peterhouse in Cambridge.
5. Cokayne, 3184.
6. Stukeley, MSS Eng. Misc e. 121.
7. Stukeley MSS Eng. Misc. e. 139.
8. Cokayne, 3178.
9. Cokayne, 3179; the baptism record is in the Northampton County Archive; Anne was twenty-seven when John was born. Laundon, 65–66, gets the date right as November 17, 1714.
10. Theophilus subsidized its publication.
11. Haycock (2002), 42–43.
12. Bod MS Eng. Misc, c 553, f. 28v.
13. Theophilus Hill (1720).
14. *Inspector* 50, April 30, 1751.
15. The word appears to have entered English in the 1760s but this nevertheless is what father and son did.
16. *Inspectors* 71, 165, 209, 224, 229, 305, 319, 389, 505, 718.
17. Stukeley moved to London in 1717.
18. Stirling, chapter 4 for Denham in the 1720s.
19. Manuscript notes compiled by English genealogist Colin LeMessurier.
20. Venn, entry under "Theophilus Hill."
21. Longden, vol. 7, 17–19.
22. *Inspectors* 23, 77, 86, 114.
23. A. D. Morris, notes sub 1728–1735; Rosenfeld, 127, records that an actor named "Hill" showed up at one of "Yeates' booths."
24. Copeman, chapter 4; Earle, chapter 3, an authoritative source for the life of London apprentices in the 1730s.
25. Society of Apothecaries, London, eighteenth-century Medics Register.
26. JH (1754c).
27. Sources for the material discussed in this paragraph include C. J. S. Thompson; R. Porter (2000); Gentilcore.

2

Amidst the Trees in Sussex

Hill also had a *third* talent. His early years spent "botanizing" with Theophilus Sr. taught him about English plants and flowers, especially their nomenclature according to John Ray's classifications. As the mid-1730s evolved, young Hill considered how to make use of his botanical skill. He had already demonstrated ability on the stage as an itinerant quack, and had been apprenticed to an apothecary. It remained to fuse the three strands.

He was healthy, tall, and agile, if still gawky and raw toothed, but he needed cash. Perhaps he already pondered securing a patron, through aristocratic and royal networks. When John Bartram,[1] the young American botanist, implored his sponsor, botanist Peter Collinson—about whom we shall hear more—to help him, Collinson advised him to petition the king. George II balked; no appointment was made. An alternative route to patronage, through Whig lords, was the avenue Hill would take, together with other aspiring young botanists like himself. Years later, he applauded Bartram's achievement in his *Inspector* columns,[2] and was awed by the degree to which Bartram's humble origins resembled his own.

For now, this aristocratic route seemed promising. He had no royal contacts, and without a university education could not hope to gain easy access to botanists in Cambridge or Oxford. William Sherard, the power broker in Oxford working in tandem with his famous German assistant J. J. Dillenius, was already dead, leaving only Peter Collinson; now in London, he was the "other" prominent botanist than Sherard of the 1730s who knew everyone in the botanical world at home and abroad. A lifelong Whig, Collinson was familiar with Sir Hans Sloane and the Royal Society, of which he was a Fellow, and close to many of the great Whig lords—Petre, Richmond, Newcastle, Northumberland, and to botanist Carl Linnaeus in Sweden too. Young Lord Petre was Collinson's finest protégé, and the master spent much time with Petre at Thorndon, in Essex, consulting about his gardens and vast arboretum. Hill sought an introduction there and obtained it through Stukeley—the kindly Stukeley, still his most faithful supporter.

Stukeley had befriended Robert James (1713–1742), eighth Lord Petre and the oldest son of the prominent Catholic family very much at the heart of the closely knit Catholic community in England's southeast. His father was the "Lord Petre" who had naughtily clipped a lock of Arabella Fermor's ringlet at a party in Berkshire, setting in motion the events leading to Pope's famous mock-epic poem, *The Rape of the Lock* (1712–1714). Our Lord Petre, the botanical Petre, he lived to plant trees.[3] Stukeley had met him at the Spalding Society, and when he approached him about employing young Hill as an assistant, Petre's response was positive. Petre's gardener, John Gordon, was overworked, and in the years around 1736–1737 Petre was greatly expanding his planting.[4] He could use another assistant intimate with the ancient languages and botanical nomenclature. Young Hill was waiting in the wings and quickly removed himself to Thorndon Hall in the village of Ingatestone, in Essex.

Petre's passion in trees was the propagation of exotics and shrubs. He was still a precocious adolescent when he had been elected FRS, having been sponsored by the two best botanists of the day: Philip Miller, as keeper of the Chelsea Physic Garden and by now well ensconced in Chelsea, and John Martyn (1699–1768), soon to be elected the first professor of botany at Cambridge. By twenty, Petre was importing seeds and plants from Collinson's botanists in the Carolinas, the already mentioned John Bartram and Mark Catesby. It was Bartram who sent him, in 1736, the very first evergreen American species, *Ro maximum*, to be planted in England. He also corresponded widely with botanists abroad, especially Linnaeus, and during the summer of 1736 when Linnaeus was leaving Holland for England, Petre employed Hill.

Petre was a precocious collector even by the standards of the decade, his large library unparalleled in natural history; and it was in this library that Hill expanded his horizons, as well as learned the names of the American botanists conducting these schemes: the Catesbys and Bartrams who, like Hill at the end of his life, would be recognized as distinguished botanists by the Swedish crown. Petre bought several copies of Linnaeus's revolutionary *Systema naturae*, which had recently appeared in Latin in 1735, and kept himself *au fait* with developments in the botanical English scene. Here, at Thornton Hall, Hill first heard about the activities of such "FRS" as Hans Sloane and Martin Folkes, both presidents, who visited Petre, as well as the great Whig lords intent on seeing the gardens. It was an education to stand Hill in good stead for many years to come.

Petre was also an integral member of the circle of planters that included the Dukes of Richmond, Argyll and Bedford, but he himself was no mere "planter." He was a naturalist who had absorbed the taxonomic transformation set in motion by John Ray, Petre's late neighbor in Essex who died in 1705 and Theophilus Sr.'s hero.[5] Petre had heard much about Ray's "research mill" at Black Notley, a few miles up the road outside Braintree on the other side of Chelmsford, and visited it. Although Ray was dead, Petre took Hill to see the place "for inspiration." His assistant learned fast; besides, Petre was less than a year older than Hill and they got on well. Petre was a willing teacher, keen to mentor his able botanical student whose Greek was remarkable for someone who had never attended university. Soon Hill, who spent much of his time in Petre's library, was making entries in Petre's "Hortus Siccus Muscorum Americanus." For example: "Whitish, brittle, upright Moss.—Brynum trichoides, erectis capitulis albidum fragile," with annotations that this moss "was gather'd in a moist Place in Virginia."[6] Many entries in Petre's multi-volume herbarium are in Hill's hand. A good case is spleenwort, *Lonchitis aspera*, described in volume fourteen as "growing in woods and shady Places as in Cane wood & on Hampsted [*sic*] Heath."

When botanist Peter Collinson came up to Thorndon to catalogue England's largest "American garden," as he referred to it, having been commissioned by Petre, he was dazzled by the plantings of Petre's protégé; singling out his "skill in all the liberal arts, particularly architecture, statuary, planning, and designing," and for "painting with Living pencils."[7] Petre introduced camellias to England, and his hothouse, one of the largest in Europe, was filled with exotics (bananas, guavas, and pineapples). By 1741 he had planted more than 40,000 trees, including 10,000 American trees and shrubs, and, according to one estimate, had a total of 220,000 trees on his estates.[8] Linnaeus, in Sweden, named over thirty American species after Petre and dreamed of visiting Thorndon.[9]

But tragedy loomed: death from the lethal smallpox was at hand in July 1742, when Petre was only twenty-eight, bringing closure to the great expansion and huge plantings, and leaving Hill bereft, without a patron. The abandonment of Petre's forests of exotica during his illness and after his death (1741–1742) remains one of the great untold stories of British botany. Even Collinson mourned that Petre's demise was botany's largest loss in English botanical history. Sadly, Petre's wife had no interest in the venture except to auction off his trees. The upshot for Hill was plain—he must leave Thorndon.

Visitors to Thorndon included another aristocratic planter, the Duke of Richmond, who was building his own garden in Goodwood, Sussex. Richmond, like other great Whig dukes of his generation, had an income in excess of £20,000 a year, then an extraordinary annual sum.[10] His two passions were gardens and sport, especially hunting and horses. Petre had already sent Hill on a few missions to Goodwood: to convey specimens, exchange books, collect rocks, shells, fossils, and flowers—all displayed in Richmond's brimming cabinets of curiosity. Petre was generous to Richmond and allowed his assistant, Hill, to work at Goodwood when the duke needed him. By 1739, when Hill had been resident at Thorndon for about two years and already acquired Richmond's confidence, and when Petre's death would soon lead to the auctioning off of his American tree collection, Hill was instrumental in placing Richmond's generous bid first. This was the acquisition enabling Richmond to expand his own groves at Goodwood.[11]

But Hill now had no fixed patron, and moonlighted among the itinerant charlatans. He became known for these returns, as will emerge later in his life. For now though, Richmond was almost ready to employ him fulltime, but Hill had to cut the right figure, for Richmond's universe was entirely different from Petre's: more extroverted, more expansive, more intellectual, and he "lived" for far more than trees. To start, he was an active politician and military man, a figure of state, and by temperament more sociable and interested in other realms than the botanical one cultivated by his late friend in Essex. He mixed regularly with the FRS and was on good terms with Hans Sloane, their president from 1727 onward, when he succeeded Newton. Sloane was curious about the gardens Richmond was building at Goodwood and Hill's name must have come up more than once.

Figure 2.1. Engraving of Goodwood from the front, seat of the Duke of Richmond, c. 1750. A watercolor by an unknown hand.

Reproduced by kind permission of Professor George Rousseau.

Goodwood in 1740 was a small stately home lorded over by a duke in his early forties, who inherited the place at only twenty-two when he succeeded to the title. It was a pastoral paradise giving no intimation that the government of its country was at war in Europe. Richmond, who was politically active in the British decision to enter the War of the Austrian Succession, was determined to turn the place into an unparalleled rustic showpiece—*res in urbis*—as a physical adornment to his deeply polymathic life. He was a model specimen of the gentleman of the Republic of Letters who navigates smoothly within its codes. Timothy McCann, his most learned recent biographer, has described Richmond's urbanity and versatility when commenting on the Goodwood Hill would have found around 1740:

> He was one of the first patrons of Canaletto, and his dining-room at Goodwood was framed with the paintings of allegorical tombs of famous Englishmen commissioned . . . from contemporary Bolognese and Venetian artists. Richmond's scholarly interest also led him to the study of medicine, science, and antiquity. In 1728 he was awarded a doctorate in law at the University of Cambridge, and in June of that year he was elected a fellow of the Royal College of Physicians. In 1741 he was president of the London Hospital, and he was one of those responsible for the hospital's move to Whitechapel Mount. He was elected a fellow of the Royal Society in 1724, and in September 1728 he was invited to attend a meeting of the Acadèmie Royale des Sciences in Paris. These were not simply honours paid to his rank and station. Richmond patronized early inoculators in Sussex, he collected information on local earthquakes in 1734 and the Chichester smallpox epidemic in 1739, and he observed and reported on Abraham Trembley's experiments on hydra in 1743. He was elected a fellow of the Society of Antiquaries in 1736, and in March 1750 became president.[12]

Richmond's activities exceeded these: his polymathic curiosity drew him to the study of medicine, science, and antiquity, which led, in turn, to the award of a doctorate in law at the University of Cambridge, and fellowship at the Royal College of Physicians, where he was active in promoting exercise and good diet. His message about health, once amidst his groomed horses and splendid trees at Goodwood, was that all types of motion—walking, riding, running, every sport—were conducive to well-being, and more than one medical work dubbed him "the greatest Professor in the *Gymnastic Exercise*."[13] Richmond promenaded his guests under the cedars of Lebanon trees he had planted with Hill; they, in turn, remembered their unique visits there. Naturally, for all this honors were paid to more than to his rank and station, as Timothy McCann has commented; to recognition for his thought and action.[14] Richmond was also one of the founding governors of the London Foundling Hospital, which had just received its Royal Charter from George II.[15] He attended committee meetings there and took part in the baptism and naming of the first children accepted by the hospital in 1741,

Hill several times having asked to tag along. Such a prominent lord was in constant demand at London's best houses, reciprocating by inviting his hosts down to Goodwood.

He was also magnanimous: after Trembley, of sliced-polyp fame, had tutored him during a brief stay in Leyden, Richmond awarded him a foreign pension. If any Whig aristocrat of the mid-eighteenth century fits the bill of the perfect gentleman of the Republic of Letters, Richmond was that person.

No patron can have been a better role model for the young Hill, who worked in the gardens and supervised in the sandpits. He watched the duke introduce Petre's Virginian oaks and tulip trees, the latter from seeds brought from America and showing leaves like "cowboys saddles." He also worked with other woodsmen, in Charlton Forest and at the estate's High Wood containing the menagerie of animals and birds that visitors from far and wide came to view, and he planted the cork trees that eventually grew to be taller than those in Mediterranean France.[16] Hill collected plants and animals on the nearby Downs, and took time off to ride horseback in the summer's penumbra. Most of all, he learned firsthand what it is to be a gentleman "of parts" in that epoch of manners and morals and great country houses.

Richmond proved to be the ideal patron: amiable, inspiring, and hardworking; the type of mentor Theophilus Sr.—for all his piety and thrift—could not be. Richmond had married Sarah Cadogan, daughter of the first Earl, William Cadogan, who brought a vast dowry with her to Goodwood, and by the time Hill arrived Richmond had also become a Grand Master Mason, which often took him away to London to the Premier Grand Lodge of England, and also brought masons down to Goodwood. The social life here was altogether different from anything Hill had seen at Thorndon. Richmond's Masonic meetings in the Great Hall at Goodwood accommodated throngs of the great and good, including the philosopher-statesman Bolingbroke, about whom Hill would later write, and many of the FRS. Hill may not have attended these séances, but his eyes were open as he watched the goings and comings of the philosophers and scientists.

Life at Goodwood was divided into avenues literal and symbolic, the former presided over by Tom Hill (no relation to John), Richmond's lifelong *majordomo* who perfected its country-house order. Years later, our Hill described its "American Grove" (the gardens Richmond planted with Petre's saplings) as a "Paradise," and he remembered observing "the whole Trunk of a young Tulip-Tree" with his enviable patron, a "Master of this Paradise."[17] He admired Richmond in a way he could not Theophilus Sr. and helped him to adorn the exotic "shell house"—Richmond's gorgeous grotto containing shells brought from the West Indies by a heroic captain in the navy, Charles Knowles, and boasting marble floors with inlay of wild horses' teeth. The gentlemen of the FRS who came to visit, especially Martin Folkes, their president, were agape. They sent Richmond specimens and rocks, and inevitably met the developing botanist Richmond was mentoring—"the puppy Hill," as Richmond came to call him.

Hill also encountered Peter Collinson again, a frequent visitor, and it was Collinson, among Richmond's favorite botanists, who dined on thick turtle soup with the duke in London when en route to visit his (Richmond's) estate at Aubigny, in France, which he inherited from his great-grandmother. Richmond was the ideal antidote to Theophilus. Eminent national figures, as well as international celebrities, came and went through Richmond's salon, in the arts as well as sciences, for which bent he acquired the nickname "the radical duke," although he himself was far from radical in his politics.[18] As Jonathan Swift had earlier educated himself in the library of his patron Sir William Temple, in Prior Park, so did Hill, botanically, in the library at Goodwood. He had begun four years earlier in Petre's library, but there was more leisure now. One day Hill came upon Elizabeth Blackwell's *A curious herbal, containing 500 cuts of the most useful plants,* and wondered whether female botanists were entering the newly competitive network of naturalists.[19] We get ahead of our story to look at competitive botany, but two years after Richmond's death in 1750, from bladder cancer, Hill lamented him, even beatified him as "His Grace, whose love for natural knowledge was as great as any Man's I have known."[20]

Henry Pelham, the future prime minister, and his older brother Newcastle, also visited; especially Newcastle whose seat was at Laughton, in East Sussex, and who was becoming Richmond's closest ally and friend.[21] Hill met Newcastle on several occasions, as he would remind him in subsequent years. Stukeley also came down, having met Richmond at Thorndon, and told Richmond that the "budding botanical connoisseur" Hill was promising.[22] A man in his mid-twenties, Hill must have been thrilled at the prospect of life here: he had the gardens and rolling West Sussex countryside, could go up to London at brief notice, while also enjoying the arts of this unusual country house. Did he travel up in the spring of 1742 to hear Handel's new *Messiah*? His letters are silent about Handel, but reveal that he rode up to see plays and witness the entertainments of t'Town.

Nor did he lack for excitement, especially the visiting French contingents who often formed the week's high points. Upon occasion, Hill was invited to dine with them at Richmond's "high table"; many attracted hither by the new "Anglomania" seducing them across the English Channel. Those who came and went were numerous. The celebrated Montesquieu of *De l'Espirit des lois* fame, as well as Antoine Réaumur (1683–1757), who philosophized about "social insects":[23] the little creatures whose intimate relations are as puzzling as human ones. Réaumur had also, bizarrely, devised a novel way of breeding chickens by artificial heat—Hill remembered his theories later on when in pressing need.[24] Hill was dazzled by Réaumur's pronouncements on phenomena ranging from ants and bees, the two most sociable creatures in the kingdom of insects,[25] to turquoise stone and the velocity of light—no wonder Hill later dubbed him "the indefatigable Réaumur."[26]

He also met Montesquieu's young son, Jean Baptiste de Secondat (1716–1795), a lawyer passionate about botanizing (which then included "geologizing"), with whom he corresponded after the Frenchman left Goodwood.[27] The adolescent Secondat had traveled to Guyana, in South America, to observe exotic birds; at home, in Bordeaux, he had become scientifically engrossed in the cultivation of grapes for wine and become an expert enologist. Hill's long-distance association was based on their joint interest in botany and geology, and they exchanged letters as if ensconced in the Republic of Letters: that crucial and borderless network of hardly imaginary correspondents scattered throughout Europe. He also met English naturalists: for example George Edwards, the artist and ornithologist who would inspire him to write a novel named after him, and whose mineralogy Hill incorporated into his geological writing.[28]

How the foreigners dazzled him at Goodwood: their accents, their costumes, their gaits, their mannerisms and perfumes. They were more erudite, if also pedantic, than figures he had encountered in his so far largely provincial orbit. Secondat, to whom he took in a big way, particularly attracted him. Hill began to imagine himself as a French or German university-gentleman-of-parts; even contemplated dressing like his formal French lawyer friend—Secondat—who was so ardent about botany. Once, on a trip to London, Hill bought foreign clothes in a small alley shop tucked into the lanes behind Spring Gardens, then began to walk the streets donned in them. Another time, he went "abroad" disguised in Venetian dress, masked and powdered, in plain daylight, as if en route to some Vauxhall ridotto. He passed brilliantly for a Dutchman too (was he not an actor?), and superadded the idea of selling his wares in this outfit as if some medical graduate of Leyden University: pills, potions, herbal panaceas, botanical concoctions, everything he had learned in his trade. He strutted forth, transformed his normal gait, confidently announced his merchandise, and modulated his English country accent to suit the platform occasion and day's exotic garb. The difference was that this was no London masquerade—it was John Hill trying out as many foreign costumes as he had acquired distinct personas.

Was he not an "author"? He was indeed, and an actor too. He was an "author" in his own right, he thought, who devised a new typology as a "Foreign Empiric," and the crowds were starting to jump up and clap.[29]

Yet the genuine dynamics of the virtuous "Republic of Letters" altogether eluded him: how you entered (assuming it was something one actually "joined"), stayed in, and its complex unwritten codes. He was attempting

Figure 2.2. "The Author [John Hill] in the character of a Foreign Empiric, c. 1742."

Reproduced by kind permission of the Trustees of the British Museum.

to gain admission, no less than his acting friends—itinerant or stationary—were trying to break into the sock. Richmond was never available to explain the Republic, nor does Hill appear to have asked him. He also heard, perhaps from some Swedish student of botany passing through Goodwood, about Linnaeus's successes in the Netherlands, and how he was moving to a professorship in Uppsala. Young Linnaeus had just spent several months in England, having been sent by the millionaire hypochondriac George Clifford: the Dutch collector who had employed him to catalogue his collections at Harderwyck in Holland. When Linnaeus made a case that he needed to watch the English botanists at work, Clifford sponsored him. Linnaeus had three specific goals in England: he wished to consult Philip Miller in Chelsea, William Sherard toiling on his acres in Tower Hill with Dillenius, and meet aristocratic lords like Richmond whose seats were being turned into botanical museums. He arrived, introduced them to the new system of binomial classification he was developing, and gifted them copies of his new book, *Systema Naturae*.

This visit proved significant for botany, introducing Linnaeus to England and England to Linnaeus. More locally in 1737–1740, it served to galvanize our young botanist: if Hill's time assisting Petre had not been sufficiently long to convert him to Linnaean binomialism, things looked differently now to a man in his twenties who absorbed everything quickly. It remains unknown whether he actually read the *Systema Naturae*, but copies were lodged at Goodwood, and the duke was too ardent a bibliophile not to have purchased a copy and discussed it. Hill was inspired by the book's utopian wish to compile lists of all the plants known in the world, and the further dream to collect and classify them according to securer systems of classification than Ray had devised.

The first edition of Linnaeus's *Systema Naturae* had appeared in Latin in 1735 but had not yet adopted the binomial system. Linnaeus waited until the end of the 1740s for that; and later, in 1758, the tenth edition of the *Species Plantarum* codified these binomials into an organic system of nomenclature. For now, late in the 1730s, while Hill was resident at Goodwood, the accounts he heard from visitors about Linnaeus's botanical ardor inflamed his imagination. The Swede was destined to become John Ray's successor: not merely inventing new taxonomical knowledge but applying self-generated taxonomies to the whole living world, not just its flora. This animated optimism about cataloguing and classifying the whole living world endured for decades beyond Hill's lifetime, as when Jean-Jacques Rousseau much later sent Linnaeus the message: "Tell him I know no greater man on earth," and when Goethe wrote "with the exception of Shakespeare and Spinoza, I know no one among the no longer living who has influenced me more strongly."

These views hint at botany's status: its newly elevated niche in the developing sciences of the Enlightenment, as well as its aesthetic and moral dimensions. Frances Hutcheson, the philosopher, noted around this time that botany, more than other pursuits, arouses the senses to "love Nature."[30] So powerful are the images the eye takes in. Linnaeus's binomials in the 1740s appeared to be systematizing the whole natural kingdom and rendering its symmetries more accessible than without them. At least it seemed so to Hill.

Hill's other side was also surfacing: by turns silly and pretentious, histrionic and sycophantic. Richmond playfully referred to these traits when asking Collinson, "is he not a puppy?"[31] The duke's question intended to amalgamate derisory connotations of mindless, almost canine, pride with affability.

He noticed Hill's affected speech, his rhetorical bouquets of flattery, his indulgence and self-aggrandizement, even in ordinary conversation. But the indulging Richmond overlooked them. Hill had too many solid virtues to compensate. Others were less understanding.

Hill was also acting on the stage at Goodwood that had attracted some of London's best actors, many soon to become noteworthy, and Richmond could forgive a "player" his verbal self-indulgences. The performances brought out Hill's weird charisma, not least because he was in love for the first time, and with Peg Woffington (more about lovely Peg in a moment). On the stage—his first pursuit before botany—he demonstrated the prideful side. He was learning a type of competitive intelligence, prompted by a spirit of rivalry, and noticed in the scant surviving correspondence between Richmond and Peter Collinson, who began to wonder about Hill's character.[32]

Hill's jaunts to London included visits to its theaters and probably prostitutes. He became a habitué of the vicinity extending from Covent Garden to the playhouses further west, attending plays and acting in them. His silly quarrel in 1739–1740 with John Rich, the well-established actor, took everyone by surprise. Hill had watched Rich on stage, and heard he was about to produce a pantomime in February (1740) based on the myth of Orpheus and Eurydice. Hill crept into the rehearsals, slyly copied passages, and embellished them with his own lines, beating Rich to publication in December (1739).[33] Then he delivered his printed "opera" to Rich's town house in Bloomsbury Square, and within twenty-four hours gave out that Rich had plagiarized from *him*.[34]

Rich was astounded. He was already a London presence well-known to its celebrities, having founded the Beefstakes and socialized with its members. He protested that years earlier he had written his pantomime for Lewis Theobald's (the erstwhile dunce of Pope's first *Dunciad*) *Orpheus*, and offered to have both versions read aloud before a neutral group of judges.[35] Rich recited his own version while Hill delegated his to the actors; when the judges found for Rich, Hill denounced them saying "he would refer it to Mr. *Pope*, Mr. *Littleton*, or Mr. *Glover*."[36] The literal-minded Rich countered Hill's further threats by producing piles of evidence to demonstrate he had been working on his "Entertainment of *Orpheus and Eurydice* upwards of twelve years."[37] He obtained affidavits from Theobald affirming that Rich applied to him in 1723 to write a musical entertainment—when Hill was just nine. "To have printed mine instead of his [own] . . . in which Opinion I am the more confirm'd," Rich wrote, seemed incredible. Hill's text was so inferior, he claimed, "there was no *Person* so *low in Life* as would lay the *least Claim to it*."

This affair entailed more than puppydom and the wagging of tails. Whatever propelled Hill to proceed so recklessly remains unknown, but Rich's labeling him the "poetical Apothecary" during the furore is telling.[38] You could make a small fortune then if you were a sought after apothecary with the right portfolio of pills, potions, and personality; by the 1740s apothecaries had swelled to such numbers, and adopted so many different styles, that notoriety was gained by difference. Hill exploited more than his literary capability, as we have seen; everywhere flouting his "foreignness," his degree of erudition, as well as his florid rhetoric and rhymes. He could be English when necessary, but also a foreign French or German quack. He "acted" his "cures," peddling them by "dramatizing" pills and potions in the sequence of illness and recovery. This is what Rich meant by the designation, suggesting that Hill was unique—there was no one else like him. Naming him the "poetical *foreign* Apothecary" would have been even more exquisite to describe this *lusus naturae.*

The unique strategy saved Hill from chastisement, for the English public had become jaded about the apothecary's trade by the 1740s. Contemporary commentary on this matter is plentiful.[39] "To talk like an apothecary; to use hard or gallipot words: from the assumed gravity and affectation of knowledge generally put on by the gentlemen of this profession, who are commonly as superficial in their learning as they are pedantic in their language"—this was one common view capped by further defamation as the proverbial "charlatan" and "quack."[40] Such aspersions, cast at performing quacks such as the legendary Dr. Richard Rock—apothecary-charlatan-mountebank *par excellence*—did not faze Hill.[41] He enlarged himself as "rhyming apothecary," cultivated charlatan, quipping quack, and was determined to acquire these metropolitan roles, especially when he discovered they were no obstacles to social rise. When some hack scribbled these verses, readers thought they described Rock: "Powders for Children, Cakes for Worms; And thus you've trod all Paths by turns."[42]

Figure 2.3. Dr. Rock, c. 1730–1740, an itinerant vendor of medicines, selling his wares from a horse-drawn carriage to a crowd; John and Charles Wesley are preaching in the background. Engraving, 1743.

Reproduced by kind permission of the Wellcome Library, London.

In 1739–1740 Hill had not yet moved up to London but was becoming known, as Rich's phrase suggests, as a type of charlatan: the "rhyming apothecary." It was the product of his ingenuity to pursue pills and plays, medicine and literature. Was it fallout from the small war with Rich that caused him to leave Goodwood in 1742? The chronology does not fit: if the scandal with Rich had taken a serious toll at Goodwood in 1740, Richmond would not have kept him on. If anything, the duke was fonder of him in 1741–1742 than earlier, although far from blind to his foibles. The likelihood is that Hill broke away in search of urban celebrity. Fracases, such as the one with Rich, can strike our sensibility as morally reprehensible, but were the way of the world in the eighteenth century and far from sufficient to ruin the young aspirant in Richmond's eyes.

Besides, Hill was already a savvy virtuoso mountebank, accustomed to makeshift platforms, foreign garb, and gullible audiences. The transition to the makeshift stage at Goodwood proved easy and was wrapped in luxury too. It amounted to a visiting theater company populated with actors who regularly came down from London to perform in its courtly productions. To the young Hill all this added luster to its *dolce vita* ambience: a place as privileged as Cambridge or Oxford he longed to attend and had heard so much about, capped by these migrant celebrities. Among them was Peg Woffington (1720?–1760), the dazzling young actress then barely twenty who was brought down by theatrical impresario Owen MacSwiny (1676–1754, often called Swiny or Swinny). He was old enough to be her grandfather, which precipitated endless gossip at Goodwood, and a theater manager partial to the new Italian opera then so fashionable in London.

Decades earlier MacSwiny had taken refuge from bankruptcy on the Continent, where he combed Italy for musical scores and singers, and was said to have wildly sown his own seeds. There he met Richmond while a young man on his (Richmond's) Grand Tour, who invited him to be his secretary. MacSwiny accepted and began to commission paintings from contemporary Italian artists. The paintings Hill saw hanging on the walls of the great rooms at Goodwood—by Caneletto, Piazetta, Cimarola, Mirandolesi, Sebastiano Ricci, and others—were mostly commissioned by MacSwiny. They hung in the great dining room and saloon. And MacSwiny had recruited Caneletto to England in the 1740s, to be Richmond's special painter. This was the artistic and scientific milieu Hill witnessed at Goodwood. But MacSwiny also had other sides. Long before this time, in 1705, MacSwiny's scabrous translation of Molière's *The Love Doctor* (1665) caused such consternation, especially among the proponents of the new reformation of manners; it was withdrawn from the London stage.[43]

Its recall did not end MacSwiny's amorous stage pursuits. Newly fired with desire for Woffington around 1739–1740, he began another translation of *The Love Doctor* while down in Goodwood, this time as a farce. He retained Molière's original characters but—to enhance the farce—increased young daughter Sganarelle's [*sic*] visits to the street charlatan to purchase Orviétan, or Venice treacle, the legendary remedy alleged to cure any illness, including hers. And he offered Woffington the part of Sganarelle: the purest proof of his love. Woffington, then green and willing, accepted, while Hill's rising star disappeared into a black hole in her emotional universe.

Now the plot thickens. Hill persuaded himself that MacSwiny's amplification of the scenes with the charlatan quack (in act two) were satires on *himself*; in other words, the literary text was charged and coded. MacSwiny took no notice. He reported directly to Richmond, whose agent and secretary he remained. Yet the more Richmond calmed MacSwiny, the further agitated young Hill became, who lusted for Peg as avidly as old man Owen and naively believed his tender years counted for more than sexagenarian MacSwiny's overtures. When MacSwiny further pursued Peg in distant Bath, while obsessively engaging her to play Sganarelle there, Hill followed on a horse; a public tussle occurred, fisticuffs were given, and Richmond apprised that the "good gentlemen of his court" were embarrassing him "in this Realm" too. But MacSwiny was unrelenting and continued to follow lovely Peg down to Goodwood, on grounds he was her amanuensis. The infatuation swelled and, a decade later, he willed his fortune to her, leaving her a rich woman when he died, aged almost seventy, in 1754.

The incident at Bath alerted MacSwiny to his rude-headed, if not ruddy, competitor: Hill. The two men came to blows yet again, in London, leaving Woffington in the middle, wondering how she would navigate these troubled waters between the Scylla of age and Charybdis of naiveté.[44] In despair she confided her dilemma to "little Oroonoko," the black African page who had been gifted to Richmond by Sir Thomas Robinson before Hill's arrival, who sent his patron this fashionable libation when posted as governor to Barbados.[45] The triangle's passions heated up again in the weeks leading up to Christmas 1742, as they prepared for some dramatic performance.

But mischievous Peg was also culpable and gave Hill hope: "a Little double Meaning touch," as she charmingly described it to Oroonoko. Was she impressed by Hill's height and good looks? She naughtily answered his letters, even after rebuffing him at Bath—this while infatuated Hill burned hers for its "expressions too tender and passionate . . . to be shewn."[46] He boasted about her "compliments" to MacSwiny, which Peg claimed were intended not "for him" at all but for their *joint* acting success at Drury Lane that spring, where Hill had appeared side by side with her in Wycherley's *The Provoked Wife*, where she played Lady Brute and he the "young Gentleman."[47]

Woffington also went to watch him play Carlos in Colley Cibber's *Love Makes a Man*, and she was shocked to witness "the attack of his foes, armd with Catt-calls and other Offensive Weapons." This was the last straw. When she later "hugged" him—whether in London or down at Goodwood is unknown—he construed the gesture as further encouragement and trumpeted his conquest. Peg claimed she gave him just "a Little double Meaning touch, on the expressive and gracefull Motion of his hands and arms" to demonstrate how he should *not* move on stage—a comedy of errors ending in Hill's tears.[48] Woffington herself was mythologized after her Goodwood sojourn, especially in the role of actress as whore, but her role in this triangle is no myth. Surviving letters prove it.

This comic welter prompted mirth at Goodwood and scandal in t'Town, amusing the duke too, and it is to Richmond's credit he did not permit it to detract from his sense of Hill's genuine botanical capability. Hill nevertheless packed his trunks and left Goodwood by the summer of 1743. Not a word in his correspondence laments the absence of Sussex meadows and trees, or the countryside he had known as an adolescent. In London he attended the botanical lectures periodically offered under the patronage of the Apothecaries' Company in Blackfriars.[49] He may he "fallen in love" with the capital's atmosphere of pleasure, captured that May (1742) in the opening of Ranelagh Gardens. Or he may have felt overwhelmed early on trying to attend to his duties at Goodwood while also assisting Petre's grieving widow down at Thorndon. A biographical entry in his *Inspector* papers suggests he traveled to Ireland that summer, but no further evidence for the trip survives. By 1744 he has opened an apothecary's stall in the Savoy, in the Strand, and is living close by, drawing on contacts he had made at Goodwood. To what extent he thanked his patron before departing for all Richmond had done for him is unknown, as are the terms on which he left.

Six years later, in 1750, Richmond was dead, eulogized by novelist Henry Fielding: "[the duke] was one of the worthiest of magistrates, as well as the best of men."[50] Hill could not have wished for a better patron. Whether he believed he had found him in Richmond remains doubtful, and the events of 1746–1749 cast long shadows on their relation. Dark clouds were gathering, not in utopian and paradisiacal Goodwood but within three miles of the river Thames, at the point where it wraps itself around central London.

NOTES

1. The botanists in this biography are identified in the Dramatis Personae.
2. *Inspector* 17.
3. See the works by D. D. C. Chambers, McLean, and Oliver.
4. D. D. C. Chambers, passim.
5. C. E. Raven (1946); C. E. Raven (1986).
6. Petre' s *Herbarium* was bought by Mayor Sutro, California, while in London in 1898 and brought to San Francisco, where it is now housed at the Sutro Library. It has never been published. For its contents see McLean, 36–39.

7. D. D. C. Chambers, 107.
8. Keith Thomas, 227.
9. James E. Smith (1821), 37–42; McLean, 37–38.
10. See McCann, xxxii; Olson, chap. 4–5. Comparisons with later periods are invidious and often incorrect, but there is no question that Richmond would today be considered a multimillionaire.
11. William Hayley Mason; Bonney, passim; the notes to McCann's introduction.
12. McCann; *DNB*, life of the 2nd Duke of Richmond.
13. Fuller, 27.
14. McCann; *DNB*, life of the 2nd Duke of Richmond.
15. McCann, xxxiv.
16. The visitor to Goodwood today can still view them.
17. JH (1752c), 7.
18. Olson, passim; Gordon-Lennox cannot be trusted on the duke's politics.
19. Blackwell; Shteir, chapter 3.
20. JH (1752c), 16.
21. McCann, xxiv–xxvi.
22. Stukeley, MSS Eng. Misc. d 719/1.
23. Theorides, 62–76.
24. Réaumur, passim.
25. John Baker (1952), chapter 6.
26. JH (1752c), 336.
27. Delpit, passim.
28. For Edwards's mineralogy see George Edwards (1770); JH discussed later him in JH (1771b) and (1772).
29. Caricatures of JH as a "foreigner" begin to appear by 1743; see BM Satire AN355224001 reproduced here (figure 2.2). The curators at the BM have correctly identified the subject as JH.
30. Hutcheson (1726), 22–23.
31. LPH, 6–7
32. LPH, 3–7; McCann, xxix.
33. JH (1740a).
34. Rich (1739); JH (1740a); JH (1740b).
35. Rich, (1739), 19.
36. Rich (1739), 17.
37. Rich (1739), 20.
38. Rich (1739), 22.
39. R. Porter (2000), 122–43.
40. J. G. Burnby, 94.
41. See Rock (1740) for the apothecary's language at this time.
42. Coltheart, 16.
43. MacSwiny (1745); MacSwiny's letters to Richmond are in the West Sussex RO, Goodwood MS 105.
44. LPH, 5–6.
45. LPH, 5.
46. LPH, 6.
47. The editors of *The London Stage* record a manuscript entry stating that JH received the part "By Particular Desire"; see Stone, vol. 3, part 1, 975–78.
48. LPH, 5–7.
49. Burnby, 176.
50. Henry Fielding (1751), 69.

3

Apothecary Hill, Almost FRS

In 2000, Dr. Richard Palmer was the archivist and librarian of Lambeth Palace, since 1610 the London seat of the Archbishops of Canterbury. We had been friends during the years when he worked as a curator at the Wellcome Institute for the History of Medicine, but afterward we lost touch. I forget how we reconnected but we did, and soon afterward Hill's name arose. Palmer knew I had been working on him for years.

"Have you seen the portrait of him as a young man," he inquired, "hanging in the great hall of the Society of Barber-Surgeons in London?" A portrait of the young Hill? I had been searching for one for decades, to no avail, and replied in the negative. "Well, I'm pretty sure it is Hill," he said, "but you'd best check." So off I went thinking it would turn out to be another false alarm: few portraits of early eighteenth-century apothecaries survive. It was a hot summer morning when I wended my way through the streets around the Barbican and the old London Wall in search of the Barber Surgeons Hall in Monkwell Square. Then there it was, hanging in the great lobby: almost certainly a portrait of the young Hill based on the provenance its archivists had collected.[1]

I spent a few hours in a chair gazing at the portrait while simultaneously pouring through an article about its owners after Hill's death in 1775. Dozens of questions arose about artist and sitter, and how it was passed down through generations and eventually bequeathed to the Worshipful Company of Barbers. But nothing in the smile or cheek position suggested a heartbroken Hill, freshly aggrieved from his disappointment with Peg. Or had he been painted a few years earlier, in 1740–1741, around twenty-seven, perhaps by some visiting artist before he left Goodwood? I never found out but construed this first known image as an omen.

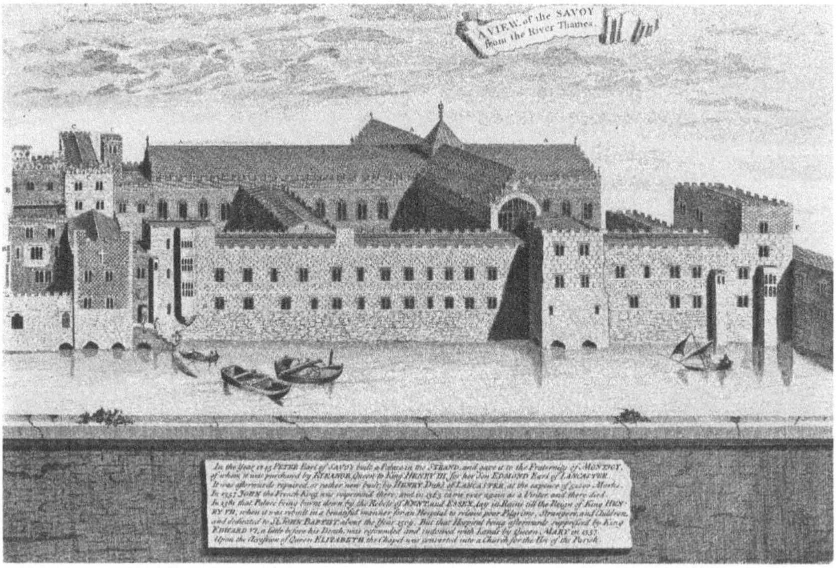

Figure 3.1. The Savoy in the Strand, c. 1733.
Reproduced by kind permission of the Wellcome Library, London.

In London, Hill worked for himself—the itinerant apothecary-botanist turned entrepreneur. His social sights were stratospheric and had been developing ever since Goodwood days. If asked their vocation, nine persons out of ten in the street would then have replied "quack," the tenth "apothecary," but the borderland between them was murky depending on qualifications, the quack's positioning of himself, and his degree of geographical fixity.[2] Hill had not been settled for almost a decade but he had a sense of his future, where he wanted to go. Fixing himself in the Savoy was a step to stability.

Moreover, "stationary" apothecaries, as distinct from "itinerant" types, were just beginning to earn large sums if diligent, persistent, lucky, and imaginatively marketing themselves. Oxford botanist William Sherard's brother James accumulated a small fortune as a London apothecary by dispensing new preparations claimed to be "made from rare botanical plants." It enabled him to buy a country estate (in Eltham outside London) and hire his brother William's botanical assistant, the illustrious Johann Jakob Dillenius, to catalogue his collections.[3] Other overlapping designations still competed without distinction in the popular mind: charlatan, empiric, mountebank, quack—and choice also depended on the speaker's intention, whether to describe or denigrate when labeling. "Quacks" often called themselves "doctors," but were rarely confused with physicians, despite performing many identical tasks for a fraction of the charge, as did the young "Dr. Hill" newly arrived in London. Thirty years later he was still being listed as "an illustrious quack" selling mercury medicines to those afflicted with venereal

Figure 3.2. An apothecary sitting in his shop, sorting through materia medica, surrounded by paraphernalia of his profession. Engraving by Dr. Rock, c.1750, after W. Shakespeare.

disease. For now, early in the 1740s, he had set up in the Savoy compound: a palace that gave him abundant visibility and included military quarters, several chapels, state rooms, and a prison.

His shop was a stall, a space in the palace with tables to sell to the public. Hill displayed his goods, which included plants and seeds brought up from Goodwood. He may not have moved out and periodically returned, riding back to Westminster with the goods. The conquest of disease was not one of Hill's goals, neither particular patients nor to improve society. The historical moment played a small role in this attitude: at home England was relatively peaceful in 1740–1742, numbers of her sailors and soldiers not yet assigned abroad as they would be later in 1744 when the French threatened to invade. That summer—1744—he wrote letters to Stukeley, still up at his living at All Saints' in Stamford where he had moved after his ordination into the Church of England, describing his routine.[4] He had turned thirty; was working hard, reading prolifically, and began to harbor a sense of himself as a "man of parts who will live by his wits." He is gathering natural medicines and promoting them. He recommends books such as Joseph Randall's new *System of Geography* to clients interested to learn more about botany, but doubts Randall is sufficiently familiar with the natural history of Pennsylvania, about which he has written in some detail.[5] This "poetical apothecary" can also be the "pedantic apothecary," eager to display his learning.

THE "ADAM AND EVE" TAVERN, 1750.

Figure 3.3. The Adam and Eve public house, c. 1745. George Walter Thornbury (Edward Walford), *Old and New London*, IV, p. 475 (1880–1886).

Reproduced by kind permission of Professor George Rousseau.

By 1745 he signs his letters as from "Adams Court, on the Broadway in Westminster," today just off Victoria Street behind the St. James's Park Tube Station. He meets the Earl of Burlington, idol of the recently deceased poet Alexander Pope, and takes up with Burlington's steward's daughter, Susannah Travers,[6] while keeping on the lookout for new patrons. Early that year he was sufficiently confident to cash in on the flurry of works appearing after Pope's death the previous May, and commented on "Squire Ayre's *Memoir of the Life of Mr. Pope*" addressed as "A Letter to Mr. Edmund Curl, Bookseller."[7] He also married Susannah in 1745 who perhaps imagined herself as the proverbial apothecary's wife: busy, frugal, protective of her husband's trade and mindful of his secret recipes—all this to join into the "middle rank" of London life, as economic historian Peter Earle has called it, and help her husband get rich.[8]

Figure 3.4. Dr. James Parsons, physician and antiquary. By B. Wilson. Reg. No. 560, c. 1762.

Reproduced by kind permission of the National Portrait Gallery.

Hill now began to follow the routine that would sustain him for a decade. He lodged between the Savoy in the Strand and St. James's, and remained here until he moved into the parish of St. James. He did not yet have the resource to live in style, but already cut a dapper figure in the local public houses and taverns. He strolled the capital's pleasure gardens in search of company, lute in hand, and wrote his own songs. This song became popular and Lewis Granom, the German flutist in London, set it, and others, to music:

> Bid me when forty Winters more,
> Have furrow'd deep my pallid Brow
> When from my Head a scanty store
> Lankly the wither'd Tresses flow;
> When the high Tide, that bold and strong,
> Now rolls impetuous on and free,
> Languid and slow, scarce steals along;
> Then bid me court Sobriety![9]

He was seen at White's fashionable "Chocolate House" in St. James Street, opened in 1693 by Italian immigrant Frances White, and at the Bedford coffeehouse, which the Fielding brothers frequented, located under the Piazza in Covent Garden. He shuttled between his base in the Savoy and his rooms in Adam's Court eastward into Fleet Street and St. Paul's, often ending the day nearer home to his wife Susannah, and it may have been there that he first encountered the naturalist Emanuel Mendes da Costa.[10]

Da Costa was an odd type striving to become a prototypical man of the Enlightenment Republic of Letters: assiduous collector, compulsive classifier, polymath, addicted to amassing specimens at any cost—a noticeable Jew living in a generation in England when, for the first time, he could hope to rise from humble origins by dint of ability despite the religion of his birth. A few Jews of great wealth—Samson Gideon was the most glaring example—had been embraced by England for pouring money into it. Gideon started out with a large patrimony in the Painter-Stainers's Company and ended up a billionaire (if you convert his accumulated wealth to our equivalence) by investing in stocks, insurance, diamonds, and the East India Company, and making loans to the nation.[11] But Hill and da Costa were miles apart, even if both embarked on their own modest sails. They also differed in religious temperament: the Jew pious, if also corrupt, Hill an occasional believer without sustained commitment to the Church of England.[12] Barely three years apart—Hill was the older—they nevertheless discovered common ground.

Stukeley prepared the way. By 1740 he was corresponding with da Costa about the philosophical meaning of the Psalms,[13] and they remained friends to the end of Stukeley's life, Stukeley joining the Jew for Passover services and suppers, and involving him in the paper sketch he was reconstructing for "Solomon's Temple."[14] Antiquarian and Christian Stukeley was fascinated by the attempts of Jewish archaeologists to resurrect models of earlier synagogues, and both were members of the Spalding Society where they first met before 1745. Da Costa was also Martin Folkes's friend, by now president of the Royal Society after Hans Sloane pleaded illness in 1741. Folkes had often visited Goodwood while Hill was in residence, and invited him to attend a meeting of the FRS, which he did. Folkes then wrote to da Costa that "all sorts of natural knowledge" crazes the duke (Richmond), who is "the most humane and best man living there ever was."[15] When Hill came up to London, he not only visited Crane Court but—thanks to Richmond—da Costa.

Da Costa was born in the London parish of St. Christopher-le-Stocks, within Cheapside, in a family that spoke Ladino (the old Spanish of the Jews before the Inquisition), Hebrew, and French at home. His devoutly orthodox father educated him in these languages and in the law, and paid to have him apprenticed to a notary. Other Jews also contributed to his education. Israel Lyons the elder, a Polish Jew who kept a silversmith's shop in Cambridge, tutored him in Hebrew on his jaunts down to London. Lyons's son, Israel Jr., was an erudite botanist and mathematician and would later sail with Joseph Banks and Constantine Phipps in search of the longitude. Da Costa soon caught the bug of natural history and by twenty-one was collecting and classifying butterflies, making a transition from law to natural history that may appear puzzling to us today but perfectly understandable to da Costa's learned father. One butterfly led to another, one field junket to another little exploration, and in 1740 da Costa was inscribed as a "merchant" member of the Aurelian Society—gentlemen who gathered to observe birds and bees—followed by his official election.[16]

At that time, the Aurelians met at the King's Arm tavern in Cornhill and had been collecting insects for a generation, having compiled a catalogue used by the great John Ray. Benjamin Wilkes, an ardent lepidopterist himself who died in 1749, documents their activities in London up to the year 1748—when da Costa was still active among them—in his book about English moths and butterflies.[17] But Aurelian life came to an abrupt end that March (1748), while members congregated in the Swan Tavern in Change Alley were nearly burned alive in the fire that broke out. They escaped, but their entire collection, library, and records were destroyed. Da Costa, and perhaps Hill too, may have been in the Swan that night. The loss so disheartened the fellowship that they never again regrouped.

By then da Costa had amassed an extensive collection of shells, minerals, and fossils, and generated an impressive network of correspondents who assisted him in obtaining more specimens. He was also gathering a reputation as one of the key fossil experts of the day, corresponding with celebrated

European naturalists while struggling, more locally, with adversity. His wife, Leah del Prado, was a third daughter without fortune, and his father unable to increase his son's funding. Besides, da Costa spent whatever he earned on his collections. And his financial problems swelled by 1754, when he was imprisoned for debt and his cabinets held in bond, despite the need to feed Leah (they were a childless couple). He was approaching forty and still receiving financial support from his father. When released the following year, he continued to prepare his long-promised *Natural History of Fossils*, first proposed in 1751 as a two-volume work.[18] Only the first part of the first volume appeared in 1757, and was highly praised by Linnaeus and his students. But the biographical picture was checkered, even stained, and by 1763 da Costa, although by now a respected member of the scientific and antiquarian communities, was a naturalist with a "history" and a prison record.

Antiquary Stukeley proved himself the generous enabler yet again. His public influence was diminishing but still palpable, and through his efforts da Costa was elected clerk of the Royal Society on April 3, 1763, following the death of Francis Hauksbee, as well as its librarian and keeper of its finances: the "Repository," as it was then called. Relieved of financial worry da Costa married (around 1766) a second wife, Elizabeth Skillman (or Stillman), with whom he had one daughter. He was now being paid £50 per annum, a handsome sum, and was housed rent-free on the Society's premises at Crane Court in Fleet Street. He had been in post for five years when he was found to have embezzled about £1500 of the Society's funds. Responsible for the collection of subscriptions as part of his duties, he misappropriated more than a hundred members' fees. He was dismissed in December 1767, the family of three evicted from Crane Court, their possessions sold at auction, and, five months later, by May 1768, was taken to court by the Society, and committed in November that year to the King's Bench prison in St. George's Fields. Penalty followed upon penalty, and he was also expelled from the Society of Antiquaries, his personal library and specimens confiscated, sold at auction, the purchase of which had hurled him into debt in the first place, charged by the government with fraud, and imprisoned a second time.

He remained in prison until October 1772. While incarcerated he attempted to support himself by writing articles about natural history, and gave lectures on fossils. Friends like Hill also sent him books. With these at his side, in his jail cell, he annotated Gustav Engestrom's English translation of Swedish chemist Axel Cronstedt's much discussed essay of 1758 on the "new mineralogy,"[19] and translated into English Dru Drury's book about insects, *Illustrations of Natural History* (1770–1782).[20] Alone, hungry, disappointed, he toiled away in his cell and was paid by the word. In 1772 he was discharged from prison under the Insolvent Act, and from then until his death almost twenty years later, in 1791, he struggled to support himself, living from hand to mouth.

But we get ahead of ourselves. In 1744–1745, when Hill and da Costa first met, they talked about botany as the new frontier and conjured joint projects. One wonders how two such dissimilar figures could calibrate their botanical discourse in joint publication: Hill educated in classical languages by his father, da Costa privately tutored in the law. The latter turned out to be far more *au fait* with the universal language of natural history, then emerging from Latin into English, than the former. Although da Costa had not attended university (Jews could not in the 1740s), his English was perfect and his Latin almost as good. It is not clear how he acquired first-class Latin, having articled himself to a London notary, but somehow he did, reading prodigiously, talking to and corresponding with other naturalists, and addictively joining their learned societies.

Da Costa was the only Jew Hill befriended, and his influence on his slightly older colleague must not be minimized. To be Jewish in London in the 1740s entailed cultural difference as significantly as anything else: a distinct heritage as well as mythologies long since hardened about Jews as moneylenders and money hoarders. Da Costa was atypical; no other Jew was then so promising in science. His drive to forge his way, as an outsider, into closed scientific circles noteworthy. Contrast him with Samson Gideon, just mentioned, and their differences of character and interest is palpable, not merely the financial disparity but because Gideon was a keen naturalist and had also been, like da Costa, elected to the Spalding Society. Wealthy Gideon even bought estates near Spalding just to be close to the meetings. Da Costa's singularity, in contrast, was the vastness of his correspondents and natural history collections. This international network of "learned men" dazzled Hill when they first met through intermediary Stukeley.

Da Costa was not the only Jewish scientist in London then but was the most energetic, which enthralled Hill. Activity, energy, and movement had always impressed him. He himself would grow restless *nonpareil*. They corresponded prolifically, drew increasingly familiar, and addressed each other—as Republicans then did in the virtuous Republic—as "dear Friend" and "Fellow Labourer."[21] The younger da Costa took the lead, especially when collecting shells and fossils, and he was destined to become one of Europe's most distinguished early geologists.[22] Soon they lodged in the same square on the Broadway, sharing friends, ideas, and news, perhaps visiting the Royal Society's private club housed in the Crown and Anchor public house in the Strand (which permitted visitors), and perching themselves at the more literary Bedford coffeehouse with port in one hand and rock specimens in the other for show to other collectors.

They also traveled together in the service of notable lords. "Mrs. Hill" was no encumbrance to the bachelor da Costa who did not marry Leah del

Prado, as we noted, until April 1750. Da Costa's excesses soon proved too glaring to stave off his creditors. But, again, we get ahead of ourselves.

Hill also made the acquaintance of several FRS, including Sir Hans Sloane (who would not die until 1753), Martin Folkes, William Watson, Henry Baker, and James Parsons. He spent the summer of 1745 "botanizing and mineralizing" with da Costa in Ireland[23]—his first time across a sea—in search of rare specimens and to supply his apothecary shop in the Savoy. He was back in London by September when da Costa took him to Crane Court, perhaps for the first time. Hill had long since sensed "the fire of botany"; the question now was how he interpreted its "gentlemanliness" and ever-increasing sociability.

Within months the two grew especially interested in bezoars—those mysterious properties believed to have the power of a universal antidote against any poison—and were corresponding about them. Bezoars had been sought for centuries, and, recently, Isaac Newton and William Woodward, the naturalist, had bitterly disagreed about their origins.[24] The Scriblerians lambasted them for their controversy *a deux*, especially in the *Memoirs of Martinus Scriblerus*, but the debate continued after their deaths, oddly within a few months of each other in 1727–1728. This was before Hill became interested. What Hill knew and thought he could believe was that the class of bezoars was widely distributed throughout the natural world: a drinking glass that contained a bezoar could neutralize any poison poured into it. As long ago as 1575 the surgeon Ambroise Paré described an experiment to test the wondrous properties of bezoar stone, and ever since then experimentalists had been searching for its secrets. Quacks and apothecaries in Hill's time routinely peddled many potions as "extract of bezoar," the magic name for instant sales. Even today, bezoar stone is extolled in *Harry Potter* as an antidote to the deadliest poisons.

Hill and da Costa also planned a collaborative project—"the prosecution of our Work," as da Costa continued to refer to it—one facet of which involved Hill's preparation of a modern translation of *Theophrastus's History of Stones*.[25] There were others too, including projected books about fossils. The rationale was straightforward: no English translation existed, and the Latin version by Flemish scholars Anselmus de Boodt (1550–1632) and Joannes de Laet (1593–1649) continued to be used. A first English translation would broadcast Hill's knowledge of Greek—always a sensitive topic to the fledgling who had not attended university—as well as demonstrate his comprehension of ancient history and natural history. Da Costa continued to maintain that a new edition of this classic of geology that included the Greek text was sorely needed, and that Hill alone was eminently suited to produce it. Even Hill's later antagonist, Christopher Smart the poet, complained early in the 1740s while still a Cambridge scholar that he could find no Greek text.[26]

To the modern student of geology and paleontology, Theophrastus's ancient text appears seminal for breaking new ground in the medicinal uses of stones. But this practical value had been lost for decades by Hill's generation owing to the work's inaccessibility. Hill's translation from Greek would remedy that. He titled his book "an English version," followed by "critical and philosophical notes: including the modern history of the gems, &c. described by that author [Theophrastus], and of many other of the native fossils . . . to which are added, two letters, one to Dr. James Parsons, F. R. S., on the colors of the sapphire and turquoise, the other to Martin Folkes . . . upon the effects of different menstruums [*sic*] on copper, both tending to illustrate the doctrine of the gems being coloured by metalline particles."[27] Both the named figures, Parsons and Folkes, could be counted on for their support, as could the deserved dedication to Richmond; both had encouraged Hill, and Richmond was still a quondam patron despite Hill's attempts to add John Boyle, the Earl of Orrery (1707–1762) to his repertoire.[28] Orrery was then furnishing his new town house in Leicester Fields, and Hill had been assisting him to collect curiosities of all types for his cabinets.

In Hill's era, Theophrastus had come down as a genius second only to Aristotle and as his protégé and successor in the Lyceum; as a wide-ranging thinker whose writings extended from biology and physics to ethics and metaphysics; and whose surviving work on stones had been a landmark, according to Pliny in the study of the history of the earth. At the end of the century, Cuvier, the French evolutionist, would repeat Pliny's estimate of the importance of Theophrastus and claim that the science of mineralogy, and ultimately geology, arose from his early texts, a position also reiterated by modern historians of science. But in 1745 Theophrastus was not yet a household name: this would change in part owing to Hill's translation, which inspired numerous naturalists, including the radical Whig John Wilkes, to follow in Hill's lead and turn for guidance to Theophrastus's natural history. The shift in emphasis was palpable. Before Hill's translation Theophrastus's *Characters*—studies of moral stereotypes—had been the main, preferred work; often reprinted and intriguing diverse thinkers in the span from Descartes to Newton who thought they could construct sciences of character types based on it. Theophrastus's grip on the European imagination continued into the Victorian world when novelist George Eliot refashioned his "precious characters" as a vital presence in her intellectual mind-set in *Impressions of Theophrastus Such* (1879).

Flashing back to Hill's milieu, the new botanizing was also arousing widespread curiosity about stones. Geology was not yet a "science," but it is difficult to name anyone among the ancients who had commented more astutely about it than Theophrastus.[29] His reflections on stones classified rocks based on their behavior when heated, grouping minerals by common properties, such as amber and magnetite which both have the power of attraction. He had also observed the effect of heat on minerals and their different "hardnesses," which proved more promising to the students of stones of Hill's world than any modern thinker. The former dominance of La Bruyère's (1645–1696) French translation of "Theophrastus Characters" was soon replaced by Hill's publication, shifting the gravity of attention from moral stereotypes to natural phenomena. And it is no surprise that Hill's book, with its copious notes providing the most far-ranging picture of eighteenth-century mineralogy to date, was welcomed and praised.

The list of subscribers to it was as impressive as its price. All London seemed to take notice. Nothing like it existed. Da Costa had secured many who were delighted to fork out the hefty price of almost £4 to buy it.[30] *GM* announced it as having appeared on or about September 7, 1746, fittingly dedicated to his erstwhile patron, Richmond—he who had so far opened all doors to his puppy-prodigy.[31]

Within days of its publication Hill was posting letters about its appearance. One was directed to William Watson FRS, the medical botanist interested in electricity, ostensibly about "the Chrysocolla of the Antients," a mysterious substance useful in the soldering of gold, but more pressingly apprising Watson of the appearance of *Theophrastus on Stones*.[32] Da Costa, for his part, profusely congratulated Hill, sent out his own letters praising the new book, and posted further greetings to "Mrs. Hill" and the Shrimptons, Hill's sister Anne and her husband Ferdinand Shrimpton, who still lived in Denham.[33]

Meanwhile, sister Anne had given birth to another child, a girl, and frail Theophilus was hanging on for life. He would be dead in a few months.[34] Hill occasionally rode down to Denham see him, while collecting specimens on the way, but his closest collaborator remained da Costa, who proved to be more than fellow toiler in the botanical and geological fields.[35] During that autumn of 1745 and winter of 1746 he worked in his stall in the Savoy and resided in the Broadway. He was thirty-one, the age at which most men have formed the friendships that will endure for a lifetime. He had made none at Goodwood: da Costa was the main figure in his orbit; corresponding with him when they were not collecting fossils and plants, especially in the East Anglia Hill knew so well from his youth, or dissecting passages together at Dr. James Parsons's house in Red Lion Square, as we shall see. By February (1747) Hill was back in London, eager to help da Costa campaign for his own election to the Royal Society,[36] and to read a paper on "The Seeding of Mosses" in the Society's *Transactions*,[37] soon followed by another paper on the unusual properties of "The Windsor Loam."[38]

Hill basked in the reception of *Theophrastus.* Finally, the kudos he sought was forthcoming, he thought, and squarely positioned him in the virtuous Republic of Letters. Several FRS, not merely his mentors in the Royal Society, saluted his "Greek competence," as one admirer called it. Yet murmurs of plagiarism were whispered, in light of his lack of university education. Plagiarism from where? No English edition of Theophrastus existed; temporarily the whispers were aborted. Yet it proved to be a charge frequently made against Hill when he displayed knowledge of the ancient languages.

Da Costa remained loyal. He had identified a good friend and knowledgeable collaborator, validated by the "botanical Duke" Richmond for taking on Hill at Goodwood; Hill himself was reading papers in Crane Court. It was only a matter of time before he would follow in da Costa's footsteps as FRS. Da Costa's associate was a busy bee who attended over forty meetings of the Society between 1746 and 1747.[39] The future looked rosy *ne plus ultra* for this second son from the fenlands, formerly without prospects.

The success of *Theophrastus* energized Hill. In just two years—1745 to 1746—he struck out in many directions, contacting "gentlemen of science," presenting himself to them as a "gentleman-scholar." Da Costa introduced him to John Turberville Needham (1713–1781), the first Catholic priest to be elected FRS, which election occurred in January 1747,[40] while da Costa's nomination was still pending. Needham had aroused interest through microscopy and the newly discovered electricity, but also for his reproductive biology.[41] During the 1740s a view was developing that biological understanding about reproduction initiated by Leeuwenhoek and the Dutch anatomists could only improve by the introduction of newly strengthened microscopes. When Needham challenged the preformationist view that microorganisms do not grow from eggs in a series of talks in Crane Court, men of science took note and elected him.[42] He had already been corresponding with Buffon in Paris, who would use his results in his widely read *Histoire naturelle*, but it was Needham's gauntlet thrown to the biological preformationists that made a lasting impression on Hill.

Hill came under his sway when Needham was a frequent guest at James Parsons's "Wednesday afternoon meetings" in Red Lion Square, Bloomsbury.[43] Parsons was a decade older than Hill and inclined to mentor the younger man. He was a man of genial character, generous with his time and hospitality, but Hill perplexed him. Having been trained under leading professors of medicine and natural history in Paris, Parsons had traveled in Ireland and the Low Countries, and glimpsed other worlds than those the gentlemen of Crane Court inhabited. Once back from France he converted his house into a research center: holding seminars and mini-conferences where *tout le monde* gathered, especially antiquarians and artists. Stukeley was a "regular," as were Arderon, Baker, da Costa, Needham, William Hogarth the artist, and many others. Here Hill sauntered from his quarters at the Adam and Eve, his first proper introduction to the Republic of Letters on an equal footing.[44]

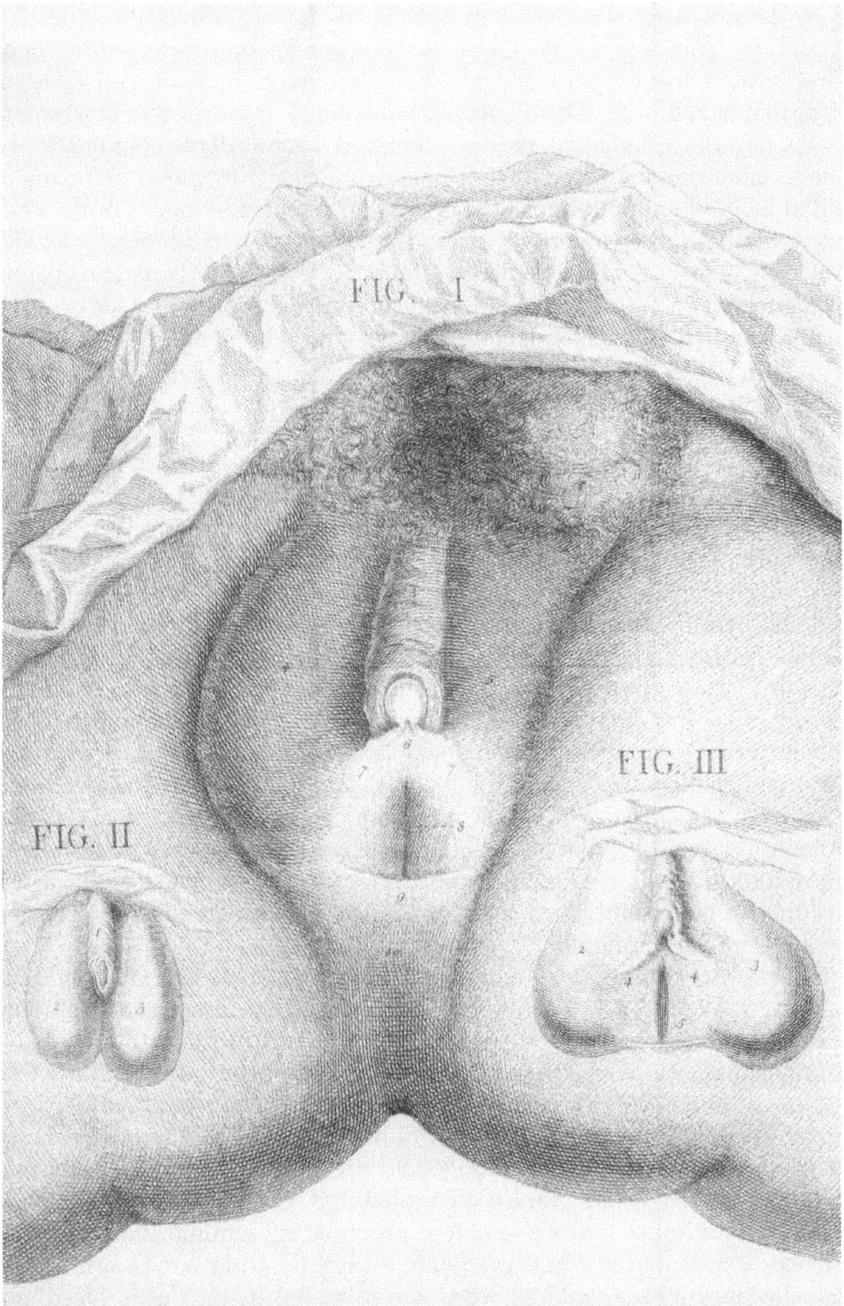

Figure 3.5. An engraving from James Parsons, *A Mechanical and Critical Enquiry into the Nature of Hermaphrodites,* 1741.

Reproduced by kind permission of the Wellcome Library, London.

The Royal Society's constituency was then divided into groups, or segments, defined by the interests of its members: astronomers, mathematicians, natural philosophers, natural historians, antiquarians, polymaths, gentlemen virtuosi, each vying for influence and sway.[45] Parsons typified the small, polymathic wing, his interests ranging from anatomy and antiquarianism to painting and physiognomy. His curiosity far exceeded the domain of natural history, although this subject intrigued him. He had little interest in natural philosophy, and was especially eloquent in communicating the interconnections of various fields. He dabbled in everything "natural": from freaks of nature—human and brute—to sea life;[46] and when a "hermaphrodite from Angola" was presented in Charing Cross, he exposed her as a fraud.[47] He also understood the function of publication as a legitimating activity and became one of the most prolific contributors to the Society's *PT*.

Hill attended his Croonian Lectures on physiognomy over three successive years in 1744–1746.[48] The topics Parsons presented were visually illustrated in drawings, paintings, and charts;[49] and when he lectured on physiognomy, he illustrated his beliefs about how the sentiments of the mind physically impinged of the muscles of the face.[50] A generation before Casper Lavater put his imprint on this ancient "scientific system" explaining how "faces" could be studied to discern "interior character," Parsons was probing its mysteries, as the young Hill watched with the others, in the wings in Bloomsbury.

William Hogarth, already an established artist whose works had included such medical prints as *The Company of Undertakers* or *Consultation of Quacks* (1736), was much taken with Parsons's theories and befriended him at this time.[51] Even before Hill began to attend around 1744, Hogarth recognized the force of Parsons's physiognomic theory about the face and its relevance for portraiture. Hogarth claimed to learn much about "art and anatomy from Dr. Parsons," and applied Parsons's view of physiognomy to his own history paintings; this while Parsons waxed lyrical when illustrating his theories of the passions and expressions of the skeletal face with his own hand. Hogarth also witnessed the young Hill in action: commenting on talks, asking questions, already puffing himself. By 1750–1751, Hogarth could have told you a thing or two about Hill while Hogarth assisted his friend Henry Fielding to combat the gin epidemic by supportive satirical prints of "Gin Lane" and "Beer Street." Hill's books featured in these prints, alas at the bottom of a heap, as we shall see when we approach those years. For now, the "research tank" in Red Lion Square is center stage, and it seemed to accommodate all Hill could desire, except a theatrical stage to act on.

Viewed in hindsight, Parsons remains an important if sadly neglected Enlightenment physiognomist for stressing the crucial role of the visual arts. He was not merely adept in medicine and natural history but masterful in drawing with colors what he imagined. Words were insufficient: each idea had his image. His interests stretched beyond physiognomy to linguistics and music (he was a gifted flutist who performed at his own house concerts).[52] Hill may not have attended the concerts, but only in Goodwood's international atmosphere had he witnessed anything resembling Parsons's personal range, and the polymathic knowledge held by those visiting from abroad.

One thing is clear from the extant correspondence: Parsons held Hill in high esteem.

But the politics began to mount. By the autumn of 1747 da Costa's nomination for election as FRS was circulating, warmly sponsored by Parsons and Folkes, two of its most influential members. His candidate's white card sat on the front table in the foyer at Crane Court, his election guaranteed. Da Costa encouraged Hill to exploit his contacts at Parsons's club meetings to get himself nominated. The two friends still roamed the countryside in search of specimens, while collecting for nobles. That spring they visited Burton Constable in south Yorkshire, the country seat of the Catholic bachelor William Constable (1721–1791).[53] Constable had earlier met the inimitable J. J. Rousseau on the first of his Grand Tours, and discussed gardens with him while collecting fossils and shells; when Constable moved to Harley Street around 1742 to study medicine, he met Hill and da Costa and retained them. They gathered all sorts of "marbles," perhaps in tandem at first, afterward primarily by da Costa as Hill's gout curtailed his travel. Contacts such as Constable added luster to Hill's profile, but nothing elated him so much as the prospect of his election as FRS.

He thought he might need more publication and proof of competence; the reality was otherwise: he already had too much. He could not grasp that what he *represented* counted for more than what he *did*—manners and morals above all else. True, Sloane had recently tightened the criteria for election, conveying the message to prospective fellows that they should be competent researchers, but Hill was a law unto himself and already demonstrated in Red Lion Square the traits that would take their toll. While da Costa was naively encouraging him to read papers and finish his translation of Theophrastus, Hill continued to edit pages in the *British Magazine*, begun early in the winter of 1746, which provided income while devouring time.

Yet not even its monthly print run of three thousand copies could compensate for lost time. Hill's contract with Charles Corbet, whose offices in Fleet Street had Addison's head affixed to the entrance until the end of the century,[54] does not survive, but the first issue appeared in March-April and continued until the summer of 1750.[55] The aim was to improve on the *GM*, its unstated model; to increase its size and include more illustrations, aiming to please and instruct in equal amounts. Hill may have raised subscriptions but is more likely to have borrowed the money from friends to launch it. An

"Occasional Spectator" essay occupied the first pages of the opening numbers, which Hill probably wrote, having fixed the *Spectator* papers in his mind, but he later changed the titles to "The Moralist." The magazine also had a silly side, parodying other magazines, travestying Shakespeare, and mangling established classics from Homer to Lesage. The finest tribute it received came from a Scottish imitator entitled the *British Magazine; or, the London and Edinburgh Intelligencer*, which began life within one year of its appearance.

Hill wrote most of the articles (all unsigned) dealing with metropolitan culture, the theater, and plants and collecting—they echo his views too closely not to be his. From this venture he learned to produce fluent copy and work to deadline. He also bought shares in the *British Magazine* from the proceeds of his earnings as an apothecary. He moaned to da Costa that "the enterprise was dissipating" his finances and it probably was, but even his purchase of shares could not keep the magazine afloat beyond December 1750. The worrying element was that neither his thought nor style were maturing or mellowing. His attention was elsewhere: enviously watching da Costa's election during the autumn of 1747—no clear-cut election for a Jew, no matter how well esteemed—and wondering what his own fate would be. The plan was that once nominated, da Costa would propose him to be FRS: one member of a "minority" promoting another, both men thinking of Hill's defect in formal education rather than religion or birth. Time would prove them wrong. Before they knew that, Hill the *arriviste* stored up anxiety about the ordeal until something untoward happened to aggravate it.

Then the ax struck. Da Costa was elected, pro forma on November 30th, his Jewish status overlooked, to the Society's credit, but immediately upon election he stopped canvassing for Hill. Unbeknownst to Hill, he scrapped their former plan and confided his reason to Needham:

> [He] designs to begin by the fossil kingdom, consequently that his work & mine [da Costa's projected *History of Fossils*] will in that particular clash together: yet he never . . . thought of undertaking a natural history of fossils till some months after I had declared publickly at Mr. Bakers[,] Dr. Parsons[,] Mr. Sherwoods & other places my scheme of my work, & even drew up a kind of plan of it wch I showed them all, & mentioned the work as a quite new design, an intire nat: hist: of the fossil kingdom having never been made before.[56]

Plagiarism, not vanity, is the charge. Yet da Costa had been praising Hill to the skies, most recently to Needham: "[his] capacity & knowledge [are] extensive."[57] His endorsements to Needham could not have been more superlative but it took time for the reality to dawn on da Costa, and he resisted the betrayal when realized. Da Costa's leak to Needham is the first surviving piece of evidence of the specific charge—after this time da Costa bit his tongue and broke off correspondence with Hill, which left the aspirant stranded in relation to the Society, with no one but Stukeley to lobby for him. Not even Richmond would support him, which seems odd—had he changed his mind about his former assistant?

Ebullient for several years by his productive working relation with Hill, da Costa had overlooked Hill's manner of promoting himself and "approaching" gentlemen without proper introduction. For example, the long letter from Hill to William Watson, already mentioned, demonstrates Hill's tactics: he wrote out of the blue to Watson as if he himself were an established member of the virtuous Republic, calling Watson "a most Esteemd Friend . . . whose knowledge, and Love of Science, have renderd you an Ornament to our Profession."[58] They may have, but modesty would have served Hill better and his reference to his friend "Mr. DaCosta" as yet counted for little. Watson himself had taken a path not entirely different from Hill—apprenticed to an apothecary, devoted to botany, writing papers about rare plants, aware of the apothecary's prospects then for upward social mobility—but he stuck out his apprenticeship to a fault and never replied to Hill's letter.[59] Besides, he had become engrossed in important experiments about electricity by 1746. Hill took too many liberties, had not learned to curb his pride, and wrote straightforwardly without balance between deference and flattery, the unction dripping from his quill.

Da Costa's discovery of the plagiarism of his *idea*—not his words, for the two books turned out to be very different—grated. The more he backed away, the more obsessed Hill became. Nor was obtuse Hill remorseful: he was driven to arrive first in cutthroat competition. When the moral lapse stared him in the face, he failed to understand. We might call this psychological denial, but no apology, betrayal, denial, or morality occupied space in Hill's mental orbit. The end justifies the means—he would win at any cost. Only success counted. He harped on his lack of university education as the culprit as da Costa's sudden change of heart; but neither Henry Baker (FRS 1741) nor William Arderon (FRS 1745) were university educated, and they had been supportive of his development to a point short of endorsement. Baker, Defoe's son-in-law who endowed the Royal Society's Bakerian Lecture at his death in 1774, was especially nurturing. He rose the hard way: apprenticed to a bookseller he knew what life in Grub Street was like, and eventually made a good living devising a system for the education of deaf mutes.[60] He knew a good deal about Hill's background, and sympathized with his predicament as a second son from humble origins whose father had no means to educate him. Baker had already published *The Microscope Made Easy* (1742), won the Society's Copley Medal in 1744 for work in microscopy and crystallization, and was becoming a leading popularizer of science.[61]

He was shocked more than most when Hill's bombshell dropped.

NOTES

1. For its painter, Allan Ramsey (1713–1784), and provenance, see chapter 11.
2. Holbrook, passim; Roy Porter (2000), 87–114; Riskin, passim.
3. Dillenius, passim; Linnaeus referred to it as "salutary."
4. Stukeley MSS Eng. Misc. C113, p. 171.
5. Stukeley MSS Eng. Misc. C133 and Randall 1744.
6. All traces of her have disappeared except a parish record, recorded in Morris MSS, f. 54, of their marriage in 1745. What did JH see in her? Or was her father, the steward, the attraction?
7. JH (1745); *GM* announced its appearance in February; *GM* 15 (1745): 112.
8. Earle, 118–22.
9. *Lyra Britannica*, vol. 1, 250–52; "the words by Dr. JH, set by Dr. Boyce and Lewis Granom." This was Samuel Boyce, the writer and hack who later joined JH's cabal at the Bedford coffeehouse.
10. They had married by the summer of 1745; in September da Costa sent "Mrs. Hill" his "hearty Services" ; LPH, 9–10.
11. Yogev, passim.
12. Rousseau and Haycock (2000): 131–64; no portrait of him is known to survive; his biographical profile here is reconstructed from *DAC* and the DAC Archives. See also Whitehead, 1–24.
13. Stukeley MSS Eng. Misc. d 719/12, 1751.
14. Stukeley MSS Eng. Misc. e. 138 and 139 for 1760; some of Stukeley's admiration was grounded in da Costa's religiosity, whether Jewish or Christian being indifferent to Stukeley.
15. Nichols, vol. 4: 636.
16. Harris, passim.
17. Benjamin Wilkes, passim.
18. Rousseau and Haycock (2000): 146–47.
19. Da Costa's English edition was published in 1770 as *Essay towards a System of Mineralogy;* Baron Cronstedt (1722–1765), a mining expert who headed the Swedish Bureau of Mines, discovered nickel in 1751; he described it as *kupfernickel* (the devil's copper) and also discovered tungsten, meaning "heavy stone" in Swedish.
20. *Illustrations of Natural History* (1770–1782).
21. LPH, 13–24.
22. Porter (1977), 42–49.
23. *LDA* September 12, 1751; Richmond may have joined them.
24. Royal Society MSS Journ. Bk. IX, 245–47.
25. LPH, 19, and no. 14.
26. Sherbo (1967), 42.
27. Translations into French (1754) and German (1770) soon followed; a second edition of 1774 contains "Notes, including the modern history of the gems described by that author; . . . To which are added, two letters: I. On the colours of the sapphire and turquoise. II. Upon the effects of different menstruums on copper. . . . The second edition; enlarged by the addition of a Greek index . . . Also observations on the new Swedish acid, . . . and with an idea of a natural and artificial method of fossils."
28. Rousseau (1986a), 182 for JH and Orrery.
29. Roy Porter (1977), 46; Laudan; Rappaport; the most vigorous recent case for the importance of JH's geology, especially his mineralogy pertaining to amber and "Jew stone" when used as medicaments, is found in Duffin, 9–57.
30. LPH, 24.
31. *GM* 16 (1746): 500.
32. LPH, 29.
33. LPH, 17; da Costa's friendship with JH's sister indicates how far their association extended by then. It is wrong-headed to think they were merely scientific associates.

34. He had few funds to leave to his children; see Theophilus Hill (1746).
35. Rousseau and Haycock (2000), passim.
36. The election took place in November 1747.
37. *PT* 44:1 (1746-47): 60–66; LPH, 27.
38. *PT* 44: 1 (1746-47): 458–63.
39. Kevin Fraser (1994), 44.
40. Needham (1748).
41. Needham (1748).
42. Needham (1749), passim; Mann, passim; Roger, passim; Bonnet et al., passim.
43. LPH, 18–45. Read ahead for Parsons, who remains one of the most understudied FRS of this period. Useful material is found in Schiebinger (1996a).
44. Proper in the sense that he was an equal to the others and in no one's employ.
45. While there is no agreement on the precise interplay of the various groups, a large literature already exists on their maneuvers; see Lyons; Feingold; Fraser (1994); Gunther (1979); McClellan III; D. P. Miller (1989); Rousseau and Porter (1980), 97–113; Sorrenson (1996). Feingold's study is particularly insightful.
46. Parsons (1745).
47. Parsons (1741).
48. Published as a separate work in 1746; see Parsons (1747).
49. S. West (1990), 75–82.
50. Parsons (1747).
51. Paulson, vol. 2, 473 and West (1990), 74–81 for the material in this paragraph.
52. Parsons was also an able linguist who anticipated Sir William Jones's theories about the common origins of Indo-European languages.
53. Rousseau and Haycock (2000), 138–39, 165, no. 61.
54. Status was then conferred in the workplace's ostentation rather than in the home, as in our era.
55. JH (1746a).
56. BL Add. MS 28540 f.200/64, July 7, 1747; no reply from Needham survives. Needham's ties to Buffon made him especially attractive to da Costa, who was well aware of Buffon's influence throughout France as director of the Paris Jardin du Roi. Hence he puffed his own natural history to Needham from 1746 until his first imprisonment. Theirs is a model of the polite correspondences typical of the international networks within the Republic of Letters. Da Costa never uses the word "plagiarism" in this outburst, but accuses Hill of something more egregious: the betrayal of stealing your scientific collaborator's, and friend's, main idea. As da Costa notes: " . . . he never thought of undertaking a Nat. Hist. of fossils till some Months after I had declared publickly . . . at Dr Parsons . . . & other places my scheme of my Work, & even drew up a kind of plan of it, which I show'd them all, & mention'd the Work as a quite new design, an entire Nat. hist: of the fossil kingdom having never been made before" (BM Add MSS 28,540 f. 64). Hill rarely "plagiarized" copy verbatim; he was too fluent and clever for that. Instead, he sussed out works and ideas in the making and got there first, in the type of intellectual theft often impossible to prove but galling to the victim. Time would prove both men—Hill and da Costa—fatally flawed; the irony was that even now, in the mid-1740s, they deserved each other. Sherwood, an ordinary medic and amateur virtuoso, routinely attended Parsons's gatherings with his young son, John Sherwood Jr. Da Costa appointed the elder Sherwood to manage his affairs when he departed for his extensive European tour in the summer of 1748.
57. Rousseau and Haycock (2000), 147.
58. LPH, 29–32.
59. Pulteney (1790), vol. 2, 295–340.
60. G. L'E. Turner (1975): 55–70; G. L'E. Turner (1981), chapters 4–6.
61. Henry Baker (1764), passim.

4

Deranged by Disappointment

Failure to find two sponsors practically demented Hill. He never imagined this outcome. Years of collecting specimens came to nothing, his writing counted for little at the critical moment of deciding his worth. Many FRS had been elected on much less. He had published the first volume of his trilogy on natural history—the book on fossils—in the spring of 1748.[1] It should have strengthened his case for nomination and was significant in the development of mineralogy, but could not offset his abrasive conduct—the image he already cut. His new edition of Pierre Pomet's *History of Drugs* appeared later, in September;[2] those canvassing to nominate him also overlooked it.

The FRS had elected dozens of fellows who published nothing, but Hill was an exception to the rules. If only he could have taken to heart Samuel Johnson's dictum about "The Man of Moderation"—he who "discovers failings with unwillingness, and extenuates the faults which cannot be denied. . . ."—he may have fared better. Instead, he lashed himself with the whip of disappointment, proving the validity of Johnson's further observation that these "are the arts by which the envious, the idle, the peevish, and the thoughtless, obstruct that worth which they cannot equal." Hill could not.

He imagined them roaring with laughter and whispering their gossip about him in close corridors. The loss of da Costa's support was colossal; all the more so because "the little Jew," as one FRS scurrilously called da Costa, never provided Hill with the reason.[3] Stukeley, for his part, had become ineffective in Crane Court: avuncular yet aging, he was now close by at his living in St. George the Martyr in Queen Square, Bloomsbury, regularly attending the Thursday night meetings, still hobnobbing with the FRS, but more likely waxing lyrical about patriarchal druids than John Hill.[4] As for da Costa, he was not talking to Hill by late 1747, and only years later did they reconcile their differences after he (da Costa) displayed his own dishonest streak.[5] The key document is a letter dated November 22, 1762, where Hill notes that they continued to be civil toward each other.[6] Da Costa replied within four days, affirming Hill's point about the continuation of their friendship despite strain.

Stukeley himself was falling out of favor, his disgruntlement with President Folkes threatening to go public.[7] Folkes was neither fool nor pushover; he held out for his positions, one of which allegiance to the large camp of mathematicians within the Society. By mid-century huge divides had developed between those emphasizing mathematics—"mixed mathematics" as the FRS called it—and the natural historians in whose cohort antiquaries like Stukeley and da Costa counted themselves. They viewed Folkes as the embodied enemy: he liked antiquities but debunked natural history. Hill repeatedly excoriated him for knowing nothing about the new botany, and was probably right. The main point is that the Society did not then consist of a unified phalanx of FRS with a common goal. The cabals were as disunified as the Hill-Stukeley-da Costa wing claimed they were ignorant of natural history.

The consequences of all this division and exclusion of Hill were formidable. He lost his creative urge and ceased writing reviews for the *MR*. His pride and vanity rushed forward. He took to gambling and dancing masters and neglected his wife Susannah, who drops out of sight altogether. Did he ditch her? Did she die?[8] He began to whore and philander in grand style. Whether he met "Madame Diamond," his alleged later mistress, at this time is unknown but by 1750 she was considered apparently installed. Her name is scribbled on the verso on several of his extant manuscript letters,[9] while his name appears with hers in the *Town and Country Magazine* for the same year 1750: a well-known scandal sheet with a regular monthly *tete a tete* about the "ladies" of t'Town, their addresses, their comings and goings and newest liaisons. Little is known about this "Diamond" apart from her association with Hill. She certainly enjoyed an intrigue with Beau Tracy, the amorous beau about town, but Tracy dallied with women of all types, married as well as courtesans.[10] The main trait Diamond apparently displayed was hysterical fickleness, described in Hill's account of their relation.

Hill published it in 1752, but had been storing up material for a couple of years. This is a racy fifty-page epistolary narrative inviting anyone who wishes to read their letters to peruse them here.[11] Half the letters "pass" between Diamond and Hill, Hill clearly hoping to appeal to the same readers attracted to *Peregrine Pickle* for its inclusion of the scandalous *Memoirs of a Woman of Quality*. In the first letter Hill describes meeting Diamond "by Accident" and falling madly in love with her. Thereafter she pretends not to know who he is: "I would not call a woman fool, in whose eyes I have read more knowledge than in all the Volumes of Locke and Addison." But Diamond plays hard to get, refuses to meet him at Ranelagh for an assignation, while confessing she loves him: "I love you still, ungrateful, insolent, destructive Devil."[12] Three weeks pass without letters. In the end Diamond persuades herself she can only be happy if she avoids the "Devil," while Hill sails off to be married to someone else. The characters are named "Diamond" and "Hill" but the story may be no more autobiographical than other scurrilous amorous accounts. Hill often wrote to turn a pretty penny; besides, he did not marry his second wife until a year later (1753).

He was in his mid-thirties, free, fancy-loose, and well turned out; tall, noticeably thin, like a stake pole, and stylishly dressed. Any number of women would have turned their heads to be noticed, as they did later on when he landed an aristocrat with a sizable dowry. One would give much to know the details; for example, what charisma or charm his remarkably sleek, ectomorphic appearance had and what his conversation was like then. References to it in Richmond's correspondence may capture a younger Hill: greener, clumsier, less *au fait* with cosmopolitan London. By now he had made the rounds of the noble gentlemen of science in Crane Court and spoken out freely—too freely, as at Parsons's Wednesday meetings, which proved his nemesis in a nutshell. The shy adolescent had undergone a London education and complete transformation, and was now more likely to be seen with a whore on his arm than a "gentleman of science."

On April 26, 1749, he attended the "famous entertainment at Ranelagh" described in the monthlies as the "Grand Jubilee Masquerade, in the Venetian taste," to celebrate the peace of Aix-la-Chapelle. Fireworks were displayed in Green Park for several days to commemorate the peace. He womanized and pranced about in fine clothes and gloves. He heard Lewis Granom, the music conductor in charge at Cuper's Gardens and resident there, and visited other central London "pleasure gardens" as well. No account survives of his monthly moods, and he never wrote personal memoirs of them, but the likelihood given his personality type is that he was periodically "up and down": high for a few days followed by bouts of despair.

In May, Ralph Griffiths launched the *Monthly Review* with the assistance of others, including Hill. Within weeks they had a full cadre of assistants, grubs of the type Alexander Pope had denounced in his *Dunciad*. Their purpose was "to enter no farther into the province of criticism, than just so far as may be indispensably necessary to give some idea of such books as come under our consideration"—in other words the prototype of the current weeklies summarizing books just published.[13] Griffiths covered literature himself and in the long run wrote more reviews than anyone else, but as his duties as manager increased he relied on others: especially John Cleland, who had just published his notorious *Memoirs of a Woman of Pleasure*, William Rose, a penny hack, and his collaborator in the *British Magazine*, Hill himself.

Hill and Griffiths did not fall out, as Griffiths did with so many of his staff and reviewers.[14] Hill may have thrived on the bellicosity and ferocity of print rivalry exceeding any correlative imaginable today. He and Griffiths shared many qualities: both men were ambitious, uncouth, and tough skinned. But they were not friends in our sense, nor did their lives overlap outside the world of print. Neither had proved himself in any way other than in entrepreneurial ventures; neither had a university education or was a "gentleman" (i. e., owned property). And each could stoop as low as the other in Grub Street. One conjures what Griffiths thought when he awakened a few years later, on the very last day of 1755, to read Smollett's savage attack on him in the manifesto for his (Smollett's) new *Critical Review*, contrasting the new plan of 1755–1756 with Griffiths's *Monthly Review* of 1749: "This Work will not be patched up by obscure Hackney Writers, accidentally enlisted in the Service of an undistinguished Bookseller, but executed by a Set of Gentlemen whose Characters and Capacities have been universally approved and acknowledged by the Public: Gentlemen, who have long observed with Indignation the Productions of Genius and Dullness; Wit and Impertinence. . . ."[15] The barb at Griffiths was the "undistinguished Bookseller"; the one to Hill only slightly less direct as "Impertinence," for by this time, in 1755, Hill had been personified through this one word *ad nauseam* and he would continue to be down through the 1750s, as when the irritable Smollett, always enlisting invective and irony, called him "the profound, the candid, the modest Dr. H-ll" in a review chiding Griffiths as well as merely "serene."[16] The cupola of Griffiths and Hill was welded by 1750.

Hill did not see himself bonded to the commercialism Griffiths typified. His scientific endeavors had always given him hope that he could shape public taste: in Smollett's words in the manifesto prefacing the *Critical Review* that he could rise to a "Patron of Genius and Science." But something else was at stake here in the fate of dullness and commercialism: the camp of Griffiths-Hill may have lacked the critical bite of their antagonists but their magazine sold well—far better than its rivals. It hauled in readers and made its owner and proprietor, Griffiths, a rich man. Hill himself rapidly climbed the economic ladder in these first few years; coupled to his other frenetic business deals he too became rich. The *Monthly* filled a gap in coverage and breadth no competitor could replace for decades. Smollett's rival group could profess to be the arbiters of "true taste" but their highbrow *Critical Review* never sold so well nor endured so long. Its notices—full-blown reviews—were longer and denser; its inclusion limited to literature, natural history, and occasionally—because Smollett himself had been trained as a physician—to medicine. Already then, by the 1750s, we see a prototype of taste high and low that would develop in our time and the stakes involved. Today it is the difference between the book reviews in weekly newspapers—the *Times*, *Financial Times*, *Telegraph*—and the highbrow literary journalism of the *New York Review of Books* or *New Yorker*.

Oddly 1748–1749 are black holes in Hill's adult life: emptier than his adolescent years and less well documented than any later year. Only his vanity remained constant, if also on the rise. He lost da Costa's trust and perhaps his wife too. He was retooling and processing psychological changes that would cause others to notice him as a startling "Proteus." He stored up disappointment without knowing whether he would ever again possess creative outlets. Perhaps he would have been amused if he could have known, for instance, that John Rutty, a Dublin physician of some note in Ireland, praised his book on fossils to his correspondent William Clark, a physician practicing in Wiltshire with whom he had studied under the famous Doctor Boerhaave in Leyden.[17] Rutty sang Hill's praises as working for "the Glory & the good of mankind," calling him "a learned man tho an Apothecary." What did these men know, Hill may have whined to himself—one across the sea in Dublin, the other almost as far, they could not help his cause. He needed two nominators and nothing—not the praise of any number of *virtuosi*—could substitute for that. These responses suggest a Hill driven to extremes by the façade of external recognition, but inside, "interior Hill" was empty.

Yet while becoming *persona non grata* at home he gathered notice abroad. By the autumn 1748 the great Albrecht von Haller, by now professor in Göttingen duly having been elected FRS from afar through the intervention of George II, was petitioning his correspondent Johannes Gesner to send him Hill's papers and books.[18] So too Linnaeus and many other Continental scientists who were diligently reading Hill by this time. Hill's book on fossils had aroused widespread interest, even if not at home, while for Hill himself, the long period of despair was followed by bouts of temporary hope: the eternal wish that some *deus ex machina* would intervene to elect him.

Sometime in 1750[19] he petitioned the very young Francis Hastings (1729–1789), described by Horace Walpole as a "rising genius" and only twenty.[20] He had become a genuine antiquarian on the Grand Tour, passing "hours with Dr. Cocchi and his medals" as Walpole wrote.[21] Hill heard about him from the powerful cabal gathered around Newcastle, which included Hastings, Thomas Robinson, and other diplomats. Robinson had just returned to England from Aix-la-Chapelle after helping the embassies sign a much-awaited peace treaty and was being feted. Newcastle said he would make Robinson secretary of state if he could: "If I was to chuse for the king, the public, and myself, I would prefer Sir Thomas Robinson to any man living."[22] But Robinson had been instructed to vote against Hill, who partly recovered from his initial disappointment at the directive and further resigned himself to exclusion: "My Purpose," he wrote in his supine letter to Hastings, "was to have Servd the Society."[23] While writing he hid his shock that Hastings had "directed" Robinson and others not to vote for him.

Figure 4.1. Albrecht von Haller, c. 1750.

Reproduced by kind permission of the Wellcome Library, London.

Hill's source about Hastings's "directive" may not have been correct but his letter shows how far he was willing to go. He was aware of the relatively new competition among candidates, especially within botany, but still thought he deserved election. In his mind support and enmity counted for more than ability, though he knew he possessed much, and by now he had learned that even the invulnerable then had enemies, the great Sloane himself notwithstanding. No one was more generous or modest than much-loved Sloane, yet even he stirred up antagonists, none more vociferous than Dr. John Woodward (1668–1728), as envious of Sloane as he was of all Sloane represented. Woodward, like Hill a generation later, had cleverly framed his criticism of the FRS in relation to their *PT*, declaiming that their content demonstrated to what appalling degree Sloane had neglected experimental research during his presidency and—*faute de mieux*—that he lacked the intellectual capacity to advance it. The analogy today might be the charge that a vice-chancellor of Cambridge or Oxford, or indeed the president of the Royal Society, lacked the acumen to distinguish first-class research from pedestrian rehash.

Hill versed himself in Woodward's experience although he was too young to have met him. He apprised himself of Woodward's argument that Sloane practiced a form of cronyism favoring the theories and projects of his chums while excluding others outside the circle, Woodward included. Recent appraisals have demonstrated substance in Woodward's claims despite his droll manner of publicly challenging others.[24] Woodward was not alone: before he struck out, William King (1685–1763), the elegant Oxford don who some were touting as the new biting Swift, anonymously published a scathing satire of Sloane's policies in the Society.[25]

These antecedents fascinated the now devastated Hill, even if Hill's exclusion did not include expulsion from the Royal Society's council, as it did for Woodward (i. e., after insulting Sloane and refusing to apologize he was thrown out). Woodward's stinging criticism of the Royal Society focused on the relation of original ideas to empirical observation and laboratory experimentation, his charge hovering in their interstice: especially experimenters not encouraged to observe new phenomena, and an endemic favoritism. Hill for his part saw the feud as less than a quarrel between "ancients and moderns," as had Woodward, than one located in the poison of patronage.

Patronage was old, its competitive edge new—this was the reality at mid-century. The recent frenzy of collection among aristocrats gave rise to a whole class of underlings now able to earn a living in their employ. The *virtuosi* had been collecting for generations, but once Walpolian wealth translated into their coffers after the 1730s the pace intensified, as did the psychology of the collectors. Furthermore, the new Whig lords were collecting everything curious and rare in what amounted to a new type of national craze.[26] The practical uses of such amassment were beneath their notice, but once Linnaeus's new classification system was adopted in Britain in the 1760s all this changed; nowhere was the Linnaean effect more powerfully felt than in botany, whose imperial and commercial value was apparent. The plant world energized this transformation; not only because its products translated into self-evident commodities to be bought and traded—teas and coffees, medicinal herbs and extracts, flowers and rare plants—but as the result of swelling populations profiting from lower mortality rates while hungry mouths waited to be fed. Had Hill been born just three decades later—into the sea-hungry world of Joseph Banks, for example, who was born in 1743—his collecting career and search for patronage would have been different: he would have been forced out to sea.[27] His death in 1775, as the effects of Linnaean classification were taking hold of commercial decisions in the aftermath of the 1766–1770 Banks-Cook expeditions, occurred near the fault line of transition from amassing for its own sake to collecting for commerce and empire. But in Hill's earlier generation—the 1740s and 1750s—patrons still collected anything they could, and men like Hill were much in demand, all the more so if they worked hard and had eagle eyes for novelty.

Hill's ordeal was to maneuver the ropes of patronage: no simple routine even for stable personalities but a complex strategy nevertheless. Power brokers in the field recognized one's ability: in botany such figures as Hans Sloane or Philip Miller at the Chelsea Physic Garden. They recommended you to aristocrats wanting you to collect as well as take their sons on the Grand Tour: hence the coveted Georgian institution of the "tutor" that differed from earlier incarnations by dint of the importance of the new natural history.[28] Once established as a knowledgeable and reliable tutor,[29] you passed from one aristocratic family to another; your earthly needs cared for, your pastimes and avocations indulged, your collections of botanical specimens—as in the case of William Sherard[30]—funded. The recipe was dual: ability and reputation. Hill eschewed these and went for ingenuity. He had already demonstrated the oblique novelty he would display throughout his life: an intuitive sense propelling him to get there first; a protean ability to keep refashioning himself even when he appeared to have hit rock bottom; an inborn penchant to go on the attack—always to lash out without thinking through the consequences. These would not endear him to collectors now, let alone fathers concerned for the welfare of their sons.

Besides, Hill had already displayed his mettle to aristocrats and power brokers like Sloane and Miller and perhaps by 1748 even Richmond. Richmond had been his lynchpin of hope, and when a number of FRS established the "Club of the Royal Philosophers"—an exclusive dining society that met at the Mitre tavern on Thursday evenings before or after the Society's weekly meeting—in 1743–1744, just as Hill was setting up in London, Richmond was its leader. The idea was his and he was ideally poised to guide it.

He also brought in members of the Society of Antiquaries whose president he then was, and Folkes too, who had recently become president of the Royal Society (1741) upon Sloane's resignation owing to poor health. The club aimed to formalize an old tradition in which cronies, many of them FRS, dined just before or after society meetings. It was the perfect setting for Richmond to puff his "puppy Hill" but something went wrong, and by the time Folkes became the club's first recorded president in 1747 he too might have promoted Hill. What happened?

Da Costa was neither habitué of the Mitre nor member of the "Club"; but he was more sociable and intentionally enlarging his acquaintance. His friendship with Hill was on the rocks, in part because the latter was becoming strangely solitary: a quality viewed suspiciously in the virtuous Republic at mid-century that prized collective cooperation and community far more than individual achievement or talent. Hill's possible plagiarism from him notwithstanding, by 1747–1748 da Costa was also changing his view of himself. He had begun to reach out and collaborate with others, especially George Ehret (1708–1770), the most distinguished botanical painter of his generation. Born in Heidelberg, he trained as a gardener and—also like Hill—apprenticed to an apothecary. While working on the estates of German nobility he painted flowers as a hobby, his first major sale assisted by Dr. Christoph Trew, an eminent physician and botanist of Nuremberg, who recognized his talent and became patron and lifelong friend. Early in the 1730s, Trew taught Ehret the botanical importance of floral sexual organs and advised him to expose them in detail in his paintings.[31] Ehret then traveled through Switzerland and France, working as a gardener and selling his paintings, and eventually crossed over to England armed with letters of introduction to patrons including Sloane and Philip Miller—the very men of science Hill would have courted if he could. Ehret next spent several months in the Netherlands at the garden of rare plants of George Clifford, the banker and director of the Dutch East India Company, where he met Linnaeus who was then formulating his new classification. Ehret painted a "Tabella" (1736) illustrating the bisexual system, which so impressed both Clifford and Linnaeus that Ehret's paintings of the exotics were engraved in Linnaeus's *Hortus Cliffortianus* (1737).

Ehret returned to England to settle in Chelsea at the moment Hill was setting up in the Savoy. One success led to another for Ehret—the apothecary turned painter—and in 1748–1749, while Hill was waking up to his prospects Ehret took the post of head gardener at the Oxford Physic Garden. The recent death of Dillenius, Oxford's only "professor of physick," left a gaping hole, its botanical gardens sinking into neglect. But Ehret soon returned to Mayfair to lead the type of life Hill dreamed of. Even if they never met Hill would have heard about his success through de Costa, who befriended him. Ehret was particularly eager to paint fossils and shells, recognizing their remarkable potential for color. He came to believe that shells had even greater potential for artistic detail than flowers. Nothing delighted da Costa, London's leading conchologist, more. Soon after meeting the two men started a correspondence; one plateau yielded to another and soon Ehret was nominating da Costa to join the "Academy of Naturalists" in Nuremburg and Berlin, who was elected as "Plinius Quartus": "Pliny the Fourth" for da Costa's distinction as a well-rounded gentleman of natural history.[32]

Further fallout arose from the da Costa–Ehret friendship. Ehret related much to his Jewish friend about his former German colleagues in Nuremberg who were members of the local Academy of Sciences, especially about his closest contact there, Johan Ambrosius Beurer, almost as gifted in botanical illustration as Ehret. To da Costa these Bavarians seemed more ardent than the currently negligent FRS to unlock the secrets of botany and geology; and he was intrigued to discover from Ehret that most of them were practicing apothecaries, like his former accomplice Hill. Da Costa also developed the view that Ehret's Germans displayed none of the bureaucratic idiosyncrasies of their English counterparts. Believing that action was needed, da Costa initiated a philosophical exchange along the lines of the Republic of Letters developing in France and England. He drafted a letter to Beurer proposing "a philosophical correspondence . . . to advise each other of their Literary Affairs" and asked Ehret to translate it into German.

Hill also figured in, but the international exchanges never occurred, each side claiming ownership of the group without da Costa apprising Hill of any developments. Hill never forgot this Bavarian Academy: years later he himself germinated a more outrageous idea, as we shall see, derived from da Costa's plan of 1747 that had died an embryonic death. For now, in 1748–1749, Ehret was rising in London esteem and giving instruction in painting to the highest nobility of England, while da Costa's employments ran out despite now—since November 1747—signing himself FRS. He had turned thirty, looked forward to marriage, despite few avenues to support a family. Hill had recommended him to Richmond but the endorsement was not heeded, perhaps because Richmond was now so much less enthusiastic about his "puppy." Instead da Costa turned to Ehret with the hope of securing something: early in 1748 war still raged on the Continent, especially in the low countries, and Ehret secured commissions for da Costa as army doctor; he shipped out to treat the wounded in the modern-day Belgium around March, a further reason why his correspondence with Hill is silent after 1747. But da Costa kept up with his quondam patron Ehret, writing and cultivating him for the future, when the temporary military commission would run out. "Pray go to see Sir Hans Sloane," da Costa begged him that May (1748), "give my service to him, how he does, and write about it."[33]

Across the North Sea, the FRS were also on da Costa's mind. And Hill? He had been at work alone on his *General Natural* for over a year since the breakup with da Costa; his big book had appeared both with and without colored illustrations soon after da Costa shipped out.[34] It may have been "too large," as da Costa reported to Needham, but it nevertheless placed Hill on the map as securely as *Theophrastus* had, because a "general survey" covering the whole natural world was sorely needed, coming in at 506 pages, and too grandly promising everything.[35] It claimed to be "Illustrated by a general review of the knowledge of the ancients, and the discoveries and improvements of later ages in these studies: including the history of the *materia medica, pictoria, and tinctoria,* of the present and earlier ages: As also observations on the neglected properties of many valuable substances known at present and attempts to discover the lost medicines [sic], &c, of former ages in a series of critical enquiries into the *materia medica* of the ancient Greeks." The title's "great Number of Figures elegantly engraved" were only twelve and were produced in color but not by Ehret.

Da Costa knew that Hill's hyperbole was legion. Hill could seem to be advancing within the Republic of Letters but his best friend suspected something darker and Stukeley was too sidelined himself to see Hill anymore for what he was. A decade later, while da Costa was still riding high and had not yet been imprisoned for serious fraud, he assessed Hill to Peter Ascanius, the Danish scientist who had heard a great deal about this "celebrity"; da Costa described him as "the famous Dr. Hill scorned & abandon'd by all that knew him formerly on account of his scandalous tongue & his lying faculties. . . ."[36] It was a shocking indictment embodying deterioration but da Costa remained mindful of his turncoat-friend. His manuscript letters in the British Library number 2,487 autographs, which constitute a small fraction of the total he wrote, yet no name before 1750 crops up more repeatedly than John Hill's.[37]

NOTES

1. *LM* (March 1748): 144.
2. JH (1748a); volume 2 deals with plants and volume 3 animals; see chapters 5–6 below.
3. Rousseau and Haycock (2000): 127.
4. Haycock (2002), 224–27.
5. Correspondence between them from 1747 to 1762 has not disappeared; until then they were unreconciled.
6. LPH, 129.
7. For the evidence see Rousseau and Haycock (1999); Haycock (2000); Haycock (2002), 225–27; Feingold (1999): 281–309.
8. My searches for a death certificate produced nothing.
9. Especially in BM Stowe MSS 155, folios 112, 116, 121–30, where Diamond's name is mentioned on several of the rectos of JH's letters; JH also printed some of his alleged letters to her in JH (1752f).

10. Murray, vol. 2, 40.

11. JH (1752f); the solitary copy of this work in the BL contains marginalia reading "to a courtesan known by the name of Diamond."

12. JH (1752f), 22.

13. *MR* 2 (1750): 260.

14. For example, Tobias Smollett the novelist and fellow editor of the *CR*, whose books Griffiths blasted in the *MR*.

15. *PA*, 30 December 1751.

16. *CR* 6 (September 1758): 226.

17. LPH, 36–37.

18. LPH, 37–38.

19. LPH, 39; this letter is difficult to date; hesitantly I assign it to 1750 but a case can be made for 1758.

20. *HWC* 20: 457.

21. Antonio Cocchi (1695–1758), the Florentine doctor and naturalist who amassed one of the largest collections of medals of the century.

22. *HWC* 20:17.

23. *HWC* 20:17.

24. See Levine, passim.

25. His barbs at Sloane and the FRS extended Swift's line about the corruptions of modern science.

26. Rousseau (2006), 228–40.

27. Gascoigne (1994), passim.

28. Grosley, vol. 2, 45–69.

29. Poet-naturalist Thomas Gray is another example; see W. P. Jones, chapters 4–5.

30. Tutor to Charles, Lord Townshend; while enjoying the privileges it afforded he complained he had little time to "botanize"; see Pulteney (1790), vol. 2, 141–50.

31. Nickelsen, 20–28.

32. Calmann, 78; their correspondence is in the BL; the Berlin Academy was making strides in the 1740s.

33. Calmann, 79.

34. *LM* (March 1748): 144, where it is anonymously reviewed.

35. The practice of natural history in mid-eighteenth-century Britain and Europe remains understudied; a good start is Sorrenson (1999).

36. BL Add MS 28535 f. 96/132, September 26, 1760.

37. BL Add MS 28534–44; for his manuscripts and their locations see Rousseau and Haycock (2000): 159–61.

II

5

Three Strikes in Revenge

Da Costa's indictment trumpeted "lies," a "scandalous tongue," and, he should have added, a "fluent pen" capable of writing at phenomenal speeds—so swiftly Hill could usurp whole projects, as he had in the first volume of *A General Natural History*, and finish them within months. No one could write faster. He composed at great stretches and rarely revised, his gift narrative eloquence and an easy style. And when the bombshell burst early in January 1750 it proved to be the fiercest and most stinging criticism the Royal Society ever endured—at least in living memory. Pope's dunciadic rebukes were muted in comparison. Hill published his censure before the FRS recovered from their Christmas holidays, let alone adjusted themselves to January slush. He called it *Lucina sine concubitu: A Letter Humbly Address'd to the Royal Society*—fifty pages of the best prose satire he ever wrote.[1]

The first reviewers identified it as by "Dr. Hill," indicating that Hill's strife in Crane Court had reached the ears of Fleet Street.[2] Its primary target was the "infidel Folkes," as Stukeley had referred to him for his lack of religion. Hill's charge was otherwise; that Folkes had an abysmal understanding of biology, forming the heart of the "natural history" of the time. Stukeley's reversal was striking; a decade earlier he waxed lyrical about the Society—"here we meet, either personally or in the works, all the geniuses of England, or rather of the whole world, whatever the globe produced that is curious, or whatever the heavens present."[3] More recently his praise turned to blame and after Thursday night meetings he often returned to his diary to vent his spleen.[4] Eventually his animosity burst its

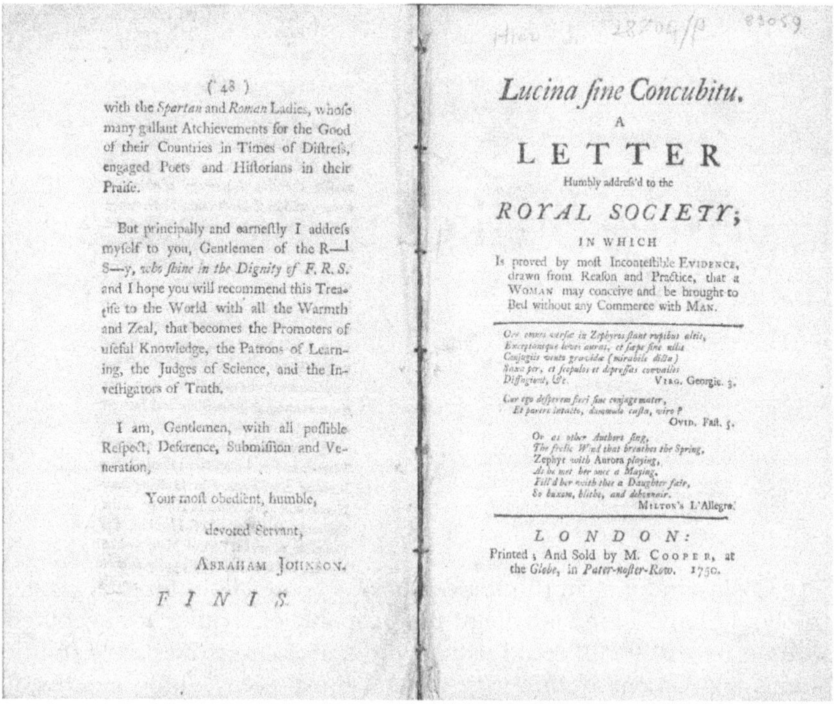
(48)
with the *Spartan* and *Roman* Ladies, whose many gallant Atchievements for the Good of their Countries in Times of Diftrefs, engaged Poets and Hiftorians in their Praife.

But principally and earneftly I addrefs myfelf to you, Gentlemen of the R—l S—y, *who fhine in the Dignity of F. R. S.* and I hope you will recommend this Treatife to the World with all the Warmth and Zeal, that becomes the Promoters of ufeful Knowledge, the Patrons of Learning, the Judges of Science, and the Inveftigators of Truth.

I am, Gentlemen, with all poffible Refpect, Deference, Submiffion and Veneration,

Your moft obedient, humble, devoted Servant,

ABRAHAM JOHNSON.

FINIS.

Lucina fine Concubitu.

A

LETTER

Humbly addrefs'd to the

ROYAL SOCIETY;

IN WHICH

Is proved by moft Inconteftible EVIDENCE, drawn from Reafon and Practice, that a WOMAN may conceive and be brought to Bed without any Commerce with MAN.

VIRG. Georgic. 3.

OVID. Faft. 5.

MILTON'S L'Allegro.

LONDON:

Printed; And Sold by M. COOPER, at the *Globe*, in *Pater-nofter-Row*. 1750.

Figure 5.1. Title page and last page of John Hill, *Lucina sine concubitu*, 1750. Note the alias, as if written by "Abraham Johnson."

Reproduced by kind permission of the Wellcome Library, London.

bounds and he sent off this diatribe contra Folkes to the geologist William Borlase in faraway Cornwall:

> He constantly refuses all papers that treat of longitude. He chuses the Council and officers out of his junto of Sycophants that meet him every night at Rawthmills [sic] coffee house, or that dine with him on Thursdays at the Mitre, fleet street. He has a good deal of learning, philosophy, astronomy: but knows nothing of natural history. In matters of religion an errant infidel & loud scoffer. Professes himself a godf[athe]r to all monkeys, believes nothing of a future state, of the Scriptures, of revelation. He perverted the Duke of Montagu, Richmond, Ld Pembroke, & very many more of the nobility. . . . He thinks there is no difference between us & animals; but what is owing to the different structure of our brain, as between man & man. When I lived in Ormond Street in 1720 he [Folkes] set up an infidel Club at his house on Sunday evenings, where . . . [many] of the heathen stamp, assembled. From that time he has been propagating the infidel System with great assiduity, & made it fashionable in the Royal Society, so that when any mention is made of Moses, the deluge, of religion, Scriptures, &c., it is generally received with a loud laugh.[5]

This was not the ranting of a senile believer who had seen better days. Stukeley believed Folkes had sunk the Society into disgrace for neglecting the *PT*: the Society's crown jewels. Da Costa agreed and laid out the details in a letter to Borlase who replied: "'Tis shocking to think how your Society has been exposed. . . .'" Borlase had recently been elected FRS but wept nonetheless "to see the dignity of knowledge so prostituted . . ." and replaced in disgrace by "the chit-chat of old women and the blunders of the ignorant." He was the nation's living authority on Cornwall, especially its antiquities, and horrified from afar at what the Society had become.

Hill was less bothered by dereliction, although he used them to his benefit in *Lucina*—his bombshell—and more vexed by his exclusion, yet it was one thing for the nation's most honored poet Pope to have referred fleetingly to the *virtuosi* a few years earlier in couplets of *The New Dunciad Book Four*, even when he named the culprits by name, and another for this upstart—this Hillian parvenu. "Who breaks a Wheel?" Pope's narrator wittily asked. The FRS who read Pope's lampoon a few years earlier were delighted to find themselves so charmingly reproved by the greatest poet of the century; others even complimented that Pope, dead as recently as 1744, took such notice of them. Richard Mead, almost seventy but still vigorous and remarkably rich for a jobbing physician, was delighted to have been immortalized in this Popean way.[6]

The FRS were not amused when *Lucina* struck. Some construed it as a prose dunciad with themselves in its epicenter, others as a disgusting *Fanny Hill* targeting themselves as villains. Part of their vexation is accountable through our speech-act theory: all depended on who hurled the stones and obscenity and Hill, they thought, should throw none. Yet he did by burying his bitter disappointment and landing on the idea of the mythological goddess—Lucina—who conceives without a man. Some germ of the idea doubtlessly derived from Joseph Tuberville Needham's earlier influence, especially his attack on the biological preformationists. Hill had never forgotten listening to him combat the standard FRS preformationist view that life springs from eggs in which the newborn is fully formed, and he remembered how the Catholic Needham was derided even after election as FRS by those who nicknamed the priest "Mr. Spontaneous Generation." Hill was no Catholic, not even a churchgoing Anglican, but Needham's dramatic defenses at the Wednesday club made a deep dent on him. Now he deployed their shafts in prose satire.

Lucina was an abusive joke wrapped in a shilling book subtitled *A Letter Humbly Address'd to the Royal Society*, signed "by Richard Roe," a *nom de plume* conjured for its alliterative ring. "Roe" and his alleged adversary

"Abraham Johnson" are names invented for the purpose of puffery, and within a year Hill changed these to female names as he entered a cross-gendered phase. He paid Mary Cooper to publish *Lucina*; "ingenious Cooper," as he called her, who had her own agenda contra authority, and even if she herself did not read Hill's lampoon, she basked in the prospect of the ruckus it would cause. Lesser jokes complement greater ones, and "Hill as Roe" cheekily inserted two jibes in his postscript.[7] First, he announced that the FRS were diverted from replying to his "modest proposal" because London was threatened by three earthquakes on the eighth day of the first three months of 1750,[8] and, secondly, he invited "All Ladies willing to breed [i.e., asexually] to favour me with their Companies [*sic*] before the 20th of *April* next."[9] The narrator describes himself as a "midwife" and country practitioner of "physic," who "stumbled" upon his discovery while attending the "sick daughter of a Gentleman" whom he delivered of child without her "having had commerce with a man."

The father confirms his daughter's story. Startled, the narrator claims to have rummaged through medical history for similar cases. While reading William Wollaston's (1659–1724) *Religion of Nature* he found pages about traducianism (the entry of souls into bodies) and discovered the account of another young woman who had bred by inhaling "seeds" (*animalculae*) from the air that "served as a certain hot Bed for them to dilate and expand themselves."[10] He paused, the narrator writes, at the notion of asexual breeding, wondering whether the seeds circulated through the air, or whether they were "lodged in the Loins of Males." Lucretius had long ago explained how these animalculae were dispersed during the atomic creation of the world, but Wollaston omitted the Lucretian account. If in male loins, then how, the narrator wonders, did the seeds proceed from loins into the wind that blew them about?

A fantasist might allow his imagination to run riot at the possibilities (including onanism), but the narrator looked elsewhere for an authoritative explanation. He remembered that Virgil had written in the *Georgics* that the west wind impregnated "certain Mares of his Acquaintance."[11] Persuaded that these "floating Embryos" permeated the air,[12] he set about in good Newtonian fashion—as a dedicated projector—to invent a machine capable of catching them: "a cylindrical, catoptrical, rotundo-concavo-convex Machine."[13]

The narrator further recounts how he reached for his microscope and found "little Men and Women inside the animalcules." He passed a further year repeating the experiments on the seeds, and eventually decided that the likeliest explanation was "a Doctrine of Winds and Embryos";[14] wind, which in good Stoic fashion circulated all elements in the air over seven seas and continents, also scattered these "floating embryos." But dissatisfied that he had found a solution, he located a sickly chambermaid on whom to try his experiment: without injecting her, he made her inhale millions of "floating embryos" collected in his machine.[15] QED: the chambermaid became pregnant, case proved, conception without a man.

Hill-as-Roe,[16] the author incognito, ought to have desisted but he soldiered on for twenty further pages[17] to the slight detriment of the sustained joke, turning to three of his hobbyhorses—Bishop Warburton (the noted textual editor), plagiarism, and venereal disease—without augmenting his case for the virtues of asexual, non-pleasurable, reproductive technology. Nevertheless, his skirting on the fringe of science and pornography was deft, yet concerned that his readers would think he had "stolen the discovery" (the embryo-catching machines) from others, he ransacked ancient literature to determine whether immaculate conceptions had been known apart from Mary's birth. He found discussions in Galen, Hippocrates, and Ovid's *Fasti*, where Juno eats cabbage as the impregnated Flora sits hard by "ravaged by Zephyrus"—the "fecund wind" that will impregnate her.[18] Milton, he says, had this Ovidian passage in mind when versifying the same idea in *L'Allegro*: "The frolic Wind that breathes the Spring, / Zephyr with Aurora playing," only to meet her once and "fill'd her with thee a Daughter fair,/So buxom, blithe, and debonair."

It was a daring move at a time when the backlash against John Cleland's "filth," as one critic called his "pleasure books," extended to such correctives as the English translation of foreign works about the glories of Mary and her virgin birth.[19] More practically, Hill referred to French biologist Antoine Réaumur's (1683–1757) chicken-breeding ovens that reproduced avians without roosters. Much was made of these ovens in Hill's generation: a technology no less problematic than Hill's machines.[20] For the third strain—venereal disease—Hill's narrator waxed lyrical and pedantic by turns: first he offers a potted history of this medical condition,[21] followed by a descent into bathos in the name of sublimity to show that he is a confused projector: the claim that he has elevated his style to be able to describe the malady's ravage on the human body. He concludes these digressions with a dig at the ever-increasing tribe of cross-dressers in his day, noting that not all those clothed as women actually *are*: "If all in female Shape (for I dare not call them all Women) . . ."[22] The detail can seem to have no place in his yarn about virgin birth, yet within three years, by 1753, Hill will alter his all-male repertory of *noms de plumes* to female, adopting the name "Juliana Susannah Seymour" as his favorite and further invigorating the rumor that he was biographically a modern satyr dancing around pornography's circle in glee.[23] At the end of *Lucina* Hill clinches his case about the benefit of immaculate conception by querying whether "single-distill'd Infants" will be as healthy as those "who pass thro' the seminal Vessels of both Sexes in the old way of Generation." He may have learned this structural trick from Swift who also saved it for the end of the *Modest Proposal* (1729).

Hill's Swiftian conclusion is that asexually produced children are timely: his new machine will produce "Offspring robust and healthy" as any generated in the old heterosexual way.[24] He "will apply for a Patent" for his new machine to guarantee the trinity of "maidenly virtue," the abolition of matrimony, and the demise of sexually contagious diseases.[25] The narrator's goals seemed sufficiently original to cause readers to take notice.

Lucina inspired all sorts of fraught aftermaths, some as productive for Hill's reputation as the reproductive tropes of its brilliantly satirical text. But soon a row broke out with his rascally inventive printer Mary Cooper. When she published Vincent Miller's *The man-plant: or, scheme for increasing and improving the British Breed,* Hill was certain Miller—an alias—had plagiarized the idea from him.[26] So many similarities existed: unusual births, abnormal conceptions, ways to increase population, faux projects à la Swift to preserve a nation. How could Cooper have permitted it? Hill was annoyed. But reproductive tropes—not merely satirical parodies—were in the air and Miller's *Man-Plant* was not the only botanical brainchild of the early 1750s inspired by La Mettrie à la Linnaeus. Some readers were certain the Hill of *Lucina* must also be the Hill of the *Man-Plant*—the Linnaean analogies of the latter were too glib not to be. But the FRS took a dimmer view. They were far more concerned with the *Lucina* satirizing *them* to be deflected by Linnaean analogies and fanciful *Man-Plants.*

It is anyone's guess how many FRS read *Lucina,* and the press was silent about its reception throughout 1750, but word quickly circulated that they ought not to. Those FRS who did *not,* heard the gossip that it was an assault on their collective enterprise through the appalling deceit of pornography. And they further understood that any reader could identify its target: the Royal Society. But however salacious to refined tastes, it was silent on more pressing problems of discovering the longitude, perpetual motion, or squaring the circle—well-worn riddles that then seemed impossible to solve but which continued to dominate FRS thought. In *Lucina* Hill had gone for the jugular of the natural historians. He sought to satirize his *own* camp: those who should have supported him but did not, and he narrated his story about Lucina who conceives *sans* a man with such finesse and polish that it was impossible to identify which particular FRS—if any—were his targets. The "mathematicians" within the society appear to have been indifferent to his election, indeed they may have supported his case if the natural historians had nominated him, but not one of them would;[27] so Hill targeted those closest to him and built their concerns into his robust satire: biological birth, sexual pleasure, and—most apparently—the raging contemporary debate about the veracity of preformation versus epigenesis in reproduction.

After *Lucina*'s publication in January, Hill kept a low profile for the rest of 1750. He tried to gain admission to a few meetings at Crane Court but was refused: on June 28 Stukeley confided to his diary that "the Dr. had abused the Society, in the brittish [*sic*] magazine" and was ejected.[28] Stukeley knew of the multiple "abuse" and must have wondered what lay next in store for his late mentor's son—just as well Theophilus was dead. Otherwise the year was uneventful. Hill bought himself a medical degree from the University of St. Andrews; the earthquake he predicted first struck on March 8, the day thousands fled London;[29] and Richmond died of bladder cancer at forty-nine, down in Sussex, on August 8. Perhaps Hill was enjoying himself strolling in the newly opened Cuper's pleasure gardens to notice his former patron's demise.[30] If he sent condolences to Goodwood they do not survive. By the end of the year he produced a second attack: this one short: forty-seven prose pages called *A Dissertation on Royal Societies*: *In three letters from a nobleman on his travels, to a person of distinction in Sclavonia. Containing an account of an assembly of a Royal Academy of Sciences at Paris, a description of a meeting of a Royal Society.*[31]

It appeared in December and was in the shops for sale by Christmas—perfect holiday reading for satirically unsuspecting thirsty readers. This one appeared anonymously, the author "H. L. Z" pretending to be a traveler from Sclavonia (Croatia) and admonishing readers not to judge his reflections a sequel to *Lucina*. Its three parts contain "an account of an assembly of a Royal Academy of Sciences at Paris," lampooning a meeting there that any English reader could see was not Paris but Crane Court, cleverly contrasted with an ostensible "description of a meeting of a Royal Society in London," and, finally, a "Coffee-House Conversation" in which abundant potshots are taken at FRS. For this one Hill returned to *The New Dunciad* and imitated its prolegomena, apparatuses, and other "Explanatory Notes," referring to Addison, Garth, and Pope but with a different overarching purpose than they had: intuitively he imagines that "FRS" is the new badge of royalty and aspires to shatter the linkage by decrying the institution. Hill moved away from natural history and closer to Grub Street when taking this satirical step. His immersion in Pope's poetry of duncery paid off: *Lucina* contains no iambic verse couplets but hurls its barbs at the "FRS dunces" as pointedly as Pope had directed his at Theobald and Curll. In bathetic scenes, like one where the traveler visits the London coffeehouses specifically to observe "two FRS"—Warburton and Hill—he finds them transformed into other men. The narrator reduces them to size by citing Pope again in a passage soon to be repeated ad nauseam about himself:

> So Proteus, hunted in a nobler shape,
> Became, when seized, a puppy, or an ape.[32]

Worse yet, the traveler notices a "Newfoundland Spaniel" tagged with an "FRS."[33] The conceit is that Hill yokes himself to Warburton, together as if friends, to disguise his authorship.

Hill's antagonists in the *Dissertation* are not so much condemned as mocked and savaged. William Arderon appears "Hardyrun," Henry Baker as "Bokur," and the *PT* castigated as so much stale tittle-tattle. The attack

Figure 5.2. Henry Baker, FRS.

Reproduced by kind permission of the Wellcome Library, London.

on Arderon's "Norweech" (Norwich) is especially callow: Arderon's having spent his whole life as an excise office in Norwich was no argument that his observations were worthless. In the third letter Hill puts down President Folkes: the "P——t" and his officers for their collusions and conspiracies. It reads as a literary amplification of the rant Stukeley had written to Borlase about "the infidel's sycophants"—Folkes and his men. But all three characters derided—Arderon, Baker, Folkes—are so minimally disguised that if there been libel and defamation laws in place, as there are now, its author might gone on trial. For the unsuspecting who read the *Dissertation* cold its anonymous author was, of course, just a "lover of Sclavonia," that faraway place on the Adriatic Coast.

Hill's belittling satire is puerile—the president grotesque, a fat and lazy Hogarthean caricature, more interested in food than philosophy, ever reluctant to be raised out of his "Seat of Ease."[34] Worse yet, the society consists of a rowdy, "Motley Mixture of all Kinds of Men": "Instead of the Decency and Order of the *French* Academy, every thing here was Irregularity and Confusion."[35] When Daval read the previous meeting's minutes, "People snarled, and scolded, and grumbled at it," and when the president introduced the first paper, "I could not for some Moments learn the Occasion of a Multitude of different Monosyllables that I heard uttered during the Course of this Prelude to the Paper: They were, as near as I can recollect, Pish !-Poh ! Shsh ! Shaw ! Pshaw ! and the like, and were accompanied with an amazing Variety of inarticulate Grunts."[36]

Hill's attack on Folkes tallies with Stukeley's and da Costa's charge that the "infidel" surrounded himself with sycophants he had appointed to committees to rubber-stamp his programs. But his assault on Arderon-Baker was different and cuts to the FRS procedures at mid-century.[37] It amounts to the view that a *virtuoso-amateur* (like Baker) brought an even lesser amateur (Arderon) into his orbit and saw to it that he was elected FRS and his papers published in the *PT*. Hill had a point. Arderon in Norwich communicated his observations to Baker in London through a correspondence that endured for a quarter of a century until Arderon's death in 1767: Baker was the star, Arderon his satellite. The star relayed his satellite's findings to the Royal Society, who elected him one of their number in 1745, as "a Gentleman well skilled in Philosophical Learning, a person of great Curiosity, and a most diligent and zealous promoter of Natural Knowledge."[38] Twenty-three of the "satellite's" papers were published in the *PT*: Hill saw this as recompense for supplying the star (Baker) with data when he himself had little to offer; and the satellite (Arderon) also contributed to Baker's works on the microscope as gratitude for the favors of election and publication. In a nutshell, Hill saw it as the old-boy system abused to extremes through correspondence. Even Arderon's recent biographer concedes that he "cannot be said to have made any lasting mark on the history of science" and that "it is tempting to regard Arderon as a quintessential amateur naturalist of the 1740s and 1750s."[39]

Hill further claimed that Arderon's cultivation by Baker arose from a system of patronage calculated to promote mediocrity: an armchair-naturalist Arderon feeding an incompetent Baker data. Still worse, Hill argued that such epistolary transmission sans verification amounted to "bad science." His analysis of Arderon's papers and Baker's can withstand the test of time despite Hill's having focused his criticism of the *PT* too single-handedly on them—indeed he had become obsessed. Yet their observations and conclusions are flawed even if Hill had not proved them wrong and despite Hill's not having been a better scientist himself. He was a whistle-blower whose wrath would serve to reform the Society in the long run, but nothing happened overnight.

By the time Hill's third attack appeared six weeks later in January 1751 (old style)—*A Review of the Works of the Royal Society of London*—the secret about authorship was out.[40] So much talk had ensued that everyone knew. Hill wrote at great speed over the Christmas holidays: almost three hundred pages of prose dissecting individual papers in the *PT* for their scientific flaws. He signed himself a member of the "Academy of Bordeaux" to which he had been elected and chose a passage about "thy giddy Dulness"—reflecting the blockhead FRS—from the third book of Pope's *Dunciad,* which he had at his side as he composed. A "Dedication to Sir Martin Folkes" unfolds as inverted irony, with every compliment intended as a dig, followed by a preface claiming that the Society is being ridiculed abroad, especially in France, for having fallen into disrepute. This is followed by a preface harping back to his obsession—Arderon and Baker—and the debased state of the *PT.*

The "author" has steeped himself in Addison's earlier criticism of the Royal Society in *Tatler* 236, and writes variations on the theme that whenever he meets a blockhead he "concludes him to be a Fellow of the Royal Society," then he then plunges in to the eight sections of his *Review* interrogating the *PT* papers in eight fields: arts, antiquities, medicine, miracles, zoophytes, animals, minerals, vegetables—covering the whole spectrum of the terraqueous globe. His division of knowledge reflects taxonomies of the time, when it would not have been thought bizarre to include "arts" and "miracles" in this anatomy. Hill needed these less didactic targets to launch his attack on Arderon and Baker. By "arts" he targets inventions and projects and accordingly begins with a paper on the "method of killing rattlesnakes" only to demonstrate its ineffectiveness in every capacity. Soon he complains that the Society is wasting its time publishing papers about "a method to catch roach and dace" or "A Way of making vines grow over the roof of a house"—both submitted by Baker from correspondence sent him by Arderon.[41] And so the *Review* continues for almost three hundred pages,

A

REVIEW

Of the WORKS of the

Royal Society of LONDON;

CONTAINING

ANIMADVERSIONS on *ſuch* of the *Papers* as deſerve PARTICULAR OBSERVATION.

IN EIGHT PARTS:

Under the ſeveral HEADS of

ARTS,	ZOOPHYTES,
ANTIQUITIES,	ANIMALS,
MEDICINE,	VEGETABLES,
MIRACLES,	MINERALS.

By *JOHN HILL*, M. D.

Acad. Reg. Scient. Burd. &c. *Soc.*

———*Like a rolling Stone*
Thy giddy Dulneſs ſtill ſhall lumber on,
Safe in its Heavineſs can never ſtray,
And licks up ev'ry Blockhead in its Way.

DUNCIAD, Book III.

LONDON:

Printed for R. GRIFFITHS, at the *Dunciad* in *St. Paul's Church-Yard*, 1751.

Figure 5.3. Title page of John Hill, *A Review of the Works of the Royal Society of London*, 1751.

no particular FRS criticized more repeatedly (in order of their appearance) than Baker, Arderon, Miles, Mortimer, and Folkes.[42]

Hill intends to name and shame them—the natural historians—but it is hard to know how to assess his *Review* apart from its *ad hominem* attacks. Much of it reads like Swift's satire of the Academy of Lagado in *Gulliver's Travels* (1726), in which Hill had immersed himself as deeply as Pope's *Dunciad*; and his jibes are made, like Swift's, at the folly of the projectors: an Arderon wasting his time on "People not born to be drown'd" or Baker on "The unicorn's horn." His reasons for exposing Cromwell Mortimer and Henry Miles are no less clear, even if they appear less frequently. Mortimer had been the Society's secretary ever since Hill had come to London and—as Hill viewed it—Folkes's most dedicated sycophant; entrusted with incorporating the Society of Antiquaries into its much larger cousin, a plan rendering Folkes even more culpable. Mortimer remained its secretary until his death in 1752, editing all the volumes of the *PT* during Hill's electioneering years. A vain man, he kept promising to publish a history of "the learned societies of Great Britain, including the Royal Society," but never did, much to the complaint to Samuel Johnson.[43]

Miles was an armchair minister elected FRS in 1743: just the sort of "dissenting amateur" who revolted Hill. His knowledge of natural history was minimal, yet he published several papers in the *PT* on the effect of electricity, the weather, and plant seeds that could live at the bottom of rivers and then transform themselves into flying insects. Hill detailed the mechanism of its publication as owing to Baker's folly in passing on to Mortimer any communication he received for quick publication.[44] Likewise Thomas Allen who sent in a communication on hermaphrodites—a physician now so obscure that he is nowhere to be found; but Allen was certain he had examined a genuine hermaphrodite claimed by Hill to be a "woman passing as such."[45] Hill had seen the freaks in Charing Cross: chimpanzees speaking French, hermaphrodites with fully formed male penises, and an alleged centaur with human face, this one his joke on the Royal Society who, he claimed, believed it existed.[46] But he was not about to be imposed upon, even if the FRS had been.

Baker figures the arch-villain, and Hill recounts one occasion in Crane Court—early in the *Review*—where Baker exhibited a louse under his microscope before the Duke of Montagu and others; when finished he discarded the insect and was forced by Montagu to retrieve it with his "Small and Delicate fingers."[47] Hill lost no opportunity to revenge himself against both Baker and Arderon in this humiliating way—the reason it seemed to them, and others, a personal vendetta. Hill would have taken a much larger sample of papers had he intended to perform an objective assessment. His limited number of scrutinized FRS detracts from the assessment and leaves him vulnerable to the charge of "sour grapes" over exclusion. But it does not invalidate the criticisms made of the FRS wing of natural historians or the criteria used for publication. The latter is the substantive criticism that hit a nerve within the Society and caused it to become enraged. Hill knew his protagonists, especially Arderon and Baker, and had been tutored by da Costa and Stukeley in the criteria for publication. He concluded, as Swift had in his equally scathing *Modest Proposal*, that he wrote to restore and reform rather than from personal animosity: "It remains only to add, that not a Hatred to the Royal Society, but a Love for the Studies that Society was established for the Promotion of, has occasioned the Publication of this Refutation of the Errors advanced by its Members."[48] How shrewd to end on a note cautioning that the virtuous men in the English Republic ought not to forget foreign places: "We cannot but wish the Men of Eminence in other Parts of the World may be informed, that the Ignorance of the Royal Society is not Epidemic among us, nor would suffer them to suppose they have a Right to say, the English are in an Error on any Subject, because an erroneous Account of it appears in the *Philosophical Transactions*."[49]

If the *Dissertation* hit a collective nerve within Crane Court, its longer successor, *A Review* elicited letters of reproof as well as support—balanced reception. A "Mr. Urban" wrote to the *GM*, for example, calling Hill's *Review* "judicious," his capability "ingenious," while conceding that his treatment of the FRS was uncivil.[50] "Urban" agreed that the topics treated needed correction: nothing was "miraculous" about the proposed cure for "fresh Wounds," as the "author" claimed, or the "Child terribly wounded in its Mother's Womb"; it was farcical to entertain the notion that "Demons" resided in "Lead-Mines"; the "*strange Creature called* Bakera," with the "a," did "not exist." The Hill who had grown up in the fen country would not hear of a LochNess–style monster named "Mer-Men," or the artificial "making of Rain," or "People born [not] to be drowned," or "the Production of Geese out of Shell-Fish," which Hill considered no more promising than Swift's mockery of earlier FRS extracting perfume from dung. And "Urban" agreed with him, especially with the pseudo-experiment Hill reported about "Incontestible [*sic*] Proofs of a strange and surprising Fact, namely, that Fish will live in Water."

Hill fiercely ridiculed all the topics investigated, as in the series of papers about "stittlebacks": small, three-spined fish who hunt by quickly pushing their jaws forward so that the food is sucked in and then grabbed by the stickleback's tiny, sharp teeth.[51] Hill claimed that these pests of British streams and rivers were not worth the trouble. Small wonder that Hill's infamy was now news: as such he filled the pages of the *GM* even before the magazine ran a proper review:

> In the preface [of the *Review*], which gives some account of his [Hill's] difference with the Society, he thus writes—"If I am merry in some places, let it be considered that the subjects are too ridiculous for serious criticism."—That the work however, might not be without its real use, an error is no where exposed

> without the establishing the truth in the place of *it*: and the author has no wish to regard *it*, but that the Society may by means of *it*, become ashamed of what *it* has been, and that the world may know that he is not a member of it, till *it* is an honour to a man to be so.[52]

Hill's *Review* was feckless but no one then—or later—could claim it missed its target: a century later Charles Dickens came upon it, read it with relish, and incorporated the material about stittlebacks into *Pickwick Papers*.[53] Hill also criticized the prizes the Society offered to projects he considered worthless—further evidence of cabals and collusion, he said.

His conclusion is plain: he has written to reform the *PT* that had sunk, as Stukeley, Borlase, and da Costa all complained on their own, into disgrace, but the ulterior motive was disappointment. Historians looking back unaware of his mortification can think his intention selflessly altruistic: a desire to restore, the need for reform is implied on every page. But Hill could not have written as he did—thrice—without the blow. Chagrin and disgruntlement drove him to revenge more than reform, even if the best historians of science studying the evolution of the *PT* without knowledge of Hill's biography must concur he was right—they had sunk into a parlous state.

Historian Anne Goldgar has adroitly demonstrated that the most noteworthy change in the early eighteenth-century Republic of Letters was the "conduct" of its members, which extended to the collective community.[54] Hill's unexpected behavior rocked the Society because conduct had taken precedence over ideology and scientific strategy in the two generations before Hill, and proof lies in the way a president so lacking in scientific imagination as Folkes appealed to the majority of FRS who elected him unanimously in 1741. He was a team player who liked presiding over committees and who reinforced the hierarchies and values of the community, however defective they may have become since Newton's death. The critical point was not, as throwback Stukeley thought, that he was an "infidel" or, as Borlase claimed, that he "neglected" natural philosophy and natural history, but that his FRS colleagues found his *conduct* acceptable. Conduct—the amalgam of manners and modesty—was the issue and counted for more than content or vision. Embedded in this required good conduct were not only codes of behavior but attitudes to gossip, faction, and quarrel, and those who failed to follow the assumed but unwritten protocols were not merely prevented from becoming *hommes illustres*, as Goldgar notes, but also derided and excluded in the short run, as Hill would be.[55] Modesty, rather than pride, was the first requirement *ne plus ultra* of each citizen; the system rewarded the mediocre and those below mediocrity, provided they took their place in traditional hierarchy. If conduct was constituted in these terms, then not merely the Royal Society but Hill too lay at its nerve center.[56]

The worst offense an aspiring "republican" like apolitical Hill—eager for FRS election—could commit was confusion between fame and infamy.[57] He was indeed becoming notorious: for ignominy rather than the prized modesty. His three reprehensible attacks on the Society excoriated not merely the top rank, President Folkes and his cabal, but those lower down the ladder such as Henry Miles and faraway Arderon, who almost never set foot in Crane Court; by so doing Hill shattered the illusion of harmony and community within the Society and replaced it with a farrago of shameless incompetence and collusion. Goldgar has put it well when describing the fragility of the virtuous Republic: ". . . stories of cabals, of posses out to protect the integrity of the great, of false botanists, pretended theologians, and insane pamphleteers, show us how fragile in many ways the structure of the Republic of Letters was."[58] So too the Society while Hill was trying to get himself elected. More recently, historians of institutions have wondered what to make of Hill's—and the Stukeley wing too—behavior and criticism, often confusing Hill's vanity with the degree to which the Society had sunk after Newton's death. Had Hill aspired to election when Newton was president it is unthinkable he would have lashed out at a "great man" in this reprehensible way. But the Society had weakened after Newton and become even more fallible and degraded in Folkes's time. By exposing Folkes and his cabals Hill had only shown his own shameless vanity, they claimed, rather than shattered their collective image.

Many FRS, not merely the two protagonist *betes noires* Arderon and Baker and the natural history wing, read his attacks in shock. They barely recognized Hill who appeared feral in this scathing satire as well as indecent. This was not the colleague they knew but the product of "Vanity, pure Vanity." He appeared to proceed on a principle that "the more people you annoy, the more you can take it for granted you are being recognized." Baker, a sober-thinking man, reported his version of the events to William Arderon: "A man who is not of it nor ever will be, who has abused the whole Society, the President, the two Secretaries, yourself and me, with the utmost Scurrility and without the least Reason in a Pamphlet just now published. . . ."[59] His diatribe followed while Arderon harangued: "As for that ungrateful Monster, Hill, I am fully satisfied, he is a mean designing, undermining, Fellow, and may from some secret grudge have longer endeavored to injure you, than you have been advised of. . . ." Another countered: "That worthless Fellow Hill has lately published a Book in Quarto," until another desperately wrung his hands because the savage attack was "particularly against our most worthy President."

Gossip and epistolary rumor flew in all directions. Thomas Shipley, still a drawing master in London who would go on to establish the Society for the Encouragement of Arts and Manufactures later in the decade, was outraged; he told Baker as much.[60] In June 1751 William Freke FRS (1688–1756), who combined interests in electricity with botany and who had recently published a work about electricity in the "sensitive plant," requested Hill's presence at a paper he would read but the Fellows denied the request.[61] Guests who were not FRS were required to apply and obtain tickets—Hill was denied and would continue to be from now on: persona non grata and demonized. To call the reception of *Lucina* and its two successors in 1750–1751 frosty is an understatement. It was icy—bitingly cold for Hill's having inveighed against the FRS and courted prurience and lasciviousness. Arderon, pegged to his desk in Norwich, folded the paper to Baker before its seal dried: "he has entirely stolen from every Body he could plunder. . . ."[62] Parsons, who had been spared, capitulated and agreed with them.[63]

Plagiarism in time proved the most damaging charge, even greater than vanity; it haunted Hill and forced printers and publishers alike to proceed with caution when they published him: usually on a proviso of anonymity or the use of a nom de plume. Its toll in fiction and commentary was less severe but in scientific works, to which Hill would now increasingly turn having burned his other bridges, it spelled swift doom.[64] In 1751 it ruined the reception of the second volume of his *General Natural History*, dealing with plants, the one work capable of leading him to secure patronage. Published in May of that year, it advocated Linnaeus's system of sexual classification. Linnaeus had introduced his revolutionary "system" to the world in print around 1730, although it would not be translated into English until 1754 after Sir William Watson touted its virtues in the *GM*.[65] But the Society condemned it, giving out that Hill had stolen Linnaeus's thunder and applied the Swede's new system to his work.[66] Hill's approach was actually mildly critical of Linnaeus and not until 1757, in *Eden*, would he fully endorse the bisexual system. But it was too late—he had made his bed with the FRS. Now he would lie in it.

The Society swiftly announced alterations to its methods of selection in the *PT* through the formation of Lord Macclesfield's so-called "1752 PT committee." It was the first step he took after becoming president.[67] The publication committee still ruled by closed majority vote, but a quorum had to be in attendance before votes could be counted. Macclesfield's greater gesture—at least for future historians—was his definition of the qualities required of every "FRS": birth and family, university education, papers read to the Society, acquaintances local and foreign, travels (on which Folkes had also placed considerable emphasis), correspondence, the branch of science worked in, and the "services or good offices he did to the Society." His own travels were limited; all he saw were "the learned Academies." This list sharply differs from the criterion Charles Babbage, putative inventor of the computer, listed in 1830 when he wrote at book length about the decline of the Society in the eighteenth century: "At the end of ten weeks, if A. B."—the hypothetical aspirant—"has the good fortune to be perfectly unknown by an literary or scientific achievement, however small, he is quite sure of being elected as a matter of course."[68] Babbage is as ironic here as Hill had been. Furthermore, what Hill failed in Macclesfield's criteria, especially in education and travel, he more than made up for in correspondence, but his branch of science—as Stukeley and Borlase charged—counted heavily against him, not to mention his unforgivable pride and vanity.

It is hard to imagine any impartial historian of science today praising the *PT* during Folkes's presidency, even when they are judged within the contexts of eighteenth-century science.[69] Perhaps this is why the *PT* ran disclaimers to the effect that endorsement of a publication was merely "civility," not to be confused with "approbation of the scientific validity of the publication or its substance"—conduct and community again over substance. Readers in 1752–1753 were reminded that the Society had been "remiss" and thereby "exposed [itself] to prejudice."[70] More defensively, that the Society would "defer [its] publication till they can furnish a sufficient number of papers to complete a volume," an approach miles away from its earlier inclusions of every paper printed in chronological order no matter how useful. Macclesfield's "1752 PT committee" declared with Hill in mind:

> . . . [be it] resolved that for the future their council should be a committee, and, if necessary, call in more assistance, in order to approve all the papers to be published in their transactions, for their honour and reputation, which has been much injured by an enemy to that body of which he attempted, but in vain, to be a member; and when convinced of mistakes refused to correct them.[71]

Immodest and spiteful Hill had been, but his vanity hurt him more than the Society. The Stukeley-Borlase camp would not be persuaded of the Society's innocence. Stukeley continued to believe the "council is only a junta of such as is herd [sic] together at taverns and coffee houses and exclude all members that know more than themselves and no papers are permitted but what are agreeable to them."[72] This is benevolent Stukeley at his severest, but he and the others in his wing of antiquarians and naturalists had witnessed how Hill was demonized and now felt they had nothing more to lose. Hill might congratulate himself that he had exacted a major alteration in the Royal Society no one else in his generation would dare attempt, but it was small recompense for a young man in a hurry. Later on he changed his mind. For now, the personal cost was great. His reputation was no longer controversial but monolithic—he could be hated, he could be loved, but he was no longer neglected, as the newspapers soon discovered.

NOTES

1. JH (1750d).
2. *MR* 2 (January 1750): 255.
3. Weld, vol. 1, 526.
4. For the evidence see Haycock (2002): 226–27.
5. Stukeley (1880-83), vol. 1, 99–100. Newly elected FRS, da Costa corresponded with Borlase (soon to be elected FRS himself) for a decade (1748–1758), most prolifically during 1748–1749 when da Costa was on his Grand Tour in northern Europe (see BL Add MSS 29,535). In Cornwall, Borlase hungered for information about the contentious natural history wing of the RS and da Costa's activity in the Bank Coffee House where he was an habituèe. Topics in natural history permeate their letters: especially its relationship to antiquarianism and botany; its "nobility" and "romantic sublimity" among the sciences; the special role of fossils and geology; the impropriety and weaknesses of Linnaean classification; Hill's revenge on the FRS and his growing reputation as a botanist in Europe. Current students of the development of Enlightenment natural history and its politics within the mid-century RS will find a treasure trove in this unpublished correspondence.
6. His opulence made a dent on JH's imagination who never forgot the sight of him driving out to his country house near Windsor in his coach and six horses, which JH imitated in a short time.
7. JH (1750d), 49–50.
8. Rousseau (1968): 438–50.
9. JH (1750d), 50.
10. Wollaston, passim.
11. JH (1750d), 12 and Virgil, *Georgics*, book III, which JH read in Dryden's translation for which he made his epigraph in "Roe" (1750g), accompanied by passages from Ovid and Milton.
12. JH (1750d), 13.
13. JH (1750d), 15.
14. JH (1750d), 17.
15. JH (1750d), 20.
16. JH (1750g).
17. JH (1750d), 31–49.
18. JH (1750d) 29.
19. Liguori, passim; Warner, chapter 3, see especially p. 42.
20. Réaumur, passim; Corea, passim.
21. JH (1750d), 41–45.
22. JH (1750d), 45.
23. See afterword.
24. JH (1750d), 46.
25. JH (1750d), 47.
26. Vincent Miller (1752). Many guesses have been made about the author's identity but one thing is certain: it was not JH, who continued to disown authorship. In contrast, when it was sometimes claimed he wrote *An Account of a Centaur*, also published in 1751–1752, JH was not so quick to deny authorship. He even claimed he would be present in Charing-Cross when the centaur was first displayed; see *Inspector* 19.
27. No evidence exists that the so-called mathematicians were his adversaries.
28. Bod. MS Eng. misc. e. 129, f. 151.
29. See *DA* for March 9, 1750; Rousseau 1968.
30. Wroth, 251.
31. JH (1750d).
32. *The Dunciad* II: 129–30.
33. JH (1750b), 45–46.

34. JH (1750b), 17.
35. JH (1750b), 17 and 19.
36. JH (1750b), 18–19.
37. The debate about the degree of disrepute into which the Royal Society had sunk continues: see Miller (1989); Sorrenson (1996); Sorrenson (1999); Feingold.
38. Royal Society election certificate for William Arderon.
39. Giles Hudson, *DNB* life of William Arderon.
40. JH (1751h) from which my citations are taken; Griffiths printed the first edition, Robert Dodsley a second edition in 1780 with different pagination indicating continuing interest.
41. JH 1751h, chapter 8: 15 for "dace" and 14: 21 for "roof."
42. For the statistically curious: Baker is mentioned thirty-eight times, Arderon twenty-four, Mortimer eight, Miles four, Folkes two, and several FRS or foreign corresponding members once each, e. g., da la Pryme.
43. Nichols, vol. 6, 2–3, 99, 144–45.
44. JH (1751h), 79–81.
45. JH (1751h), 97–102.
46. *Inspector* 19, April 2, 1751, and Rousseau (1986).
47. JH (1751h), 5.
48. JH (1751h), 286.
49. JH (1751h), 286.
50. *GM* Feb 1751: 21, 69–70.
51. JH (1751h), 122–26.
52. *GM* January 21, 1751: 47.
53. G. R. Potter (1923), 49–51.
54. Goldgar, 6–7; see 236–37 for the conduct rules.
55. Goldgar, 6–7, 155.
56. Goldgar suggests it was; see 6–7, 150–71.
57. Goldgar, 6–7, 172; Goldgar's example is Dutch polymath Prosper Marchand attacking Pierre Bayle, and the parallels with JH are noteworthy.
58. Goldgar, 6–7, 173.
59. LPH, 40.
60. Allen, 183–84.
61. Stukeley MSS Eng. Misc. e. 129.
62. LPH, 46.
63. For Parsons's career and relation to JH in more detail see Rousseau (2010), 63–65.
64. The consequence of stealing the other person's *ideas* is minimal here.
65. See chapter 14.
66. JH (1751b).
67. Weld, vol. 1, 519.
68. Babbage, 51.
69. Haycock (2000): 82–84.
70. *MR* 9 (July 1753): 37, reviewing *PT* 47.
71. *PT* 47 (1752): 69–70.
72. Stukeley MSS Eng. Misc. e. 131, 1751: 379.

6

Man of Letters

Hill was now a force majeure, if not yet famous then becoming fashionable and already somewhat notorious. Within one year he had written three biting satires, all demonstrating how fast and fluent his revengeful pen had become. His barbs may have been "lies," as da Costa gasped in horror, but they frazzled nerves and provoked gossip. The response to *Lucina* exceeded Hill's wildest expectations: he had already developed a thick skin as the petty war with John Rich augured but now—to think—he managed to arouse the largest national society of scientists. He attacked first, then prepared further for his own retaliation by inciting the foe; and on the intuitive belief that all publicity is good publicity this sequence energized him for further verbal assault. The publicity in the aftermath of the three satires assured him he had arrived in the Republic of Letters via Grub Street. Some said it was entrée as a latter-day Popean dunce, "Curll the Second," but with luck, he thought, he would secure patronage as an imaginative writer.

Hogarth was one of the first to take notice. "Beer Street" deals with the tumble-jumble of London life and includes "a large hamper of books" directed for a bookseller in St. Paul's Churchyard. Closer inspection reveals that the books themselves are destined "for waste paper" and include Hill's *Dissertation*. Hogarth either saw a copy of Hill's *Dissertation* or read it, having met him at Parsons's Wednesday night meetings, and one recalls Charles Lamb (1775–1834) commenting that "his graphic representations are indeed BOOKS: they have the teeming fruitful, suggestive meaning of words. Other pictures we look at—his prints we read."[1] If Lamb was right, here was Hogarth's "reading" of the worth of Hill's attacks.[2] Hill licked his chops, operating on the principle that gossip was good: the more talk, the more copies of

Figure 6.1. William Hogarth, "Beer Street," showing Hill's *Review of the Works of the Royal Society* (1751) in the basket in the lower right-hand corner.
Reproduced by kind permission of the Wellcome Library, London.

the *Review* he might sell at this steep price of 7/6, and all this while Baker plied Arderon and Miles with detail demonizing the devil:

> None of the Royal Society or indeed of any character will keep him company: whatever he writes hereafter will . . . be treated as it deserves. This Man's insufferable Pride and Vanity . . . have puffed him up with such a conceit of himself that for some time past he has been insupportable and seems now to be raving mad.[3]

Whether deranged as a modern-day Proteus or Cain, or Swiftian hack, the monster motif is dominant: not merely described as feral in his verbal attacks but for his audacity to satirize the FRS as brutes stuck in the rut of repetition. For their part Arderon, Baker, and Co. reduced him to some type of wild beluga roaming the land or, alternatively, a groveling puppy wagging at whoever praised him—a silly thing licking the dust with his flappable pride. Hill's satires had portrayed them as dissecting creatures in their sessions; preoccupied with "freaks of nature" (hermaphrodites, troglodytes, weird insects) who titillated their colleagues rather than instructed them about science—this at a moment when at mid-century monstrification was on the tip of many naturalists' tongues, some of its reification owing directly to Hill's three satires.

But he had not yet pondered his life's goals or reflected on the fallout from *Lucina* for the long haul. He needed a patron to survive, and his rush into print in *Dissertation* and *Review* had been the worst decision of his life in respect of his dire financial circumstances. From another vantage it was the best: he knew that literary life *outside* the Royal Society differed from its secure interior networks provided patronage had been secured. Grubs and hacks scribbled in the hope of economic survival at a moment when the mid-century novel was starting to swell to great numbers despite not having yet solidified into a distinct genre. Count the fictions published in the years leading up to 1750, or 1755, and their quantity and quality is extraordinary: not merely the acclaimed *Tom Jones* and *Clarissa Harlowe* that became best sellers but lesser prose fictions whose plots entailed adventure stories cast as some sort of "bios": the "life" of a hero or heroine from birth to death. Hill's three prose satires (he was no poet and knew it) prepared him to explore the form further.

Then, in December 1750, just as he was preparing to launch both the *Dissertation* and *Review*, he discovered that Tobias Smollett's *Peregrine Pickle* was half printed—an event Hill had been closely following. The huge success of *Roderick Random* two years earlier added to its advance publicity. Even Richardson took an interest in its imminent appearance, partly as printer but also on moral grounds given what he knew about the contents of the second half: the *Memoirs of a Woman of Quality* based on the notorious life of courtesan Frances Vane. While Hill was correcting his proofs Richardson lamented on December 6 to his confidante Sarah Chapone, to whom he offered to procure an advance copy of *Peregrine Pickle*, that the lady of its inserted "Memoirs" is "a very profligate Woman" indeed. The more notorious she appeared, the more Hill perked up from his recent demonization, regenerating himself with further writing projects.

One was a set of memoirs of a courtesan: *The history of a woman of quality: or, the adventures of Lady Frail*, which he wrote at great speed and published on February 8, 1751, just *before* Smollett could place the finishing touches on his "true" account.[4] "Frail," unlike Vane, was the product of his imagination;

Figure 6.2. Tobias Smollett, author and physician.
Reproduced by kind permission of the National Portrait Gallery.

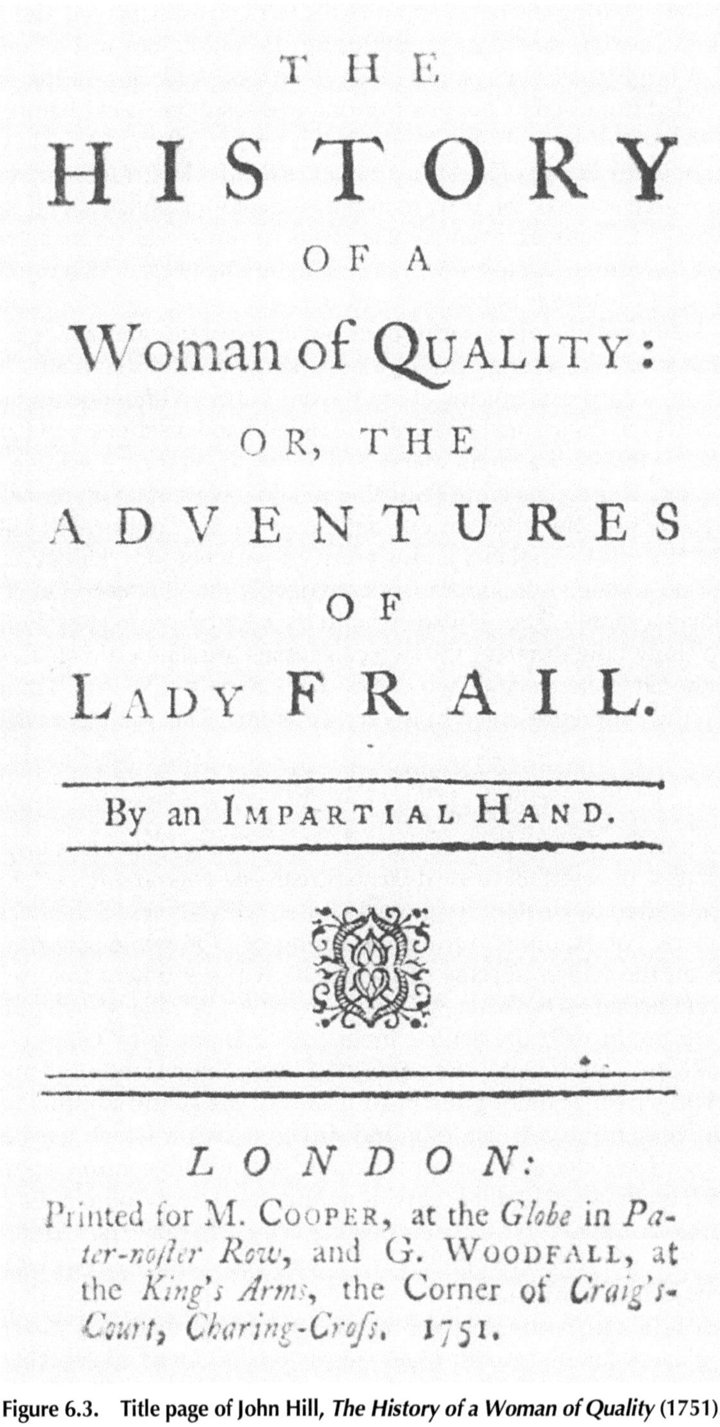
THE

HISTORY

OF A

Woman of QUALITY:

OR, THE

ADVENTURES

OF

LADY FRAIL.

By an IMPARTIAL HAND.

LONDON:

Printed for M. COOPER, at the *Globe* in *Pater-noster Row*, and G. WOODFALL, at the *King's Arms*, the Corner of *Craig's-Court*, *Charing-Cross*. 1751.

Figure 6.3. Title page of John Hill, *The History of a Woman of Quality* (1751).
Reproduced by kind permission of Professor George Rousseau.

yet Smollett, hearing the news about Hill's tactic, was dismayed and placed adverts in London newspapers imploring the public not to be "imposed upon." It brightened Hill's spotlight in the press. And despite the protest, copies rolled from Mary Cooper's printing presses three weeks before Smollett's *Peregrine Pickle* did, just as the town criers bellowed the news that winter about the Prince of Wales's premature death.[5] Mistress Diamond may have provided some of the "raw material" for composition, but Hill also ferreted Smollett's sources; even so, 239 pages of prose was no mean feat for someone to write in just a few weeks coming on the heels of two prior prose satires—and Christmas holidays.

Lady Frail contains more satire than novel; exposure and ridicule rather than character and setting. The plot sufficiently follows Smollett's "Memoirs" to cause further suspicion about the line between imitation and plagiarism: Lady Frail flees from Lord Frail in England and disappears to Paris. On the way she takes up with all manner of lovers: noblemen, a soldier, and—juiciest—a Creole she meets in Paris that would have cast a different slant on Hill's racy fiction, but after various dalliances on the Continent "Frail" sees the light, returns to England, and is reunited with her lord. Hill's *Lady Frail* received no acclaim, nor ought to, but cut deeply into the reception of Smollett's novel a month later. It also cut into its sales by contrasting Frail with Vane to show how different the two courtesans are. Hill claims: "Upon the whole, the Characters in the Two Books are extremely alike in all Things; but the light they are represented in is very different." The argument was lame.

Despite these publications and the debacle in Crane Court it is erroneous to think they turned Hill toward Grub Street—he was *already there* by 1747 when he started to write shilling works, often with a medical theme, for the booksellers. For example, during the spring of 1750 while congratulating himself on the winter success of *Lucina*, he wrote a timely treatise about actors and acting—*The Actor: A Treatise on the Art of Playing*[6]—dwelling on (what we might call) the actor's inner self. Theater critic George Taylor aptly calls this inner being the actor's "subconscious creativity" and considers Hill's treatise among the most useful of the century in this regard.[7] Yale University theater historian and director Joseph Roach goes further to adjudge *The Actor* as the most lucid mid-eighteenth-century treatise for elucidating what is actually occurring within the actor: "John Hill's pivotal exposition of sensibility, the nervous capacity whereby the vibrations of the passions are registered on the mind and body and without which energy would be meaningless."[8]

Roach brilliantly pinpoints the achievement. Hill believed that *passion* drives players far more than ideas—even preconceived ideas. Yet Roach opines that Hill established more than "passion." His extensive analysis of

The Actor demonstrates how Hill organized the major philosophical ideas of mid-century—sensibility, passion, nervous energy, movement, character, inner and outer selves—into a unified system of acting making sense to *both* actors and audiences.[9] Unsurprising for a decade (the 1750s) dominated by Hume rather than Locke, passion prevails over reason and the actor's inner-self shines through a deceptive exterior. Hill shows how the passion every actor understands best is "within him"; so profoundly he cannot constructively articulate it. It nevertheless reflects, and then represents, that "self within" his acted part.[10]

Hill also dissects personal physique and physiognomy, advocating perfect verisimilitude wherever possible, so that courtiers need not surround a Hamlet or Macbeth if the intended effect is realism. Taylor and Roach are in unison about the strange neglect of Hill's elucidating treatise.[11] Hill's first readers in the decade of the 1750s were more supportive, if sales of *The Actor* are indications. Bookseller Ralph Griffiths was happy to publish it with Hill's name on the title page in 1750. It sold so many copies within five years that Griffiths reissued it in 1755.

Hill's subtitle about "the art of playing" also claimed to be based on *Le comédien*, by P. Rémond de Saint-Albine. St-Albine (1698–1778) is an obscure figure who apparently flourished in Paris during the 1740s as both actor and dramatist and oddly wrote a *Mémoire sur le laminage du plomb*—Memoir of the Metallic Lead Plant in Paris (it was founded around 1730 but St-Albine's reason for writing this work has disappeared)—but no copy of *Le comédien* has ever been found and it may be that Hill invented it to add authenticity to his treatise. Either way it was his first work demonstrating that the stage is an imitation of real life rather than identical to it: "All dramatic fictions please us the more, the more like they are to real adventures and occurrences."[12] In comedy the audience is most "moved by ease" and "naturalness"; the actor should "deliver what he has to say in the very same manner that he would have spoken it off the stage if he had been in the same circumstances in real life that the person he represents is place in."[13] He sought a definition of "Truth" and found it when moving toward realism as the "natural state."

The 156-page work is an intelligent discussion of the art of acting governed by three key words: feeling, force, sensibility, all three arising naturally from "inside" the actor. Nor did his agenda prevent him from doling out praise and blame. For example, he chides the celebrated but corpulent actress Hannah Pritchard (1711–1768) for assuming the title role in Rowe's *Jane Shore*, the fat lady of Wapping: "no woman can speak Jane Shore so well as Mrs. Pritchard, but a lady so much *en bon point*, makes an odd figure dying of famine."[14] Goldsmith agreed with Hill and lifted his passage, almost verbatim, in his "Remarks on our Theatres" in *The Bee*.[15] In pleading for verisimilitude Hill added his voice to a later litany also calling for it. More generally in *The Actor* his implied reader is one who frequents theaters, as he himself did, and is familiar with playwrights and the style of their works.

Some of the most eloquent pages relate to specific scenes in *The Beau's Stratagem, Venice Preserved,* and *Othello*, where Hill writes astutely about the actor's responsibility in portraying—for instance—the death of Desdemona, as well as "Old Adam" and "Touchstone" in *As You Like It*. Hill knew the major dramatic tradition and had acted in many plays but his insights derive too uniformly from his medical learning, as when he comments that "players are, more than all other ranks of men, afflicted with nervous disorders."[16]

He also published a didactic tract on "the plague and pestilential fevers"[17] and the sequel to author-printer Robert Dodsley's *Oeconomy of Human Life*: 155 pages of maxims about the way to forge a better life allegedly based on a translation "from an Indian manuscript, written by an ancient Bramin . . . In a letter from an English gentleman, residing in China, to the Earl of ******." Addressed to Chesterfield, its subtext is patronage, its genre parodic of the Oriental tale in the mode of others who had exploited the form and as Goldsmith would soon perfect it in his *Citizen of the World* (1759).[18]

Hill had done business with the Dodsley brothers before—indeed John, Robert's older brother, had distributed the stinging *Review* and Hill would have many dealings with them in the future. For now, early in the 1750s, having burned his bridges with the FRS, he turned his gaze squarely on Grub Street. He could supply instant text on demand on almost every subject and wrote by rituals of discipline but was also becoming an entrepreneur whose publication cannot be understood apart from his relation to the London booksellers.[19] Anticipating the coming wave, his biographer glimpses that in over three decades he will produce more than one hundred original titles with approximately twenty different publishers. It is hard to name another Georgian writer who reprinted more editions of his own works (usually identical texts with a new title page).

The four publishers—in descending order of the works by Hill they took on—were Robert Baldwin, Mary Cooper, Thomas Osborne, and Ralph Griffiths.[20] The four were similar types at mid-century: the "work-horses" of the industry who acted as our modern agents for Hill. That is, he paid them to take on his publications and parlay his works to publishers who physically printed them. But Hill usually insisted on retaining copyright with all his booksellers. The Copyright Act of 1709, enacted early in 1710, had given authors the first legal right to do so and Hill availed himself. Cooper and Baldwin were indispensable middlemen without whose guarantees Hill could not have churned out his work at such speed.[21]

Two of his big publishing contracts with Thomas Osborne (1704–1767) of Gray's Inn Road survive, the Osborne who also published the early biographies of Samuel Johnson, and they may be sufficiently representative of the way Hill entered into binding printing agreements.[22] Both reveal his custom to sell his copyright outright for large sums; if a particular work—for example, his three-volume *General Natural History*—exceeded anticipated sales

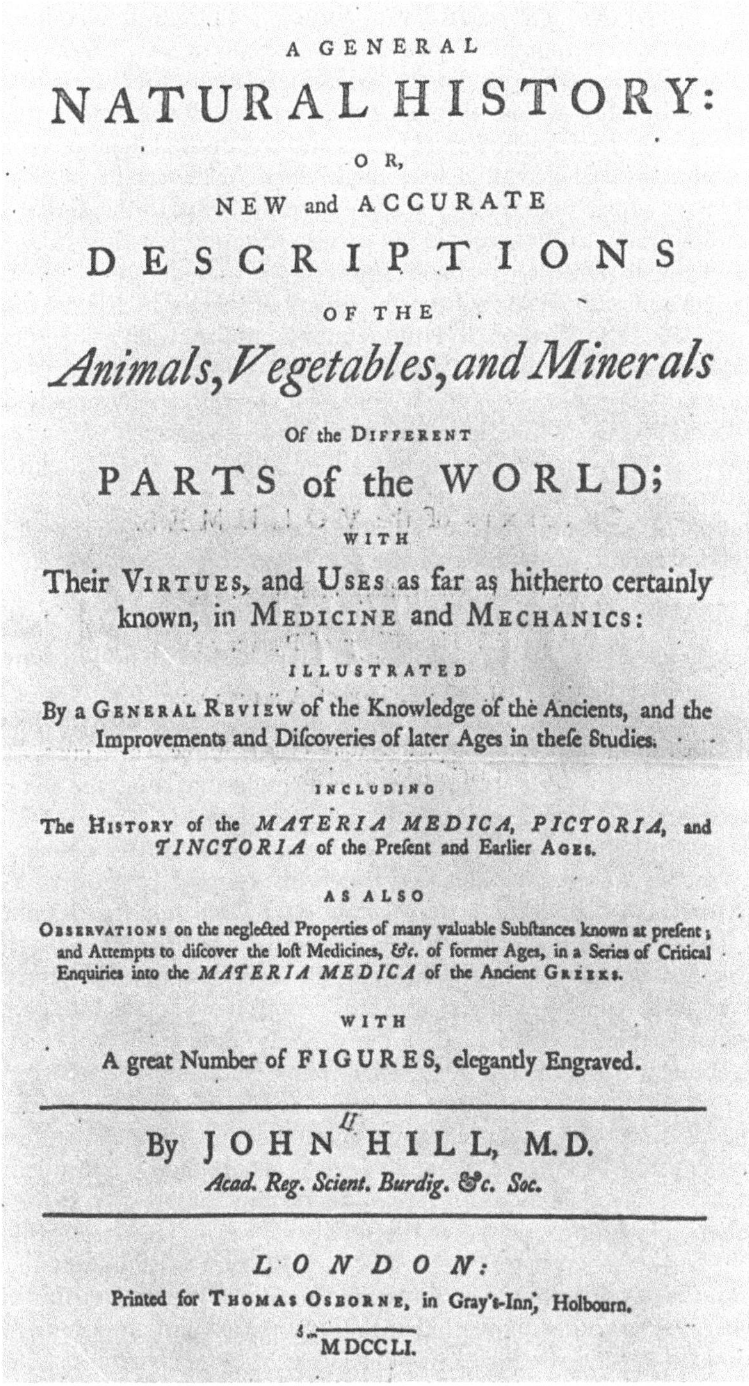

A GENERAL

NATURAL HISTORY:

OR,

NEW and ACCURATE

DESCRIPTIONS

OF THE

Animals, Vegetables, and Minerals

Of the DIFFERENT

PARTS of the WORLD;

WITH

Their VIRTUES, and USES as far as hitherto certainly known, in MEDICINE and MECHANICS:

ILLUSTRATED

By a GENERAL REVIEW of the Knowledge of the Ancients, and the Improvements and Difcoveries of later Ages in thefe Studies.

INCLUDING

The HISTORY of the *MATERIA MEDICA, PICTORIA,* and *TINCTORIA* of the Prefent and Earlier AGES.

AS ALSO

OBSERVATIONS on the neglected Properties of many valuable Subftances known at prefent; and Attempts to difcover the loft Medicines, *&c.* of former Ages, in a Series of Critical Enquiries into the *MATERIA MEDICA* of the Ancient GREEKS.

WITH

A great Number of FIGURES, elegantly Engraved.

By JOHN HILL, M.D.

Acad. Reg. Scient. Burdig. &c. Soc.

LONDON:

Printed for THOMAS OSBORNE, in Gray's-Inn, Holbourn.

MDCCLI.

Figure 6.4. Title page of John Hill, *A General Natural History* (1751).
Reproduced by kind permission of Professor George Rousseau.

Osborne forked over a stipulated sum and so forth each time counts were taken, much in the manner of modern royalties. However, Hill's contracts with Mary Cooper, who printed the second largest number of his titles, do not survive but may be less enigmatic than those with Osborne in that Hill brought her his most controversial works and she printed them on a pay-up basis; that is, *he paid her* rather than the reverse for the total cost of a print run. If fewer copies than the run sold he bore the brunt of the loss, if more, then they split the profit according to precise formulas now lost to time.

Mary Cooper (and her husband Thomas, with whom she worked) was a different type of bookseller from the others in this list; so risqué that she often appears a counterpoint to Hill's cunning publishing ploys, and her list in 1750–1753 reveals so many Hill-like titles that a reverse principle of attribution can appear likely. Namely, that by appearing anonymously on her list Hill can be assumed to have been the author. He probably was not, but if more were known about her dealings they might be extrapolated to Hill. Now, two and a half centuries later, she lingers in shadows.[23]

Finally, Hill's printing relations with Robert Baldwin are the least problematic of the four, for by the time he published Hill's *Conduct of a Married Life* in 1753 (the first title Baldwin took on) Hill's "literary days" were more or less over—as we shall see—and Hill made no attempt to use Baldwin's printing house for any remaining literary titles; besides, Baldwin's own list was primarily scientific and he may have declined the publication of Hill's literary titles. Baldwin was known for his "industry" and "integrity," which Nichols claimed were "proverbial";[24] he was widely liked, and considered a cut above Mary Cooper's crude commercialism despite being the same type of bookseller specializing in news and the retail trade.

This leaves Ralph Griffiths, the most significant of Hill's publishers not merely for the number of titles he printed but because he launched Hill's literary career and undertook the all-important *Daily Advertiser* containing Hill's *Inspector* columns.[25] The salient question about Griffiths is biographical: how can a bookseller who watched Hill scoop Smollett over the publication of Lady Vane's memoirs (with *Lady Frail*) have gotten into bed with someone like Hill in 1749–1750? Even this question raises larger general issues about the role of scooping, plagiarizing, and—most of all—publishing, especially the economics of publication among the early Georgians. Our modern biases predispose us to construe publication as a positive force indicative of achievement. Hill's era, however, was driven by contradiction on this front: on the one hand publication was coming into its own as the proof of entitlement leading to access and even distinction, as we saw in Hill's war with the Royal Society;[26] on the other it was still tainted as the refuge of the desperate hack—the amoral scribbler churning out words for a farthing—and Hill's career demonstrated that nothing undid him so definitively as his unrelenting scribosis. Had he published little, or even nothing, he would have fared better and never have been vilified.

Hill, for his part, justified his partnership with Griffiths on financial grounds—he was broke despite raking in advances on books. But he misjudged: he was becoming a household name for his satires and needed "quality writing" rather than further puffing, but he did not see it that way. His attention during the early spring of 1751 was far from focused on Smollett's possible retaliation but on plans to launch the *LDA*. Smollett revenged himself not once but many times, as did Hill against Smollett, lambasting the Scot as "Mr. Smallhead" and scurrilously announcing that the judges of Licencing Hall had passed an edict prohibiting Smollett from producing subsequent novels until "he understood more of Human Nature."[27] Instead of worrying about Smollett Hill, and Griffiths and their cohorts puffed the forthcoming newspaper aimed "at an audience of the common people," eschewing "Parties of the Great," and claiming that existing outlets such as the *Magazine of Magazines*, which reprinted extracts from original pieces, would be no match for it. The pair—Griffiths and Hill—unfurled the right flags about the four-page paper to be launched in March.

The idea underpinning "the Inspector" remains murky but the most informed guess is that Hill conjured it and Griffiths agreed. Samuel Richardson's alleged role—*pace* Arthur Morris (1891–1982)[28]—is without basis and there is no reason to think the novelist-printer in 1750 would have been willing to enter into a *quid pro quo* arrangement in exchange for Hill's so-called "favor." The "favor" itself remains mysterious and has been summarized at length by Richardson's biographers.[29] Briefly, when Richardson's friend, Thomas Edwards, leaned on his printer-friend to get editions of Medieval English writers published Richardson thought the newly launched *LDA* a good prospect for excerpts. Richardson apparently appealed to Hill—so the line goes—who "with some Difficulty" agreed on condition to include them in the new periodical, and they began to appear in the May issues.[30] But had Richardson made Hill's acquaintance? Had he met him? If Richardson sought him out before February, when *LDA* was being launched, Hill may have asked for a "favor" in return but the dates do not jive—they are too late: the *LDA* was planned by the end of 1750 and Edwards's correspondence with Richardson occurred in April and May 1751. The date is not too late for the appearance of the excerpts themselves, but the suggestion cuts against Richardson's business policies. It is likelier that Griffiths, and Griffiths alone, cut a deal with Hill, who already owned shares in the venture; and that Griffiths himself—as Richardson's appeal to Hill makes plain—who was already known in Grub Street as the putative editor of the forthcoming weekly magazine, made a deal with Richardson.

All of which points to the curious character Griffiths was. An ex–watchmaker's apprentice from Shropshire, he migrated to London like others from the provinces to seek his fame and fortune. Ambition propelled him, especially the desire to launch a project with himself as its epicenter. He could consider this because he had tasted fame and established a reputation as a possibly seditious printer in the years after the "1745" (Bonnie Prince Charlie). He exploited the public's fear over the Jacobite cause in his ephemeral writing, then brushed with the Duke of Newcastle by writing a gossipy tract called *Ascanius, or the Young Adventurer*, which presented Prince Charles Edward as the perfect romantic hero, and—in 1748, while Hill was trying to get himself elected FRS—seized the opportunity to print *The Memoirs of a Woman of Pleasure*, known today as a classic of early pornography, and perhaps in Soho later in the century plainly as *Fanny Hill*. With the fortune he made publishing it—some estimated it to be more than £10,000—he launched the *MR*, in which Hill would play a leading part as one of the reviewers.

Griffiths' luck with *Fanny Hill* was the type of success story publishers dream of today. It was ostensibly written by a hard-up gentleman who had left the East India Company under a cloud—this was the conceit promoted by its author John Cleland, who eventually owned up and surrendered his rights to the work to Griffiths for a mere twenty-pound note. Griffiths, forever on the lookout for talent and printing opportunities, recognized its potential and took every precaution to issue the book under a false imprint. But the law kicked in nevertheless; visited Griffiths' premises at the "Sign of the Dunciad" in Paternoster Row near St. Paul's Churchyard, ransacked his warehouse and found nothing. Cleland was then summoned before the Privy Council and rebuked rather than imprisoned, perhaps by the intervention of Lord Granville who agreed to award Cleland a pension of £100 per annum.[31] The case's dismissal allowed Griffiths to continue to print and reprint *The Memoirs of a Woman of Pleasure* and use the proceeds to establish the *MR*, which by any standards was one of the most successful monthlies of Georgian England. The equally literary *CR* could not compete with its sales.

Griffiths was less educated than the men he employed but had a knack for selecting winners: James Kirkpatrick who wrote medical reviews; his brother-in-law the Reverend William Rose, a Presbyterian much touted by Samuel Johnson, covered theology; James Grainger the poet; Oliver Goldsmith who reviewed all "polite literature" and whose first genuine paid assignment this was; last but not least Hill who could divagate on everything. These men would continue to write for Griffiths, but Hill, already in his thirties and by now living beyond his means in St. James, never signed for the duration nor did he remain in Griffiths's employ for long.

The reasons shed light on Hill's character. Griffiths drove a hard bargain—he gave away nothing and milked his hacks. By this means he survived the peaks and valleys of a publishing empire down through the century, much like Rupert Murdoch in our own time, until his death at eighty-three in 1803. He outlived Hill by many decades but the more impressive fact is that whole chapters can be compiled to document his ruthlessness in dealing with his writers, to the degree of clapping them into prison if they defaulted on their deadlines or owed him books they failed to review. He was one of a pair of eagle-clawed publisher-printers—his wife was the other—for whom survival indicated vigilance to deadlines and word counts rather than style or quality. Within this preoccupation his lady, Isabella Griffiths, was an integral part of his publishing machine. She fed and housed a contingency of hacks in Peckham but was no mere cook: she supervised deadlines and revised reviews and—according to Smollett—even wrote some. A decade later Goldsmith bitterly complained about her "gross interferences," especially her revisions: it was the reason he quit and was almost sued by her husband, but this gets us ahead of our story.

One would give something to learn when Hill first met Griffiths and whether Samuel Richardson really had played a part; as well what their encounter entailed, but no evidence survives. Even more so what the youngish Hill represented to this former clockmaker's apprentice who had spent his formative years exploring clock mechanisms rather than English or Latin syntax, as had Hill in his youth. A decade later, around 1758–1759, Griffiths hit the buffers and almost went bust but earlier, in the 1750s, during the years when Hill was reviewing for him, the *MR* became so well established that Griffiths could afford to enlist any writer. When he had launched his Review and needed to fill pages, Hill appeared the ideal catch: he could write overnight, on any subject in any field—especially natural history, botany, medicine—and when he did, he appeared in the vanguard. He produced copy, and the *MR*'s most meticulous modern scholar, Benjamin Nangle, has identified which reviews were his.[32]

Hill now charged ahead in the further aspiration that his name was becoming fashionable. He converted colossal disappointment over non-election into the most firebrand discharge of creative energy—1751 was indeed becoming an *annus mirabilis*. In May he brought out his *History of the Materia Medica*, which received a very lengthy review in the *MR*.[33] By June Osborne had printed the second volume of his *General Natural History* to considerable acclaim, this one dealing with plants and following his fossils.[34] He wrote so prolifically and quickly that all sorts of works were attributed to him; for example, the *Memoirs of a Man of Pleasure, or the Adventures of Versorand*, a two-shilling book containing "tales, fables, maxims," and "other little Lessons of Morality in Prose and Verse," but no "male equivalent" of *Fanny Hill* despite its dedication to Samuel Foote, a controversial actor who fled to the Continent in semi-disgrace. Hill had kept his eye firmly on Foote since his failure to be elected FRS, judging Foote to be the all-around "wit" he himself aspired to, but cautioned by Foote's flight.

A further reason *Versorand* was attributed to Hill was that Osborne advertised it on the end-cover of Hill's *Adventures of George Edwards*.[35] It may have been Hill's and claimed to be an English adaptation of a book by Henri-François de La Solle (1698–1761), still alive in France and not to die until 1761 about whom nothing is any longer known. De La Solle's *Mémoires de deux amis, ou les aventures de messieurs Barniwal* (1754) exists in French versions, as do a few other of his amorous fictions of the 1750s, but no French original has been located of the *Memoirs of a Man of Pleasure*, which gave rise to the erroneous notion in 1751 that Hill invented it.[36] No one then judged it to be Cleland's and it might seem the sort of base work Hill would compose, especially those aware of the strategy Hill's comrade Griffiths had cashed in on its female version. Its three hundred–plus pages are stylistically not Hill's and it lacks the plot and punch of any accomplished narratist. But Hill spent the bulk of his time writing his editorials for the *Inspector* to which we turn in the next chapter—for now it remains to be seen how rapidly he propelled himself into central Grub Street as one of its leading figures and most lucrative worthies.

He did this primarily by turning his hand, not to the novel but the *anti-novel*, which requires explanation.[37] It was then a minor developing form without cache or profile. Others had tried their hand at it, especially women, without contemporary recognition: so impressive were the novels of the 1740s, especially masterpieces clustered around 1747–1750—*Roderick Random, Tom Jones, Clarissa Harlowe, Peregrine Pickle*, even the pornographic *Fanny Hill*—that they overshadowed the upstart anti-novel. Besides, Hill had a surfeit of the gene, as it were, of satire to write fiction of any type—this was his main limitation: an imagination of parody and replica. He was too angry and anxious, too fearful of failure, to imagine characters and plots in the leisure the fictive and moral imagination of novelists requires. By mid-century he had published biting satires, in addition to all sorts of scientific works, but nothing—certainly not *Lady Frail* or other prose ephemera—indicating he could succeed as a novelist. But in anti-novels he might just squeak by; and this state of affairs he intuited, as he had on so many prior occasions taken stock of the landscape, probably without articulating the reasons to himself. It was therefore hardly surprising that his contemporaries thought his latest transformation to be "Versorand," another maker of minor anti-novels as its name playfully suggests.

Six months before launching his scathing *Dissertation* and *Review*, in the spring of 1750, he brought out the first of these anti-novels: *Adventures of Mr. Loveill, interspers'd with many real amours of the modern polite world*, where the "real" is essential; two volumes totaling 695 pages of derivative, imitative romance about Lady Juliet-Scheme and her accomplices—Busy, Sir Solomon Single, Lord Tawdry, and dozens of others—in Bath. It has been attributed to others (sometimes to Mary Lloyd, who had died a year earlier, but whose imagination was very far from its concerns) but is much more likely Hill's.[38] The evidence is stylistic as well as contextual, and to add weight to the style a shadowy biographical figure called "Lovell"—or "Loveill"—then frequented the Bedford coffeehouse, one of Hill's haunts, as we shall see.[39]

He likely paid Mary Cooper to print it as "a second edition" on the alibi that this "reissue" had merit.[40]

The narrator claims to be "a woman," asking "her" readers not to blame "her" for idealizing Loveill and presenting him "in a much less perfect picture than I have given of him."[41] If "a woman writes," as Hill's narrator claims, then this particular female is "an angry woman" because she has been enraged by the way her sex has been abused. Eventually "Loveill" and his desired mistress Cynthia, a chambermaid eager for a career on the stage, appear, to the chagrin of the spurned Lady Juliet. Their identities are revealed, the disguises wear thin, when enter a band of itinerant actors, who are so well depicted that it gives further credence to the biographical strain about Hill's adolescent years spent among them. By the end, Loveill's amorous fraud is uncovered, Cynthia punished, and Lady Juliet vindicated. Restoration comedies had teemed with this strategy and the fiction here is such a throwback to the moral concerns of an earlier generation that one would think no one could have considered *Loveill* a work of merit. Except for the cross-dressing conceit—one Hill will use throughout the 1750s.

But this is to read *Loveill* apart from its satiric thrust. The "stage" Hill refers to is repeatedly the *arrière-pensee* of *Loveill*: its *leitmotif* as well as the plot's engine for suggesting to readers that they could identify the originals if they read closely enough. But the stage is also the work's most interesting metaphor for the polite metropolitan world in which these flat characters move and may even function as a metaphor for Hill's own life in 1751: the stage on which he saw himself as player rather than biographical figure engaging with life's choices; the platform for his surreal charades and outrageous risks rather than for actions with moral consequences. Lady Mary Wortley Montagu relished *Loveill* while traveling in northern Italy early in 1752—she confessed to Lady Bute "tho there is [only] one character in it that I can find out"—and clearly could not put it down.[42]

Even if Hill was not its author, its variety of adventure based on romance in polite society demonstrates that works of this type were routinely being attributed to him; and the reason that its sequel, the *Adventures of a Valet*, was not merely widely attributed to him but self-proclaimed as his own.[43] *Lucina* had set him ablaze on this path: writing satirical fiction of the type Smollett was producing in finer pedigree. Those reading *Loveill*, like Lady Mary who relished it "night and day," like some custard never to be finished, did so for the plot of its satire while aiming to identify its original targets.[44] Like all else "Proteus Hill" touched, he did not stick with it for long. He was no celebrity yet acted as if he were, scribbling hither and thither and boasting as proof that works were being attributed to him at random.

Did he do anything other than write? It can seem so but not through statistical proof. His output in word counts was incredible by any standard of measurement but matched during those years by Fielding, Richardson, and Smollett. The last, with whom Hill often compared himself, had written the sprawling *Peregrine Pickle* in record time—this feat coming on the heels of *Roderick Random*. But Hill could juggle three or four large works simultaneously, in addition to producing his biweekly "Inspectatorial" editorials. He had become a veritable writing machine in 1751–1752, the main reason his contemporaries labeled him "lusus naturae," but he also learned from his mistakes.

His next novel, a weird amalgam of satirical fiction, realism, and erudition, was the *Adventures of George Edwards, a Creole* published in July 1751, and sets off on a new tack that incorporates learning while dropping the romantic mold.[45] The "Creole," Hill's protagonist who travels from the Caribbean to London and immerses himself in the Royal Society, is based on George Edwards (1694–1773), the ornithologist and artist whom Hill had met at Goodwood, and who later performed research, in the 1760s, into rare birds and the "vegetating fly" that could allegedly turn itself into an insect.[46] Hill's choice of protagonist could appear sensible in 1751. Edwards was a member of the best learned societies in London. He was a neutral, rather than controversial, figure among the FRS. He would have no reason to complain about Hill's unfair treatment of him even if he is a vehicle rather than developed character in his own right. Nor did he—when Edwards read the novel he apparently smiled.

A decade earlier, when Richmond brought Edwards to visit Goodwood in the 1740s, while Hill was still there, he was already a known ornithologist who had worked with Mark Catesby (1683–1749), the naturalist who taught him how to etch in the Carolinas, and the Bartrams in Philadelphia, as well as with corresponded with Linnaeus. His chief patron was Sir Hans Sloane, then president of the Royal College of Physicians who employed him as the bedell and keeper of the library, giving him a base from which to disseminate his hand-colored etchings of birds. By 1750 Edwards was an established figure within London scientific circles and was the best-known illustrator of birds in England.[47] Why fictionalize him in a novel? The more focused question may be, why choose him rather than others?

A clue comes from the novel's printing, especially Hill's decision to contract with Thomas Osborne rather than Mary Cooper to print its almost three hundred pages, which can suggest it was intended as something other than a lampoon. The preface contains the usual pieties about romance and realism, folly and vice as more pressing than individual character, but also insists that the hero—the "Creole" Edwards—has no real-life original: "the Writer of these Adventures declares, that there is in the World, no such Person as the Hero of them, or as any other Character described in them: The Persons are all, so far at least, *Tom Jones's* and *Clarissa's* [*sic*] . . . [and] are intended as Characters of various Vices, Follies, &c."[48] Perhaps they are, but Hill knew better when propagating his ruse. And he was so steeped in *Tom Jones* that he simultaneously imitated many aspects of its construction except the choice of protagonist—this white Creole son of a wealthy plantation owner in Jamaica. It was a sound choice two decades before the composition of Richard Cumberland's play *The West Indian* (1771) describing the London fortunes of a naïve white Creole called "Belcour"—if only Hill had risen higher in other areas of plot, form, and character than the choice of his "Hero."

The story opens with Edwards voyaging to England, befriended en route by the young and equally naïve Spence, an uneducated white Creole. In London they find Edwards's uncle Jeremy at Will's coffeehouse. The wise, if duplicitous, uncle takes nephew Edwards under his wing, thematically emphasizing the uncle-nephew kinship attachment so important to the Georgians, and pretends to introduce him to the best London society while doing so for his own gain. Once settled Edwards soon becomes a "Man of Pleasure" devoted to women but quickly loses interest in the hedonistic life; in book III he becomes a "Philosopher" in search of scientific truth. The minor characters are flat—"Dr. Single Dose," "Mr. Storm," "Mr. Pliant"—but sufficient sensationalism is included of the type Hill had already used in *Lady Frail*; and in one chapter "Our Hero makes violent Love to the celebrated Mrs. Conquest" (238–43) which almost undoes him. The book closes with Edwards winning the lovely Miss Wentworth and returning home to the West Indies just before his father's death to inherit the fortune he has left him—but not before the curtain comes down exposing deceptive Uncle Jeremy who dies eight months later and leaves the money Edwards repays him to his ward, "faithful Ruth."

George Edwards is an apt test case of Hill's fictional ability as it was beyond all doubt the work of his pen, and no issue of attribution can cloud any assessment of its achievement. It sustains the dramatic analogy of life as a stage from the first page—"Book the First: Containing about as much business as the first Act of a Comedy"—and incorporates autobiographical elements such as (1) the nod to his mistress "Diamond"—"The Author does particular Honour to a Woman of the Town, call'd *the Diamond*";[49] (2) the Wednesday night meetings at Dr. Parsons's when a lady "listens at the keyhole, especially on those Nights, when a Hermaphrodite, or some other Phaenomenon which concerned the Sexes, was to be the Subject of Disquisition . . .";[50] (3) allusions to "a Paper, entitled, *The Inspector*."[51]

Neither plantation life nor migration to London were original features in 1751, and Hill also wrote unaware of Aphra Behn. The characters do not lure readers then, and despite the demonstration of its hero as "a Man of great Prudence and Oeconomy . . ." there was little to recommend in Edwards's character.[52] He loves Julia Wentworth, daughter of a plantation owner, but does not tell her; she is beautiful but not wealthy and Edwards' family does everything it can to prevent his marriage to her—to the extent of damaging Hill's plot by Edwards's uncle Jeremy informing his nephew that Julia is dead so that he can marry someone else. But as the main action in London unfolds it is apparent that Hill's imagined death of Julia is just a device to permit Edwards to run the full gamut of amorous adventures in t'Town.

Hill could imitate and parody, excoriate and lampoon, but not create his own voice in fiction. The influence of Smollett's early fictions, especially *Roderick Random* (1747), is omnipresent, especially Smollett's preoccupation with money, which Hill heightens to levels of specificity perhaps not seen again until Jane Austen's fictions. His aspiration to emulate Fielding is also apparent but Hill's digressions are few and derivative, as in the "Dissertation on the modern Art of Humbugging."[53] To gloss this "modern Art" the narrator comments that "There is a Species of Wit . . . we may be allow'd to call Lying by that Name, which was very successfully laugh'd out of the World some years ago, by the *Spectator*. . . ." It was, but student magazines in Cambridge and Oxford revived it in 1751.[54] Hill fictionalizes "humbugging" at the point that Edwards meets a "Mr. Pliant" who is "good at this humbugging, with a female partner . . ."[55] Pliant marks Edwards as "a gentle Innocent, or, in his won Phrase, a Pigeon, cut out on purpose for his Plan"—"to humbug"—and enacts multiple frauds on him to the detriment of his purse and person, suggesting how well Hill understood this "art of imposition."[56] Hill's exposition antedates writer Arthur Murphy's by a year and nothing Murphy wrote adds to Hill's demonstration, not even Murphy's claim that the "never enough to be admired Art of Humbugging came into Vogue" just recently—in 1751 to be exact.[57]

Was Murphy conjuring up Hill for the public? After all, humbuggers conceal, lie, dupe, are the worst of imposters, and in his digression in *George Edwards* Hill had named it and fictionalized the "art" anticipating Smollett's enactment two years later in *Ferdinand Count Fathom* (1753), the story of a rogue "humbugger." Even so, the first readers of *George Edwards* latched on to the sections lampooning the FRS, having been prepared by Hill's previous satires. Hill's achievement must therefore be qualified: his displays of narrative clarity and the fluency of his expression, his propensity for imitation and parody, and the difficulty he had experimenting and innovating within the form. Not that formal experimentation helped Smollett's reputation either: two centuries later his name is now almost forgotten. But the verdict about Hill's prose satire must be that despite narrative clarity *George Edwards* is a throwback to pre-Fieldingesque fiction destined to leave t'Town indifferent.

It did, but Hill's satire hit its mark again and the collective FRS bellowed. When, in the novel, Edwards meets a "Dr. Single Dose" who "gave tea at five every Tuesday—the day his *Inspector* column appeared each week—for visitors to discuss philosophical subjects, readers perked up, as Lady Mary Wortley Montagu had in trying to identify the original of Loveill. Immediately they saw the Hudibrastic force of Hill's severe whip. Dose takes

Edwards under his wing and transforms him into a scientist in "no less than four Days . . . to instruct him in the Terms and Rudiments of the Science, and having furnished him with a Specimen, which was no other than a *dry'd Whiting*, that had been part of the Ship's Stores, he assur'd him of the Success of his Undertaking."[58] The "Success," of course, is Edwards's election as FRS in just ninety-six hours. But when Edwards forgets everything his tutor Single Dose has taught him, the FRS construe it "as a tacit Encomium on their own Qualifications, readily accepted the Excuse . . . ," and Edwards is "now dub'd a Philosopher"; introduced to members not according to their "Ranks and Orders," which was judged "in Consequence of the Number of learned Performances each had oblig'd the World with," but just because he knows nothing.[59]

Readers in 1751 looking for a vivid account of the live sessions in Crane Court found it in *George Edwards*, and what chaos they discovered; more madhouse à la Hogarth than laboratory of science:

> The rest [of the room] was fill'd somewhat indiscriminately, with Philosophers, Antiquarians, Mathematicians, and Mechanics. A *Scotch* Peasant produc'd a New Orrery; a *German* Mechanic, a Table Fountain contriv'd to play in a Desert, to the great Entertainment, and Bedabbling of every body present; and the Doctor's Son and Heir, the Model of a new invented Mouse-trap. The Audience consisted of the Doctor's Taylor; an *Anabaptist* Preacher; a converted *Jew* who sold Spectacles; an Atheist and two *Roman* Catholics; a blind Fiddler, who fully expected he should be restor'd to Sight by the Doctor's Nostrums; and the Master and Mistress of a Pamphlet-shop at *Charing-Cross*, with whom his Works, entire, were always to be met with.[60]

Hill's representation of a typical convocation produces such a collage of incompetents that readers extracted meaning from its reduction to absurdity: "The People who spoke beside the above-mention'd, were Mr. *Storm*, the Inventor of a new Religion; Mr. *Farthing*, a Collector of a peculiar Species of *English* Coins; Mr. *Sage*, the Author of a very egregious History of Printing, in which, one of *Swift's* Prophecies is given as a Specimen of the Letter of one of our earliest Printers, *and Maker of Bologna Sausages*, who had discover'd the Longitude."[61] Perhaps an allusion here to Hogarth's depiction of the insane astronomer in his "Bedlam" looking through a telescope; for symmetry Hill inserts his hobbyhorse—the earthquake, which he claimed to have predicted—when the meeting "is interrupted by a great noise from the room above . . . others took it for the Shock of a third Earthquake."[62] Now the risible FRS projectors stream forward, as they had in Swift's Academy of Lagado. A letter from a German with a ten-part name is read which, having heard "of the English's obsession with petrification," had sent them "some *petrify'd Flames of Fire*."[63] Here Hill exposes many papers in the *PT*, for petrification none other than a "Letter from the Right Rev. Dr. *George Berkeley*, Lord Bishop of Cloyne, to Tho. Prior, Esq, in *Dublin*."[64] And others too.

It unduly dispraises Hill not to notice his Butlerian inventiveness in the fabrication of these novel projects, as in his "account of a fat man who has the fat cut out from his body, and an account from a lady on Herculaneum and the foods cooked by the volcano found there."[65] These are as imaginative as Swift's projectors extracting perfume from dung and building houses from top to bottom. Hill's defect lies in his timing: what was novel in the 1720s no longer was in the 1750s. His "fat man" reducing his weight of over six hundred pounds by half appeared stale in 1751, and the historical fact that Cromwell Mortimer, Hill's *bete noire* as perpetual secretary of the Society, had read out the account on May 9 cut no ice.[66] His denigration of birthmarks as signs of shocks or surprises to the mother during pregnancy was still debatable but did not enhance his pungency. His amplification of "An Ichthyological Dissertation upon a dry'd Whiting," another satire on the *PT*, seems to cut the FRS down to size as unassailably as Pope had, but coming from the pen of the disgraced Hill it seemed the stuff of sour grapes.[67] Pope had nothing to lose; he was a free and self-supporting agent in no way dependent on patronage. In 1751 Hill appeared as having lost everything.

Some FRS naturalists again came to his defense after reading his "Ichthyological Dissertation" in *George Edwards*. They lauded the spoof and recognized the follies of its parallels in the *PT*, especially the ridiculous tendency then to classify everything in ever-longer Latin words. Da Costa was one. He carped to Needham, now in Paris, that "we are so fond of exotic ideas that not one English naturalist dares think for himself [that] the torrent of natural history runs all Linnaean and a student who should now affirm that skates rays or sturgeons are fish (for Linnaeus says they are *amphibia natantes*) would be ridiculed out of society[.]"[68] Borlase agreed but was stymied: had Hill himself not done so, he asked da Costa in a letter, noting that Hill "frightens every one with his long and hard names, I hope he will study plainness & simplicity & clearness much more in his Vegetables. . . ."[69]

By the fifth day Edwards' scientific education is complete and he reads his scientific paper before the FRS, presenting his rare and newly discovered animal—a mere, ordinary whiting. The Society, having heard only "the Danish, German, Swedish and learned names of the fish left his Audience no Suspicion of it's being a Whiting. . . ." Applause thundered and Edwards "was immediately proposed for a Member, and, what was much more to his Purpose, had the Honour of the particular thanks of the Father of his Mistress, and was invited to his House."[70] But in the fiction Edwards's current mistress is the daughter of FRS President Martin Folkes, claimed by Hill's narrator to be held "in nothing but Adoration."[71] Edwards visits her in Queen Square, where Folkes lived, just off in Great Ormond Street in Bloomsbury, and—strapping, amorous fellow he is—meanwhile also becomes enamored of another dozen or so women; takes them to Ranelagh and "makes violent love to the celebrated Mrs. *Conquest*," a widow who intrigues with him about *liaisons dangereuses*, when suddenly his adolescent lover "Jane" arrives from the West Indies. A wedding is arranged, the couple returns home—all too late. Edwards's father has died and left his estate to his son, Edwards repays his debts to his uncle in London, "with lawful interest only," as the comic novel's curtain comes down.

NOTES

1. Hogarth, 92.
2. For JH and Hogarth see Paulson, vol. 2, 98–103; Hogarth never again caricatured or disparaged JH and it is probably idle to speculate why.
3. LPH, 40.
4. *GM* 21 (Feb. 1751): 96; *MR* 4 (Feb 1751): 307-8; for the attribution see Rousseau (1972): 375–76.
5. See Scott, 390–91; Rousseau (1972): 375–78; Lewis Knapp (1949): 118–25; Anonymous, *An Apology for the Conduct of a Lady of Quality . . .* (1751).
6. JH (1750a); incorrectly attributed to Aaron Hill.
7. Taylor, 60–64.
8. Roach, 103; Roach's superlative analysis (pp. 99–106) paves the way to further explorations of JH's neglected work. At the very least Roach lifts by several notches JH's reputation within early modern theater history.
9. *The Actor* shows JH to be philosophically up to the minute rather than glancing backward to a prior generation; for JH's version of sensibility see Rousseau (2004), 229–33.
10. See Coxe (1980) for the mid-century "inner self" as the new stranger to be discovered.
11. Roach's treatment (n. 8) adds JH's dramaturgy as another field in which JH shone.
12. JH (1750a), 156.
13. JH (1751a), 187.
14. JH (1755a), 257; JH added the point to the 1755 edition.
15. Friedman, vol. 1, 362.
16. JH (1750a), 47.
17. JH (1750e).
18. JH (1751g).
19. James Raven (2007), passim.
20. See appendix A for the statistics.
21. Even so, the number of JH's published titles remains approximate.
22. LPH, 52–54.
23. Important preliminary work has been presented by Beverly Schneller (1994).
24. Nichols, vol. 6, 443.
25. Lewis Knapp (1939): 199–204.
26. Rousseau (1998a), 196–201.
27. *Inspector* 14, 75.
28. English amateur medical historian A. D. Morris, mentioned in the afterword, claimed to have found evidence that Samuel Richardson suggested JH to Griffiths as the right man to compose the daily columns of his new newspaper; after a long search I have found nothing to confirm the view; see Morris MSS, entries for 1955–1958, where Morris is burrowing in the old North Library of the BM through newspapers for those years.
29. Eaves and Kimpel, 330–31.
30. *LDA,* May 22, 1750, and issues on the following days.
31. Granville's reasons for intervention remain unexplained; one argument is that he had known Griffiths as a boy.
32. See Nangle sub "John Hill" in the index.

33. *MR* 5 (1751): 371–84; *GM* 21 (1751): 239; *LM* (1751): 287.
34. *MR* 7 (1752): 437–45; *LM* (1751): 288.
35. JH (1751a), 287.
36. See attributions to JH in *LM* (April 1751): 192 and *MR* 5 (June 1751): 43–44.
37. Beasley discusses the genre's development but the form continues to remain understudied.
38. *MR* 3 (1750): 58, as does the later *MR* index; *Loveill* has long been attributed to JH by Smollett scholars such as Lewis Knapp; see also James R. Foster *PMLA* 91 (1949): 1085.
39. Anonymous, *Memoirs . . . Bedford Coffee House* (1763), 31. See chapter 8.
40. No one should imagine the duo of JH-Cooper had been alone in this commonly deployed publishing tactic; see Schneller (1994), 129–35.
41. JH (1750c), preface, v.
42. Halsband (1967), vol. 3, 7.
43. JH (1752a); for the evidence see *Inspector* 24: 102; *LDA,* January 18, 1752; *MR* 6 (1752): 110–23 also announced it as by JH and ran a complementary review.
44. Halsband (1967), vol. 3, 7.
45. JH (1751a); Scott, 389–92, located the BL Add MSS 35398 providing a key to the original characters; no doubt exists about the biographical George Edwards, the naturalist, as the work's original.
46. George Edwards (1743–1751); George Edwards (1758–1764); George Edwards (1770). James Robson, the London printer and bookseller, was also Edwards' publisher and on his death in 1773 sold his huge library; see GM (1806: ii, 783, 871). For the "vegetating fly" see George Edwards (1758–1764): vol. 3 [1760], 262–65; Edwards based his research on the observations of Spanish naturalist José Torrubia (1698–1761).
47. Catesby (1748), passim.
48. JH (1751a), preface, v.
49. JH (1751a), 223.
50. JH (1751a), 158.
51. JH (1751a), 140.
52. JH (1751a), 3–4.
53. JH (1751a), 100-109, chapter 7.
54. *The Student* 1751; no evidence exists that JH saw any of these student newspapers.
55. JH (1751a), 102.
56. JH (1751a), 105.
57. *Grays-Inn Journal* (1752), no. 11.
58. JH (1751a), 157.
59. JH (1751a), 160–61.
60. JH (1751a), 163.
61. JH (1751a), 164–65.
62. JH (1751a), 165.
63. JH (1751a), 176.
64. *PT* 44 (1746–1747): 325–27; an addendum appears on pp. 328–29 from a letter to Dr. James Fothergill dated August 8, 1746.
65. JH (1751a), 177.
66. See *PT* 47 (1751–1752): 47, published as "A Letter from Dr. *T. Coe,* Physician at *Chelmsford* in *Essex,* to Dr. *Cromwell Mortimer,* concerning Mr. Bright, the Fat Man at *Malden* in *Essex.*"
67. The original paper is *PT* 46 (1749–1750), 518–20, "The Description of a *Fish,* Shewed to the *Royal Society* by Mr. *Ralph Bigland,* on March 22, 1749–1750: Drawn up *by C. Mortimer,* M.D. Secret. R. S."
68. BL Add. MS 28540 f.224/93, March 18, 1760.
69. BL Add. MS 28535 f.280/62, letter of May 7, 1751.
70. JH (1751a), 186–90.
71. JH (1751a), 195.

7

Puffing "*Inspector Hill*"

The *Inspector* columns began to roll from the press on March 5, 1751, and appeared biweekly on Tuesdays and Fridays.[1] They occupied some of the newspaper's front page and continued until June 30, 1753, totaling between 713 and 720 numbers depending on whether "letters to the editor" are included in the count. Griffiths and Hill numbered them consecutively irrespective of the daily paper's number until July 1751; afterward they were placed in sync with the same *LDA* number and from July onward.[2]

Newspapers of the time customarily prepared their first and fourth pages—the "outer forms" as they were called—in advance of the inside news, the procedure being to reprint essays, or editorials, from other London newspapers such as Johnson's *Rambler* and *Idler*, Hawkesworth's *Adventurer*, Dodsley's *World*, Colman and Thornton's *Connoisseur*, and later on Wilkes's *North Briton*. Hill's *Inspector* often joined their company and extended his visibility to the provinces. The *Inspector* appeared, for example, with some regularity in the outer pages of the *Salisbury Journal*. Afterward, these editorials were bound as self-contained single or double volumes by different printers, often by Griffiths, as in the two-volume set Griffiths issued in 1753.[3]

Hill guessed well at his readership, and within weeks they began to write letters addressed to him that routinely appeared in the main weeklies and monthlies where he was fast becoming a staple featured as routinely as any politician. For example, a "Tradesman" wrote a long letter printed by the *LM* about his business and domestic life, and asked for advice about his future prospects.[4] The editors of *LM* attached this note to the letter: "This paper [the *LDA* in which the *Inspector* columns appeared] made its first appearance about three months ago, and seems to gain ground, being writ with great accuracy and spirit." Hill himself may have penned some of the letters and sent them to himself, but most were genuine—at least for the start.

Fakery or not, he was now obliged to produce a biweekly point of view to the tune of approximately one thousand words. His editorials were too long to resemble our blogging but derived from some of the same impulses. He reserved Saturdays for religious columns—a day before the Sabbath—including his own religious biographical development,[5] which he chronicled unabashedly except for the attraction he claims to have felt for a sentimental deism derivative from the closest observation of nature.[6]

At first he had little notion how his opinions would be received; how gentle or forbearing his readers would be and to what degree his *persona*—real and imagined—would influence the responses. This uncertainty was fundamental to his enterprise: every columnist, even in the mid-eighteenth century, knew that he cut a public figure, as Addison and Steele had learned and as Johnson and Goldsmith were learning in the 1750s. Hill may have misgauged his own but was not so naïve as to forget that he possessed one. After his recent debacles—still lodged in public memory—he was on guard not to appear contentious, ungracious, or patently ignorant; and soon latched on to the idea that a "roving inspector"—someone wandering "t'Town talking to strangers in search of news," a combination of the generic Enlightenment spy and modern policeman—would serve his cause;[7] would lend him research credibility, in our current sense, by promoting the view that he was not merely generating these "opinions" from an idle armchair.

Nor did he. He had wandered plentifully, on horse and foot. He had spent a decade in London's taverns and coffeehouses, pleasure gardens and watering holes, and knew every lane and gilded coach and was, besides, already a familiar face to many in the capital. He had watched the erection, in Whitehall, of the Horse and Guards Buildings, and sauntered through the new Berkeley Square Gardens, north of Oxford Street. Had called in on the Hunter brothers at their School of Anatomy in Covent Garden while talking to printers and booksellers in the stalls surrounding it. Had heard Thomas Arne's newfangled music while strolling through the Thames's sweet-scented pleasure gardens, especially Cuper's—his favorite—situated near Lambeth yet still capable of overlooking Somerset House.[8] And his imagination soared as he watched William Kent's fine town houses being erected along St. James's Square and in Arlington Street, especially at number 22 so close to where he himself would soon move. Nothing in his orbit, however, rivaled the magnificence of Vauxhall and Ranelagh, appealing to all the senses with their myriad of entertainments in the form of musicales, fireworks, illuminated groves, spectacular balloon rides, pantomimes, and theatricals. He knew most of their extensive walks, private arbors, supper boxes, rotundas, and Chinese pavilions. Why then should he not be the grand "inspector" of all these places and comment on their goings-on?

The new "Inspector General" had pretenses and aggrandized himself but was assuredly metropolitan. The invention of a "roving inspector" was as innovative at this moment as Addison's "Spectator," who gazes and gapes, had been a generation earlier, or Johnson's "Rambler"—also walking despite the different connotations of Johnson's metaphor—at the same moment early in the 1750s. The name soon caught on, not least for its novelty, and further disseminated Hill's own name to such degree that "Hill" and "Inspector" were soon interchangeable designations. It gave his biweekly editorials a brand name—"The Inspector"—and introduced its author by a code just as British "Inspector Morse" has done in our time. It presented Hill as "walking the city" and "roving in his chariot," at a time when London's newly curious, and often fawning, inhabitants were also compulsively strolling. The mental picture his "Inspectors" offer is one of his being followed around by eighteenth-century paparazzi, almost as if he were royalty. Certainly of having joined the celebrated.

Hill rode to some of his locations but his columns made clear that the "inspections" were accomplished mainly on foot, as John Gay's imaginary walkers have done in *Trivia* (1716). The moral advantage of roving was not merely to improve mankind, although Hill hardly disclaimed such benefaction would follow from his effort, as to provide the most accurate up-to-the-minute information—to take the t'Town's temperature. And he wrote as if he also expected deference, if not reverence, to be shown toward his attempt.

Walking was then becoming the new national pastime, leading to the shopping that soon followed and led to the rise of leisure and the cults of consumerism associated with the Age of Walpole.[9] Hill wisely tapped into the newly fashionable ambulation but whether he roamed, strolled, or promenaded it soon became apparent in the columns themselves that he was the center of attention far more than the expanding city. He visited places its inhabitants had not seen, or—if seen—whose finer details they had not observed. Between 1720 and 1750 London had transformed its Thames landscape and buildings, and expanded so far to the west and north that few could keep up with the alterations.[10] Hill's "rover" satisfied these curiosities while delivering dollops of morality.

Churning out the words presented no problem. He wrote fast yet fluently, quickly found his voice despite its vanities, and realized that the production of "opinions" develops like a muscle that improves with use: the more you moralize the stronger it becomes. He also sensed which "opinions" were more appropriate than others, and did what he could to beef up the undernourished ones; he never wrote "Inspectors" artificially and was dedicated to topics about which he genuinely felt. Nor did he construe their production as journalistic slumming; on the contrary, he cultivated them as further entrées to the patronage and status he avidly sought.

As the "roving inspector" he professed to be "obliged to wander t'Town for news" yet did so for amusement as well, especially its pleasure grounds and music halls and gardens. He heard the celebrated diva Giulia Frasi at Ranelagh,[11] and next year the ravishing Maria Bennet at Cuper's Gardens, one of their last performers before fire destroyed the place.[12] Three weeks later, in March 1751, the monthlies announced forthcoming reviews of his *Dissertation on Royal Societies* and *A Review of the Works of the Royal Society of London*.[13] The "Inspector" had reached only his third issue when Hill turned literary critic. The first editorial gives a brief statement of purpose as primarily literary and then plunges into pungent praise for Gray's *Elegy in a Country Churchyard*—"one of the best in the English language" he writes—comparing Gray favorably with the parlous state of other professional authors. He even isolates out Gray's "moping Owl" for its hoot: "It is this species which utters the cheerful and agreeable hooting, which we hear on evenings."

The second *Inspector* moved to the "Progress of modern Amour," a topic bound to have wide readership. And the third quick to take note of the failings of Fielding's account of the origin of their paper war, a theme he would sustain.[14] During that first week of publication the editor of the *London Advertiser and Literary Gazette*, another weekly, wrote: "We would be ambitious to make this Paper [the *London Daily Advertiser*], in time, the general Channel of Literature and Amusement."[15] It struck them as a modern *Time Out* magazine with the "Inspector" targeted as the main attraction.

During this first month of publication—March 1751—Hill included nonliterary topics as well: the new calendar coming into effect in a few weeks (March 25); the perception that crime was sharply increasing, especially forgery and perjury; the proper way to understand gardens historically as both micro- and macrocosms of the real world; whether animals have both "reason and instinct"; the need for police protection in the newly criminalized world of metropolitan London. But there is not one reference over its three years of life to the Royal Society or any of the FRS. Hill has turned over a new leaf in his career—he has been refashioned.

But not without courting t'Town. Hundreds of letters written to him as "the Inspector" have inevitably disappeared; among the surviving ones it is clear to what extent he made an impact throughout the metropolis.[16] For example, Sir John Fielding (1721–1780), the half brother of the novelist who founded the Universal Register Office to "bring together ingenious persons of all kinds . . . [to] meet with those ready to employ them"—an early type of clearinghouse functioning as an employment agency.[17] Fielding had found it difficult to obtain space in London's newspapers, but when Hill touted his cause in the "Inspector" his luck picked up.[18] In gratitude Fielding, who also was first to give the metropolitan area police protection (the origin of London's contemporary Metropolitan Police), wrote to Hill a few days later: "the great concourse of persons of Fashion that have lately appear'd at our Office, many of whom professing that it was from your recommendation of it that made them venture thither, convinces me of the happy influence Mr. Inspector has over the polite World. . . ."

John Fielding's correspondence with Hill also makes clear how widely known Lord Orrery's recent patronage of the "Inspector" was.[19] No wonder Hill later dedicated the collected *Inspector* papers to him. Not a letter from Fielding elapses without some reference to his "lordship" whose biography of Swift had appeared that August (1751). But not all the "Inspector's" topics were metropolitan. A few weeks earlier he wrote about "Cleora, a nobly born but poor girl, who when orphaned cannot support herself"—he sent her too to Fielding's Universal Office. References to feral children are also evident, perhaps glancing at the story during Hill's adolescent years of Peter, the "Wild Boy," found living naked and mute in the woods of Hanover in 1725. Peter was still alive and described in 1751 by Hill as "more of the Ouran-Outang species than of the human" when he churned out his early *Inspector* columns.

Hill was "roving" all over the place—town, country, and further afield—and suddenly he was also doling out praise to the other Fielding production: the rival *CGJ*, and though it was thoroughly inimical to the "Inspector," to put it mildly, Hill now called it "inestimable"; doling praise as well to Johnson in the *Rambler* as a model of virtuous humanity couched in classical prose. About James Thomson's *Seasons*, recently reprinted after the poet's recent death, Hill wrote a balanced *précis*: the right amount of praise and blame. But what he gave with the left hand he withdrew with the right for some authors, as when labeling Smollett "a killing satirist,"[20] or tactfully taking on Fielding's pamphlet, *On Robberies*. Fielding had claimed that "irreverence" was the basic fuel of modern robbery; Hill rejoined that "people should go to church twice on Sunday" to eradicate it. He believed it and perhaps went himself, although the record is silent.

He also deployed his editorials for biographical purposes to verify and deny. He explained in the literally hundreds of references to himself—some useful, others so self-aggrandizing as to be risible, as when he claims that an eminent physician in London commends his ancient Greek so profusely as to suggest he compose all remaining "Inspectors" in Greek—recounted "why the inspector goes on many excursions,"[21] and, later, denied that he had penned *Lady Frail*. He ran columns on microscopes, physico-theology, and philosophical attitudes to the difference between animals and man. He reviewed dozens of new books and included letters to the editor, whether real or fabricated letters never to be known although he claimed most were his. By the summer of that first year, 1751, his role and style have considerably developed: he claims to be receiving numerous letters and publishes his replies; advice is given out; he prints the public's speculation about who he is; and he lets his readers know that the coffeehouses and taverns are abuzz with conversation about him.

The columns also demonstrate Hill manipulating them to incite feud and fracas. A stunning instance involves Henry Woodward, the actor at Drury Lane, and a gentleman named Fitzpatrick. In November 1752 Fitzpatrick threw an egg at Woodward for a shoddy performance that disrupted the play and caused it to terminate; Woodward gestured to Fitzpatrick from the stage as if to challenge him to a duel, which would violate the codes of dueling in that a common actor was challenging a "gentleman" (Fitzpatrick) to duel. Hill penned the story,[22] and came down on Fitzpatrick's side on grounds of the conventions of dueling, which encouraged the gentleman to prosecute Woodward in court. Henry Fielding was the magistrate when the case came forward and he found for Woodward; claiming that Hill had incited all of them because he was "the meanest and basest fellow that ever took a trumpet in his hand" and because "he had the imprudence to declare in the camp [of Wits], that he [Hill] was the leader of the town."[23] Repeatedly, these incidents reduced to battles of egos warring because the new dunce marketed his celebrity as few had done in a generation.

No one, however, dared deny his genius for PR—he was his own best publicist, "puffing" himself *ne plus ultra* in the lingo of his era. Yet after almost three centuries it is difficult to describe adequately how he struck his contemporaries. In our era Norman Mailer once published a book called *Advertisements for Myself*, which at the time offended the genteel segments of his readership; and Hill's puffing proved even more offensive than Mailer's because he focused on himself so routinely. He could have avoided the trap, in part, by dwelling on issues and topics without any mention of himself, and let his readers judge for themselves. But not even this ploy—difficult for him—would have succeeded: he was already irrevocably tarnished, a man with a history he could never live down despite extraordinary ability and flair for writing.

Moreover, Hill did not merely puff: he parodied and mocked his *own* puffery; lambasting his self-endorsements from afar, as if someone frenzied by the contempt he held for it, and even plagiarized (his own) travesties. Today, our postmodern sensibility might celebrate someone so naughtily inventive and judge his mischievous antics inventive and playful. In his day, however, he was reviled for desecrating propriety in this contumelious way, a severe attitude enduring into our time among those offended by his jests and pretenses. Puffing was not, of course, unique to Hill; it was becoming widely disseminated and practiced in different forms and shapes. It was already developed in Pope's generation even if the word had not yet come into its own.[24] The paper wars in Grub Street often started over violation in some protocol or other of its practice. Trace the *Inspectors* week by week and you glimpse into the mind of a genius at self-promotion. That his strategies ultimately backfired depended more on temperament—especially his arrogance, pride, and vanity—than the tactics themselves. Someone more humble practicing them would have succeeded brilliantly. He puffs each of his books in ways not entirely dependent on language but on timing too. "I have been long sensible . . . [that] there is hardly a Man in Town more generally known than the Author of these Papers":[25] so patently ridiculous an assertion that the reader stops dead in his tracks and by beggaring belief Hill has achieved his purpose. Or when seriously claiming that all London coffeehouses must order not one but *two* copies of the *LDA*.[26]

Arthur Murphy, the actor-hack soon to become Hill's next *bete noire* for assisting Christopher Smart in the large-scale mock-epic poem *The Hilliad*, classified the varieties of "puffery" then, claiming some were ordinary, others benefited the community, while others had an opposite effect.[27] Hill's "Inspectatorial" varieties embraced all three but were transparent rather than subtle, and he was also masterful at the direct hit.[28] He also "puffed" by inversion and innuendo: by attacking *himself* and then claiming he was now compelled to set the record straight, or by spotting offense and malice where none was intended and making fusses—or mountains—over molehills. His *vis operandus* was the belief that every man has the right to defend himself; so, in the first instance, especially among unsuspecting readers, he proceeded as every decent Englishman would. Among those who knew better, like Smollett or Johnson, or for those who were reading his *Inspectors* closely and continually, the ulterior motive seemed contrary to the affirmation. As commentaries on the paper wars of mid-century, especially with Fielding, Smart, and Smart's "gang," the columns form a key primary archive. Nothing else describes their chronology, evolution, and factions more exquisitely. Fielding especially occupied a region of Hill's mind that no one else could for his competing columns in the *CGJ* and when teaming up with those producing for the *Drury-Lane Journal*. The three organs published their issues with the other in mind: watching its rise and, often, much to be desired demise.

If Hill's *Inspectors* appear marginal to us today in this domain it is perhaps because our sentiments situate this type of dunciadic warfare opprobrious and politically incorrect. We aim to be a culture of transparency rather than slippery allusion and innuendo buried in mountains of verbiage. But Hill's columns thrive on it; the veiled statement in his fabricated "letters to the editor," in his dozens of invented characters, and in the yarns he spins. Even the moralities derived from his stories are veiled so far as his personal lot is concerned: does he mean to endorse or slam particular positions?—the reader is baffled over and again. Other moralists avoided the dilemma, but Hill straitjacketed himself by the creation of so many fictional characters in the *Inspector*.

The columns flowed for over two years, 1751–1753, without any hint of recalcitrance on Hill's part, most columns in the early days dealing with literature as a refraction of the current social climate but soon segueing into discussion of whatever his audience would find up to the minute: modern ladies, the menace of dueling, cowardice among men, extravagance in dining, the need for better food, pretentiousness, embalming and mourning rites, the lack of religion in t'Town—the topics grew increasingly diverse by the column with religion the "Inspector's" *arriere-pensee*. He wanted everyone to know that he stood for the traditional Church and its historic English values.

Only politics as a major topic was eschewed, although unsystematically, perhaps because the "Inspector" did not feel comfortable speculating about it, as his correspondence also shows. By 1753 he is carping about the deleterious effects of all things French, especially the English love affair with imported French goods. His style also grew more conversational, less formal, relying on epistolary vocabulary and cadence. He took a few weeks' holiday during August in both 1751 and 1752, which invited further familiarity—the "Inspector" was a family friend, someone you could trust and rely on even when he sauntered. Only during the last six months of publication (January–June 1753) will this familiar style wane; not because Hill saw the Inspector's decline on the horizon but because the multiple paper wars in which he was engaged were grating on him and causing him to turn inward. It was one thing to take on the Royal Society, another all Grub Street.

He also worked away on the third volume of his trilogy about natural history, his book about animals.[29] He was drafting this work during the spring of 1752, while also churning out the *Inspector* columns, and finished it in the autumn. *A History of Animals* was announced as "published" in December,[30] and must have appeared around then if any time was allowed for the reviewer to read it before publishing his long review in the *Monthly*.[31] This is perhaps the most original of Hill's trilogy, if perhaps not the most far ranging, and the one where he coined the word "paramecium" to describe these microscopic animals. The classes of paramecia, he wrote, are "animalcules which have no visible limbs or tails, and are of an irregularly oblong figure."[32] The paramecium is a single-cell organism, much studied in recent biology. It belongs in the kingdom of Protista, and to the phylum of Ciliaphora, and is often loosely called "Lady Slipper." To this species Hill added two other types of paramecium which he had viewing since boyhood with his father, from the time when Theophilus Sr. gave him his first simple microscope. Decades later Otto Frederik Müller, a Danish naturalist, published his own study of paramecia, without knowledge of Hill's prior work, nor did he apprise himself in the 1780s when Müller attempted to classify all the paramecia.[33] The first palm doubtlessly must be awarded to Hill.

Hill was also immersed in contemporary fiction; not merely in the novels he had already written, as we saw, but in the proportion of invented epistolary authors in these pages. Their names are as indicative of their characters, and one-dimensional too, as those in the fiction of the 1740s: Jack Trueman

(Hill himself?), John Bullock, Jack Trifle, Jerry Wildfire; Martha Mildew, Chloe Brickdust, Susan Fret, Emma and Jessica without surnames; not to mention the prolific "Philo" characters who are proponents of this and that. Increasingly the columns show him presenting abbreviated lives of one character to demonstrate contemporary morality: the evils of wealth; childrens' duties to their parents; the crucial importance of luck. Many must have struck his readers as real, as in the colorful account of the "Orphan Cleora" who lives with her son and maiden aunt, or the tale of "Jerry Wildfire" and his wife and their hunting exploits as a duo. He courts fancy and probes the improbable too, as when speculating about the myth of the centaur, an "electrical cook" he has heard of, and several extraordinary nocturnal dreams, and even sleepwalking, presented.

Some papers originated specifically in dinner talk, as when Doctors Stukeley, Lyn, Cobden, and several others (for these medical friends, now largely lost to time except for Stukeley, see page 121) found themselves debating "the perniciousness of bread as now made."[34] Hill turned the controversy into an entire *Inspector*. They thrashed out the biblical justification for unleavened bread during Passover, highest of the Jewish holy days, and Stukeley remembered that Theophilus had "always eat [*sic*] bread made of flower, water & butter only for twenty years before his death saying that yeast was poison."

Others referred to the current lot of Jews, whose status and rights were being widely discussed in the nation (the Jewish Naturalization Bill would follow soon). Yet other papers mentioned unexpected consequences and a few led him straight to the brink of court. There was the pathetic case of "Miss Arria G—n" in the *Inspector* of May 30, 1751 (Hill claims to have changed her real name). He reports having received a letter from her aunt recounting the sad, almost Popean, affair. Dalton, her fiancé and an only son, took her snuffbox out of a generous impulse to prevent her from overindulging in snuff. His friend Paul naughtily gave her a pinch, and then also snatched her snuffbox. Arria demanded its return, but before he could return it Dalton intervened, they scuffled, and fought. That evening a very sullen Paul returned the box by a messenger: not to Arria but to Dalton with a note requesting a "gentlemanly meeting"—read "duel"—around midnight. Dalton was killed, Arria's life wrecked.

The notion that Arria's aunt would write to the *Inspector* indicating that her coquettish niece deserved what she got is improbable. But it is what Hill claimed. After publishing the aunt's letter t'Town spoke of nothing else for one week according to the newspapers and weeklies. By the second week a twenty-two-page *Vindication of an Innocent Lady* appeared condemning Hill and inquiring what his motive can have been: financial gain, personal spite, "a desire for fame"?[35] Whatever the reason, Hill's readers began to lose faith in his so-called morality. Not in his exposé of Arria's coquetry: unwittingly she had precipitated the duel out of rage at Dalton's interference in her consumption of snuff. But for Hill's fabrication of the aunt's letter, and his lack of compassion for Arria's loss.

This time the author of the *Vindication* requested Hill to apologize to the real Arria; later he would be threatened with court action for columns like these. He professed to "provide news" under the gun of producing constant copy without assistance, which is true. No others collaborated with him except for reliable Stukeley who certainly contributed several *Inspectors* despite our difficulty in identifying which ones. Stukeley himself wrote that he had supplied material for the "philosophical ones," but also offered jocular Hudibrastic verse passed between himself and an obscure clergyman in Lincolnshire over twenty years earlier. Always hungry for copy, Hill printed them.[36] Even so, it was a gross miscalculation—his readers were bored and found nothing in them.

Stukeley studiously continued to read the *Inspectors* and commented on some in his diaries, but he was of Theophilus Sr.'s generation—no one on whom son John Hill ought to have relied. Yet he did: he took sexagenarian Stukeley's advice, printed Stukeley's comments and letters as his own, lifted snippets and sometimes whole papers, a miscalculation for which Hill paid dearly. Stukeley was not the only voice feeding him—he also relied on acquaintances; but Stukeley was loyal as few others were, always ready to serve and be useful. Hill needed what he sorely lacked: a few astute young friends with ears to the ground who could have told the roving "Inspector" what was hot, sexy, topical. When Stukeley read a paper to the Society attributing earthquakes to electricity, Hill mentioned it in his *Inspector* column.[37] This time the topic *was* timely: two years earlier there had been predictions of earthquakes set to hit London and large populations vacated the city. Hill exploited both the recent fear and Stukeley's new theory, placing the matter in the incendiary context of the French theft of English discoveries.

Hill also relied on Stukeley for topical natural knowledge: having been excluded from the one place—the Royal Society—where he would have gathered up-to-the-minute facts, he turned elsewhere, to London's coffeehouses and taverns, but their value was unpredictable—entailing luck and the pick of the day. Stukeley continued to be a regular attendee of meetings at the Royal Society and apprised Hill about papers presented there and the ensuing discussions. He continued to supply Hill with content for *Inspectors* all spring and summer in 1752: a piece on "the picture of human happiness,"[38] verses addressed to Samuel Foote, whose career Hill still watched curiously and which Hill used in *Inspector* 271.[39]

Hill's detailed biweekly account of metropolitan culture for two years, 1751–1753, would repay further exploration if it were not—as we now will see—riddled with caveats. Within weeks the "Inspector" was the talk of t'Town, its most recent household name: not merely for his positions but for the true identity of the man lurking behind it, its success guaranteed by the extreme topicality of these subjects, as well as fascination for the mystery of the author's background. Who was he? Some readers thought they knew when they claimed to see him riding about in his chariot and six. The ladies were particularly drawn, especially outside London, as when bluestocking Elizabeth Carter wrote to her constant correspondent Catherine Talbot in September 1751 that she was enthralled by his views, even when she did not agree with them.[40] They filled a niche, she thought, which nothing else did. The "Inspector" was unique.

That September Thomas Birch, the diligent biographer and compiler of histories, lamented to her that sales of Johnson's concurrently running *Rambler* were tapering off. Carter was bewildered; she had told Talbot that "the *Rambler* is grown very agreeable this summer" because its topics were relevant to people like the two young women.[41] When Johnson hit out at Hill in *Rambler* 106, a paper on "the vanity of an author's expectations" referring to "the oracles of the age and the legislators of science," both Carter and Talbot protested. Clearly his "Inspector" had impressed the young ladies precisely as "oracle and legislator"; they found this combination attractive and professed to being incapable of putting it down. But Johnson, the wiser moralist who focused on the general rather than the particular, had seen through the façade of this spectacle of ambition. His choice of subjects in the *Rambler* was more restricted than Hill's, and he never pretended to know a fraction of what "Prince Proteus" did.

Morality's part in Hill's columns should not be underestimated: every story ends with the moralizer's adage—in tune with the temper of the era—but the "Inspector" is not sufficiently general in his treatment to extract pith. He numbers the streaks of the tulip rather than gazes at whole gardens; and when pondering, for example, the uses being put to tea in England he gets bogged down in trivia about the varieties of contemporary tea—so much that some readers thought it an advertising ploy to sell his own brand: "I have been myself many Years in the [tea] Trade, I hope with an unblemished Character."[42] The morality was defective. No wonder Johnson protested.

Hill also leaned on the fictive realm, which so routinely pervades the columns at center stage that morality can seem to assume second place. The "Inspector" cannot resist, for instance, the prototypically ruined young woman, or the young man who comes to the metropolis for the first time and falls into a bad crowd, or the dying father who turns against his son on his deathbed because he realizes with his last gasp that inheritance has brought his offspring to his side—all elicit stories. Johnson had sparingly indulged these tendencies in the *Rambler*, resisting the fictive and the sentimental and allowing only Richardson to enter the temple of his imagination because his moral sense, Johnson opined, was so perfectly hewn. But Hill—Johnson thought and we agree—was misguided to court stories so explicitly at the expense of profundity, and to adopt the autobiographical pose against the backdrop of his reputation. He would have fared better to continue writing third-person fictions (they had not yet coagulated into our modern sense of "novels") where he could conceal himself behind new Loveills and George Edwardses.

It was not to be. For Hill, the "Inspector's" roving adventure was exhilarating, and it made him financially richer than he would ever be despite glaring contradictions between what he preached and how he lived.

Women, marriage, and a broadly based natural science—in this descending order—encompass the *Inspector*'s other main concern. Women hold first place and education comes fourth, particularly the superfluity of a university education.[43] Yet Hill was no emancipator. Women should be educated but their proper place is in the home; their intellect must be nurtured but only to a degree; Latin is "a Language not proper for the Study of Women."[44] Men have just as rough a ride: Hill depicts them either as bored with, or quitting, university, nor does he approve of the black robes they wear in college. A young physician discovers that his university education in medicine is worthless; he learns how to practice through apprenticeship with other practitioners. The *Inspector* returns to a Theophilus-like father figure who lives quietly in the country and has shut up his son in his library to learn Greek and Latin. Dozens of papers abound with these sorts of autobiographical topics—a far cry from Johnson's wider ranging morality dealing with the eternal dilemmas of birth and death, joy and pain.

The "Inspector" impugns immodest women, for their dress and behavior, and those "too garrulous, brash and overbearing." The ideal female companion should possess a good understanding but not excessive education or erudition. Virtue is the highest quality she can possess, and if she is also fortunate to be beautiful and modest she has everything a man can want—a fairy-tale view; a throwback to a pre-1740 mentality *sans* everything Richardson the moralist had found diabolical in English life and built in to his fictions about "Pamela B." and "Clarissa H." Hill's "Diamond" demonstrates all three virtues and Hill includes five accounts of her as both ravishing and intelligent.[45] Later in his columns, a woman with an undisclosed nickname appears who displays equal wit and distaste for domesticity.[46] She travels to the capital from the country to reside with a family, meets a man whose conversation stimulates her, and is then shocked to learn that t'Town considers her his "mistress." Move in and conjugate is the moral.

Parents and children constitute another favorite sphere of concern. The "Inspector" discusses his own education (or lack of it), waxes lyrical about his indulgent and loving father (similar to Sterne's fictional Elizabeth Shandy, Hill's mother remains shadowy and never referred to), and comments on his flirtations (he boasts his mistresses and conquests): all are semi-veiled but without autobiographical clarity. He produces a letter from a son whose father is a rector in a village in Lincolnshire.[47] The father has sacrificed much to send his son to a foreign university to study medicine and decided his son should practice medicine. The resemblance to Theophilus is striking, and a few months later the "Inspector" writes straightforwardly about of his father's influence: "Christian Charity I suppose I learned from the good Clergyman my Father."[48] But his failure to do well at this foreign university contributes to his mother's early death.[49] He is drawing on biographical evidence when the occasion suits him, yet in most instances he needs rapid copy above all.

The *Inspector* refers to "mothers" so frequently that one wonders how painful the loss of Anne Turner was for him during his biographical adolescence. One "Inspector" almost seems autobiographical: the drift is that his mother died when he was young, his father whom he adored indulged him and did everything possible to educate him.[50] Then, as an experiment, his father locked him in the library for two hours every day for a month, and this is how the young Hill acquired his love of reading and knowledge of the classics.

The columns also discuss the state of the English language, especially as used by Spenser and Milton, but Hill adds little to the contemporary post-Swiftian debate. Natural history and natural science occupy a sizable portion, and one could continue statistically in this vein from most to least favored subjects but the approach misses the point: Hill's assertive tone of righteousness and callow degree of hurling blame. It is too self-assured, even cocky, without offering the reader a chance to decide for herself about most subjects, and his mean streak may surface at any moment. The "Inspector" was generally "nice" but when he felt threatened, attacked, or—worse yet—slighted, he lashed out; he rarely forgot offense and once having been crossed, as in the paper wars heating up, the transgression brought out the worst in him. All aspects considered, he is more fascinating for his persistence—he just will not surrender—than for views he held: *the moralist himself rather than the morality*.

The most authentic use of the *Inspector* columns is biographical, especially the stage it sets for paper warfare as the key to the developing Georgian public sphere. Such heated fracas among the "wits" was proof that metropolitan print culture had come of age, and it continues to remain so well over two centuries later in our much more complex world. For example, when the "Inspector" received intelligence that Fielding's *CGJ* would cease publication he was more disappointed than overjoyed for the loss of his oppositional sounding board. Fielding's last paper bombastically opened trumpeting these words: "JOHN HILL, Doc. Soc. Burg. &c. alias Hill the Apothecary, alias Jack the Herb-gatherer, alias Player-Jack, alias Hilly Pilly, alias Silly-Hilly, alias Jack the Trumpeter, alias Jack the Spectre of Great Britain, &c. &c. &c."[51] The mirth was poked at Hill's expense but no one should think the preoccupation unidirectional. Hill was as much on Fielding's mind as vice versa, and when the "Inspector" blasted, much earlier, that he sought no involvement with "the Author of *Amelia,* whom I have only once seen . . ." no one cares if it was biographically true.[52] Fielding and Hill need never have met; each man loomed large within the other, and each man, each magazine, inadvertently puffed the other.

Hill had begun his "Inspectors" by invoking Addison and Steele as his muses, explaining how he preempted Steele's "Lion Head" at Button's, the carved wooden head of a lion perfected by Hogarth and intended to serve as a receptacle for letters and contributions, and affixed it at the Bedford coffeehouse for the receipt of letters.[53] External confirmation in the published memoirs of that coffeehouse verifies its move there, and when Hill printed the text of Steele's letter in the "Spectator" complaining of "cruel and groundless censures" thrown upon Steele's character, he indirectly refers to his own predicament.[54] This appeal recurs, perhaps genuinely, as Hill finds himself commenting that he is grateful for having his "faults" pointed out.[55] He may have been, but in 1752 his critics were growing louder by the day.

How to assess the columns? As social history they offer a useful guide to the era, especially for its metropolitan values, although all positions must be revaluated for the voice behind them and for Hill-as-victim: not victimized by individuals but collective literary culture, already so fiercely competitive that biographical Hill could not imagine life without it. His behavior cannot be exonerated but interpretation made from different approaches—not merely for the *Inspector*'s content—would repay the effort. In his day, the "Inspector" would not be let off. Within one year of commencing publication, when he had produced half his editorials, a tract appeared fiercely criticizing them in *Remarks on the Life and Writings of Dr. John Hill, Inspector-General of Great Britain.*[56] Its author had read Hill's prior works, followed his rise from rags to riches, his chief charge now arrogance: not incompetence, not egoism, and certainly not plagiarism (although he spotted some of the misrepresented original letters) but an unbridled arrogance. It was a public milieu in which spades could be called spades without our tiptoe hesitations. Some kindly hack came to Hill's defense in the *GM* declaring that for all his flaws Hill was an "ingenious writer" and that his works deserved "a *good* criticism from which he would profit."[57] "The doctor," he opined, "doubtless has his faults as *writer*, and as a *man*, and had these faults been *candidly* represented to him, it might have tended to his reformation, instead of provoking him to resentment. . . ."

Reformation apart, he always had more enemies than allies, and the debate about the *Inspector* demonstrates the extent to which both his talent and flaws were recognized. But the "Inspector" had become an irrefutable urban phenomenon; a metropolitan fixture of print culture on which readers relied. He may have begun life as a country boy, wandering and collecting in the state of nature, but since the late 1740s he had not strayed far from a five-mile radius of Covent Garden and had imbibed its values so well that he was now "notorious"—then a word capable of conjuring fame as well as ignominy.

When suppressing his natural arrogance and vanity and not groping to emulate Johnsonian morality, he can make constructive, practical observations, such as the need for an efficient postal network. He gathered the facts, evaluated the cost and worth of a Universal Register Office—then just forming—and showed the benefits it would have for the metropolis. He can even be philosophically persuasive, as when he taps into the stoicism of the time and weighs hedonism in relation to temperance, coming down on the side of the latter and claiming that the "high life" cannot be salutary for the human condition in the long run—not even for the young. Translated to the personal level this position sheds light on interactions among human beings. The "Inspector" hits the mark when observing that "the most friendly Office one Man can do to another is the telling him of his Faults."[58]

Hill did not live by these principles, as some in t'Town knew. Neither temperance nor candor nor the ability to learn from criticism played parts in his character that was fonder of excess and pretense than restraint and fair dealing. Still a youngish widower, he hired servants who helped him to entertain at his lavish accommodation in St. James, and despite public rows on many fronts the guests came in droves. Stukeley's diary provides some of the names: Doctor Lyn on February 26, 1752, who was a regular at the "Inspector's table and had debated the horrors of "modern bread," together with a Doctor Cobden and others who were not medical.[59] Two weeks later, on March 10, Stukeley accompanied Hill to a breakfast at Ranelagh when Henry Purcell's hymn "Twice the Ten Thousand Deities" was sung. That spring Hill entertained profusely, using the income from his *Inspector* columns to pay the bills. On June 7 he accompanied a certain "reverend" to dine at Stukeley's more modest table at his house in Queen Square, Bloomsbury. More often the banquets were laid on his own candlelit tables in St. James's.[60]

Hill was less hypocrite than naïf, and the difficulty his columns pose for modern assessment rests in the biographical realm rather than as "texts" to be evaluated apart from their contexts. If you read them as a key to understand the man you can become ensnared. They are more valuable if construed as part of the literary and printing history of mid-century and in relation to the rise of competition among men of letters; less so in the biographical realm. Reliable biographies of most of the persons the "Inspector" discusses—Pope, Fielding, Newton, Stukeley, and dozens of less well-known Georgian figures—have already found their biographers even if Hill has not. So when he writes on January 16, 1752, that Bonnell Thornton

(1725–1768)—the writer he courted because Thornton too started an anti-Fielding campaign—"today published the first issue of the *Drury Lane Journal* to appear every Thursday," it has become a fact of literary history. The 720 *Inspector* columns are permeated with similar details of utility to literary historians of the eighteenth century.

The essays are also useful for estimating the status of knowledge then. Historically it was a transformative moment betokening the breakdown of universal systems of thought into specialized discourses. Professionalization had not yet been institutionalized in the way it would be in the next century, but the unity of thought was not so intact as it had been—as augured two generations earlier, "the circle was breaking." Hill played a small part: he thinks it important to scold those who collect shells but do not study creatures, and he warns his readership about the perils of the current vogue to assemble without purpose collections into cabinets of curiosity.[61] Did he overlook that *he* was that person? Plausibly he describes his presence at a "learned society's dissection of the nerves," explaining why the nerves are physiologically significant yet never lets on to the FRS debacle. He expands on "how to succeed in a profession" without having done so himself. Another responds "to people who say one man could not be writing all these different papers"—not the specter of plagiarism but multiple authorship of the *Inspectors*. It had been largely *one* man, but at what price to himself? No editorial exists on the toll taken.

In September 1751, when the *Inspector* columns were widely being read, he claims "still [to be] leading a medical life," practicing the art and dispensing the potions.[62] It may be true. Then he sketches his own formers marriage to "Susannah" and names her, instilling the confidence that he is biographically reliable.[63] Susannah Travers had been his first wife, but she was dead by the end of 1750. Nothing more is known about her. Later in the *Inspector* he performs an about-face and writes about his "looming marriage." Was he fantasizing or sending up his readers?

Almost on the last day of 1751 Hill announced that the "Inspector-General of Great Britain intends to marry"; eleven months later, in November 1752, "Amelia [is] now the Inspectress of Great Britain—the Inspector is married." Hill was certainly not married to a woman at the end of 1752—that would occur late in the summer of 1753 by which time the *Inspector* had ceased to exist. For now, by late 1752, he has invented a character named "Amelia" (another taunt at Fielding?) who will stimulate further interest—he thinks—among female readers. But Amelia is a physical sphinx located at a printer's premises: the female equivalent of his lion. He presents her as beautiful and of solid understanding and he will collect letters from the ladies at "Mr. Browne's Printing House" where she is located. The "Amelia columns" provoked a barrage of correspondence from women, all sent to the "Sphynx." "Lesbia" wickedly wrote to advocate the courting of many male lovers at the same time. A colonel's mistress would not give her name but wanted to learn how best to rid herself of an unwanted lover. No one will ever know what part of this material was grounded in fact, or what the general public thought. Their responses are lost to time.

The "Inspector" churned out his columns until his (not the biographical Hill's) demise on Saturday June 30, 1753. Biographical Hill took his farewell aware this would be his last; and eight weeks later, on August 27, he married Henrietta Wilhelmina Jones, sister of the future fourth Viscount Ranelagh, of the parish of St. Anne's, Soho, at St. George's Chapel in Hyde Park Corner. About this second marriage there is no doubt, as there had been for his first to Susannah Travers, who died toward the end of 1750. When the *LDA* published a letter from an unknown "Eliza" one week after their marriage (September 3, 1753), perhaps constructed by Hill, Eliza seems remarkably similar to the biographical Henrietta. The letter extols her youth, beauty, fortune, and reluctance to wed. Yet she succumbs when meeting such a strapping man who resembles the "Inspector."

Despite the "Inspector's demise" trumpeted in the *LDA* he lived on in readers' minds as someone real. Ralph Griffiths' two-volume syndication of approximately one-third of the columns that autumn (1753) was further evidence, but more concrete proof was found in the degree to which the "Inspector" had become embedded as a region of the urban imagination. Allusions and references were made throughout the 1750s; an anthology of them could be gathered. He gradually faded in the 1760s, when international war and national politics replaced the topics Hill had addressed. But by then Proteus Hill had transformed himself yet again.

NOTES

1. *LDA*, spanning the duration March 5, 1751, to June 30, 1753; many sets of excerpts printed by Griffiths appeared in 1751–1753, for example JH (1751e). "Inspector" presented in quotations designates JH the man in this incarnation; when in italics denotes one or more editorials as it appeared in *LDA*, as well as in the 1753 collected edition. JH sometimes published on Saturdays.
2. *LDA*, July 24, 1751, *Inspector* 123 is the last column in the old system; number 124 the first in the new number system. In my designation "the *Inspector*" with italics denotes JH's columns while "the Inspector" designates the figure as distinct from his column.
3. JH (1753b).
4. *LM* 20 (June 1751): 273–74.
5. *Inspector* 57, for June 1, 1751.
6. *Inspector* 15, for August 9, 1751.
7. Forerunners of the genre had appeared by the 1720s; see Anonymous, *A View of London . . . or, The Town Spy* (1725).
8. Spring Gardens, near Piccadilly, was also a favorite, but was smaller than Cuper's Gardens.
9. Brewer and Porter, passim.

10. Phillips, chapters 3, 4, 6.
11. *Inspector*, February 12, 1751.
12. See the *Inspectors* for the months of January and July 1752.
13. For the *Dissertation* see *GM* 20 (1750): 575; *GM* 21 (1751): 45; *LM* (December 1750): 576; *MR* 4 (1751): 187–92; for the *Review* see *GM* 21 (1751): 47; *LM* (January 1751): 48; *MR* 4 (1751): 279–94.
14. *Inspector* (March 9, 1751).
15. *LDA*, issue of Wednesday March 6, 1751.
16. For example, Rousseau (1986a), 184–86, for material discussed in this paragraph.
17. Sir John Fielding (1752).
18. *Inspector* (November 4, 1751).
19. Rousseau (1986a), 185; see the "Dramatic Personae" sub "Boyle."
20. *Inspector* (March 30, 1751).
21. *LDA* (March 13, 1751).
22. *Inspector* (November 14, 1752).
23. Jensen, the paper for November 18, 1752.
24. Pat Rogers (1972), passim; Buck (1977): 199–204.
25. *Inspector* (June 1, 1751).
26. *Inspector* 223 (November 18, 1751).
27. Murphy (1754); Murphy's *Gray's Inn Journal* for March 24, 1754; Emery (1946b), 162–65.
28. James Raven (2007), 283.
29. JH (1752d).
30. *LM* (December 1752): 580.
31. *MR* 9 (July 1753): 18–21.
32. JH (1752d), 5, in part 1 ("Animalcules and Insects"), book 1 ("Of Animals").
33. In his *Vermium Terrestrium et Fluviatilium* 2 vols. (Copenhagen, 1773–74).
34. Stukeley MSS Eng. Misc. e. 134.
35. Anonymous, *Vindication* (1751): 20.
36. Stukeley MSS Eng. Misc. d. 719/12; *Inspector* 71, June 28, 1751; the clergyman was Beatniff, curate of Beckingham, Lincolnshire.
37. Stukeley MSS Eng. Misc. e. 132, p. 42, entry for October 31, 1752.
38. *Inspector* 52, May 25, 1752.
39. Stukeley MSS Eng. Misc. e. 133, p. 74 and *LDA* January 13 and September 17, 1752.
40. Elizabeth Carter (1809), vol. 2, 33.
41. Elizabeth Carter (1809), vol. 2, 33–34.
42. *LDA* (March 19, 1751), a letter on the tea trade.
43. More than a dozen papers on this approach but see *LDA* (April 6, 1751) and *LDA* (May 21, 1751).
44. *LDA* (April 19, 1751).
45. See especially *LDA* (October 8, 1751), no. 188.
46. *LDA* (July 23, 1752).
47. *LDA* (February 21, 1751). During the 1730s JH's father and only surviving brother Theophilus Jr. both lived in Lincoln, his father Theophilus Sr. having moved there after his wife Anne's death c. 1730–1732 to be close to his son Theophilus Jr. Our JH rarely visited them; if he did, his letters are silent on his visits. In any case, he was never close to his brother or his brother's children.
48. *LDA* 521 (November 10, 1752).
49. JH never studied at a foreign university. Anne Turner, his biological mother, had died in her forties, c. 1730–1732, probably not in childbirth for which she was then too old. I have been unable to locate the date of her death, but JH was emotionally attached to her, however murky a presence she was during his early life when he was itinerant.
50. *Inspector* 224 (November 19, 1751).

51. Jensen 2, 141; the dig at "Doc. Soc. Burg." is to JH's election as a Fellow of the Bordeaux Academy of Sciences, which was genuine.
52. *Inspector* dated January 9, 1752.
53. See the *Inspectors* dated October 2 and November 10, 1751.
54. *Inspector* 417 (July 1, 1752).
55. *LDA* (June 15, 1751).
56. Anonymous, *Some Remarks on the Life and Writings of Dr. John Hill* (1752).
57. *MR* 21 (April 1752): 310.
58. *Inspector* (August 17, 1752).
59. Stukeley MSS Eng. Misc. e. 133, diary, 1752.
60. Stukeley MSS Eng. Misc. e. 133, diary 1752.
61. *Inspector*, August 28, 1751.
62. *LDA* (September 20, 1751).
63. *LDA* (June 14, 1751).

III

8

The "Lion" at the Bedford

Activity in the darkly lit, smoke-filled Bedford coffeehouse, located in the piazza near the entrance to the Covent Garden Theatre in 1752, was more charged than seemed possible for a modern-day tavern.[1] It was here that John Theophilus Desaguliers, the French natural philosopher, had installed himself around 1740 and delivered scientific lectures until his death in 1744. While in Oxford, long before the 1740s, Desaguliers had been Isaac Newton's assistant. But it was here, inside the Bedford's darkened lecture room, that Desaguliers-the-showman announced to the English nation his discovery of electricity in 1741, for which the Royal Society of London awarded him—a French foreigner—its highest honor, its Copley Medal. Masons congregated here in numbers too. David Garrick often came around. Tobias Smollett, the novelist, had been so impressed with the Bedford's unusual literary and scientific atmosphere, he commented on it in his first novel, *The Adventures of Roderick Random* (1747). And now, just a few years later, in the early 1750s, this unique space in Covent Garden also became Hill's favorite hangout; his coffeehouse of choice, where conversation like his—acerbic yet commodious, informed despite its affectation, always agile and swift footed—endlessly streamed. Here the "news industry," as Hill once called it, traveled from mouth to mouth. Often the participatory mouths spoke in unison, stomping with their feet, their chorus an antidote to the quiet calm of printed news: the broadsides and pamphlets swamping them, a developing information glut.

Hill had frequented many other coffeehouses, like the "Adam and Eve" when he first came up to London, to assess their degree of welcome. But he discovered he could best spin his idiosyncratic brand of conversational magic here. Its particular conversational culture suited him; soon he saw its denizens flocked to him. The time seemed right to establish himself as a household name—to preside as a celebrity.

Hither congregated its pipe-and-port habitués, including Hogarth and George Coleman the actor, among other *luminati* engaged in the theater, as well as rogues and wags living by their wits, especially their mouths.[2] Smaller clubs gathered too. A "Shakespeare Club" met on Wednesday nights; aspiring poets and philosophers on Thursdays. These were networks within networks, but not based on commercial profit in the way Hill related to Ralph Griffiths and Mary Cooper and the dozens of printers with whom he interacted. Hill was, in fact, a loner, despite his manifold sallies into both print and social networks. His staunchest fiber was the voice telling him to make it alone; when he networked it was always for self-promotion or gain. His time in the Bedford was his least anxious because he imagined himself at the center of a cabal or network, and the Bedfordians coming over to him were proof.[3]

The atmosphere was electric with the nervous and swift pulse of their conversation and ideas being "up to the moment"; otherwise you would not know how to pair the sobriquet with its original. Cliques ruled, as well as individuals. The "Malevoli," or "Critics"—those incessant evildoers holding forth—included lynchpin Hill ("Bobadil," later changed to "Bobathill"), William Barrett (a punning apothecary nicknamed "Errator"), Henry Chitty ("Town"), Arthur Murphy ("Ranger"), Dr. Thomas Arne the composer ("Harmonicus"), Samuel Derrick ("Quinbus Flestrin"), and Francis Gentleman ("Will Dactyl").[4] Their harangues formed a main attraction for listeners, especially visitors who came to watch and gape. Illustrious guests who occasionally dropped in included Fielding, Garrick, Foote, Macklin, and many theater types, but the Bedford was not their haunt as it was for the waspish Malevoli. One habitué said that Hill could make his enemies tremble; another—"Parkington Tomkyns," a wit who has faded from memory and with whom Hill got into correspondence—noted that the "Inspector's" wish was his command. Early in the 1750s news of the Bedford's events, its debates and duels, circulated widely, and more than one man was found dead on its floors.

But these Bedfordians were not "friends" in any sentimental or affective sense. Da Costa had been Hill's first and last friend, until Hill's plagiarism, unless someone has dropped out of the record, and after his debacle with the FRS Hill was off-limits to friendship: too tarnished for anyone to court him for friendship in public, and too unscrupulous to attract any but novices desperate for recognition in private. Hill never expressed his views on the matter, unless he did so in confidences now lost to time. But he could not have been unaware of the companionless persona he projected, and even if he never sentimentalized friendship as an affective state to covet and cherish, as did so many figures in his era of sensibility, his desolate state must often have stared him in the face. He was, in brief, a friendless man.

On Sunday nights the "Board of Criticism," a group of leading figures, mostly Malevoli, collected at the lower end of the room to exchange views and gossip. One well-timed aside, whether gracious or poisonous, a well-timed *apercu,* counted for more on Sunday nights than a dozen printed tracts, crucial as publication could be. These were years—early in the 1750s—when the Bedford was establishing itself as London's seat of criticism. Its atmosphere was altogether different from nearby establishments such as Rawthmell's coffeehouse, the favorite resort of Richard Mead, Hans Sloane, and many of the science-spouting FRS who may have just emerged from some scholarly talk in Crane Court.

The Bedford was more exotic, if also less charted; it traded on news and gossip, and aimed to establish taste and fashion by the making and breaking of reputations. By the 1760s its recorded conversations, suggesting what Hill's was like, fixed the credentials of members for posterity.[5] For now, in 1752–1753, its activities were watched and weighed by the outside world, even if it is difficult to gauge how influential its "critics" were. It claimed to be the emporium of wit, the seat of criticism, forging for the nation the standard of taste, and other such grandiose platitudes, but the boasts were often gross exaggerations based on huff and puff. Hill already had considerable experience in the critical realm, judging by his lashings in the *Inspector* columns, and some Bedfordians must have judged Bobadil a larger-than-life public personality as their little club gathered ever-more attention. Judging from the number of references to it in the 1750s it would have been foolhardy for any of Bobadil's contemporaries to underestimate its dominion.

It was one of London's many coffeehouses at mid-century serving the cause of German sociologist Jürgen Habermas's public sphere: that real and imagined space where public opinion is born and debated by citizens.[6] Habermas's conception included the freedom of citizens to gather and confer in unrestricted fashion, with the freedom of assembly as well as the freedom to express and publish their opinions. These usually dwelt on topics of general interest, to the whole populace; and it is extraordinary the degree to which wit and taste dominated conversation in many of London's establishments then. But the Bedford was a particular type of establishment: prone to the formation of cliques and factions exercising themselves on individual "wits" and their status than on general concerns, and collectively the "Bedfordians" seemed obsessed by the role they cut in London's intellectual life.

They were often grilled: were they the rightful inheritors of the "rule" at Button's? Hill was asked outright: was he the authentic heir to his renowned predecessors Addison and Steele? The still unidentified compiler of the Bedford *Memoirs* pronounced on these matters in 1763 when publishing the establishment's history; so intimate was his knowledge, even if his mission was partly satirical—in keeping with the tenor of the Malevoli—that he must have been an habitué. He lists over one hundred names of members and guests, and identifies their nicknames and exposes insider knowledge, especially the flanks of alignment and opposing cabals. He understands cliques and networks and knows they are not conspirators or secret gangs but the inevitable products of "the competition in wit." Women, who were occasionally invited, are also identified, Bobadil's "Mrs. Diamond" for example. It would have been ironic if there had been more than one "Mistress Diamond" but more curious is the way all "mistresses" apparently abetted the cliques.

During the 1750s t'Town guessed about several identities behind the nicknames as part sport, part curiosity, within a milieu when public positioning was growing more important than ever. Some Bedfordian denizens revealed their identities, other remained secretive, and more must have been at stake than can be discovered now. The *Memoirs* identify Thomas Arne, the composer, as "Harmonicus," and Samuel Derrick, the aspiring author, as "Quinbus Flestrin." Derrick had more to lose by his "outing" than Arne: he was positioned in Hill's camp and would soon play a major role in the "Inspector's" defense as the wars heated up. But the Bedford historian can also be infuriatingly vague: "Mopsy" is "the beau of the age," but who was he?[7] The compiler includes anecdotes about "Bobadil-Hill," recounts how Peg Woffington, Hill's unrequited flame from Goodwood days, frequented the place from time to time but did she mix with Bobadil? Hill gets a principal part in the story and is called "this . . . Errato . . . [who] was universally styled the 'punning Apothecary.'" He was labeled this way before and would be again but can he have been so affected as to speak in rhyming cadences? Perhaps.

Late in 1752, a pamphlet entitled *The Inspectoress* supposedly appeared, claiming that the Bedford-Bobadil was a *woman*. No copy of this work survives, and it is known only from another nasty tract attacking Hill, entitled *The March of the Lion* that vividly describes Bobadil's dominion.[8] Almost immediately Hill began to receive letters at the Bedford addressed to "the Inspectoress," the name he signed in his replies, conjoint with "Amelia"—"Inspectoress Amelia"—perhaps referring to the vogue of Fielding's novel at the time. Hill himself started the gender-bending rumor, inserting the ruse about the "Inspectoress" into *The March of the Lion* to keep the public guessing at his identity. If only half the antics described in *The March* were biographically true, they still provided a strong clue to his behavior and conversation at the Bedford: how he dominated the discussions, modulated his voice, paced up and down, lashed out indiscriminately. Not one wit, certainly not Fielding nor anyone in his circle, was exempt. How shrewd of Hill to dupe the public by pretending to be two different personae, one male the other female, a lion and sphinx at the same time. Who was he? The question kept t'Town on tenterhooks.

Hill cannot have written the anonymous *Memoirs* eleven years later, in 1763. His life had moved on to other controversies by then. And the stinging opprobrium about him as a "rhyming Apothecary" was too close to the nerve even for him to bear. Typically when he fabricated rumors and tracts his goal was deception and disguise, as in his gender now, not outright condemnation. Elsewhere in the *Memoirs* the Bedfordian is more generous, conceding that Hill is a "wit" and elevating him to the leonine lair he has adopted for himself in its darkly lit quarters. Here, inside what the compiler calls the "bawdy box," he describes how ". . . I already convened the Inspector, Errato, the Town, Philocleus, Ranger, Specio, Mopsy, and Harmonicus, the eight principal members of the bawdy-box; and I shall now give a dialogue, pretty nearly as it passed between these eight wits [*sic*] on the utility of whoredom and the propriety of fornication."[9]

Both topics were capable of spellbinding the spectators. By the time the *Memoirs* were compiled, a decade later in 1762–1763, Hill's profile had altered, his public persona was *male* again, and the author might impugn him fearlessly, but for now he would have paid through the teeth for such digs.[10] Instead of wreaking retribution, imperious Hill returned to the drab of his small accommodation in Hart Street directly across from St. George's Church bordering Bloomsbury Market. Two hundred yards to the north was Great Russell Street with its imposing Montague House (site of the present British Museum) and the recessed Southampton House overlooking the grand square of that name for which the current Southampton Row is called. Hart Street is today Bloomsbury Way, then remarkably convenient for Drury Lane and its theaters to the south and the varied establishments of Holborne to the east. From there Hill often rode in his chariot to the Bedford.

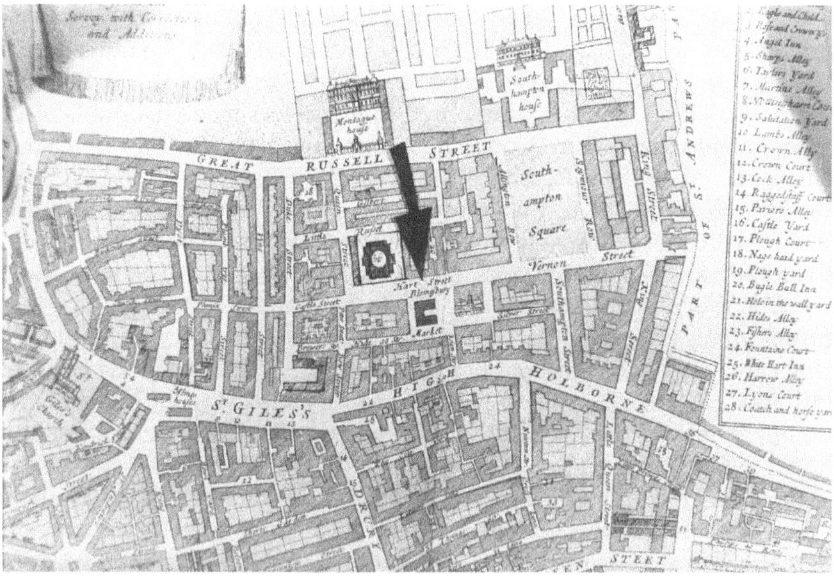

Figure 8.1. Hart Street, Bloomsbury, c. 1750.
Reproduced by permission of Professor George Rousseau.

The Bedford was an old establishment that had attracted notables even in the 1730s. J. H. Desaguliers (1683–1744), the French natural philosopher who spent much time in London, adopted it as his haunt when he came to deliver coffeehouse lectures. By mid-century its tone altered, the scientists departed, and it seemed given over entirely to wit and drollery and the vexatious matter about "succession": of course Hill was no Addison, nor was anyone else among the Malevoli, but they pretended they were and ruled unrivaled for a while despite cries that they were natural heirs to duncery and deception.

The charge was less their collective egoism than pretension, Hill's pretenses paramount beyond the others. Addison had considered Montaigne "the most eminent egoist that ever appeared in the world,"[11] but were he alive he would not have said the same of Hill. It was Hill's presumption that galled and the way he defied his "challengers" among the "gangs"—as he continued to brand the opposition and as the *March of the Lion* labeled them—never to venture there. Under his "rule" he united the Bedford's denizens by copying Addison and making use of the symbol of the lion and sphinx: two gold objects serving historical functions ranging from architectural design and garden ornament to public monument. The lion in particular was widely used in Georgian England—for the first time—to adorn front doors as part of the postal apparatus to receive letters, and it remains affixed to the front doors of English houses. Hill announced in the *Inspector* in October 1751 that a lion of "Scotch origin" mysteriously turned up in Covent Garden.[12] "Parkington Tomkyns," proprietor of the Shakespeare's Head Tavern in Covent Garden, alerted him; and Hill printed his letter to announce its arrival from Button's on the premise it would be moved to the Bedford.[13] In just three weeks' time, on November 12, 1751, his hunch as confirmed: "The Lion of my honoured Predecessors made his public Entry Yesterday into the Bedford Coffee-house, and has taken his Post in the most conspicuous Part of the Room."[14]

Hour and day named, the transmission seemed credible. According to Tomkyns, busts of Addison and Steele were also in the process of being transferred to the Bedford once they could be glossed.[15] Tomkyns swore in public this was true, which proved to be manna to Bobadil imagining himself in this Popean succession as heir to the mantle: Addison-Steele-Hill. What care he if now he did not possess the initials FRS; he had the lion—the gold lion. His strategy was ingenious even if false. Most of Hill's readers had never entered the Bedford but Hill had thrown them the symbol of an animal to focus on.

The strategy worked by keeping Hill's readers on edge about the lion's and busts's whereabouts, the leonine symbolism implying Hill's stature and the fear of some contemporaries in countering him. In hindsight it is easy to derogate these events as nonsense, as tricks; but for those who lived through them Hill could seem a plausible candidate—the new polymath among the Wits. The amazing feature is that Hill himself believed in the comparison, claiming especially in the *Inspectors* during the summer and autumn of 1752—that when he sees the types of rivalry t'Town holds up, he becomes as "riled up as the lion." He even personified himself as one dwelling within the kingdom of animals: the lion "has been aroused by injustice."[16] He asked his *Inspector* readers: "is the same Lion who roared so instructively and agreeably at Button's Coffeehouse in the Days of your renowned Predecessors Addison and Steele . . . me?"[17] He announced that "the lion has again been aroused by injustice" and swore retaliation. The most outrageous cases were those, he claimed, where the lion is aroused by Fielding's affronts.[18] Fielding had commented on the "Inspector's" prurient nose and written that Hill never set abroad without his imaginary bodyguard—a marshmallow nothing—called "Major England."

All the above was a nonsense beyond belief, spin calculated to keep the public talking. Hill reinvigorated it by exploiting his brand name as the roving inspector who never rested. The *Inspector*-lion "roamed" unpredictably from the Bedford and could surface at any time, in any place. He liked to walk, especially in his two favorite gardens at Kensington Palace and in the gardens between Spring Gardens and Vauxhall, but he could also turn up in other parts: roaming t'Town for news and priding himself as a judge of all things, especially people's behaviors and characters. Hill tells his readers in the *Inspector* that his "eye" can be upon them at any moment: "We shall have a happy Opportunity of seeing every body, but as our Ears are to be open to the Behavior of the Public, as well as our Eyes, we are determined also to hear what every one has to say to us" by writing to the "Lion" and the "Sphynx." It was an imaginative admixture of gender confusion, play and deception, and it further enhanced the sense that magic and mystery still lurked in the metropolis despite the City's urban transformations during Walpole's administration.

"Bobadil" as "Bobathill" assumed the mantle—the "Inspector" found his niche. He could boast and pontificate, he could puff and denigrate, but he committed two tactical errors: first in puffing Samuel Boyce (?–1775), the minor poet who had so far published nothing, second in the naïve belief that Henry Chitty and William Fitzpatrick—respectively "Mr. Town" and "Mr. Tongue" in their Bedfordian monikers—could protect him if the Wits declared war. They have been identified as insubstantial hacks,[19] and the *Memoirs* and *Inspector* recount how they met nightly at the Bedford after plays to adjudicate merit. "Bobadil" fell into their orbit, as well as Boyce's sphere, the latter more substantial despite having as yet nothing to support the view. Boyce appears as a flea to us now but was then possibly a rising star who seemed to be on the ascent in the firmament of poetic wit. The more Bobadil-Hill puffed Boyce, the more miserable he left the Wits; some imagining that Hill was building a rival wit-machine at the Bedford consisting of himself, Boyce, Chitty, Fitzpatrick, Samuel Derrick (who had been assisting all Hill's efforts since he arrived in London in 1751), and other hangers-on. Fielding and other Wits watched from afar this post-Popean dunciadic intrigue, saw that a wag like Hill was a sitting duck for cabalistic warfare: all they needed was a common cause to unite them—once in its possession the menace Bobadil-Hill would be dethroned.

Other coffeehouses buzzed too about the gathering of the forces: the "Hillians under the Lion" versus the Wits under Fielding; the "Junto," as Hill would refer to the antagonistic party of Smart, Fielding, Murphy, Kenrick, et al. who were conducting their opposition on many fronts: daily in the newspapers, in periodical journalism, in the maelstrom that would soon erupt as Smart's *Hilliad* took form, and—not least—on the London stage by inventing Hillian characters to be blasted. Hill, the "rhyming Apothecary," countered when he could, especially with rhymes addressed "to the Junto."[20] In contrast, the venom of the Wits was more effective by dint of striking in various forms. But Hill had never properly learned the arts of retaliation. He would typically launch out before having been provoked and take his chance that the target would not strike back, which worked with the FRS who were rarely eloquent but not with the more articulate Wits. Now, in renewed opposition to the Bedfordians, Bobadil misgauged the coalition's counterstrokes, underestimating their retaliation as well as frequency of reprisal. With revenge calibrated at this pitch Hill had no hope of success without assistance, and those he thought would accord it turned out to be protective nothings—the feeble counterblasts of weaklings like Chitty, Fitzgerald, and Derrick, and even the aspiring Samuel Boyce.

It could seem that the Bedford under Hill's rule was squelching the public sphere as it developed in the cradle; its murderous weapon Hill's avidity to retain his sway and rule without opposition. His cabal took measures not be toppled, even when this meant spin, lies, and grotesque self-delusion. No matter how well read and up to the minute Hill and his Bedfordians were, they nevertheless flourished in a combative atmosphere catering more to the making—and unmaking—of individual careers than to generous democratic principles about the rightful heirs of Button's. Hill actually believed he was his generation's successor to Addison's "Man of the Town": Will Honeycombe repackaged as the "Inspector." All of which proved the veracity of Addison's precept, now a generation old, that any upstart who tries to align himself with the front rank of literary merit will be trampled. In Hill's world this included a broadly based science, for the two realms—literature and science—had not yet broken off as they would early in the next century.

Even so, a new psychological strain of Hillian response was peeping through: denial and withdrawal. In a curious self-confessional *Inspector* column, Hill describes how he is sensitive to criticism and literally "cries" when opposed.[21] He may have been sincere, or inserted the plea to win sympathy as the underdog. Either way, it was becoming apparent that Hill, even when shielded by his Bedfordian Malevoli, his lions and sphinxes, his Boyces and Chittys and Derricks, was no match for the "Wits" on the warpath. Not all the smoke and candles within the Bedford could restrain them.

NOTES

1. Anonymous, *Memoirs* (1763); Lillywhite, 114, sub "Bedford Coffeehouse"; Henry B. Wheatley (1909), 284-86. The "genius" of the anonymous *Memoirs* (1763) functions as a topical, rhetorical convention, and the compilation may well have been the work of several hands. It was so popular that a second edition appeared in 1768, "with many Additions." The extraordinary facet of the *Memoirs* is that they bristle with almost two hundred pages of information about one of London's most vibrant coffeehouses of the 1750s and describe over three hundred biographical persons. It is here, for example, on p. 31, that we learn about the "Mr. Lovell" JH fictionalized in *The History of Mr. Loveill, A Novel* (1750c).
2. Anonymous (1763), 10.
3. It would repay the effort to study JH's career during the event-packed years 1750–1753 in terms of networks to which he belonged, which were primarily, but not entirely, print and botanical.
4. Henry Chitty and Samuel Boyce were fixtures at the Bedford and swore allegiance to JH. Chitty subscribed to Boyce's *The Rover; or, Happiness at Last* (1752). With their loyalty declared, JH began to imagine a coalition of wits forming with him at its center.
5. Anonymous (1763), 13.
6. Habermas (1989), passim; see Rousseau (1998a), 187–205 for application of Habermas's ideas about the public sphere to JH's print culture and publication milieu. JH's significance for the development of print culture at least rivals his place in the development of Enlightenment botany.
7. Anonymous, *Memoirs of the Bedford Coffee House* (1763), 22.
8. Anonymous, *Now You have all settled it . . .* The *March of the Lion* (1752). The sequence of alleged pamphlets entitled *Inspectoress* and the actually published *March of the Lion* demonstrates JH's characteristic ploy: he invented the first work's title—a fiction—trumpeting that it preposterously made some false claim about him (in this case that the "Inspector" was biographically a woman); then he replied that he had to correct her gender, and did so in a published work, *The March of the Lion*, which further confused Grub Street. When the anonymous *A Particular Description of a Certain Lady at Present Conceal'd* (1752) appeared a few weeks later, readers were further confused but some readers guessed it might refer to "Inspectoress Hill."
9. Anonymous, *Memoirs of the Bedford Coffee House* (1763), 26.
10. Anonymous, *Memoirs*, especially 7, 11, 14.
11. *Spectator* no. 562 (July 2, 1714).
12. *LDA* (November 13, 1751).
13. *LDA* (October 2, 1751).
14. *LDA* (November 13, 1751) and *Inspector* 219.
15. *LDA* (November 7, 1751).
16. *LDA* (January 9, 1752).
17. *LDA* (November 7, 1751).
18. *LDA* (September 1, 1752).
19. Rizzo (1999): 124–32.
20. See *Notes and Queries 2nd series xi* (January 19, 1861): 52–53, 198.
21. *Inspector* 218, 221, 224.

9

Riot at Ranelagh

Dudley Snelgrove, a late sub-curator in the Prints and Drawings Department of the Old British Museum, was Paul Mellon's—the American bibliophile and collector—British agent and held cache in the London picture world in the 1970s when I was looking to illustrate Bobadil-Hill. He knew of my chase and put his vast collections at my disposal, which amounted to more than F. G. Stephens's listings in the catalogue he compiled in Victorian England.[1] Among these was a print that haunted me, and still does thirty years later.[2]

It shows a well-dressed man being assaulted under the arch decorated with frescoes leading to the rotunda in Ranelagh. Inside, the stalls are filled with elegant ladies and gentlemen promenading. A man in distress—"Bobadil"—is assaulted by another on his left, Mountefort Browne, as the legend informs the print's spectator. Three accomplices flank assist their gang leader, Browne to the right of Hill. The caption reads: "A Night Scene at Ranelagh on Wednesday 6th May 1753," and is embellished at its top with the sentence, "Thus I bore my point; six rogues in buckram let drive at me?"—with the interrogative mark. Browne's accomplices watch the scene, each one engraved with a flap protruding from his neck containing words such as: "Zounds, draw your sword Libeller, if you have the Spirit of a Mouse."

Figure 9.1. Engraving of "A Night Scene at Ranelagh," on Wednesday 6 May 1753, showing Hill and Mountefort Browne at blows in an engraving probably made by Leumuth.

Reproduced by kind permission of the Wellcome Library, London.

> I am a Rogue if I were not at half Sword with a Dozen of them two hours together. I have *escaped* by Miracle. I am eight times thrust through the Doublet, four through the Hose, my Buckler cut through & through, my Sword hack'd through like a hack Saw, *ecce signum*[.] I never dealt better since I was a Man; all would not do. A plague of all Cowards[.] *Let them speak.*

An asterisk appears after the word "speak," glossed at the bottom as "the Constable and Master of Ranelagh." Then the engraver's name is identified and the date of the engraving, May 6, 1753, followed by an abstract from Fielding's *CGJ* dated May 19 and explaining how "Dr. Hill had filed a complaint before the Justice of the Peace" claiming that an attempt had been made on his life. "An eminent Physician" filed his own affidavit purporting that Hill "was not in any Danger of his Life," yet Browne was required to post bail, guaranteed by "two Housekeepers of great Credit & Substance becoming his Sureties."

The anonymous cartoonist is sending up Hill and can do so because the whole "Town is talking, the newspapers and weeklies brimming over with accounts of their own." Mid-Georgian England thrived on visual entertainments of this sort; hundreds of satirical prints are extant but few capture a figure of fun so riotously, if also so pathetically. There can be no doubt about the protagonist identified in the main caption as "the Inspector."

For several years I believed that the figure of the "Inspector" was the key to unlock the chest of Hill's private life and public image. But a speech-act riddle—the sense that nothing Hill could write or say would escape his critics' ire and that Browne was the public's convenient agent—intervened. If you are already doomed, determinism sets in and nothing you do or say counts, even if biographical reasons existed for Browne's caning of Hill. During the hours I spent gazing at the engraving, Hill's pathos resonated: his wig ripped away, hat thrown on ground, head stripped bare, ears protruding, eyes expressing pain. It seemed a scene of male rape in the presence of women, suggesting past *hubris* and present *transgression* committed by a tarnished man, even if the cartoon itself does not define the excesses beyond the labels "Rogue" and "Coward." The engraver adroitly frames his subject's grief, and contrasts his distress with the night-scene's mirth. But biographers are not merely engravers of the ephemeral, they must present more—even for a figure like Hill; must explain which events triggered fiascos like this one precipitating a brawl on this scale.

Then Snelgrove joined me—we both gazed at the engraving in silence. He chuckled that Hill must have inspired many more caricatures if he was the paradoxical creature—ambitious, cowardly, driven, vain—I earlier described to him. Hill probably did engender them: some survive and more must have been lost.

Before he was caned Hill moved to a new accommodation in Hart Street late in 1752, directly across from St. George's Street in Bloomsbury within a stone's throw to the Bloomsbury market. It then lay approximately where the current Bloomsbury Way is, a broad thoroughfare running from New Oxford Street into the southwest corner of Bloomsbury Square. Within months he was also signing his letters as from Arlington Street. Horace Walpole also had a town residence here and so did John Astley (1724–1787), the painter nearby in Schomberg House in Pall Mall. That European gadfly the Baron Poelnitz had seen it just four or five years earlier and christened St. James "the most considerable square in London, not only for its Bigness, but for the Residence of Persons of great Quality," and a few booksellers had also set up here.[3]

John Ridley's book shop was at the top of St. James Street, toward the Piccadilly end, and Ridley probably made more profit from the sale of Hill's medicines than by disseminating any polite literature. Hill strolled down the street toward the Pall Mall end with his gold cane, decked out in wig and gloves of a Sunday, recognizable for his inimitable gait.

His removal to St. James further buoyed his confidence. The Earl of Orrery, who also had a nearby town house and to whom Hill would later dedicate the bound volumes of the *Inspector*, gifted him a personally inscribed copy of his *Life of Swift*.[4] Hill was number sixteen in a list of recipients that included Chesterfield, Richard Mead, Garrick, and Johnson. For a self-made man like Hill to take lodgings here was reckless but conducive to the image he was still forging. Such eminent lodgings perfected the picture of a rising star and he also hired a carriage-and-six for setting out abroad, decked out in finery capped by hat and cane, and he also fitted out his rooms in equally fine interiors. It is unknown how plush they were, especially as it was a bachelor pad, but external commentary about its furniture and fixtures exists, even if the accoutrements encouraged his contemporaries to mythologize him further.

In January 1752 he dispraised *Amelia* as unworthy of its author—a defective work, he said, compared to *Tom Jones*—without offering persuasive critical reasons.[5] Fielding ironically replied on January 11, 1752, that "a famous Surgeon, who absolutely cured one Mrs. Amelia Booth, of a violent Hurt in her Nose, insomuch, that she had scarce a Scar left on it, intends to bring Actions against several ill-meaning and slanderous People, who have reported that the said Lady had no Nose, merely because the Author of her History, in a Hurry, forgot to inform his Readers of that Particular." Hill's attack included the company of Smollett, Cleland, and Bonnell Thornton, and as he wrote in one of the newspapers: "Sir Alexander Drawcansir Knt. Censor of the *Covent-Garden Journal*" has not honored himself. As spring evolved not a month passed, it seemed, without the papers jibing at the new Fieldingesque-Hillian rivalry:

To prop the tott'ring Credit of his own
H—l roars out, *F——'s* Spirit'd dead and gone.[6]

All year they taunted each other—until the discrediting assault on Wednesday night May 6 occurred and dramatically changed Hill's life again. Reconstruction of the events leading up to the assault is not perfectly clear, and the paper trail may be incomplete. It seems the "roving Inspector" encountered Mountefort Browne, a young buck Hill reduced to "Clody," a name as vacuous as it sounds, and described him in the *Inspector* as the "empty-headed Clody," a witless fop who strolls about London with sawdust in his head.[7] "Clody" demanded an apology, Hill refused, and Clody took revenge. Brown and a group of friends hunted down Hill at Ranelagh that night, caned him, and punched him out. No threat of a duel ensued but the bloody-nosed, black-eyed Hill gave out that he had been mortally wounded and was dying. Clody hired counsel to defend himself, as did Hill, who from this time began routinely to resort to solicitors and physicians for legal protection.

Further examination uncovers a public increasingly bewildered as it watched these events unfold. No witnesses of the assault came forward in the newspapers but the *LDA* ran the first full-length story three days later to chronicle what happened:

> Dr. Hill at first felt so little from the Hurt he received on his Breast, in the Assault made upon him in Ranelagh, that he was that Night with Mr. Lediard [Justice of the Peace], and on Thursday Morning with the Right Hon. the Lord Mayor. About Noon on Thursday he was seized with a Difficulty of Breathing, and a Spitting of Blood; but he was still well enough to be at the Crow and Anchor Concert that Evening. Yesterday it increased upon him in a Degree that alarmd his Physicians. The Perpetrators of this Fact have all made their Escape.[8]

Hill provided this evidence through his representatives. Also on Saturday, May 9th, Browne wisely consulted magistrate Fielding about his legal position, while Hill, advised that the stakes had been elevated by Fielding's involvement, retracted, claiming that "Clody" in the original *Inspector* was only a "general character," not specifically Mountefort Browne. But Hill had attacked unprovoked before, his reasons unclear; in most cases the prospect of criticism prompted him to strike first but in others no provocation was known. For the moment he struck chords of mortal danger, so much so that "the Hurt . . . I have received is not without Danger," indicating bodily harm, and that as he lay on his bed his thoughts "approached Death."[9] Perhaps they did but no one else thought so, and his physicians—whoever they were—have left no trace or record of a medical diagnosis.

Hill, we will remember, owned shares in the *LDA*, but it is far from clear whether the editors were willing to perjure themselves by concocting a fraudulent case. For a whole week Hill's health continued to be headlines and the news suggested he was collecting medical evidence for a lawsuit. Two days later, on Monday May 11th, this account appeared:

> The Physicians who attend Dr. *Hill*, are Dr. *Mead*, Dr. *Dodd*, Dr. *Askew*, and Dr. *Parsons*. They Yesterday added to the other Means, a Blister on the Left Side, where it is feared an Empyema [tumor] will be formed. On the last Consultation they gave orders that no Person should be admitted to him, that he might be perfectly quiet; and forbade even Broth as too strong for his present Condition.

Such an eminent quartet of physicians escalated the case, leading one to think Hill cannot have named them without basis in fact and permission. The notion that James Parsons would "attend him" just three years after the debacle in the Royal Society seems fraught unless Hill's condition was dire.

Again, on Tuesday May 12, Hill reappeared in press headlines, this time announcing that the editors of the *LDA* received a letter indicating that Browne's resentment was owing to Hill's having embarrassed him at the Bedford. Hill denied ever having met Browne anywhere, let alone at the Bedford; in place he claimed he had received an anonymous letter implicating Fielding in Browne's harassment. Hill further gave out that the number of medical men attending him increased since the quartet of four examined him—an alarming state of affairs—but his *Inspector* columns nevertheless continued to appear (*Inspector* columns were often written in advance of their publication and this is not an argument either way). The "Consultation of Physicians" summoned an apothecary to bleed Hill and send him into the country for "a proper Regimen of Asses Milk" if they found him improving. A hiatus of a fortnight intervened. And then the "Inspector" announced in his own column that he would "drop the Prosecution" if Browne conceded that he had acted without provocation. Browne refused, Hill pressed on, and magistrate Henry Fielding heard the case in the court of sessions at the old Hick's Hall at the junction of the Great North Road. The dailies and weeklies fell silent after May 30th, reporting on that day only that "Browne, after attending the Sessions at Hick's Hall, was discharged for want of a Prosecution," indicating that Hill probably pulled out.

The record culled from the *Inspector*—the version Fielding referred to in his *CGJ* in May—reveals a different story. On April 30th Hill wrote about an "empty-headed Clody."[10] The *CGJ* immediately noted that everyone recognized "Clody" as Mountefort Browne, a young buck about town about whom nothing biographical other than his tribulation with Hill survives. Clody demanded a retraction, Hill refused, whereupon Browne set upon him at Ranelagh on May 6th. Neither man appears to have threatened the other with a duel, and if it ensued it would have been the only one Hill fought in his lifetime, in a period when one's honor was publicly diminished if one did not submit to one.[11] The affair produced a letter in Hill's *Inspector* column proposing a law against dueling, taken up by other papers also commenting on the menace of dueling. Whether these stemmed from the assault Hill received is unclear, but their timing suggests there was discussion after the scene at Ranelagh about the reasons why the two men did not fight a duel.

Flash back to mid-May and the public had no way of knowing who was telling the truth, nor did the print trail of the subsequent three or four weeks help. On May 16th an anonymous work appeared while Hill still claimed to be recovering entitled *Libertina Sine Conflictu*, referring to *Lucina*, was discussed in the *CGJ*, and was the work of novice Arthur Murphy recently recruited to the Fielding coalition.[12] While t'Town digested the Ranelagh events the pusillanimous "Inspector" gave out on May 20th that "he must prepare for death" in an editorial as literal as it was rhetorically free of typical Hillian bombast. The public was amused, and someone—perhaps a member of the coalition—printed in June Hill's alleged will as *Libertina Sine Conflictus; or, A True Narrative of the Untimely Death of Dr. Atoll . . . and a Faithful Copy of His Will*, covering himself as "Atoll"—the toll it all had taken.[13] A few days later Hill himself, sufficiently recovered to pen the work, brought out *A Narrative of the Affair between Mr. Brown and the Inspector . . . With . . . The Inspector's Own Account of It*.[14]

Hill lamented he was dying, a pose that struck the metropolis as reprehensible cowardice. Minor Molièrean symptoms were insufficient—Hill gave out he was on his deathbed. His failure to produce reasons why he lampooned Browne was lacunary; the only persons swayed were those willing to side with the underdog. Hill could have laid bare the facts, instead he retreated to his Cave of Spleen and reported which organs were impaired, which bones broken, which bruises bleeding. Cowardice of many types was an ingrained trait, part of his inability to tell the truth. Yet the public remained confused. "Will Everywhere," known as "an honest storyteller of t'Town for twenty years," presented his spin endorsing Hill's version. He was probably a Hillian creation—one of many—presented in an *Inspector* column.[15] The myth-making aspects of the incident were noted, especially the way that pride and cowardice combined in someone too ambitious for his own good.

Hill was blind to his own cowardice. What he knew was that he worked day and night; why could the public not understand that his word was worth more than a young ruffian's who had assaulted him? He could never face up to the truth that he was of the second—or third—rank, creatively and imaginatively, and this psychological predicament is ultimately what is both engaging and pathetic about his whole life. "Will Everywhere" (Hill) commented that the *Inspector* "has a thousand good qualities but no one knows them; scandalized with a character which he by no means deserves."[16] But t'Town appeared deaf and produced more printed replies. Besides, the coali-

Figure 9.2. Caricature of John Hill as "Le Malade Imaginaire," 1753.
Reproduced by kind permission of the Trustees of the British Museum.

tion gathered force to show that this was a case of flagrant cowardice shown up and that Hill was nothing more than a bungling figure of fun—a jack-a-napes rapscallion who would eventually do himself in when Fielding's farce "The Mock Doctor," a take on Molière, was revived at Drury Lane later that spring, the casting made in such a way, and the lines inflected, to point to the vilified Hill. Both "doctors"—Molière's target and Hill—were *"malades imaginaires,"* as the recent cartoon claimed.

Hill suffered more this time than when sensing himself triumphant with the "gentlemen of science." His body may have racked with pain but his psychological anguish is more difficult to assess and certainly colored his subsequent public persona. It is facile to dismiss the *"scandale à la Browne"* as another publicity stunt for Hill, but it may be that this time he suffered physical pain that triggered his various illnesses of the 1760s. Besides, Browne's afterlife was checkered to say the least, and he continued to get himself into similar types of trouble; so much so that hindsight must exonerate Hill to some degree at least.

If this line has any validity, the sequence would have been approximately this: Browne assaulted him; he grew ashamed that he had allowed himself to be so vulnerable; he compensated by lashing out; the more he struck out the greater his public shame in a vicious circle of psychological sadomasochism. If only Theophilus Sr. could see him now—just as well he was dead.

But simultaneously Hill was growing more entrenched in Grub Street. In November Ralph Griffiths announced that *Whipping Rods . . . for Scribblers* had appeared, printed and promoted by the irrepressible Mary Cooper.[17] Griffiths had no clue about authorship—so he said—and drubbed him as "a punster" and "unhappy pretender to authorship."[18] The "Inspector" features from the first page, together with Foote as "the mouth of the lyon [*sic*]," his "bombastic style and . . . dunghill flowers . . . of rhetoric" contrasted with Fielding's purer ones. His Bedfordian life is criticized: lion, sphinx, and Malevoli all denounced; his attempts to court Bolingbroke excoriated (they will surface over the next two years); and finally the suggestion made that he is Foote's catamite. The fifteen-page "Dedication" amounts to an exposé of post-Popean hack life until this wrangling exposé divulges its maker as "K——y": John Kennedy, a hack now lost to time, if he ever existed.[19] But the anonymous author has done his homework; has read Hill's recent *Observations on the Writers of the Present Age, and Their Manner of Treating Each Other*, which appeared in the autumn of 1752, complaining further about the abuse he had received by Fielding's gang.[20]

Whipping Rods . . . for Scribblers was intended to topple Hill forever, its sprawling parodic paragraphs, notes, and apparatuses heading for his jugular. To accomplish its goal it satirized him well beyond the style of *Inspectors*, to include detailed criticisms of his Theophrastus translation—substantive repudiation as well as verbal assault—mock "Receipts for the Writing of Inspectors," and the generalized claim that not only was the *Inspector* a repository of falsehood and calumny but an assault on its readership too. It was the most extreme attack on Hill to appear yet, so no wonder that even Griffiths had recently grown more judicious: ". . . dr. *Hill,* with all his ingenuity, very frequently deserves the severest chastisement of true criticism, and that we have so good an opinion of his candour, as to think he would profit by it." Griffiths and Hill had not fallen out—Hill could claim these taps were puffs. But Griffiths's review also takes Hill's psychological temperature: "The vanity and egotism of Dr. Hill, together with the freedom with which he has treated several of his cotemporary [*sic*] writers, has made it a sort of fashion for the little scribblers of the age to attack him. . . ."

Every week, it seemed, brought some new verbal assault, so many that a list of this year alone—1752—would tax the limits of the diligently inquisitive. Inquiry also poses a quintessential question about motive and expectation: what did all the participants think they were doing when each attack led to further attack and further attack to renewed paper wars? Or was the contemporary hack's fluency so remarkable—especially Hill's scribbling pen—and the finances involved in printing copy so miniscule, not to mention the time expended, as to enhance this sociology of fracas? This is the question post-Popean duncery has occasionally posed without answers.

In December comedian Henry Woodward attacked "Bobadil," calling him the greatest of all buffoons.[21] Hill replied as "Simon Partridge,"[22] and before the snow of Christmas had set in he himself also penned the *Inspector's Rhapsody on the loss of his WIG, In a scuffle with some Irish gentlemen at Ranelagh,* his version of the caning at Ranelagh cast as a "rhapsody" mawkishly to capture his emotional pain as well as capitalizing on this growing popular sub-genre. The fallout from the caning at Ranelagh could also be seen in reviews: the big wigs—Fielding, Richardson, Smollett, and Johnson—would no longer review anything he wrote. Only Cleland, who in financial desperation wrote many reviews for Griffiths, penned one, a review of Hill's *Dissertation on the Royal Society.*[23] Even Griffiths's prolific reviewers hesitated or feared reprisals in print and Griffiths himself reviewed only one work by Hill: the *Inspector's Rhapsody* just discussed.[24] He sent out Hill's books for review but had a difficult time finding reviewers. Those who did review Hill are undistinguished: John Ward, a minor hack, four reviews; Joseph Leman, another, and William Bewley, two each; and one each for Hirons and Hugh Rose—scant showing for a phenomenon who had recently taken t'Town by storm.

Hill wrote over a dozen reviews for Griffiths's *MR,* including reviews of two of his own books: the *Actor* and *Loveill,* a practice so repulsive to us that it would take another chapter to explicate its custom in Georgian England, but at mid-century it was not unknown despite Hill's forlorn abuses. He also reviewed books about natural history, accepting whatever Griffiths sent his way. These included Thomas Short's *Discourses on Tea* (1750) and—far more interesting for their topicality—newly certified physician Ralph Schomberg's (1714–1792) *Medical Aphorisms*.[25] Hill may have written differently about Schomberg, not to be confused with his twin brother Isaac, also a physician, if he could have had a crystal ball prognosticating the parallels that would develop in their lives: excess, plagiarism, prolific scribbling on all types of topics. But he did not, and wrote blandly; relying at times on reviews like these to settle scores, as when he savaged the *Philosophical Transactions*.[26] Yet most of his early reviews are too diverse to locate a pattern of response, as when he favorably reviewed David Jeffries's *Method of Finding Diamonds*, William Shirley's *Black Prince*, and William Whitehead's (1715–1785) tragedy *The Roman Father*, all works without literary merit Hill should have castigated.

Browne's assault at Ranelagh was extraordinary even for Hill, and its coverage in the newspapers was disproportionate to the event. But Hill was already a *cause célèbre*. The purpose of its discussion in this chapter is demonstration of how far matters had progressed for "Bobadil" rather than exhaustive coverage. Earlier dunces—Theobald, Curll, and Cibber—had not been caned and publicly assaulted, but Hill was a different kind of creature. His speed-writing and wicked tongue had become so pronounced that whenever an anonymous title appeared the first attribution was now to him, and when a two-volume anthology of "Modern Characters" issued forth in 1753 stitching together almost six hundred pages of "real lives" the reviewer were *certain* it was Hill's:[27]

> They [the lives] appear, by the lively and not inelegant style, to be the work of a gentleman, whom another author has thus briefly characterized, "Warm passions, a quick conception, and a ready expression characterize most of ****'s productions. He writes much, because it is *necessary* he should, consequently correctness and regularity are less studied."—If the reader would be further informed concerning this writer's talents, we refer him to our account of the adventures of *Lady Frail*.[28]

The *MR* editors inserted a cross-reference to the passage, but *Modern Characters* was probably not Hill's.[29] They were swayed, they claimed, by "Warm passions," their euphemism for prurience and scurrility.[30] Hill's culpability intensified when *The Man-Plant* was also attributed to him: a quasi-pornographic prose satire devising a scheme à la *Lucina* for the improvement and increase of British dogs by serial copulation among proven human breeders. Hill's *métier* was growing alarmingly censorious and when Mary Cooper printed an anonymous novel entitled *The Eunuch*, narrating the adventures of young shepherd Harry who is taken up by a rich, also corrupt, Booby-like London family who encourages him to enter into illicit amours with a mistress, Hill was again suspected.[31]

Hill's "affair" with courtesan Diamond, published as "letters," as we have noted, added fuel to this developing persona.[32] No doubt whatever existed about Hill's authorship: "these letters," the *MR* reviewer confidently wrote, "contain the particulars of the rise, progress, and breaking-off of an intrigue betwixt Dr. H. and Mrs. D. They are written with uncommon spirit: but whether they are genuine or not, is as yet a secret to the public, and to us, further than that an advertisement has appeared in the papers, disavowing them on the part of the lady."[33] "Diamond"—whomever she was—existed and disowned their authenticity (how could she not when Hill wrote to her that "you were born to give happiness to thousands"?); and Hill—still a widower and allegedly sowing seeds all over t'Town—kept his inspectatorial readership on tenterhooks.[34] But his enemies continued to assemble. The "Junto," their *nom de guerre* that would gather strength over the next year, was also becoming more coordinated in its warfare, as captured in this vacuous ditty:

> The wish should be in form reversed
> To suit the Doctor's crimes,
> For if he takes his Physic *first*
> He'll never read his rhymes.

To this Hill epigrammatically replied in kind "To the Junto":

> Ye desperate Junto! ye great! or ye small!
> Who combat Dukes, Doctors, the Deuce, and them all;
> Whether gentleman scribblers, or poets in jail.
> Your impertinent wishes shall certainly fail.
> I'll take neither essence, nor balsam of honey—
> Do you take the physic, and I'll take the money.[35]

NOTES

1. F. G. Stevens and M. D. George and their magnificent catalogue; see Stephens. JH's frequent appearance in the caricatures of his time is considerable and would repay a study in its iconography. My inclusions represent a small part of the total. Many have surely been lost to time and, for this reason, eluded Stevens and George.
2. Stephens, vol. 3, satire 3183.
3. Poelnitz, vol. 2, 23.
4. Houghton Library MSS Eng. 218.14, Harvard University.
5. *LDA* (January 8–9, 1752).
6. *London Evening Post* (January 18, 1752).
7. *LDA* (April 30, 1753).
8. *LDA* (Saturday May 9, 1752).

9. *Inspectors* 372 and 374.

10. *Inspector* 372.

11. See Peltonen, chapters 3–4, for the relation of cowardice and dueling at the time.

12. Jensen, vol. 2, 740; see n. 13.

13. Anonymous, *Libertina Sine Conflictus* (1752); this is a different work from Christopher Smart's exposure of Hill by the same title; see Smart (1752).

14. Anonymous, *Libertina Sine Conflictus* (1752).

15. *LDA* (June 11, 1753).

16. Victorian compiler Thomas Wright recast the episode for softer Victorian tastes; see Thomas Wright (1867), 218–21.

17. John Kennedy, *Whipping Rods . . . for Scribblers* (1752).

18. *MR* 7 (1752): 394.

19. *Whipping Rods* (1752) and its imitations have not been discussed among those studying these ongoing paper wars; Rizzo (1999) was first to attribute it to Kennedy.

20. JH (1752g).

21. Henry Woodward (1752).

22. Partridge, passim.

23. *MR* 4 (1751): 187.

24. *MR* 8 (1752): 190.

25. Ralph Schomberg corresponded prolifically with da Costa and, like him, overspent, embezzled, and stole to compensate. He sued his frail and aging father in Chancery for fictitious debts; the very father who, like JH's father Theophilus Sr., had done everything possible to enhance his son's medical career. His twin brother Isaac was a less scribbling physician much involved with Hogarth and Garrick. Yet Garrick condemned the scribbler—Ralph—while receiving the non-scribbling brother Isaac with open arms.

26. *PT* 49, part 2 (1750–1751): 134 and part 3 (1751–1752): 241.

27. Anonymous, *Modern Characters* (1753).

28. *MR* 9 (1754): 144, reviewed in the July issue.

29. *MR* 4 (1751): 307.

30. Aware that Griffiths had published *Fanny Hill*, a few reviewers also attributed *Memoirs of a Woman of Pleasure* to JH, claiming there was good reason for its protagonist to have been named "Hill."

31. The copies in the Bodleian Library of *The Man-Plant* and *The Eunuch* both identify JH in eighteenth-century hands as the author on their title pages.

32. JH (1752f).

33. *MR* 6 (1752): 145.

34. JH (1752f), 7.

35. *Notes and Queries* 2nd Ser. (June 11, 1861): 198.

10

Hill and the "Fame Machine"

To be famous is usually to accomplish something noble. Celebrity too thrives on recognition yet is less demanding of nobility and often courts its opposites, especially among politicians and media "stars," not to enlist criminals and thieves. But notoriety—the radical of both fame and celebrity and a phenomenon far more elusive than its kindred cousins—cannot survive without widespread coverage in newspapers and other media. Celebrity and notoriety were often yoked in the half century before Hill's adulthood. Is Defoe's protagonist Moll Flanders, in his novel of that name, notorious or celebrated? The overlap is tricky and any sharp distinction entails slippage. Even while in Newgate Prison, hints abound that Moll aspires to become a "gentlewoman" and join the ranks of the "celebrated," no matter how criminal she may be. Perhaps her aspiration embedded the moral of the myriad "celebrated lives" written during the early Georgian era: that such persons were famous no matter how notorious.

Soon after Hill's death some compiler claimed he had been the most "Extraordinary Character," which not even his enemies denied.[1] Over two decades earlier, as spring turned to summer in 1753, the compiler's claim was verified, by the appearance that June of a remarkable caricature entitled *"Lusus Naturae, or Carracaturas of the Present Age,"* including Hill in the left foreground amidst illustrious contemporaries. It was one of dozen of prints showing Hill, often as the centerpiece. Here were Chesterfield, Cumberland, Johnson, and Hill; Hill prancing in the lower left with Elizabeth Canning—the girl he will "save" in a few weeks—in front of Whitehall, a scrolled broadside under his feet reading "not to know me argues thyself unknown." It was no mean feat to have reached this exalted echelon for originally humble Hill. In 1753 his contemporaries still squabbled

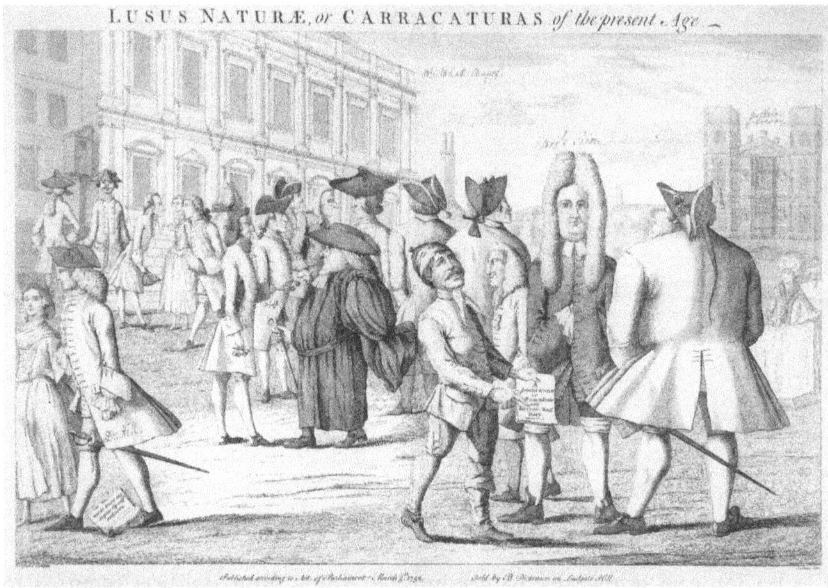

Figure 10.1. "Lusus Naturae, or Carracaturas of the Present Age," 1753, showing Hill in the left foreground amidst the most remarkable of his contemporaries.
Reproduced by kind permission of the Trustees of the British Museum.

about his stature despite the monolithic aspersions of the so-called "Junta" conspiring to demolish him.

The caricaturist assembles human portents betokening the rise of a new type of individualism, and frames them into a political space suggesting their relevance to the public sphere. But not all were attention-seeking extroverts craving celebrity, although their individualism is collectively captured as phenomenal; a remarkable achievement to rise so high in their respective fields: Chesterfield as responsible politician, Cumberland as dramatist, Johnson as moralist—and Hill? He alone appears with someone else—the Canning girl he has vindicated, as we see in the next chapter—making it difficult to pinpoint the locus of his "*Lusus Naturae.*" So far Hill, the genius for acquiring notoriety, had achieved nothing to classify him among these men, unless his release of Canning was considered analogous to their works, which is unlikely. The caricaturist may also be proceeding on an aesthetic principle grounded in "the art of contrast," as Fielding had described it in *Tom Jones*, with Hill the foil to these other prodigies and the space left between him and the others supporting the contrary direction in which he walks. If Francis Bacon's old saw that "fame is like a river, that beareth up things light and swollen, and drowns things weighty and solid," is true, then the noteworthiness of Hill's notoriety suggests cultural decline—in Bacon's sense he belonged to the lighter detritus auguring decay.

Meanwhile, Fielding's *CGJ* ceased publication and "Smart's gang," as Hill called them, was forming to strike. They found good cause in his earnings: in 1752, Hill had earned more wages than in any other year of his life. His contemporaries saw him as rich; a further reason the caricaturist places him among these "curiosities." Horace Walpole exclaimed in disbelief: "Hill has now become the highest paid."[2] Eyes were fixed on the *arriviste*: some, like the caricaturist in partial awe, partial disgust, others incredulous, and his enemies waiting in the wings to topple his forming empire of dullness. No one knew how he climbed to such heights: was it through hard work and talent, or their opposites in luck and ignominy? If Hill's reputation reached the furthest corners of London, some observers asked themselves what his "reputation was *for*." He had indubitably become a household name: the new condition for popular success of the developing self-made man. But in 1752–1753 no one could have explained precisely *why* or *how*.

They were aware of Hill's constant barrage of the public sphere with feuds, fights, and furores—and, of course, publications. After his debacle with the FRS and his caning one might have wondered what spectacle remained but Hill had more tricks up his sleeve; or, his chicanery and duplicity had more avenues for expression than these. Few episodes titillated the public more than his new fracas with the young Christopher Smart, recently arrived in London from Cambridge, begun when the two men met in the summer of 1752 on the premises of Francis Newbery, the bookseller who was now also Smart's father-in-law.

Still widowed during that summer, Hill was curious about Smart's recent marriage to Newbery's stepdaughter and could see how it benefited Smart. Heavily in debt it solved the young Smart's cash crisis: he and his bride had moved into Newbery's premises at the "Bible and Sun" in St. Paul's Churchyard—that row of showplaces along the side of the church—as one of Newbery's resident hacks. Newbery lived behind the shop and the debt-ridden Smart had a dimly lit bedsit there. Having left Cambridge in debt he was taking stock.[3] His arrangement with Newbery was typical and involved him assisting a busy publisher, Newbery, then engaged in multiple profit-making projects. The penurious author would eek out a living as a freelance writer does today, and also had his room and meals provided gratis. Smart hoped the arrangement was temporary and resented Newbery's constant demands deflecting him from writing poetry, especially preparing for the publication of his first volume. He had been bruised by Robert Dodsley's rebuff in his search for patronage and was thrilled when Charles Burney, the musicologist, introduced him much earlier that year (1752) to Newbery, who was then looking for someone to edit *The Midwife*.[4] Smart was merely one of Newbery's fleet of hacks living in his back rooms.[5] When he also began to contribute to Newbery's quondam periodical *The Student* that fall (1752)—this in addition to editing *The Midwife*, nicknamed *The Old Woman's Oratory*—Newbery realized what a bargain he had struck and was eager to retain his protégé.

Figure 10.2. Portrait of Christopher Smart in his study at Pembroke College, Cambridge, with his mock-epic poem *The Hilliad* on his bookshelf.
Reproduced by kind permission of the Master and Fellows of Pembroke College, Cambridge.

One summer Sunday Hill turned up unannounced. Smart was already well predisposed against Hill who represented everything he loathed: ambition, ostentation, prevarication, and self-aggrandizement. Newbery for his part steered clear of Hill, reducing father and son-in-law to the spectacle of being infringed at their private premises. Witnessing the cool reception, Hill thought that by inviting both men to supper they might bite, but they did not and he left in a huff. When Hill eventually realized how he had been rebuffed he struck out, claiming that Smart was a mere "poetaster" and "hireling": a hack with no ability who would scribble for anyone who greased his palm.[6]

He also claimed *he* had been responsible for bringing Smart from Cambridge to London, and compelling Newbery to employ him, none of which was true and for which fables he later apologized.[7] For the moment—in December 1752—he announced to his inspectatorial readers in the *LDA* that he must punish this "ingrate" who has begun to read "an abusive Poem, a long and elaborate work . . . at Alehouses and Cyder Cellars." This was Smart's in-progress mock-epic poem *The Hilliad*, whose origins lie in the paper wars more than elsewhere. True to form the *GM* immediately reprinted *Inspector* 544 in its Christmas issue, titling it "Mr. Smart Selected for Chastisement by the *Inspector* and thinking it would make for entertaining holiday reading."

Hill had reviewed Smart's *Poems on Several Occasions* acidly the previous August 8th, followed by a further attack in an ephemeral newspaper called the *Impertinent*. These were Smart's juvenilia and he had not yet been declared mad or composed the religious lyrics for which later generations remembered him. Hill found it especially difficult to tolerate the latter written by a new author just having published his first volume of poetry under duress and trying to demonstrate how versatile he was. Five days later, on August 13th, Hill attacked himself—Hill—in the *Impertinent*; readers could not have been certain Hill was the author but he was, and then, at the end of August, he published a second, this time balanced, review of Smart's poems in the *MR* to confound the track record. Within a few days—still in August—the *GM* announced that the "Impertinent" and the "Inspector" were one and the same man.[8] The trick boomeranged. Smart for his part had done little to antagonize Hill: neither wrote for the *MR* or other weeklies or monthlies and Smart came to the view that Hill's tactics were unprovoked.

Hence when Smart awoke on December 8th he was appalled and stunned to find himself lambasted. He soon regained his equipoise and was encouraged by Newbery to retaliate on several fronts. First he took out advertisements in London newspapers denying he had ever written by the word and returned Hill's catcalls. Then he rushed into print a little satire—*Libertina Sine Conflictu*—printed by Newbery and mocking Hill's *Lucina*.[9] It bore the same title as Arthur Murphy's excoriating attack, showing what a profound note *Lucina* had struck.[10] And Smart colluded with Newbery, explicitly as "Mr. Smart Selected for Chastisement by the *Inspector* to run his own statements setting straight the record of the 'Sunday imposition.'"[11] His *piece de resistance* was announcement of the imminent appearance of *The Hilliad*: "I am determined to follow my friends, and bring the *egregious coxcomb* to poetical justice, in the *Hilliad*, the first book of which will be published with all possible dispatch."[12]

This swollen lampoon published early in 1753 names names, contains "Notes Variorum," and portends to be a new *Dunciad* for the 1750s; one to catch the ear of t'Town and propel the weeklies to rush into print with accounts of the bruising battle.[13] No wonder Hill had complained to Smart that "he [Smart] had not Reason to make me the Hero of a *Dunciad*." Perhaps not, and all this further fallout could be proof of the resonance of Pope's original dunciads, but the dailies and weeklies—the *DA, London Chronicle, LM, St. James's Magazine*—quickly ran features on the fracas. The *GM* took out a small supplement to chronicle the threats both ways.[14] New Year 1753 would be the merrier for such pugnacious paper wars even if we wonder centuries later why such battles existed, what they accomplished, why they had become so firmly institutionalized, and what they revealed about the public sphere in the 1750s. The matter is, of course, one of the fundamental points Hill's notorious life raises, its juncture of authorship, celebrity, and the quest for patronage in crisis.

Smart did not compose his own "Notes Variorum" for the new work—this task he left to Arthur Murphy, the strapping Irishman recently arrived from Cork who was not yet a playwright.[15] Murphy was recruited to the coalition and no stranger to feud, having worked for Fielding at the *CGJ* and, more recently, as an editor for the *Gray's Inn Journal*. To sharpen his blades he produced a short prose imitation of Hill's *Lucina* entitled *Sine conflictu*, taking the toll of satires and parodies of it to over a dozen in just a couple of years, and portraying Hill as "Slender," a conceited fellow given to "manifold employments."[16] He often wrote under the pen name "Charles Ranger," issuing announcements of the forthcoming "beautiful Piece of Mock-Epic-Poesy" without divulging that he—a "veritable exegete"—had written the notes for *The Hilliad*, and conceptualized the coalition as transformed from the former "Junto" against the enemy Hill, with Smart's couplet-verse as ammunition and his notes the much-needed fodder. The engine of siege was Hill's attacks—all of them—and "the behemoth of Bobadil" awaited extermination. These were not metaphors: Murphy had mastered the Popean parody of dunciads and went for the jugular in his "Notes Variorum." His message: Hill's fall alone would restore the virtuous Republic to its former honor.

Here Hill is satirized, vivified, and demonized in ways the FRS never contemplated by further transforming "Proteus" into animal, mineral, vegetable, and insect too. Collectively the FRS, especially its natural-history wing, possessed little bravura as vilifiers. But now the cadres of attackers included Dr. Kennedy (who outed the "Inspectoress"), Fielding, Garrick, Murphy, and, later, William Kenrick, who possessed a fierce tooth in lashing post-Popean dunces.[17] Often the group published under a single name; for example, "Henry Woodward," writing in *A Letter from Henry Woodward,* reputed to have sold out the whole run in just four hours.[18] They could pose as latter-day Scriblerians, and here, in *A Letter*, a spurious doctor named "Dr. Bobathill" writes a mock-*Inspector*, number "524," parodying Hill as "Bobadill" with two letter l's, poking fun at Hill's herbal penchant and spinning variations on Hill's Bedfordian sobriquet. "Bobathill" also demonstrates in *A Letter* that he is a better writer than the biographical Hill presented here as no "gentleman" at all.

On other occasions they exploited current events: after Hill had been kicked, caned, and de-wigged at Ranelagh in May 1753 they issued an epigram by "the Epigrammatist" urging Hill only to appear in public in a black wig. They fixed on the loaded word "pert" to describe him. "Pert" circa 1750 denoted dullness of a particularly *active* type: that is, someone remarkably unclever who is never at rest, or always in motion; a quality of particular interest to that mid-century, post-Popean milieu we have lost. "Pert" is shown to be "the scribler [*sic*] who publish'd the load of personal abuse, that excited the indignation of the public, and produced the most *pert*, assuming, and short-lived of all the periodical pieces that have lately appeared."[19]

On another occasion they enlisted David Henry, an editor of the *GM* and acquaintance of Smart, to take on Hill in *An Essay on the Rationality of Brutes*, subtitled a *Philosophical Comparison Between Dr. Codghill* [*Hill*], *Inspector General of Town-Island. And Mango, the Great monkey* [*Smart*], *Director General*. . . .[20] It considered whether animals are endowed with reason, its conceit the theory of the transmigration of souls as proof; and by so proceeding it vivified the "real soul of an animal" in a human body, "Dr. Codgill's," who had been a "rattlesnake" in a prior life, with that of "Mango," a "monkey," casting Codgill as Hill and Mango as Smart. The point of the lampooning *Essay* was demonstration that in every category of human nature—disposition, docility, honesty, simplicity, and sincerity—"Mango" was the superior soul.

When Fielding's *Mock Doctor* was acted in a new production at the end of 1752 at Garrick's theater in Drury Lane, it featured Woodward mimicking Hill. He wore high shoes to look taller, like Hill, and fancy frocks. Smart wrote the new prologue where Woodward was slated to appear in the costume of the old "Mock Doctor," staging all to persuade the audience the "old doctor' was Hill, who sent his lawyers forth and compelled the Lord Chamberlain to suppress the play everywhere except in the newspapers.[21] Even so, young Smart remained the most aggrieved of the coalition, unable to forget or forgive Hill's criticisms in his *Inspector* and periodicals. Hill's prolix assessment of Smart's poetry in the *MR* was unforgivingly savage, winding up Smart as the most promising poet since Pope and "at least the equal of Gray and Mason" but "careless in cultivating poetry."[22] Hill found his verse to contain absurdity, pompous neologism, bold "pilfering," and uneven "flowers . . . over-run with nettles and briars." It was a patronizing blow to the fledgling poet: he deserves "a place among the first of the present race of English poets," and if he should learn from criticism such as Hill's to perfect his poetic craft, "there is no doubt of his becoming equal to most who have done honour to the last or the preceding age."[23]

Smart endured these blows for months but now he retaliated in *The Hilliad* and lost no opportunity to be implicated in the coalition's jibes.[24] These included their "March of the Lion" attacks: parodies claiming that even if Hill were the "Bedford lion" he was a papier-maché "lion."[25] Then the alliance proceeded to attack and counterattack *itself* in just the way Hill had puffed himself, gathering barbs from "Bobadill-Bobathill" to "the savage of Bedford Coffee-House" as Hill was often dubbed.[26] Mary Cooper, Hill's printer, printed many, her palm having been greased by the coalition.

Smart's taunts in *The Hilliad* relating to Peg Woffington, the actress with whom Hill had been in love, galled the "Inspector" most. Woffington had since become famous and joined David Garrick's acting company at Drury Lane Theatre, celebrated especially for her skill in "breeches parts"; and whenever she appeared as a man, in "different dress" as one critic put it, it was with a Hillian edge. When Smart once put the words "I either sex can ape" into her mouth they referred equally to a woman imitating a man (as Woffington often did) or man imitating woman, as in the case where Smart made it the subject of a riddle. Earlier Hill had hit out at Smart's cross-dressing as "Mary Midnight." But savvy readers of 1752 could not so easily be fooled: they guessed the subject of the riddle was "Mary Midnight," alias of the same Smart who edited *The Midwife* where so many satires of Hill appeared. Elsewhere Smart took on Hill's waddling gait, as in *The Genuine Memoirs . . . of a Very Unfortunate Goose-Quill*, again through the convenient squib of Mother Midnight. Here Hill is cast as "H Waddle" and compared to a monkey. The image of the goose-quill is used to lambaste him, and George Russel, a hack and sometime member of the coalition, used it in his own satire entitled *The Adventures of a Goose Quill*.

Dozens of these ephemera appeared in 1752–1753—enough to provide a sense of the *Dunciad*'s outreach after mid-century.[27] Ralph Griffiths, never one to lose out, watched the fracas grow from the bleachers and published his own version in the "Miscellaneous" column of the *MR* December issue, ostensibly a review of Woodward's reply to Hill but fast-forwarding to focus on Smart and the avalanche of replies the *Hilliad* would bring.[28] He aimed for neutrality, commenting that it was now the "fashion" in London to attack Hill, but cunningly backs "the remarkable Inspector": "this gentleman has solely carried on for almost two years, and still continues to support [the *LDA*] with growing success." Both Griffiths and Hill owned shares in the *LDA* and it was not surprising that the entrepreneurial Griffiths would measure success by "sales."

Griffiths glimpsed what was coming and apologized for Hill's lapses—"who might not sometimes under-write himself?"—and occasional miscalculations.[29] After such litotes the shoe dropped:

> . . . unluckily, the doctor has let slip no opportunity of expressing the highest opinion of his own performances, at the same time he has shown the most absolute contempt of the works of almost all his contemporaries. 'Tis therefore little wonder, that authors less successful than the *Inspector*, stimulated both by envy and revenge, have taken advantage of the openings afforded them in the doctor's own writings, for the most ample retaliation. Hitherto, however, he has only met with critics whose efforts he has scarce taken more notice of than they deserved. . . .[30]

Having augured what was coming for readers of the *MR* who may not have heard about the imminent appearance of the *Hilliad*, Griffiths added this note: "*The Hilliad*—To be speedily published" and then returned to the review he presents of Woodward contra Hill, where Hill, surprisingly, comes out ahead. All lights soon to be on *The Hilliad* aroused Griffiths's Grub-Street sensibility. He glimpsed how Smart's mock-epic poem would precipitate an overgrowth of Hillia and burgeon it did. Every week, it seemed, a new scourge appeared from the woodwork: in January the *Monthly* advertised almost a dozen works lambasting the "Inspector."[31] These embraced defenses of Woodward, including one by a "Simon Partridge," and another claiming to have been written by "the honourable the Earl of ****" who remains unidentified, but given that his old friend Mary Cooper printed it one wonders if it can have been another Hillian ploy. A bookseller calling himself "W. Reeve" published *A Lick at 'em All; or The Moderator*, but the *MR* dismissed it as worthless as the name was invented.[32] Reeve urged the world to forego Smart's private concerns and doubted the veracity of Newbery's claim that he had never paid Smart to write.

The most fanciful of these replies was *The Geese Stript of their Quills: Or, Proposals for Depluming and Rusticating the Rival Literati*, which Mary Cooper also printed, the principal "Rival Geese" Hill and Smart, and arguing that *both* should be expelled from the "Republic of Letters" (the author's phrase).[33] The author selects his epigraph from the advertisement that had just appeared in *Inspector* 548—that he means to chastise both parties—and regrets that all "*modern Geniuses* have opened with Exclamations against the Multiplicity of their Competitors."[34] His solution recognizes the culture of ambition and competition in which they struggle, warning them not to be so "ambitious as to transgress the Limits prescribed to them."[35] Griffiths' review summarized its plot this way: "all that now remains in the power of the *rivals in abuse* . . . is, publickly [*sic*] to exchange forgiveness *as Men*."[36] They did not, of course, and the idea itself was preposterous by this stage of the bellicose endgame. The author also suggested that both men be compelled to read only the writings of others and forbidden to scribble: Hill limited to observing the natural world through his microscope, and Smart to "collect his random thoughts on various subjects, and range them in proper *declamatory* order"—a further dig at his propensity to ramble.

The truculence heated up again in February and March 1753, with pieces pro and con appearing in almost every issue of every newspaper and periodical and adding new detractors such as William Kenrick who had an ear for dunces, as he was one of their tribe.[37] He had captured the Republic's sham in the hack sphere in *The Town* (1748), followed by the more complex but equally splenetic *Old Woman's Dunciad* (1751), an appendage to the Grub-Street wars of the prior decade. In *The Pasquinade* (1753)[38] he followed on from *The Hilliad* as a new member of the coalition and reminded readers about *Lucina* and Hill's scandal with the Royal Society, as well as more recent paper warfare, but nothing Kenrick wrote ever won him public recognition, and neither abuse nor flattery produced his much-desired patrons.

By the time *The Hilliad* appeared Kenrick had not yet become the black sheep of Grub Street—that was coming. A decade later he had burned his bridges by attacking Samuel Johnson's *Dictionary of the English Language*, excoriating William Warburton, decrying Goldsmith's learning, claiming that David Garrick had had a homosexual love affair with the disgraced Isaac Bickerstaff (which would have ended in a libel case in court if Kenrick had not suppressed it), writing his own savage reviews, and landing himself in prison for debt—all rivaling Hill's notoriety. He capped these by failing in other pursuits too: as Shakespearean actor, playwright, and controversialist. Soon after his paper war with Hill, he made one smart decision to travel on the Continent for a number of years. This way he acquired foreign languages and could work profitably as a translator of, and commentator on, the contemporary Continental Enlightenment scene after his return.

But he continued to sully his reputation through unjustified attacks on more famous contemporaries, Hill included. And he puffed himself and reviewed his own works negatively to drum up interest. His *Grand Question Debated; Or, Being an Essay to Prove that the Soul of Man is Not . . . Immortal* (1751) failed more notably than any of Hill's similar works and when it did, he followed up with a sequel to prove the opposite. In energy and apparent learning, for unwavering arrogance and irascible temper, he rivaled Hill with whom he deserves comparison except that he had none of Hill's brilliance for natural history. He was a scribbler of parts, as demonstrated in *The Pasquinade*, although not so diverse as Hill, or as fluent in the divisions of knowledge. He too struck out without reflecting on the consequences and imprudently imagined himself equal to any task that financial need imposed. Pathetically, he never found a long-lasting patron as Hill eventually would.

Kenrick was still green in Grub Street when he issued *The Pasquinade* contra Hill whose career he followed closely. It was Kenrick who first attributed all three of Hill's novels—"*Valet, Loveill,* and *Creole*"—to the right author and who commented upon the gender transformations of Hill's aliases.[39]

Figure 10.3. Engraving of William Kenrick, from a portrait engraved by Worlidge.
Reproduced by kind permission of the National Portrait Gallery.

Pasquinade opens by invoking "the doctor" and devotes a full fifth of its first canto's 250 lines to him. Then Kenrick displays him sunk in the arms of his "Chloes, Daphnes and Amandas," striking an alarm bell by reminding readers of what they already knew: that the pre-1753 Hill philandered even more than he scribbled. Kenrick then moves to the "Muses Nine" with whom Hill boasted intimacy—"By the soft vows of your Inspector's Love"—and spends the rest of his time describing the rival provinces of "Dulness" and "Pertness." "Pertness" discovers that "In none, immortal Hill' can she shine so brightly as in his kingdom. Inflamed with love, "Pertness" signs a truce with her sister "Dulness" and vows to shield her son:

> Whom still my arm protects to brave the town,
> Secure from Fielding, Machiavel, or Browne;[40]
> Whom rage nor sword e'er mortally shall hurt—
> Chief of a hundred chiefs o'er all the *Pert*.

Kenrick's claim is that the realms of the "pert" were "vacant" before the 1740s; that by narrating in this new vocabulary he will fill them, so to speak, and explicate the difference of the two offensive domains: the dull and the brazen. The former, he suggests, crested early in the 1740s when Pope lodged his latest attack on the "new dunces"; the latter was just coming into its own, Hill its emblazoned Anti-Christ. Whatever "pertness" is (and it is not, of course, any longer that in current usage), it thrives on the *act* rather than the *artifact*. Its chief strands—archness, cockiness, disrespectfulness, impertinence, impudence, roguishness, rudeness, and waggishness—attach to actions rather than works, to behaviors rather than publications, and amounts to the position that scandal is the pert man's natural habitat.

Kenrick's emphasis on Hill's dalliances with "women of quality" distinguished him—Kenrick—from other detractors. His "Notes Variorum" glossed "Hill's women" with the carping meticulosity of a classical exegete. The reviewer in the *MR* picked up on Kenrick's highlight and drew a tie between Hill and Smart as kings of the dunces: "[this is] A satire in imitation of the *Dunciad*; . . . Mr. Smart and Dr. Hill are to be the heroes in chief, attended by the whole tribe of inferior writers: a noble subject, and worthy of the author [Kenrick]: who endeavours to copy Mr. Pope's manner; but, alas!"[41] Alas indeed, Kenrick was no Pope; was as dunce-like as Hill, his contribution to *Pasquinade* limited to stale explications of "pertness" at mid-century. Meanwhile Hill also had his defenders, if fewer than Smart's and now Kenrick's, and not so well organized into a coalition, especially scribblers Richard Rolt, Samuel Derrick, and John Henley. "Orator Henley"—who conveniently bore the same initials as "JH"—was no fan of Smart, loathed Newbery against whom he held a vendetta, and was willing to go public in his debasement of Smart's *Impertinent* and *Hilliad*. His own life had already turned for the worse and he would be dead in three years. He saw Smart and the coalition as part of the new politico-religious degeneracy about which he railed in his sermons and Hill as a truthful underdog, like himself.

Hill's team was disorganized and lacked numbers. It was a scribbling, depopulated phalanx of the second rank. Derrick (1724–1769), an Irishman in his twenties who attached himself to Hill around 1750, probably in the Bedford coffeehouse whose memoirs he contributed to, was also aspiring to patronage.[42] He had much less auspicious early start than Hill, as he recounts in *Fortune, A Rhapsody*, dedicated to Garrick and written in the rhapsodical sub-genre then flourishing ("rhapsody" indicating fervid feeling rather than a tone of cool reflection). Having grown up in Dublin he resisted migrating to London but recognized that only there could he establish himself, and then, having failed to find a place on the Dublin stage, he crossed the Irish Sea as well as installed himself in Bath where was promoted to Master of Ceremonies, some said because he moved freely among "ladies of easy virtue . . . and sacrificed his unhappy life to the shrine of *Venus*."[43] Small wonder Boswell later found him a suitable first tutor into the "ways of London." He was as diminutive and deformed as Hill was tall and straight, and also melancholic, qualities the Smart coalition found an easy target when they crowned him in the *Hilliad* as "Quinbus Flestrin": the "man mountain," the name the Lilliputians gave to Gulliver for the way he seemed to prop up the sky—as did Derrick Hill. Hill in turn saw Derrick as a protector, and when opportunity arose to show his loyalty Derrick grabbed it and pounced on *The Hilliad* in print.

He called his "pasquinade" *The Smartiad* and included the discovery he made that Samuel Foote had refused to supply Smart with the notes for *The Hilliad*, a barb he now used in Smart's hide. He accused Smart of being as dull as any dunce; an irritable pest who lashes out without the least provocation, the very picture of grotesque literary ambition:

> No pompous Marble shall preserve thy Name,
> No flatt'ring Stone shall tell imagin'd Fame,
> But Death, victorious, shall in Triumph ride,
> Trampling the poor remains of Envy, Scorn, and Pride.[44]

One visualizes Hill's glee; how he must have basked in this glow levelling the score, how he grimaced in imagined triumph. Nevertheless, the reviewer in the *LM* assumed Hill wrote it.[45] Consisting of only seven pages, *The Smartiad* is far shorter than *The Hilliad* yet parodies it, with biting couplets, annotations, and variorum notes. But Derrick could not rival Smart's mock-poetry of allusion and Hill, for his part, was still churning out biweekly *Inspector* columns and relying on former allies, like Griffiths, to buttress him; which Griffiths did when lamenting early in March that all the parties are so "deeply engaged in such dirty work."[46] But Griffiths was cautious: he had commissioned Hill to review Smart's poems the previous August, which

Hill trashed, as we saw, and now found himself caricatured by the coalition as "Gabriel Griffin," a money-grubbing printer devoid of aesthetic sense. Griffiths was no friend, predictably, of Smart and he disliked Newbury, and to bring off his review of *The Hilliad* he assumes the persona of the disengaged man of letters recoiling in front of such "abrasive performances."

By April and May 1753 the flames crescendoed, t'Town ablaze with "paper war." The response of hacks, far and wide, is documented, but not the general public's. Were they aghast that the whole tribe of hacks was so vexed? One scribbler, never identified, enumerated "rules for being a wit": avoid fracas at all costs, while also observing that the public was no more interested in Smart's troubles than disputes between "two monkeys in his [Smart's] Oratory."[47] And he added that writerly pride was now an "illness" rather than sin. The term itself—"paper war"—was now reserved for "Hill's war" rather than any other within the virtuous Republic. And when another unidentified hack—weekly they spawned like insects—chimed in that Hill was "contemporary humbug," recalling the earlier fray over the use of the term and crowning Hill "king of 'em all," he plotted the warrior's succession:[48]

> . . . with the Courage of Pompey, and pen of a Hector,
> First Woodward then Smart now Newbery he'd [Hill] maul,
> But if you'd believe him he'd *Humbug* you all.[49]

The fad of "humbugging" as an imposture, deception, or fraud had lingered for a few years as an afterlife, as it were, of dunciadic existence; some restricting its use just to denote class and rank, as when a university student wrote in 1751 that humbug is "that exalted species of wit which is now practised by gentlemen of the brightest parts under the elegant denomination of a Humbug."[50] This, of course, did not say what it was. Another student contributed a whole article on "the Superlative Advantages arising from the use of the new-invented Science, called the Humbug."[51] Fast-forward two or three years to 1753, and t'Town was cloyed and trouncing humbug, as when the Earl of Orrery, who Hill would also suck up to for patronage, was vocal in denouncing it as so much spin: "Single words, indeed, now and then broke forth; such as odious, horrible, detestable, shocking, Humbug," he claimed of the early 1750s.[52]

Specifically about humbug he carped: "this last new-coined expression, which is only to be found in the nonsensical vocabulary, sounds absurd and disagreeable, whenever it is pronounced." Then he moaned that "Our pretenders to wit . . ."—here thinking of Hill and Smart—"when they talk of Humbug, etc. they seem to be jabbering in the uncouth dialect of the Huns."[53] Restless and up to the minute, Hill too had devoted *Inspector* 28 in

April 1751 to the assessment of humbug, noting that Samuel Foote, a "very sensible man," had coined the term to ridicule folly and absurdity. But Hill failed to notice that "humbugging" could turn itself against truth, as had the "humbuggers" in this battle.

He may have found temporary solace in Griffiths's publication that spring of a two-volume set of his selected *Inspector* papers.[54] Griffiths himself favorably reviewed the pair but the paper wars nevertheless continued for years;[55] even after Fielding died in 1754 and Smart moved on to other pastures, soon to be committed for insanity to St. Luke's by his father-in-law Newbery and other booksellers.[56] In 1756 the alliance was still parodying Hill, as when they struck against his notion developed in the *Inspector* that actors could be compared to painters.[57] This one was probably spearheaded by Smart, who called the essay "On the Multiplicity of Modern Authors," and signed it "S. Gelasimus," as in one who is, etymologically speaking, a "mocker."[58] The alliance added and lost members, especially the aforementioned Rolt who changed sides, and they were now less united than when they launched *The Hilliad*; but Hill was lying low after 1753 and if he tried to start another venture similar to the *Inspector* they would pounce. So, when a new periodical called the *Critical Review* started up early in 1756, Rolt and Smart were sure Hill was inherent to the new machinery. But its editor was none other than Tobias Smollett, Hill's archenemy who had never been coerced to join the alliance. Did they forget about Hill's earlier paper battles with Smollett? Overlook that Hill had tried to ruin him? We cannot imagine any type of alliance between Hill and Smollett but the Junta was not yet in possession of this crucial fact. Proteus as "Lusus Naturae" had changed his colours and shapes so many times it might just be true.

The last *Inspector* paper appeared on July 7, 1753, by which time even indefatigable Hill was exhausted. Thomas Birch, the FRS who was now working away at his history of the Royal Society and who had avidly read the biweekly columns, lamented their demise: "The Inspector expir'd this Day without any previous Warning than that of his growing Weakness as a Writer."[59] Which "growing Weakness" had Birch spotted: factual, political, or stylistic? The claim is vague. Then Birch announced that "he is to be succeeded by the *Monitor* . . . three times a week"—a new periodical—and a few days later he confided to his constant correspondent, Baron Hardwicke: "he is his own Successor, for the new Composition [the *Monitor*] is evidently from the former Hand, tho' it affects Modesty."[60] It continued thus from periodical to periodical while Proteus reinvented himself.

One thing was clear: no victors emerged from the paper wars, and Hill came away bruised but more than ever notorious. He had failed on many sides, not least for his idiosyncratic notion that you are what you publish and his obsession with self-promotion. His feeble alliance—the Derricks and Henleys—ultimately amounted to protective nothings; were no matches for the Junta and Smart alliance, especially in the early days when Fielding was active. Furthermore, Hill's party did not refer to each other's works in ways that collectively puffed them—Hill had too much pride for that—and lacked an avuncular benefactor of Newbery's well-greased caliber.

If Samuel Johnson, one of the original figures pictured in the "Lusus Naturae" of 1753, was watching, his morality would have been plain: never write too much or too quickly, do not ruthlessly attack your contemporaries, and avoid paper warfare. He might also have noticed that the persona who emerged was pointedly the Fame Machine's arch-villain, not the "Inspector General" as imagined by the great-and-good of t'Town—*that* "Hill" remains irretrievable.

NOTES

1. *Annual Register* 18 (1776): 61.
2. LPH, 122.
3. Sherbo (1967), 59.
4. Mahony and Rizzo (1984), 54–75.
5. Sherbo (1967), 59; Brittain; Mahony and Rizzo (1984), passim.
6. *Inspector* 544 (December 7, 1752).
7. *Inspector* 553.
8. *GM* 19 (August 1752): 387.
9. Smart (1752).
10. Anonymous, *Libertina Sine Conflictus* (1752).
11. *Daily Gazeteer*, December 10, 1752, Advertisement.
12. *GM* 22 (1752): 600.
13. *Inspector* 543.
14. *GM* 22 Supplement (1752): 599–600.
15. J. P. Emery (1946a); J. P. Emery (1946b).
16. Murphy (1753).
17. Dunbar; Fussell; see the notes about Kenrick in Mahony and Rizzo (1984), passim.
18. Henry Woodward (1752).
19. *GM* 22 (August 1752): 387.
20. Henry (1752); the attribution to David Henry was made by Betty Rizzo.
21. Mahony and Rizzo (1984), 305.
22. *MR* 7 (August 1752): 131–43, one of the longest reviews JH published.
23. *MR* 7 (August 1752): 142–43.
24. Smart opened by appending some to epilogues he wrote for "Mother Midnight's *Oratory*," or to satires like *The Midwife; or, the Old Woman's Magazine*, consisting of Mother Midnight's endless outpourings. His variety show, *The Old Woman's Oratory*, also mercilessly lampooned JH as pompous, vain, ignorant—a "mongrel in search of a master."
25. Anonymous, *The March of the Lion* (1752).
26. Anonymous, *Now You have all settled it* (1752).
27. Works such as Anonymous, *The Inspector in the Shades* (1752).
28. *MR* 7 (1752): 470–73.
29. *MR* 8 (1752): 472.

30. *MR* 8 (1752): 472.
31. *MR* 8 (1753): 78–79.
32. Anonymous, *A Lick at 'em All* (1753), 2.
33. Anonymous, *A Lick at 'em All* (1753), 3.
34. Anonymous, *A Lick at 'em All* (1753), 5.
35. Anonymous, *A Lick at 'em All* (1753), 37.
36. *MR* 8 (1753): 78–79.
37. Fussell, passim.
38. Kenrick (1753), passim.
39. See Kenrick (1752), 5.
40. Naturalist Patrick Browne (c.1720–1790) who reenters our story later on; it cannot be Mountefort Browne of the Ranelagh riot, who makes no sense when coupled to Henry Fielding and Machiavelli. For this Browne see page 218.
41. *MR* 8 (January 1753): 80.
42. Derrick during the years 1746–1750.
43. *GM* 41 (1775): 30.
44. Derrick (1753), lines 111–14.
45. *LM* 9 (February 1753): 96.
46. *MR* 8 (1753): 151.
47. Anonymous, *Rules for Being a Wit* (1753), 6.
48. For further discussion see chapter 6.
49. Anonymous, *The Humbug* (1753), 3.
50. *Student* (1751), vol. 2, 129.
51. *Student* (1751), vol. 2, 287.
52. *Connoisseur* (1754), no. 14, 3.
53. *Connoisseur* (1754), no. 42, 4.
54. JH (1753b).
55. *MR* 8 (1753): 190.
56. Sherbo (1967), passim.
57. *LDA* (December 1751), nos. 248–49, 259.
58. Sherbo (1960) and Anonymous, *Universal Visitor* (1756), 135–37.
59. LPH, 56.
60. LPH, 56; Birch to Philip Yorke, July 7, 1753.

11

Canning and Marriage

While riveted by paper wars Hill diverted himself with a defense of Mary Squires, the old gypsy woman, against the fraud he perceived in young and conniving Elizabeth Canning, a true-life Moll Hackabout who pretended to be innocent. The case captured as much popular sentiment then as Victoria Climbie and James Bulger have in Britain in our time. It generated even more commentary in 1753 than the "dunciads" and "pasquinades" of both parties clamoring in the paper wars, although comment of a different sort, and for once it vindicated Hill—here was a no-humbug event in which his position prevailed. Since then the Canning case has ranked as one of the century's great hoaxes together with Mary Tofts, the so-called rabbit breeder, and with dozens of counterfeit maidenheads protesting too loudly; so pronouncedly that in our time a literary historian has gathered Canning's prolific materials into an exhaustive study of the ins-and-outs of the intrigue. Three novelists have fictionalized it.[1] The story can be briefly summarized.

Canning went missing on New Years Day 1753, claiming to have been abducted in Moorfields by two ruffians who robbed her, stripped her, struck her on the temple, and dragged her to a house on the Hertfordshire Road. There, she alleged, an old woman solicited her to "go their way" (become a prostitute) and when she refused the old woman, Mary Squires, she kidnapped her to a nearby house, cut off her stays, and confined her to an upstairs room, giving her only a jug of water and bread to live on. Nearly a month later she reappeared at her mother's door; she was half-naked, emaciated, unable even to swallow. On January 29th Canning escaped through a window and—thin and ailing—groped her way back to her mother's house. When she told her story to family and neighbors most thought she had been taken to Susannah ("Mother") Wells's well-known house of ill repute at

Figure 11.1. John Hill and Mary Squires, the so-called gypsy woman, 1753.
Reproduced by kind permission of the Trustees of the British Museum.

Enfield Wash, about ten miles north of London. Canning repeated her story two days later before an alderman in the Guildhall and a warrant for Mother Wells's arrest was issued.

On February 1st Canning, her mother, and a number of friends traveled up to Enfield Wash accompanied by an officer of the Lord Mayor. Canning was taken from room to room until she identified the particular loft as the place in which she had been held captive. Among the house's inhabitants that day she selected a gypsy, Mary Squires, as the woman who had cut off her stays and thrust her into captivity. A local magistrate committed Squires for trial for stealing the stays, with Susannah Wells as accessory, and six days later Canning was examined by Fielding in his capacity as justice of the peace for Middlesex and Westminster, the same Fielding who had been so active among the Junta contra Hill in 1752.

Fielding, according to a contemporary commentator, was "duped by female artifice and cunning,"[2] convinced by Canning's story and issued a warrant against all the inhabitants in Mother Wells's household. Subsequent proceedings were conducted without rigorous evidence and Virtue Hall, from Wells's house, was bullied into telling a story closely resembling Canning's, which, with the aid of Canning's solicitor, was incorporated into the deposition. Squires and Wells went on trial on February 21st before a packed Old Bailey, the newspapers having given the case far more attention than the paper wars. Conflicting evidence of Canning and Squires rocked the case, some of it related to the change from old- to new-style calendar. Squires's claim was that she and her family were traveling down in Dorset at the time of the alleged abduction. As Canning went missing early in January 1753, the change in dating styles led to considerable confusion, both at the trial of the women she had accused of kidnapping her and at Canning's own subsequent trial for perjury. Witnesses on both sides frequently were asked whether they were using old- or new-style dating ("Do you remember when you kept Christmas Day?" or "What January do you mean?" and so forth), and many of them seem to have been muddled about it.

Canning retold her tale, corroborated by Hall, while three defense witnesses supported Squires's alibi. A number of other witnesses were prevented by the mob from entering the Sessions house. Nevertheless, the jury found Squires and Wells guilty, and five days later, on February 26th, Wells was sentenced to branding on the thumb and six months in jail, while Squires was sentenced to death by hanging, which was the maximum sentence by law if she had committed the crime. Before receiving the sentence Squires pleaded an alibi in which the details differed from the defense evidence at the trial.

Now enter celebrity-Hill, whose intervention changed its course. Had he been some unknown he could not have pulled weight, but "the Inspector" had infected the whole "Town." Hill had been active behind the scenes to persuade Squires to retract her confession, and when Crisp Gascoyne, the London mayor, suspected Canning was not telling the truth their forces combined. First Hill raised a subscription from his house inviting clergymen to contribute to save the destitute old woman. Then he began to devote his *Inspector* papers to the case; in the latter he explained how "The Lord Mayor is going around taking more evidence on the Canning affair."[3] He handsomely gave all credit to the Lord Mayor and none to himself. Lord Mayor is Sir Crisp Gascoyne who, like most London mayors of the early 1750s, learned that they could not function without the semblance of transparency. He had no desire to offend Fielding, and his magistrate-tribe, but he must demonstrate the goodwill to ascertain the facts. Gascoyne obtained an affidavit from witnesses swearing that Squires was in Dorset on New Year's Day, Hill's coercion worked, Gascoyne summoned her, she recanted in his presence, the death sentence was placed in abeyance, and Gascoyne wrote to George II—so notorious had the case become—to express his doubt about the old gypsy woman's guilt. But not without Fielding and Hill having numerous exchanges. Fielding, after all, was adjudicating the case.

By mid-March Hill's account of the "story" appeared.[4] Written by candlelight from his lodgings in Hart Street in Bloomsbury and defending Canning, Hill replied to Fielding's earlier published account, suggesting the magistrate had been duped, and winning much popular acclaim in the newspapers for championing her case.[5] "The Doctor's Pen," wrote the journalist in *Canning's Magazine*, which had been started up just to chronicle the events, "that has been so long and so eminently distinguished in the polite world, in Vindication of a poor, abject, despicable old Gypsy. . . ."[6] But Fielding would not change his mind and further acrimony ensued between the chief rivals: himself and Hill. During April and May further turns and twists occurred and on May 30th, five months after Canning's disappearance, Squires was pardoned by George II and brought before the Lord Mayor to be discharged, while Wells served out her six-month prison sentence.

Four factors turned the conviction in Squires' favor: blatant inconsistencies in Canning's story, the Lord Mayor's humanity, the widespread discussion of minorities that spring as the so-called "Jew Bill" advocating the

Figure 11.2. Caricature of John Hill, with Henry Fielding, as one of "The Conjurers," 1753.

right of Jews to vote heated up—and, finally, Hill's intervention played out through his rivalry with Fielding. This was one occasion when their antagonism had a beneficial outcome both in the law and for Hill's morale. Fielding remained silent when Hill published two further *Inspector* papers on June 2nd and 7th, 1753, defending Squires, as Fielding must also have been when the court recorder read out the sentence:[7]

> It is with horror that I look back, and think of the evidence you [Canning] gave at the trial of Mary Squires, who you knew to be destitute and friendless, and thereof fixed upon her as a proper object to make a sacrifice of, at the dreadful expence of a false oath. . . . This audacious attempt, and that of calm and deliberate assurance with which you formed a scheme to take away life of one (though the most abject) of the human species, together with your youth, and the character you then had, as well as your seeming inexperience, imposed on many. . . .[8]

Hill could not have intervened so forcefully in the old gypsy's case without the experience he gained in the paper wars, and Canning's sentence—and Fielding's accompanying defeat—further boosted his spirit. The paper wars had badly bruised him, but he was a survivor and fighter. The double-header is more significant for his life at the time than the intricacies of the case over its six-month life; for example, the formation of two camps—the "Canningites" with Fielding as their head and the "Egyptians" with Gascoyne and Hill as leaders. For one thing the new feud eased Hill's obvious losses against the coalition where Fielding was so prominent; for another, it buoyed him at just the moment, in June, when it was becoming apparent that the "Inspector" must soon cease. The precise reasons for its demise remain unknown—they must have included finances and the sense that the public had been cloyed long enough—but whatever historical forces combined they nevertheless brought to a close a major phase of the "Inspector's" restless life.

Furthermore, Hill now approached his fortieth birthday, approaching on November 17, 1754, just one year distant, a significant landmark, and no matter how "amorous," he remained widowed. His search for patronage had come to naught, the *Inspector* had just "died," he was increasingly vilified even if the Canning case vindicated him—and he was a single man. He could overlook the death of his first wife four years earlier through the long period when he worked feverishly, but during the last year he heard the clock ticking. If he were to marry again and raise a family this was the time to become domesticated; both parents were dead, and he saw little, if anything, of his brother Theophilus Jr. and his family in faraway Lincoln or sister Anne. The siblings had never been close.

Inspector 158, written early in 1752, recounts how a woman conveniently called "Eliza" met a gentleman at Ranelagh. At first she does not like him.

But he strikes up a conversation with a female relation of hers, endears himself to the lady, then her family, and soon his "vast conversation" wins over the woman. Can this have been the young, Irish, wealthy Henrietta who would come with a sizable dowry? We do not say "beautiful" because no portrait of Henrietta survives, but the Hill we know would not have married an unprepossessing wife; not at this vulnerable time, when he was engaged in such frantic publication and paper warfare. The lady in Hill's *Inspector* has no title but whatever her pedigree it was niches above her future husband's.

This was indeed Henrietta Jones (?–1801), sister of Charles Jones, soon to be the new Viscount Ranelagh of County Roscommon in Ireland.[9] Their great-grandfather had been the famous Viscount Ranelagh, Richard Jones, for whom the famous pleasure gardens in Chelsea were named and about whom Jonathan Swift had penned shrewd assessments of his projects. Among his quasi-Marxist dreams was a scheme for aristocrats to marry the sons and daughters of the poor: by this intermixture and diversity the nation would be saved. But he had died in 1712 before his "project" could be enacted and his title became extinct, remaining so for half a century until Charles Jones, a great-grandson and Henrietta's brother, thought it would raise his status in the world if he revived it.

Charles was then in his twenties, an eldest son soon to inherit the estates of his ailing father; a young, swashing buck who often came to "Town" to live it up in London. The Joneses were rich by the 1750s and Charles ambitious; he would later build Monkstown House, almost at the site of the current Dun Laoghaire Harbor near Dublin, and raise sons who rose in Nelson's navy. For the moment he made merry across the Irish Sea in decadent London where younger sister Henrietta joined him and stayed the season, never again to return home. Hill did not meet her in Ireland, never having traveled there, nor would he. Somehow, somewhere, he was introduced to this marriageable daughter who came with a sizable dowry. They married in September 1753 in the Chapel of St. George in Hyde Park Corner.[10] Six years later, in 1759, brother Charles was installed as Fourth Viscount Ranelagh.

Henrietta's character must be stitched together from her husband's married life and the account she left of him thirteen years after his death. She was steadfast and determined to be a responsible mother. She probably retained her Irish accent too. Some years after Hill's death in 1775, John Wolcot, alias "Peter Pindar," visited her with a few actors. She was then a widow of "considerable age" and he found her as personable as she was still handsome, but he had been taken there without being told the name of his hostess and when asked he replied that he imagined she must be "the widow of some Irish lord." Nothing is known about her piety or beliefs but no reason exists to think she deviated from the routines of Anglican teaching. She was certainly not Catholic, nor did she bring up their children as Catholics.

Henrietta had no title when she married—just money. She was the single sister of a young gentleman in Ireland who would soon inherit land and wealth but had not yet. Years later, as we shall see, she became "Lady Henrietta Hill" when husband Hill was awarded a Swedish knighthood. For the time being her greatest asset was the dowry she brought to their marriage enabling Hill to continue his schemes in Grub Street while also permitting them to live in style at fashionable West-End residences. This time Hill married "up" and—if lapsed aristocrats can still be considered titled—he married well. But neither she nor others styled her "Lady Hill" in 1753, nor did her ambitious husband.

From the start she was remarkably loyal. Her reasons are unclear—perhaps it was in her nature—but as the years progressed her devotion increased and endured until John's death. A biographer should ask hard questions about the characters of his *dramatis personae*: if Henrietta could be reincarnated and asked one question only it would pertain to her reasons for such unflinching loyalty. History is littered with fanatically loyal wives but only a few were ever married to Notorious Hills. Henrietta outlived John by almost thirty years, dying in 1802, and continuing his crusades and fighting his cause to her last breath as a martyr-widow.

She gave him at least six children in very rapid succession: two Johns (one replaced the other in infant mortality), Joseph, Juliana, Sarah, Margaret, and Wilhelmina.[11] Not enough is known about Henrietta's psychology, or biology, to speculate why she procreated so profusely. Five children were born by early 1759, but Juliana, Sarah, and Wilhelmina did not survive infancy. Then, another three girls between 1761 and 1765, identically named to replace them, except for Catherine. Juliana, the youngest of these three daughters of the second round, was born in October 1764; her last child, the one who would never marry and remain with her mother. All totaled, Henrietta had given birth to at least ten children, in two rounds, of which five appear to have survived into adulthood.[12] Therefore Hill was, if anything, a family man; with huge domestic outlays needed to support all these hungry mouths, living and dying, in addition to his own excesses and lavish lifestyle.

The sons had such common names (John Hill, Joseph Hill) it has not been possible so far to identify them, nor did they achieve anything memorable whose record has survived. One son, Joseph Gulston Hill, became a soldier and joined the Indian Army in its Madras Cadets.[13] He left England only two years after his father's death in 1775 and remained in India for the rest of his life. Years later in the 1780s, after Hill was dead and Henrietta embattled in legal frays over the royalties of the recipes of his medicines, she was plunged into debt by borrowing £250 to buy Joseph an "Officer's Cadetship in the East India Company's Service."[14] Their other son, John, continues to be elusive.

Margaret (1754–1828), also known as Ann when young, eventually married into the Hemp family and moved to Stoke Newington, her barber-surgeon husband James Hemp (1754–1837) assuming the Mastership of the Barber's Company in 1825, three years before her death. The Hemps had been apothecaries and barbers for generations, like her father Hill. It was through Margaret Hill that the portrait of John as a young surgeon, featured on this book's jacket, came to Barbers-Surgeon's Hall in London.[15] It had hung on their sitting-room wall in Stoke Newington ever since Allan Ramsey painted it—Margaret always proud of her illustrious father who had died when she was twenty-one.

Only the second, surviving Juliana—Margaret's youngest sister named after Henrietta (Juliana was Henrietta's middle name)—has left a direct trail owing to her proximity to her mother after her father's death in 1775.[16] She would never marry or give them grandchildren but was loyal in other ways. Besides, Hill was fifty by the time she and her two sisters (of the second round) were born in the 1760s—then an old father. He would not live sufficiently long to see grandchildren even if Juliana had married. Our protagonist was too unfortunate to become a grandfather, not even through his eldest surviving daughter Margaret. By the 1750s, when Margaret was born, he was overworked. By the 1760s, when the rest of the brood came along, he was exhausted and ailing. Perhaps too worn out to lament he would never live to see grandchildren.

Flashing back to 1753 and the new bride Henrietta, they found Hill's old lodgings in St. James's too small for this growing tribe, and migrated to larger accommodation in Hart Street in Bloomsbury, near the site of the present Bloomsbury Square, a nearby road that no longer exists today. Given Hill's intuitive method of selecting topics for publication it would be characteristic if his wooing of Henrietta, occurring just as the lively debates about Lord Hardwicke's Marriage Act were being discussed, had not spurred him to write about his own courtship and marriage. This he did in the *Conduct of a Married Life*. Robert Baldwin published it in June 1753 on strict condition that Hill disguise his identity.[17]

Here Hill posed as "the Honorable Juliana Seymour"—one of Henrietta's middle names—persuaded the domestic argument would be more cogent if set out by a woman, like Henrietta, of minor aristocratic pedigree. What was this minor gender change for a man who had, a decade earlier, pretended to be a "foreign Empiric," disguised in different national costumes? The *Conduct of a Married Life* is framed as an epistolary tract pretending to be the "genuine letters" of a recently married woman to her equally young, and still unmarried, cousin. The new strategy of anonymity or de facto alias worked, if its reception was an indication. A decade later, in 1766, a young gentleman in Southampton, on the verge of marriage, or perhaps having just been married, wrote in the margins of his copy: "Miss Seymour's treatment is more realistic than that in our modern novels."[18] It may have been but was also less insightful. Hill addressed his readers in nineteen "letters" covering the main components of marriage—two partners, their appropriate treatment of each other, the affective dimensions, hurdles, problem resolution, and life outside the home—except that he deferred for a follow-up "next year" a work, which Baldwin also published, on the management of children. The new work emphasizes two areas of childhood, the affective and the moral, and divulges "I am a Female Moralist . . . and would direct my Thoughts to the Heart."

A surprising number of topics converged with those Samuel Johnson would address in his marriage debates in *Rasselas* four years later (1759) and Hill's "moral treatment" also evolves from the moral and psychological realm. "Seymour's" view has strengths but appears old-fashioned; and "her" notion marriage seems retrograde in 1753 and insufficiently problematic to satisfy the complex dynamic of what post-Richardsonian marriage had become by then. Seymour also stunned some readers when declaiming the universal weakness of women in: "The Law of God ordains it. We [wives and mothers] are weak and useless to the World, they [husbands] are our Support and our Defence. . ."; worse yet, that this view of women does not apply to just "one Country or one Time" but for "all the World, and . . . all Ages . . . in all places."[19] This part misfired as did Seymour's praise of English men for being "the least Superior" over their wives "of any country in the world," or when she strikes out at masquerades and denounces Summer Evenings at Ranelagh as "something mean in People of Virtue and Decency mixing with the Herd of common Prostitutes, and abandoned Rakes. . . ."[20]

This was odd cant coming from Hill, or was he still smarting from Mountefort Browne's lashes and newly reformed? Either way, his reputation was growing as an author who skirted the fringes of pornography. This was the new charge his opponents relished. Their old ones had been exhausted through repetition. A lascivious Hill—sexually ambivalent, prurient to the fingernails—added to their grist. Small wonder, they claimed, he dwelled at such length at the trials on the horrors of Canning's kidnap into the slavery of prostitution.

Meanwhile Hill was a new husband and father-to-be during that autumn of 1753, so his thoughts turned again to patronage and reverted to posts. For months the "Inspector" had his eye on proposals for the newly forming "British Museum," the first repository and library of national treasures.[21] Hill's correspondence in 1753–1755 with committee members and aristocratic patrons, especially Newcastle and Northumberland, demonstrates how ardently he chased a post there;[22] doing so meant gaining the favor of the selection committee that included Thomas Birch and other members of the Royal Society who dominated the committee. The mechanism for selection was complex: the Crown had entrusted the Lord Chancellor, Speaker of the House, and Archbishop of Canterbury with nomination of the officers, and a codicil to Sloane's will further mandated that the officers of the new museum would be appointed by the heads of three families: Cotton, Harley, and Sloane. The "Act for the Purchase of the Museum or Collection of Sir Hans Sloane, and the Harleian Collection of Manuscripts" had long since passed.[23] Hill judged his former ties to Birch favorable, and thought his prior supplications to Newcastle and Northumberland would count for something. Birch had been a core member of Parsons's "Wednesday circle," where he admired Hill's bravura and knowledge of the natural world, and since then watched Hill's movements with awe. He had, we recall, lamented the "Inspector's" demise on July 7, yet had also just started a term as Secretary of the Royal Society and was actively writing its history.[24] If anyone understood the debacle over Hill's election it was Birch.

When Sloane died on January 11, 1753, Birch was at the forefront of those ready to follow his will to establish the new museum as soon as possible and he served as its very first trustee. The deceased Sloane was, of course, its patriarch, and Birch, the Society's secretary, its ardent promoter. He sat in the front row of the ceremony on June 7th to open its doors—just as Canning was beginning her prison sentence—and worked hard over the next six months to pave the way for the first meeting of its fifteen trustees who constituted some of the men Hill had been petitioning.[25] Hill sought the post of principal librarian or superintendent but had no chance.[26]

The reason centered on the competition: Dr. Gowin Knight (1713–1772), physician and inventor of geomagnetic instruments, Oxford educated gentleman of science par excellence, respected FRS and other equivalent societies, as perfect a member of the virtuous Republic as could be found in England.[27] Knight embodied every quality Hill did not, especially in the techniques of self-promotion; and it counted for little that he was reclusive and irascible, that he had antagonized fellow scientists, or that he lived alone. Equally minimal that Samuel Johnson and others deplored his methods of marketing his magnets and his temperamental stealth. Knight had the right connections, even if he had lost to rival Birch the post of secretary in the Royal Society just two years earlier in 1751. And he was also close to Benjamin Wilson and Henry Baker, the same men who recoiled from Hill.[28]

Confusion has ensued about the Trustees: they were not the three families themselves but their nominated representatives. Given the prominence then of the Royal Society, it could be expected that the families would rely upon the FRS rather than Whig lords like Northumberland and Newcastle and other patrons Hill leaned on to decide. The committee probably did not seriously consider Hill's candidacy; if they had, they would have felt obliged to acknowledge that Knight would be there all the time: a hands-on man for the job. A confirmed bachelor, he had lived in Crane Court since 1750, where he was perpetually present and would do the same at the new museum. Hill, in contrast, was hands-off: gadding about t'Town, courting wine, women, and song, and even if he meticulously classified the collections and mounted exhibitions he could not be assumed to be there all the time.

The selection process extended over two years. Hill was aware of Knight as his competitor and supplicated Northumberland to intervene. He claimed to have received word from Macclesfield, another trustee with sufficient profile because he had recently been elected President of the Royal Society—that Knight "has not all the necessary Qualifications." Hill proceeded further, claiming to quote Macclesfield verbatim that he would not "obstruct" Hill's nomination nor "stir any step farther in that gentlemans [Knight] favour." It is unlikely, although not impossible that Hill fabricated the letter from Macclesfield, nor has it been found. But Knight's qualifications counted for more and their competition lingered—at least in Hill's mind—until Knight was elected on January 6, 1756.

Having won the post he remained at the museum until his death in 1772. For £200 a year, he acted as live-in caretaker, responsible for displaying the exhibits and supervising public access, and played a key role in the adoption of the Linnaean system of classification, while also carrying on the *de rigueur* international correspondence with the ever-increasing networks of the Republic to enlarge the collections. £200 would not have seemed a princely sum to Hill in his extravagant mode during his glove-and-carriage inspectorial years (1751–1753), but now, after 1754, when he had neither patron nor reliable income and a growing family, it would have more than sufficed.

Knight's own profile was far from perfect and the Trustees eventually came to regret their appointment. He was irritable and ungracious; a loner apparently given to fierce mood swings and raging tantrums with other staff. He had fewer public rows than Hill but when they occurred they amounted to unrelenting dogfights in which he refused to surrender, as in cases over the priority of his naval instruments. He persistently declined to divulge his magnetizing techniques and forged a reputation as a curmudgeon. Hill would have been more charming and could have dazzled the Trustees but the FRS botanists would not support him—without their endorsement he had no chance of gaining the post.

He fretted that he had given offense to his would-be patrons, especially Northumberland and Newcastle, Birch and Herring, for championing the gypsy woman. A pathetic letter to Northumberland captures his anxiety and demonstrates how even these powerful public figures were caught up.[29] "Pray write me word," the Lord Chancellor, Hardwicke, wrote to Birch from Cambridge very late in June, "what the general opinion is now about Canning, & whether any further Light is yet thrown upon that dark Story and Inspector Hill." Two days later, on June 30th, Birch replied, "The story of Canning is still the Subject of Conversation here, & people are impatient to see what Light will be given into the real Merits of it by the Tryals after term or at the next Session upon the cross Bills of Perjury. . . ."[30] During those "trials" Hill knew which side he was on, but not without chafing whether it had cost him the post.

Perhaps he would have taken heart from Johnson's wisdom about the great Dutch physician, Herman Boerhaave, if he could have read about it: "Providence seldom sends any into the world with an inclination to attempt great things, who have no abilities, likewise to perform them."[31] Was Hill not living proof?

NOTES

1. Judith Moore (1994); Rousseau (2001); Straub (2009); the primary literature is summarized in Moore's book.
2. Newman (1799), vol. 4, 177.
3. *LDA* (March 10, March 14); *Inspectors* 625 and 627.
4. JH (1753f).
5. Henry Fielding (1753).
6. Cited in Judith Moore (1994), 109.
7. *LDA* 2 (June 7, 1753).
8. *State Trials*: 19: 491–92, quoted in Judith Moore (1994). 163–64.
9. Henrietta was born during the years 1712–1722; much archival search makes it difficult to pinpoint her birth more definitively. The chronology of her childbearing life, as we shall see, suggests that she could not have been older than forty-seven in 1769, and was probably in her early thirties when she married JH. I owe this information, based on baptismal records in various parishes of her children, to British genealogist Colin LeMessurier.
10. See LPH, 188.
11. Most of these children are found in the Westminster Archive baptismal records and several are named in JH's Will (see LPH, 185–90); the task of identification is exacerbated by the common name Hill and voluminous records often compiled in scarcely legible hands. Two British archivists, Colin LeMessurier and Roger Power, assisted me to compile the complex genealogy of JH's children.
12. See the manuscript Records of Baptisms, St. George, Hanover Square, vol. 2, index, for the years 1757–1769.
13. I owe this information, culled from East India archives and the Madras Military Fund records, to Roger Powell.
14. See below 305–8 for her debts and lawsuit.
15. I owe this information about Margaret Ann Hemp to archivist Dr. Richard Palmer. An oil painting of her also survives, the only one of JH's children thus memorialized.
16. Juliana was a year younger than Margaret and baptized on November 15, 1755; see Baptismal records of St. James, Piccadilly, Westminster.
17. JH (1753a).
18. Marginalia by "James Hilgrove" (unidentified) on the title page of the Dublin edition of 1753 in the BL.
19. JH (1753a), 173.
20. The passages are found, respectively, at JH (1753a), 164 and 201.
21. Edward Edwards (1996); A. E. Gunther (1979); A. E. Gunther (1980); A. MacGregor (1994).
22. LPH, 61–66.
23. 26 George II, c. 22.
24. See 180.

25. MacGregor (1994), chapter 1.
26. Edward Edwards (1996), 298–309.
27. The most persuasive account is found in Fara, passim.
28. A. E. Gunther (1979); A. E. Gunther (1980).
29. LPH, 57–58.
30. BL Add MSS 35398, f. 125.
31. James Samuelson, *Life of Hermann Boerhaave,* in *Collected Works of Samuel Johnson,* 9 vols. (Oxford: Talboys and Wheeler 1825), vol. 6, 275.

IV

12

Philosophy, Botany, and History

By the end of 1754 Hill was burned out of paper warfare and going broke.[1] He had become more "notorious" than "celebrated" but was still impelled to lie low—almost to hide. Perhaps he would have agreed with Samuel Johnson's recent definition in *Rambler* 165: "I did not find myself enriched in proportion to my celebrity." Either way he took stock: the "Inspector" was effectively dead, he had roasted enemies and they him, and during the toasting had lost his network of naturalists, including his close all-important quondam associate da Costa. Only generous old Dr. Stukeley remained faithful, as he had been throughout the "*Inspectorial*" battles, and was prepared to make one-off monetary loans but had no ability to patronize Hill or offer him a pension. His securest hope was long-term patronage of the type that a post in the new British Museum would have provided through the great Whig lords he had courted.

He considered the prospects. Frederick, Prince of Wales, had supported diverse naturalists and botany was his greatest passion, but he died in 1751, leaving a hole. Pelham, still prime minister until 1754, and Newcastle, his most important minister, soon to succeed him, inherited some of this clientele provided they clearly demonstrated Whig values and could meld into a Whig world dominated by Whig views.[2] Northumberland was less politically inclined; to some he appeared singularly apolitical. He had patronized sundry types in town and country—at Northumberland House and Sion House in Middlesex—and his socialite duchess had acquired an artistic coterie shown off at their balls and gatherings. Frederick's widow, the Princess Augusta, had just employed Bute—the great lover of botany—to tutor her son George in Leicester House, their London residence, where Bute had an apartment. Hill set out to find a patron in this company.

Figure 12.1. The third Earl of Bute.

Reproduced by kind permission of the Wellcome Library, London.

Contrary to what he thought his incessant scribbling counted against him—if only he had written a fraction of it. Serious botanists published one or two books in a lifetime, if their collections merited print. Peter Collinson, Linnaeus's main English representative, is a perfect example: he was humble, sensitive, and notably lacking in publication, even in his native Swedish language. Even Hill intuited he must slow down—after 1753—and cease his attacks, so he set about writing natural history books dedicated to noble lords who might take notice. The first of these had been planned while he was still immersed in Grub Street and he titled it *Essays in Natural History and Philosophy,* a work of over four hundred pages "containing a series of discoveries, by the assistance of microscopes," and dedicated it to the Earl of Orrery, a keen botanist who had shown interest in *The Inspector* and seemed a good prospect.[3]

Hill wrote more deftly here than at any time since *Lucina.* The *Essays* do not contain original ideas when compared to the major thinkers of natural history but the power of observation is noteworthy, in part because he enjoyed a temporary respite from the obsession with himself. He names his heroes in natural history—John Ray (who had also been his father's) and John Woodward[4]—for fastidiousness in identifying specimens and stating where they found them, strews his text with classical references, and rhapsodizes the natural world—all within broad botanical reading from the English naturalists to the French botanists, especially Antoine de Jussieu (1686–1758), the Keeper of the Jardins des Plantes in Paris who is often cited.

The main achievement is making the unseen visible through words. Writing within a Horatian doctrine of *utile dulci,* instruction and pleasure, he demonstrates himself subjected to the tyranny of his anatomical eye, his "master," but still profiting from its magical powers: a position he may have transported from the roving "Inspector's eye" who wanders t'Town looking for news. For teasing out the "seen in the unseen" he has been termed a "scopophiliac" by art historians and warmly praised too: "no text [of the epoch] more cogently posed questions . . . and [proposed] purposes." He further presents natural history as "an allurement": a seductive enticement the natural object poses for the anatomical eye. The *Essays* have no plates nor do they need them; Hill's empowered "eyes" convey graphic images through vivified words. In brief, they are everything the *Inspector* columns, for the most part, were not.

He is particularly adept at dramatizing predators without sentiment, placing them center stage to show "Nature red in tooth and claw" as intrinsic in the predatory chain. His penchant for morality surfaces whenever he displays the weak revenging themselves on the mighty, yet animated description of the endless chain of destruction is his main theme. Nor does he sentimentalize the predatory moment: he seizes on "killers" large to small, each predator victimizing smaller fry and perhaps identified with them in some grubbean, eat-up milieu whose Darwinian survival tactics he knew firsthand. The "arts of death," as he calls them for their competitive edge, were no strangers to Hill and he historically was one of the first natural history writers to excel in this mode exposing nature's fiercely fanged butchery.

To achieve intimate contact between himself and the natural object within its habitat he eschews the dialogic form. Dialogic voices demonstrating different points of view are astray from his field of vision. The surprises he conveys verbally must be expressed in the first person. A generation later Jeremiah Joyce (1763–1816), a popularizer of science during the Regency, read Hill's *Essays* and was moved by their first-person animation. His pace is swift; images flow toward each other briskly, as if personified at the level of dramatic characters involved in action. Each creature is given a dominant human emotion: the caterpillar is "helpless" when "assaulted" by the predator, the minute insect "almost infantile" when snapped up by the lightening bird's speed, and so forth.

But the constant theme is the need for ever-stronger microscopes, which he calls the "great enhancer of Science," and if "Men of Curiosity would desist from repeating old Experiments and . . . launch out into new Sources of Life . . ." they would find "the eternal Charm of Novelty."[5] These stronger microscopes permit heightened vision of his rituals of death, as when the fly devoured the caterpillar: "the Violence of the Whirl put the whole Fluid scene into a strange Confusion."[6] Chapters 3 and 19, respectively entitled "On the Nature and Properties of an Insect not before known" and "On the Nature and Qualities of an Insect inhabiting subterranean Waters," amount to a series of deadly sub-optical scenes; each time the predator's triumph destroying the victim's hope for its own nourishment, for "the Creature lay . . . in Expectation of its Food" only to find itself fatally "gorged."[7] Did pre-Darwinian Hill glimpse parallels in these dances of death between the microscopic world and his own unrelenting plight? The "I" so prevalent in the *Inspector* is absent here, as it was in *Lucina* two years earlier, and Hill always wrote best when forgetting himself, overlooking offenses and slights.

He sees warlike insects invading inanimate objects, in one case infiltrating the hollow joints of a species of coralline. Elsewhere the creatures are so vicious he must reclassify their basic nature from "pacific" to "violent," and sometimes he cuts across phylogenies from animal to mineral and mineral to vegetable, in one case christening them "fierce Minims of Existence." Nor does he assume that because an animal is large it automatically is a vicious beast of prey. The passages crest to prove the validity of Shakespeare's phrase about the "minims": "We are apt to suppose Nature has lavished all her Bounty upon her larger Creatures, and left these Minims of Existence, as *Shakespeare* phrases it, unfinished, and scarce half made up."[8]

Even the smallest "devils" invisible to the eye locate smaller creatures—seemingly no larger than animalcules—which they devour in this race to death. But death is never uniform: "Every one of the hungry Inhabitants of my coralline seemed like a *Briarus*, crushing different objects at one instant in his different Arms, and dealing out Destruction so many Ways at once." From this observation into "the Arts of Death" he grows ruminative about cosmic death at large, from vermin upward to mankind, impressed by the infinite variety of destruction's forms. He teases out a type of Blakean innocence in the meek preyed upon by the more violent, and then returns to his magnifying glass to hone in on these "arts of death" in nature's "kingdom of Slaughter."

Perhaps this was Hill's main philosophical difference from fellow microscopist Turberville Needham, discussed in connection with *Lucina*. Needham's biological microscopy taught Hill one profound lesson: a universal analogy based on a vitalistic principle at work throughout the universe. But Hill sensed its ambiguity nevertheless and acknowledged its materialism—the vitalism within materialism. Observations of the teeming wonders of nature impressed Needham for the rhapsodic transport they produced in him.[9] Hill also succumbed to these raptures but was more eager to pin down the reasons; rather than rhapsodize them to dramatize them in graphic words, which heightened his observational experience rather than diminished or obliterated it.

I have dwelled on Hill's *Essays* for their visual rhetorics, but Hill also vivified his philosophical perception of the microcosmic universe and peered into the connections between botany and the sexual topics his society was addressing.[10] The latter covered a broad spectrum at mid-century, including the flood of erotica hitting the book market; but now—in the 1750s—the open discussions themselves were more notable than strands in their argument. Hill sees, for example, the "paramecium"—as he once referred to miniscule creatures too small to be gleaned by the naked eye—ruling among the "small wonders of the natural world," and superimposes his reliance on the new compound microscope to his vivid adjectives, energized verbs, personifications and sexual innuendoes.[11] This was a new style of botanical writing, particularly for its imaginative personifications;[12] within a generation it was perfected in *Zoonomia* (1786) by Erasmus Darwin who learned much from Hill's *Essays* and British herbals.[13] Just as the "Inspector" never roved without his pad and quill, Hill the naturalist never wandered without his magnifying glass. He was mid-century's microscopical prose-poet excelling in the art of minute description despite not writing verse. The poetry of botany would not take off for another generation, in Clare and Wordsworth, but Hill found his prose adequate to his purposes.

This integration of observation and expression might have provided clues into Hill's religion, which was minimal and never appears to have altered over the course of a lifetime. For the most part he was an Anglican who rarely went to church. Neither success nor failure dented his view, but the brutal designs of his microcosmic predators enforced the sense that whenever extreme assault, or violation, occurs in nature it has a logic. He is wrenched, for example, when he watches a fly murderously attack a caterpillar on a mulberry leaf. The killer fly is unrelenting, stabbing its victim a dozen times when half would have sufficed. Hill fathoms no reason why, carries the leaf home for further observation with his magnifying glass, to learn only that both fly and caterpillar are female and that the stabs are secure means to deposit eggs. Relieved, he reiterates his belief that divine order never deviates from its clockwork plan. There are no exceptions to nature's laws for Hill.

Other occasions shed light on his sexual imagination. Having written little that was explicitly sexual in the decade of *Fanny Hill*, when he could have extracted capital from it, one wonders where he stood philosophically. He had been heterosexually amorous, hardly immune to temptations of the flesh, having kept mistresses, and as someone immersed in medicine he understood the body's tugs firsthand. When he turns to the sexual dimensions of the natural kingdom, under the microscope, the predatory female fly behaves in ferocious masculine fashion toward the equally female caterpillar: laying eggs that will destroy the mother caterpillar and prevent her from becoming a butterfly. Their young appear to be neuter as they continue to gnash through the mother's flesh; not even their gnawing declares them male or female. The scene is eroticized and medicalized—especially the warring females followed by the caterpillar's inflictions, sufferings, and eventual death through implosion—but not presented according to the rules of gender.

Reviewers, overshadowed by his antics in the paper wars, ignored this whole side of philosophical Hill. Matthew Maty, a polymathic physician who, like Gowan Knight, also assumed a Keeper's post in the new British Museum, wrote about Hill's *Essays* but was oblivious to their vivid presentation.[14] One wonders how attentively he read them or whether he was so predisposed in his disfavor that he judged them not worth the effort despite his reflections. But Hill's natural history was his best writing and would remain so to the end of his life. He can seem impossibly incoherent: addicted to paper wars and adroit in verbalizing the natural world. He was regrettably divided in this way—if only he had suppressed the former.

His tendency to personal isolation did not help, and he was not—as became clear at the Bedford—clubbable unless he could "rule." Some time in 1754 he joined the Antigalligan Society that met at the Lebeck's Head, a tavern at the corner of Half-Moon Street in the Strand, fashionable in the mid-fifties for admitting the financially successful. Its spearhead was John Sherratt (1718–1788), a con artist who had already declared bankruptcy twice, the second time in concert with John Trusler, the manager-owner of the Marylebone Pleasure Gardens, one of Hill's favorite places. But his main task remained the search for patronage, and Stukeley—still alive but failing—wrote testimonials, often sending him copies, and sympathizing about the support of a family. In October 1754 Stukeley petitioned the Princess of Wales, saying that Hill would be the perfect man to shape her new gardens adjoining Kensington Palace.

His writing pace abated from the miraculous two years—mid-1751–1753—but he still produced five titles: a *Gardener's Pocket-Book* (a sort of country gentleman's *vade mecum*); a farce called *The Maiden Whim; or, The Critical Minute* that was never performed; and three scientific works: one titled *Urania* about *all* the sciences, a "family herbal," and a third book about the management of children—this last compelling for filling a gap in the growing literature about the upbringing of children.[15]

Provided he stuck with natural history and had no one to attack he fared well. In August the *GM* advertised *The Useful Family Herbal* where Hill expounded how a kitchen garden would enrich British diet and increase health.[16] Hill had filled the gap Cheyne left a decade earlier, which no one had despite the purchase power of readers wanting "how-to-do-it" books for health; not merely country folk in the shires, or Methodists who welcomed John Wesley's *Primitive Physick* (1747), but metropolitan dwellers too. William Owens's press attractively published it with the puff that every family needs a copy. It is easy to use and has a full index; its approach arising from the "natural world" rather than panaceas such as Bishop Berkeley's "tar water" or Ward's "pill and drop." It was a plug for ordinary "kitchen physic"—what every housewife should have to hand near her back door.

Hyssop had gained a following during the 1740s and is here recommended to reduce fever, and alleviate bronchitis and inflammatory disorders. So too chamomile, lavender, valerian, hobs, and catnip for sleep and nerves. The idea was to encourage the widespread planting of kitchen gardens, small and large, if one did not already have one, and it anticipated the modern "miracle herbs" movement. Occasionally Hill combined ingredients to promote potions, as when recommending "devil's bit" for wasted lungs in cold English climes; a drink of strange ingredients—nails, claws, bitter roots—which some reader-patients must have resisted.[17] Compared to the restorative chamomile and hyssop he promoted it must have struck those looking for advice about their lungs as ridiculously foul.

That autumn Hill retained his accommodation in Hart Street, just a few hundred yards down the road from the warring Wits at the "Great Room," a type of theater used for lectures and dramatic performances. For several years he had juggled personal and professional residences, often keeping multiple ones simultaneously. In December Foote feuded with his quondam teacher Charles Macklin, who established a school of oratory here at the Great Room. Foote heckled Macklin, by now an actor of stature although he had already fallen out with Garrick; Macklin avenged himself against this

"Sam Smatter, alias Mimic, alias Buffoon." Their acquaintance remained intact in that era when skins were tougher than they soon became, but Hill could not frequently look in as he was at work on a philosophical tract over four hundred pages: *Thoughts concerning God and Nature*, a reply to Bolingbroke, which he printed at his own expense and sold from his house in Bloomsbury.[18] It depleted his finances, according to his letters, and he published in the hope it would—finally—secure patronage, timing its appearance to be just before Christmas. But it was still unpublished in late February for lack of a title, according to a letter he wrote to Newcastle asking for a pension from George II.[19]

It was not so spectacular as his *Essays in Natural History and Philosophy* (1752) in resisting the late Lord Bolingbroke's (1678–1751) notion that "history is philosophy teaching by example," and evolved by ennobling those who had attacked atheism. It was an imprudent decision failing to demonstrate Hill's philosophical powers; indeed he approached Bolingbroke's deism so tangentially as to baffle his readers, some of whom had great respect for the now deceased, if flawed, statesman. William Rose, a minor journalist, endorsed Hill's treatment in a bloated review claiming that "many good things there certainly are in it; and on such a subject it would be strange indeed if there were not some."[20] But it never rose to the stratosphere of his natural history *Essays*.

The book demonstrates how his mind worked: first he came up with the idea, in this case refutation of Bolingbroke; then he imagined his patron (often the dedicatee but here it was the king) responding to the argument, here Newcastle's known orthodoxy. Then he advised the potential patron what was coming and requested his favor. Finally, he enlisted the names of other prominent figures—whether they had acquiesced to support him or not—to his patron. Here he claimed that all three archbishops "speak of it with favour," and mendaciously continued: "there are some who say I deserve a publick Reward for it [the book]: I am Sure I want it; for I have hurt my affairs extreamly by the Expence of the Publication." He concluded by imploring Newcastle whether it could lead to "a Gratuity from the King" in return for its being dedicated to him.[21]

Bolingbroke's "letters on the study of history" had been privately circulating for two decades, and approached history from a utilitarian angle, not as the product of a great philosophical mind but a distinguished politician who was sent into exile where he forced himself "to think." In France he developed a credo grounded in skepticism that led him to doubt the historian's ability to recover the distant past, and was particularly distrustful of biblical and ancient history, which he considered myth and fable embroidered with veneration. The value of history, he thought, was its moral and practical side, its promotion of social virtues; and—in this sense, and perhaps this sense only—it was philosophy teaching by example. Hill's reply, one of many since Bolingbroke's death in 1751, defended the ancients on what he understood as the legacy of Sanchoniathon (eighteenth-century spelling):[22] a Phoenician author of three lost works containing a philosophical creation story traced to the cosmogony of the Egyptian Thoth.

Sanchoniathon's cosmogony began with Erebus (the son of Chaos, said to personify darkness) and Wind, between whose forces Eros, or "desire," came into existence. The rise of Eros in turn gave rise—according to Sanchoniathon—to death, or Môt in Phoenician, in the process of whose birth the germs of life also appeared, which in turn combined to form an egg, but from this point forward the theory is unclear. Hill had grown interested in Sanchoniathon's theory of wind six years earlier when writing *Lucina*, where the all-empowering wind carries seeds to impregnate the virgin Lucina. In 1754, while preparing to counter Bolingbroke, Hill resumed his interest, as did other contemporaries, for instance Goldsmith in *The Vicar of Wakefield* and James Mackenzie, author of a much-read *History of Health*.[23] Yet Sanchoniathon had been received in Christian eras as pagan and heretical, which only a recent vogue for exotic history could camouflage. A rational skeptic like Bolingbroke had no time for him, unlike the Scottish Thomas Blackwell (1701–1757), author of *Letters concerning Mythology* (1748), who esteemed Sanchoniathon's worth while Hill, for his part, thought he could gain mileage by pitting pragmatists like Bolingbroke against traditionalists advocating him. In the end it turned out to be a wasted effort on Hill's part beyond catering to the then current wave of excitement about exotic history. Gibbon, then still a student in Oxford, recounts in the eighth book of *The History of the Decline and Fall of the Roman Empire*, how he began to write an *Age of Sesostris* extolling Sanchoniathon, which he later abandoned.

It was treacherous for the still aspiring Hill to counter a recently deceased philosopher-statesman who still commanded respect; all the more so when rumors begun that he had been the secret author of the *Memoirs of Lord Bolingbroke*.[24] He was not up to pleading the tangled cause of orthodox Anglicanism, especially for faith, miracle, and belief in the afterlife. Instead Hill's *Thoughts* proceed as humdrum Christianity in the lip service of ruling Whig lords, touting the view that practicing politicians learned little from history. Their reliance on an orthodox Anglican God would be more beneficial than all history's lessons.

Henrietta's dowry was also being depleted by the spring of 1755, and two hungry young mouths were crying to be fed. "The Book I have published against Lord Bolingbroke," Hill wrote in desperation to Newcastle, "has involvd me to my Ruin, the Impatience of my Creditors on that account has stripd me of everything: my Effects are Seizd; and the Cloaths on my back are all that is left me in the world."[25] He did not exaggerate—he was approaching the doorstep of destitution. Word spread so far that that even botanists were shaking their heads in disbelief. "Dr. Hill," the Danish naturalist Peter Ascanius who had heard a great deal about Hill but as yet not met him, wrote to Linnaeus in Sweden in April: "the too famous naturalist of England, is in the lowest possible condition."[26] Ascanius was merely a visitor in England, yet the word spread to him too and he repeated what he heard in England. "I do not think any mortal has ever written with more impudence or more ignorance," he told Linnaeus, "his only excuse is that he must write in order to exist."[27]

Nothing came of Newcastle's intervention, if he did intercede, and residual jibes at Hill continued harking back to the paper wars.[28] He was not the only aspirant to Newcastle's bounty and was even willing to relocate to the West Country for "the Post of Collector of Exeter."[29] This one a sinecure at the port in Devon that would tide him over. David Mallett, the poet, had obtained a similar post through Newcastle's benevolence. Besides, the death of Hill's latest daughter Juliana hit both parents hard. She was born on November 10, 1755, and baptized in the parish of St. James five days later. Ten days later she was dead of some illness, no injury having been given to her mother, who left them only with the two boys, Sarah not yet having been born.

The anxiety between income and purpose in Hill's life is subtle. Henrietta's dowry enabled them to live, but Hill's ego was large. He had no savings on which to draw, having squandered his earnings: he spent whatever he earned in his formerly ostentatious lifestyle. His selfhood, so proximate to his purpose, took as great a toll. He needed to preserve an image of himself as a personality who wrote, published, and cut a figure in "t'Town." Remove it, and he would have been felled more quickly than by his crippling gout. Reinvention served dual purpose, enabling activity and a paltry income while also providing the selfhood needed for psychological survival.

Small wonder then that when printer-publishers stipulated that he appear anonymously he reinvented himself as a woman: Juliana Susannah Seymour, two names he liked rounded out by an invented "Seymour" and the title "Honourable" to legitimate authorship. He named his daughters Juliana and Susannah as mementoes of these books, calling himself "George Crine" or "Archibald Douglas" when he required a male name, or, for medical works, "Dr. Uvedale." For literary tracts he was "Philologus" (then common) or—if the topic was racy as in four essays on libertinism that may earlier have been be his—"Hilario."[30] There were others, such as the fishy "Codgill" (perhaps providing his readers with a clue about his identity as a writer of natural history), but the female aliases were more extensive than the male.

Anonymity vexed Hill's printer-publishers more than Hill. His identity was embedded in verbiage and provided he wrote and published—under whatever alias—he could manage his self-image. But his printers were invested in the economics of publishing rather than egos; if copies containing his name on the title page did not sell, the printers usually bore the brunt of loss. Hill had earlier made arrangements in which he sustained the loss, but more recently his funds were depleted and the deals he cut conditional on writing anonymously or under an alias. This was common practice in the 1740s and 1750s among obscure hacks but Hill had never construed himself as one of them, not even during the black months of the paper wars. As he aged, such required anonymity increasingly grated on him and may have precipitated the illnesses soon to descend on him.

When Hill used an alias in 1754–1756 t'Town was often fooled, the reviews favorable, and many copies sold. The practice's success spawned two ideas for the future: more cross-gendered authorship and the invention of further aliases. Baldwin liked books written by "Juliana Susannah Seymour," making both printer and author royalties, but it is wrong to think Hill harbored a psychosexual fantasy through cross-dressed authorship—it was economic survival. A more useful question pertains to his never having written pornography when his ties to Griffiths were secure. The answer rests on more than conjecture: it was antithetical to his nature. But he took note when he read in the *DA* in July 1754 that "Hannah Glasse, of Tavistock St., St. Paul's Covent Garden" had gone to debtor's prison. She was not yet dead but had anonymously published the *Art of Cookery* several years earlier that ought to have kept her out of jail. Even then, in 1747, before the tirade of sobriquets everyone thought it by Hill.

He continued his low profile during 1755, no longer sending post from his old accommodation in Arlington Street St. James, or newer one in Hart Street Bloomsbury but from a pub in Dover Street, and when he heard the next March that the committee had still not appointed officers for Hans Sloane's new "museum," he petitioned Northumberland again. He had proposed Hill to no effect at the newly formed Society for the Encouragement of the Arts, the only applicant they rejected.[31] Meanwhile da Costa was faring better. He had long since returned from military duty and reintegrated himself back into the virtuous Republic. Nor did Ehret's support flag after da Costa's incarceration: many poignant letters survive from him to "Mr. da Costa at the Bank Coffee House."[32] It was through Solander, though, that da Costa received his luckiest referral of the decade to Gustavus Brander, a merchant trader and Swede like Solander. Brander's passion was in botany and the collection of fossils, and when Ehret invited da Costa to join a "botanizing party" at Lord Macclesfield's country house, at Shirburn Castle in Oxfordshire, in the summer of 1757, da Costa declined: "I am busy making a catalogue of Mr. Brander's collection which is to go to the British Museum at Montagu House."[33] The museum was not open yet but one recommendation led to another and soon da Costa was a fixture at the Royal Society. Years later, when the wheel of fortune had turned, Brander again saved him, as we will see. If only Hill had been so lucky.

The political climate in England was also changing. The Seven Years War broke out in January 1756, sounding the alarm of a French invasion. Admiral John Byng was sent to Minorca in April to prevent its capture by the French, failed, and was court-martialed for cowardice. Hill lost no opportunity to cash in on public sentiment, and when reportage of Byng's actions shifted from anger to compassion Hill wrote to Newcastle to say that he, Newcastle, was being blamed for Byng's harsh treatment in prison—anything to win favor.[34] Hill was on high alert owing primarily to the pursuit of his creditors and immune to news other than any pertaining to himself. An earthquake was reported to be destroying the distant city of Lisbon in Portugal that spring; he had his own fiscal earthquake to deal with. On March 22nd he grew desperate that Northumberland may have heard the rumor that he was the author of a new anti-government newspaper, the *Monitor, or British Freeholder*. He was not: it was John Shebbeare, the rabble-rouser and incendiary, but Hill took no chances: "a Report has been propagated," he swiftly wrote to Northumberland, "in his majestys Court that I am Author of a disaffected Paper."[35] His anxiety was grounded in an announcement made three years earlier that the *Inspector* columns would be replaced with another entitled "The Monitor," which had appeared that year (August–November 1753) without bearing on the current newspaper.

Newcastle and Northumberland appeared his best options. Newcastle had awarded him gifts over the years and thrown his way substantial amounts of £50 for this task and £100 for that, the funding of which derived from his secret service accounts.[36] Hill acted as his underground spy and could satisfy Northumberland too by keeping his "inspectatorial" eyes and ears close to the ground. At least one letter survives documenting this espionage: when public sentiment seemed to be turning in the court-martial of Admiral John Byng (1704–1757), tried for negligence at Minorca, Newcastle sent Hill out in t'Town to reconnoiter for him, and when Hill produced the goods paid him off.[37] But now, in the spring of 1756, at the moment of the rumor about Hill and the "disaffected paper"—the *Monitor*—Northumberland was the vital link to Hill's future patron: the Earl of Bute, "Maecenas of Botany," the future prime minister. They were on close terms, their children to marry in just a few years.

NOTES

1. Bank records count for someone like JH more than voting records or church attendance, but a search of the five principal extant archives for London banks in the eighteenth century produced nothing for so common a name as "John Hill," nor did any accounts under his wife's maiden name surface. JH's bank accounts might change our sense of him, but in the absence of

any I decided there was no productive purpose to wallow in the disappointment. Some of his rates survive (Westminster Parish Rate Books 1752–1758, sub "JH") but these reveal less than a long range of bank accounts would, especially if his wife's dowry was paying them.

2. For Newcastle see Owen, 127–35, for the Whig views J. C. D. Clark.
3. JH (1752c).
4. For Woodward's deserved eminence see V. A. Eyles (1968).
5. See JH (1752c), 415, for both passages.
6. JH (1752c), 11.
7. JH (1752c), 414.
8. JH (1752c), 83.
9. For Needham's vitalism and transport see Miller and Reill (1996), 10.
10. The idea is Barbara Stafford's in Stafford (2002), 184.
11. Samuel Birt, a contemporary microscopist and compiler, also documented them at mid-century but without any of JH's graphic language; see Birt (1746); Birt (1750); Nathaniel Wanley articulated an earlier seventeenth-century version in *The Wonders of the Little World. . . .* (1678).
12. JH saw the links between botany and the new pornography but generally avoided explicit sexual connections; see Samantha George (2007).
13. For Darwin's comments on JH see Blanche Henrey (1975), vol. 2, 94.
14. *Journal Britannique* 9 (September–October 1752): 184–219.
15. Respectively JH (1754d) and JH (1754e).
16. *GM* 24 (1754): 39.
17. JH (1754e), 111.
18. JH (1755b).
19. LPH, 59–60.
20. *MR* 12 (1755): 161–71.
21. LPH, 59.
22. This is one of the eighteenth-century spellings.
23. For Goldsmith see Friedman, vol. 4, 74; also Mackenzie, 43.
24. JH (1755b).
25. BL Add MSS 35398, f. 109 Thomas Birch to Whig magnate Philip Yorke, November 11, 1752.
26. LPH, 60.
27. LPH, 62–63.
28. G. A. Stevens (1755), passim.
29. LPH, 60.
30. Hilario, "Libertine" (1751).
31. Oliver, 46–47.
32. *DAC*, vol. 8, folios 22–53 passim.
33. Calmann, 79.
34. LPH, 67–68.
35. LPH, 65.
36. BL Add Mss 32,977, f. 68, 70, 72.
37. LPH, 67–68.

13

Botany and Bute

Bute was alarmed when he heard, but the prince's mathematical tutor, George Lewis Scott (1708–1780), had already been summoned and instructed to advise Hill of the predicament he was in.[1] Scott informed Hill by letter, which further persuaded Hill he was the butt of a conspiracy to eliminate him from the British Museum post. Suddenly paranoid after being buoyed by hope, Hill continued to believe that treachery was afoot—he was not after all the author—and it took some doing to clear his name from the "disaffected Paper." The fallout was grim among botanists and naturalists observing Bute's growing interest in Hill, and gossiping whether his favorite was indeed a candidate for the post.

Da Costa was especially bewildered by the accusations. Their collaboration had long since diminished since Hill had scooped da Costa, and now he watched the possible treason with alarm as it could redound to him too. His own debts landed him in debtor's prison during the previous year (1754), his curiosity cabinets held in bond. A prison sentence offered him the chance to reflect on his excesses, with the upshot that he vowed personal reform; but it turned out to be fleeting, and once released the prison respite proved temporary, as we shall see.[2] For now he set out to finish his long-promised *Natural History of Fossils*, whose first volume appeared the next summer (1757), and when it did was heralded in the pages of the *Critical Review* as "learned and accurate," courtesy of Smollett or whoever wrote that review.[3]

"John Hill Esqr," da Costa dashed off to Thomas Knowlton, the gardener and botanist he had known for years, "is by all accounts on his last legs, however his itch for scribbling [*sic*] yet remains with him."[4] He continued by imagining Hill's execution in ironic cuts: "when he is no more the whole nation must bewail so great, so good, and so learned a man." Further correspondence between Knowlton and da Costa shows them sacrificing Hill as a whipping board for their own anxiety in the challenges the new Linnaean botany was posing; and Knowlton kept replying that someone as "ignorant of it [Linnaean botany] as any person can be," uninformed as Hill, should not be "botanizing on [a] grand scale." Da Costa continued the aspersions to Knowlton for years, culminating in the verdict that "he goes on the same way and is in like manner rejected from all honourable societies. . . ."[5] Da Costa was no one to throw stones in this self-righteous way: he was already well on his way to embezzling the Royal Society out of hundreds of pounds and would soon be sent to prison for much of the rest of his life. Hill was never imprisoned but routinely brought out the worst in competitors, strong and weak.

Knowlton had recently entered the service of the third Earl of Burlington—the "Duke of Taste," as more than one poet had called him—to build his gardens in faraway Yorkshire, and he craved news of the metropolitan botanical scene, especially about Bute's possible interest in Hill.[6] Five hundred miles east, in Sweden, Linnaeus also heard about Northumberland's paving the way for Hill, and was more polite than Hill's English brethren. He was keen to learn where Hill stood about his new classification and honored when Peter Collinson apprised him that spring (1757) that "Dr. Hill has published proposals to publish your botanic works in English," referring to *Eden*, a "compleat b[o]dy of gardening" along Linnaeus's new principles dedicated to Bute.[7]

Once exonerated from possible sedition Hill returned to botanical publication: a *Compleat Body of Husbandry*, a *vade mecum* for everyone urging the return to the kitchen garden and anticipating the modern allotment;[8] *The Sleep of Plants and Cause of Motion in the Sensitive Plant*[9] and *Eden*, which deserves more notice. His fame was also accelerating in the American colonies among its botanists, especially Bartram, Mark Catesby, and Cadwallader Colden, who knew about his Grub Street wars and more about his botanical publications and the three-volume *General Natural History* dealing with fossils, plants, and animals. Alexander Garden, a promising young Scottish botanist who based himself in Charleston, South Carolina, was a mainstay of information. During the 1750s he developed a network of far-flung botanical correspondents in the virtuous Republic and sent them hundreds of specimens, recounting his botanical travels in the colonies, as well as his conversations with Benjamin Franklin and meetings with intellectual botanists like Colden. Hill often featured in these.

Colden was an intellectual whose interests ranged widely across the arts and sciences. Like Garden and other American botanists, he corresponded with Linnaeus (who named the plant *Coldenia* after him) and kept his ears open about Bute's botanical progress. His scientific letters to Benjamin Franklin still command interest, especially his attempts to modify Newtonian natural philosophy, the basis for his publication about the *Principles of Action in Matter* (1751); and his *History of the Five Indian Nations*, focusing on the Iroquois, which had appeared in London in 1747, was widely reviewed. Colden formed his own opinion of Hill's botanical stature but the question of how far Hill's row with the FRS traveled is more difficult to answer.

Colden, like Garden, inquired of Henry Baker—Hill's *bete noire* in the Royal Society—to enlighten him about Hill, which Baker did in surviving letters. Early in the 1750s Baker kept the young Garden *au fait* with Hill's botanical publications.[10] A classical Linnaean by the time he migrated from Edinburgh to South Carolina in 1750, Garden corresponded directly with the Swedish master, and Hill's name crops up, as do references to "Hill's remarkable ability." If Garden's letters praise Franklin's conversation they also express indignation at the inaccuracy of Catesby's *Natural History of Carolina* and cast doubt on Hill's "colloquies."[11]

Hill had not yet begun to sell his plants and seeds in the colonies, so he was not known as the distributor he later would become but as a rising botanical author and star. Linnaeus dominated the European botanical stage, and colonial botanists, like their English counterparts, divided according to their acceptance of his binomial classification. But Hill's massive two-volume *British Herbal* called "A History," written with Linnaeus books at his side containing dozens of references to Linnaean classification, criticizes the Swede for "his fondness for making new distinctions" that "gets the better of this author's earlier knowledge."[12] Hill refers to contradictions between the earlier *Genera Plantarum* and later *Species Plantarum*. This criticism differs from the accolade of 1751 Hill made in his *General Natural History*: "I have kept up to the arrangement of the plants in the Linnaean system, the author of which deserves infinite praise"—said to be the first *formal* introduction of Linnaeus's system.[13] Hill's contradiction about Linnaeus continued throughout the decade and would eventually take its toll.

But Hill had not yet—this is the point—he had not concerned himself with Bute's views of Linnaean classification, the aspirant pleasing the patron.

Predictably Hill dedicates the *British Herbal* to the "father of the distressed"—for Northumberland's support of various hospitals for the poor—and produces a print on his title page showing "the genius of Health recieving [*sic*] the tributes of Europe, Asia, Africa and America and delivering them. . . ." In case his dedication is insufficient, or unnoticed, he repeats in the preface the prediction that if Linnaeus had his patron George Clifford (the Dutchman who launched his career in Holland two decades earlier), England's equivalent botanist will eventually have his. Did he imagine it would be him?

The goal was to attract Bute, even if Hill might have to satisfy himself with Northumberland. Now, early in 1757, his focus was the latter, and when the moment seemed right he wrote, probably in April or May 1757,

Figure 13.1. The Earl of Northumberland.

Reproduced by kind permission of the Trustees of the British Museum.

his first known letter to Bute: "My Lord Northumberland has acquainted me that he did me the great honour of mentioning me and my present botanical Researches to your Lordship."[14] He could write this because he had just dedicated *Eden; or, a compleat Body of Gardening*, which Thomas Osborne published in May, to Bute. Here Hill professed to be a confirmed "Linnaean" but it is doubtful whether this aspect made the difference. After all, he had been a household name in England for a decade; any sense that his professed allegiance, if final Linnaean conversion it was, could eradicate vacillation between praise and blame, or his scandalous past, is unknown. Bute himself had probably become a "Linnaean" by now, but in the spring of 1757 he had more pressing matters with which to navigate during this pinnacle of his long Leicester House period. Frederick, Prince of Wales and next in line to succeed George II, had died on March 20, 1751, while Hill scribbled faster than in most years. His son, George, now became the next in line to the throne and Bute tutored him in secret, as well as advised Augusta, his widow, who was thrilled that she had found the right tutor for her son.

Augusta had engaged Bute to tutor Prince George in 1755; a year later the young George announced his preference for Bute as groom of the stole, and rumors also spread beyond court that Bute had become his mother's alleged lover. Bute's clandestine romance, as well as his politics in the prelude to election as prime minister, has often been recounted in degrees of sensationalism—what counts for Hill's story is his relation to Linnaean botany. Of course Hill heard the rumors about Augusta and predictions about Bute's bright future once George ascended to the throne, so he moved precipitously to approach Bute just as *Eden* was launched.

The Scot was persuaded that the road to Leicester House was *botanical*: both Bute and his German princess were botanical fanatics, and if Augusta was planning extensive additions to the garden—the future Kew about which the public was in 1756–1757 still in the dark—to commemorate her husband, Hill was the man to supervise them, ready and waiting. Bute's botanical life has never been properly compiled yet its outlines are sufficiently clear to construct a sketch, especially his role in the development of the Royal Gardens at Kew.[15] Frederick had laid these out as a young man, but after his death in 1751, the young George and his grieving mother began to remodel them. Bute's love of botany played a major role in endearing mother and son to him in 1755–1758, a shrewd move. He leased a house on Kew Green, expanded to contain his botanical library, and single-handedly supervised the garden alterations, commissioning Sir William Chambers to design new buildings in addition to her own small palace, including the orangery, the pagoda, and temples.

By the summer of 1757, Bute, having scanned and warmly acknowledged the huge folio *Eden* dedicated to him, appointed Hill his assistant. For Hill it was the appointment of a lifetime. He was in. Had Bute's reading of *Eden* convinced him about Hill?

Figure 13.2. Lord Bute's "Erections at Kew Gardens."
Reproduced by kind permission of Professor George Rousseau.

Some copies of *Eden* appeared with hand-colored plates, determining the book's price in this expensive folio printed by subscription and funded by Henrietta's remaining dowry. The sixty plates were advertised as "by Dr. Hill's own hand."[16] Arranged by the week of each month, it advises the skillful gardener on every aspect of his task: preparation of the soil, watering, what to do, and—more crucially—which plants to tend, where and how. Each plant and flower is beautifully illustrated for the gardener to see and to accompany descriptions of its native habitat, history, migrations, and the commentaries of different authorities. Useful tips are included on the type of effect it creates in different gardens, as well as notes on the flower's history and discussion among botanists. The daffodil, or narcissus, is presented in many varieties, spring to winter, plain to fringed, none more lovely than the "poetic daffodil" which has no rival "so honourably mention'd by all Kinds of Writers."[17] In the section on commentators, ancients to moderns, Hill's claim that "Tournefort, of all Men, is the best Authority on this Head; and he, unknowing or unthinking of this Cavil, tells us he gathered on the Banks of the *Granicus*, and about *Ephesus*, Daffodils in *December*."[18] He may have, but comes in for abundant criticism as taxonomer.

Eden's structure clarifies itself when the reader searches for roses, best discussed in the section for the month of July: beginning with the "double red rose" Hill demonstrates why it is "the Glory of Flowers, the Favourite of Mortals; and in the antient [*sic*] Expression, the Delight of Gods," annotating each claim from the works of Anacreon, Propertius, and Ovid.[19] His wide reading in natural history, especially with Linnaeus at his side, had enabled him to provide synopses and annotate facilely from both Greeks and Romans: "They crown'd their Priests with it for Sacrifice; their own Brows for Festivity. They strewed it upon the Tombs of their Heroes; and covered with it the costly Marbles on which they placed their Wines."[20] These prevailing constructions following the rigidly classical ornate style are typical of his botanical prose. Indeed he had used a different style during the 1750s for botanical prose, fiction, satire, and didactic literature.

Eden opens chronologically at the end of August, "when gardens are at their least beautiful in the summer," and comes full circle for one year. The introduction explains how a garden is to be "distributed," and summarizes how he will guide the reader through the various parts: "the Flower and Kitchen Ground, defended by Walls and planted with Espaliers, furnished with Greenhouse and its Stove, and enlarged by the Addition of its Seminary, Orchard, and Wilderness," each of which is summarized for every week of the year. The avid gardener need only follow his instructions: "he will have no more Care upon his Mind than to observe our separate Instructions."[21]

In 1757 there was no similar work in English, certainly not so handsomely written, colored, and produced. Bute read it upon publication and was delighted. It was indeed a huge achievement Hill could not have accomplished alone, running to 36 leaves, 790 pages, and 61 pages of plates containing over one thousand individual species. Amanuenses had been known to work for him throughout this decade, and they must have here, for he produced it in record time. Here he used their assistance to gather material, dictate, and tidy the information, but the ideas remained his, especially the hobbyhorses he rode: the utility of the past in botanical learning, his preferred flowers, the different seasons weighed up in relation to a Garden's beauty, and the genius of Linnaeus—"the great Swede." The last shines through.

On this Hill is unequivocal: "We shall follow the SYSTEM of Linnaeus, which we shall deliver compleatly, in the naming of every plant and flower," he states early in the preface, rejecting Tournefort as obsolete, while generously extolling the Swede. When the Linnaean classification is long and complex he nevertheless favors it. He hesitates to name the "Blue Clitoria" because the Linnaean appellation is "indecent" but feels he must follow the Swede.[22] And he continues in this fashion in *Eden* for several dozen adulating nods at the "founder of the new province of botany" without a trace of resistance, perhaps because he was so determined to secure Bute's patronage that he suppressed any hint of criticism. He may not have adopted "Linnaeus's system" wholeheartedly but he certainly endorsed it. Why then the developing view in the decade (1750s) that Hill was antagonistic to Linnaeus—or, at least, not his constant champion?

The answer is found in the only other botanical work Hill produced in 1757, which followed closely on the heels of *Eden* that September: *The Sleep of Plants, and Cause of Motion in the Sensitive Plant*, which his primary publisher of his botanical works, Robert Baldwin, printed.[23]

Containing only thirty-five pages, this pamphlet is framed as an open "Letter to Linnaeus" focusing specifically on Hill's endorsement of the Swede's method and answering Hill's critics about his alleged vacillation.[24] Hill's attitude to Linnaeus, far more than his experiments with plants in the darkness, and his observations of rising "steams" as if the "veins of plants" giving off fluids when they heat up and cool down under the influence of light and darkness, concerned these critics.

The Sleep of Plants has since become a tract of considerable interest to cultural historians of the Enlightenment and students of Romanticism, especially those concerned with the contemporary sources of "plant poetry": canonical texts such as Shelley's "The Sensitive Plant," first published with *Prometheus Bound* in 1820, and for the puzzling role of sleep in plants and humans in poems such as John Keats's "Sleep and Poetry" (1816), with its opening lines about "First the realm I'll pass/Of Flora, and old Pan." These poets absorbed scientific theories about sleeping, sensitive plants, including the views of Hill and Erasmus Darwin, and also pondered analogies between human and plant sexual organs: especially the reproductive male organ as "sensitive plant." Historians of science and medicine have also cited Hill's early tract (1757) to document Enlightenment theories of sympathy and irritability judged so significant for the development of Enlightenment sensibility, all the more so in light of Haller's seminal role in the rise of this doctrine and Hill's known biographical relation to Haller.[25] For these combined reasons Hill's tract reached out well beyond narrow botanical readership in the late eighteenth century.

Among plants it was *Mimosa pudica*, first formally described by Linnaeus in *Species Plantarum* (1753), which piqued imaginations of poets. Linnaeus noted that the species epithet, *pudica*, means "bashful" or "shrinking" in Latin, alluding to its shrinking reaction to contact, but the English debated the plant's actions far more than its indecent name; and in the same year Linnaeus's *Species* appeared (1753) *Chambers Cyclopedia* described the sensitive plant as "an herb sufficiently known to the world for its remarkable property of receding from the touch, and giving signs, as it were, of animal life."[26] This ambiguity of animal or plant haunted them for decades. For example, English author and politician Soame Jenyns compared the "sensitive mimosa" to the shellfish, noting that the "lowest" animal and the "highest" plant are both distinguished by sensitivity; the bivalve opening "to receive the water which surrounds it," just as the plant is observed "shrinking from the finger" that touches it. Hence the sensitive plant embodies the same

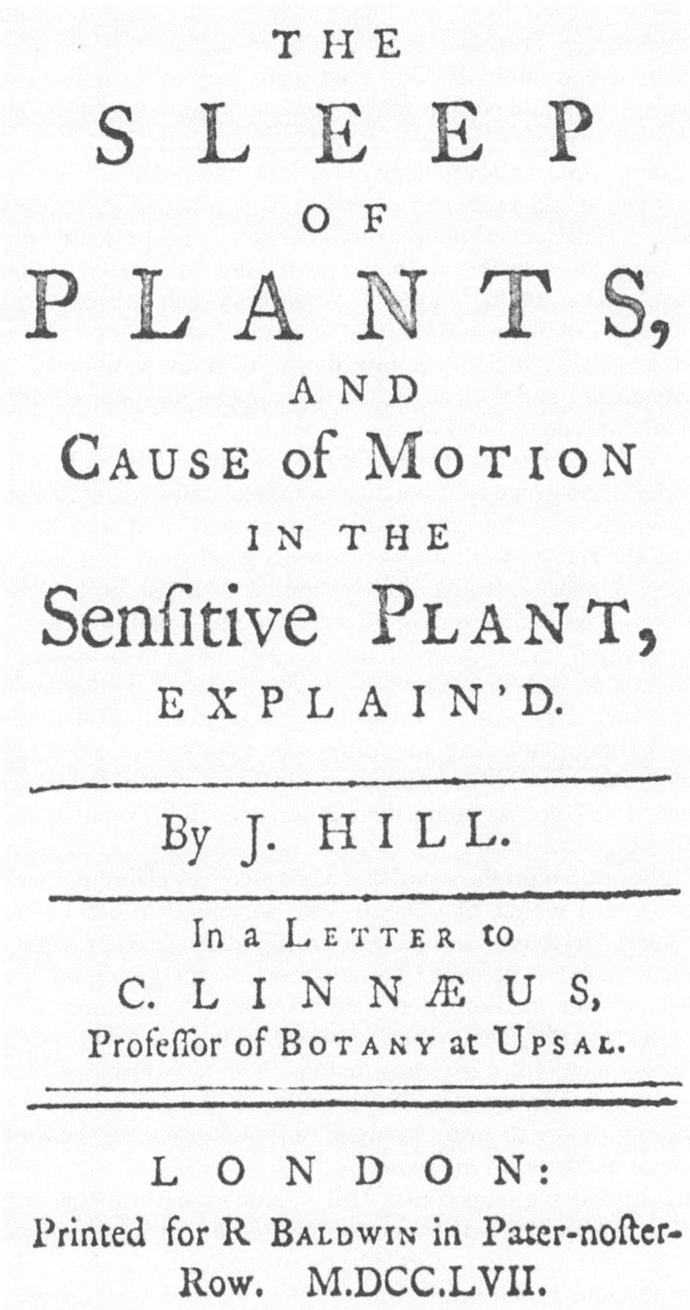

THE

SLEEP

OF

PLANTS,

AND

CAUSE of MOTION

IN THE

Senſitive PLANT,

EXPLAIN'D.

By J. HILL.

In a LETTER to

C. LINNÆUS,

Profeſſor of BOTANY at UPSAL.

LONDON:

Printed for R BALDWIN in Pater-noſter-Row. M.DCC.LVII.

Figure 13.3. Title page of John Hill, *The Sleep of Plants . . . in the Sensitive Plant,* 1758.

Reproduced by kind permission of Professor George Rousseau.

anxiety about hybrids that posed such problems for early naturalists like Hill, Linnaeus, and Erasmus Darwin: in brief because it looks like a plant but behaves like an animal. What then were they to do with those ferns, for example, which looked like animals but always behaved like Linnaeus's sensitive plant, especially in their retraction and "sleep"?

Hill's exaggerated claims to fame in the little pamphlet, which the reviewers and others (Goldsmith and Murphy) also courting celebrity noticed, tarnished him. The general estimate was derision of his professed familiarity with the king, the specific one brandished false "modesty," odious "self-sufficiency," and outright "vanity."[27] To address their sovereign with such familiarity was outrageous in their view; scandalous, as the *MR*'s reviewer observed, to classify himself among those "who are acquainted with the powers of nature," and then claim, as Hill had, that he "assured himself" he was of their elite, small number.

But in 1757 and afterward naturalists throughout England took note of Hill's work, for the sleep of plants was a much-contested topic: the mechanisms by which they "fell asleep" and "awakened" and why they needed to sleep at all. The subject intrigued foreign gentlemen of science as well, men such as Linnaeus, Haller, and Gesner, as it did naturalists at home.[28] Henry Baker, who had never recovered from Hill's denouncement of him in *Lucina*, got into correspondence in 1757 with naturalists about Hill's latest production, as did John Browning, a little-known "gentleman botanist" making his own experiments. Browning disagreed with Hill's view about the role of light in plant sleep and argued the opposite case: that light alone cannot be the reason. He communicated his theory to Hill but they seem to have reached an impasse about their difference, and Browning eventually appealed to Baker as arbiter.

Baker further fired up the scandalized reviewers by claiming that Hill was dead wrong; that plants, like people, are "sensitive" to other phenomena than light and dark but would have no truck with their controversy, having earlier been stung too fiercely: "You must excuse my giving no opinion on the subject of your correspondence with Dr. Hill, from whom I wish you may get more real satisfaction than from me . . . have long ago resolved, that I on no occasion will have anything to do with your correspondent or any of his affairs, and therefore you must excuse me, whatever happens, if I decline intermeddling in any disputes between you and desire you will never appeal to me or make use of my name. . . ."

Still, he argued the case contra Hill at some length in this correspondence: "His [Hill's] only discovery seems to be that certain plants close their leaves when put into dark places (which others surely must have observed without making any bustle about it) and their awakening or opening again he imputes to light alone, whose modus operandi he very cleverly describes." Baker was predisposed to esteem Browning's contrary case and had no view of his own: "Your discovery is certainly as good as his." But he cautioned Browning not to be drawn into controversy with such an antagonist: ". . . take warning, my dear friend, and as he is palpably mistaken in his conjectures as to the cause [of the sleep of plants], be you content with the honour of discovering a real fact, without perplexing yourself with steams or vibrating fibres. . . ." He could not forego this admission of Hill's extraordinary ability:

> I forgive him heartily, bear him no ill will, nor judge of him with prejudice. I am sensible he has some extraordinary qualifications, great application, a considerable degree of knowledge and a readiness [sic] of expression, which with a benevolent and honest mind would have made him truly deserving esteem, and I am sorry to see such parts . . . so ill employed.

Baker could not take his leave without forewarning Browning of what might arise and reminded him that years earlier he had sent Hill's *General Natural History* to the printer Osbourne [*sic*] only to be "disgraced":

> Did not you some years ago send a work of Hill's to Osbourne [*sic*] with disgrace? Have you not now made a discovery [about the sleep of plants] that overturns his boasted effects of light? And do you imagine by a little complaisance to extirpate these crimes? I find your conscience pricks you and you fear some bad consequences and therefore [I beseech you to] deposit a copy of what you have wrote to him with me.

Correspondence between Browning and Hill has disappeared but the gist is clear: Browning, having promoted Hill's *General Natural History* to printer Osborne at the start of the decade, saw how the book's reception was unfavorable and his own standing diminished. Or was Browning suggesting that Hill plagiarized his ideas? By "depositing" a copy with Baker the FRS seems to suggest he could act as insurance in case Hill had plagiarized or would make further accusations in 1757. But this was as far as Baker proceeded and here the matter ended, Browning never again to trouble Baker with his anxieties about the sleep of plants.

Bute for his part was delighted with *Eden*, as we shall see, but nothing survives—either printed or in archives—to know whether he read *The Sleep of Plants*.[29] Hill certainly gifted him a copy adorned with an unctuous letter saying that his purpose was to making botanical "studies usefull," but Bute may have been too busy with Augusta.[30] It is difficult to think such an ardent patron-botanist, who had just appointed an "assistant," could be unaware of the circulating gossip about Hill's antagonism to Linnaeus. Still, he confided to his by now bent and old uncle Archibald Campbell, the 3rd Duke of Argyll and an avid gardener himself, of his delight in *Eden*. He probably meant the dedication rather than its content, but one thing led to another, and soon Hill and Argyll, gratias Bute, were on good terms.

Argyll was no mean botanist even as he approached eighty—indeed, his botany may be more important than all his politics. Hill called on him at his country house, Whitton Park on Hounslow Heath, where he cultivated exotic trees, the source of his nickname as "Treemonger," invented by Horace Walpole and widely adopted by the botanists.[31] Old Argyll took to Hill and puffed him further to his nephew. When Hill called on Bute they discussed books and botanists, appraised the sketches of Simon Taylor, a young landscape illustrator in Bute's service who had drawn up the plans for anana hothouses at Whitton Park, and soon Hill began to act as informal advisor to both uncle and nephew.[32] He still lived with Henrietta and their children in Arlington Street, in St. James, but slept away while consulting with Bute and collecting for him. He was often gone, as he notes in correspondence: to Surrey, Berkshire, Northamptonshire, especially the sleepy town of Daventry there, an old haunt where he and Theophilus Sr. used to ramble and botanize during his youth—to all these he returned to collect seeds for them.[33]

Suddenly his prospects brightened. He felt secure in the prospect of patronage.

NOTES

1. LPH, 65–66.
2. Rousseau and Haycock (2000): 128–45.
3. *CR* 4 (September 1757): 246.
4. BL Add MSS 28539, January 10, 1756, for this and the next citations; for Knowlton see Blanche Henrey (1986).
5. BL Add MSS 28539, March 10, 1764.
6. Can he have remembered that his former Steward's daughter had been Hill's first wife?
7. JH (1757a).
8. JH (1756b).
9. JH (1757b).
10. References are found in Linnaeus's correspondence in J. E. Smith (1821).
11. Quoted in Garden to Baker, March 25, 1755, in Baker Corr; see also Catesby (1748).
12. See JH (1756a), 10.
13. JH (1751b), preface for the citation; historian of botany Blanche Henrey made a vigorous case for this as the first formal endorsement; see Blanche Henrey (1975), vol. 2, 92.
14. LPH, 71.
15. See D. P. Miller (1988); Schweizer (1988), passim.
16. *PA* (November 16, 1757).
17. JH (1757a), 495.
18. JH (1757a), 496.
19. JH (1757a), 529.
20. JH (1757a), 529.
21. JH (1757a), 2.
22. JH (1757a), 53.

23. JH (1757b).
24. Ibid, "Advertisement."
25. Riskin, passim; Rousseau (2004), 251–65; Guthke, passim; Haller (1977), 45–87.
26. Ephraim Chambers (1741–1743), article under "Sensitive Plant."
27. *MR* 17 (1757): 330, for the citations in this paragraph.
28. LPH, 72–75. For the Baker–Browning affair, see p. 211.
29. A search through the Bute Archives at Mount Stuart and elsewhere in Scotland produced nothing.
30. LPH, 74.
31. LPH, 72.
32. LPH, 77–78.
33. LPH, 89.

14

Hill and Linnaeus

Hill's *Sleep of Plants* criticized Linnaeus, but a thorough trawl through Swedish archives reveals not one hint that the Swede read it or knew of its existence despite the forewarning of his English friends. Was he aware of Hill's vacillation? Did he care? It was one thing for an Englishman to oppose him in 1751, before the appearance in 1753 of the *Species Plantarum*, and another now, in 1757, when his fame was spreading throughout Europe. Daniel Solander, his loyal disciple who would champion his master's system in England, would not arrive for another three years on the London scene; the English botanists themselves relied for information about his taxonomy on networks in the virtuous Republic, as well as accounts such as Hill's. After Solander's welcome among the London gentlemen of science everything changed—it was the start of Hill's new war with the botanical world.

Before Solander arrived the English botanists apprised Linnaeus of Hill's endeavors and views. Peter Collinson wrote to him a few weeks before the appearance of *Eden* announcing that "Dr. Hill has published proposals to publish your botanic works in English."[1] Hill himself sent Linnaeus a copy of *The Sleep of Plants*—a few months after its appearance—and wrote him friendly letters that do not mention his criticism.[2] English botanists, however, told different stories, some apprising the Swede that Hill was resisting his taxonomy in England. In Uppsala confusion was the response: how could Linnaeus know what was actually occurring across the sea with so many conflicting reports? Linnaeus formed a clearer sense after Solander arrived and sorted out truth from fiction. For now, the reports about Hill's attitude conflicted.

Confusion in England was as pronounced. Hill, for his part, praised the master; he also published criticisms, as we saw. Was there a "real Hill" assessing and contemplating the new Linnaean system?

The essence of Linnaean taxonomy was, as we have claimed, revolutionary for its simplicity and fullness but it could not accommodate the riotous growth of new facts and discoveries in the decades after its announcement in 1735: not merely in botanical realms, which it was intended to reform, but in the other sciences that also required classifying, and which often overlapped with botany. Even so, this proviso is made in hindsight. In foresight, from the perspective of 1735 and even in the 1750s, when the *Species Plantarum* appeared, it was a spectacular prospect—doubtlessly the most noteworthy development of botanical science in Hill's lifetime.

Throughout the 1740s, and more rapidly during the 1750s, the virtues of Linnaean classification were gradually recognized. Among them were that its mechanisms applied to all species throughout the natural world: no exceptions whatever existed to its method of naming. It privileged the visual sense, then coming into further prominence as the result of ever-more far-flung exploration, and it was only a matter of time (even within Hill's lifetime) when explorers like James Cook and Joseph Banks would use its binomial system to classify the thousands of specimens they brought back with them to England from the Arctic, the Americas, and South Pacific. Its double naming according to stamens and pistils also enhanced accurate classification even if it ignored natural affinities. And it inspired a new sys-

Figure 14.1A. Engraving of the young Carl Linnaeus.

Reproduced by kind permission of the Wellcome Library, London.

Figure 14.1B. Engraving of Carl Linnaeus, the Swedish botanist, physician, and zoologist.

Reproduced by kind permission of the Wellcome Library, London.

tematic language that could be generalized throughout the natural sciences; not merely in botany, medicine, and mineralogy, the fields Hill's tilled—but in anatomy and chemistry and other developing sciences as well. In brief, whatever its limitations binomial classification remained in usage until the days of A. L. Jussieu in the mid-nineteenth century.

Predictable opposition to these Linnaean principles would naturally form, and this is the site where Hill saw an opportunity to aggrandize himself. With a vulture's talons he clutched the new "philosophy" in 1751 in his first *History of Plants* and began to espouse it.[3] Concurrently, Buffon and Benjamin Franklin railed against it in the 1760s, on grounds it was artificial and violated the sacrosanct natural order.[4] Then the Germans joined the pan-European debate to assess its value, as many holding out against it and those for. Kant lost no time in Wolfenbüttel to add his dissenting voice to the catalogue of opposition on grounds it was wholly "artificial to arrange objects into taxonomies."[5] This artifice of taxonomy was their chief gripe and they would have carped against Ray's earlier system had it crossed over to Europe, but Ray's simpler classification remained hidden from most—an insular British event. When opposition developed in the 1760s, from Buffon to Kant and beyond, it was made in the name of a natural order sufficiently flexible to resist the straitjacket of monolithically universal binomial classification.

But in the 1750s Linnaean classification remained somewhat unknown in Britain save among savants.[6] Philip Miller, in charge of the Chelsea Physic Garden since 1722, had not fully adopted it despite extensive correspondence with Linnaeus himself about its components. Tournefort and Ray had formed Miller's mind, and he continued to use their classification rather than Linnaeus's binomials; many others were similar too. Hill and Linnaeus, on the other hand, had never met; were names to one another, each known in the other's country but their fascination was almost reciprocal: Linnaeus closely watched Hill's development, noting whatever he could glean from his base a thousand miles across a vast North Sea and frozen terrain of hills and lakes in Uppsala. He checked with his contacts abroad carefully to be sure he had not overlooked any new book Hill published, listed the titles in his files, and later—when receiving the book—compiled notes about it, often corresponding with other gentlemen of science around the globe especially with Gesner—to be sure he was up to date. He even preoccupied himself with Hill's geographical movements: was he still in London, had he relocated, had he discovered any new botanical species?

Haller was one of Linnaeus's informants but Haller received his information from Gesner, a fact Tissot—the anti-onania campaigner and illustrious Protestant doctor of Lausanne—also knew. In the Republic networks were everything: who corresponded with who and what their conduct was like. During the 1750s Haller's reputation among naturalists was almost as high as Linnaeus's—only with the passage of time has the Swede usurped him. Haller seemed to his contemporaries a prodigy of learning: his theories of *sensibility* and *irritability* as the basis for the biology of life particularly enabled the English to wake up and take notice as soon as those texts were available in English. Early in the decade the *GM* described his physiology and noticed his books.[7] The theories of all four had botanical consequences, and if you were a botanist working in the environs of London in the late 1750s—at the time Bute picked up Hill—you might well venerate the Swede while also harboring deep reservation.

The specific grounds only clarified themselves in time: Linnaeus was a compulsive note taker and cataloguer rather than observer, and he preoccupied himself with everything botanical, including Hill, in whom his interest appears disproportionate.[8] Hill was a gifted but not original thinker and nothing he did in botanical science could elevate him to Linnaeus's league. Even in the 1740s Hill—this was his leap—recognized that Linnaeus's new system was the only one to rival Ray's: only through him would botany in England significantly advance and this is why he applied the Linnaean binomials in 1751 in his *General Natural History*; the reason Hill kept claiming precedence.[9]

Then a competitor of sorts presented himself: Patrick Browne, an Irishman and recent graduate of Leyden, had arrived in London around 1743 to work as a physician in St. Thomas's Hospital, departed three years later for the West Indies, eventually settling in Jamaica, where he practiced.[10] Hill never met him but Browne was a keen botanist and in Jamaica studied its natural history, collecting indigenous plants and animals. He returned in 1755 to arrange for the printing of his illustrated *Civil and Natural History of Jamaica*, accompanied by engravings based on drawings he had commissioned from Georg Ehret—da Costa's collaborator. Browne's biographer writes that "his reputation as a botanist stems from the [*Natural History of Jamaica*] . . . because in it he became the first English-speaking author to use Linnaeus's system of classifying plants in print."[11] And both W. T. Stearn and F. A. Staffleu concurred in Patrick Browne's importance: Stearn calling Browne's work "the first British book to follow the Linnanean system of classification" and ten years later naming Browne "the first true Linnaean."[12]

The claim is inaccurate—Hill arrived there five years earlier in his *General Natural History*. Nor has Britain's preeminent historian of botany, Blanche Henrey, accepted this unfounded claim; her verdict is plain: "[Hill's] *History of plants*, a work in which the Linnaean system is introduced into this country for the first time."[13] How to explain these discrepancies? Patrick Browne, after seeing his *History of Jamaica* through the press, returned to the Caribbean. Linnaeus congratulated him upon its publication—high praise—and named some of his binomials after him, particularly native Irish birds and fish (including marine mammals), and they exchanged letters.[14] The reviews of Browne's *History of Jamaica* were few and made no reference to his Linnaean application. Nor is there mention of him anywhere in Hill's correspondence or any reason to think Hill was aware of his book. As far as Hill was concerned he, Hill, had been first—and he had if chronology is the test.

But Hill wrote *before* the 1753 appearance of Linnaeus's nomenclature in the *Species*; so, almost by definition, Hill cannot have been *first*. This is the prickly thorn in need of disentanglement. If, by analogy, you apply Newtonian or Marxist terminology *before* either man has published his "system" can you be said to have been the *first* to *apply* it? You may have anticipated or heard about the method and inserted it but can you—logically and rigorously—apply it? The matter requires further dismantling; it was not that Linnaeus had not yet published his "system" but that he had not yet applied a simplification embraced by the scientific community.

Biographically Hill read both Linnaeus's 1735 *Systema Naturae* and heard about his subsequent methods; and by the time Hill wrote in 1750–1751 he had digested the ideas.[15] Besides, 1735 is a crucial date insofar as it constitutes the starting point of Staffleu's study of the introduction of Linnaeus's ideas into England.[16] We must, however, become entirely clear on what appears in Linnaeus's 1753 *Species* that is absent from his earlier *Systema Naturae* capable of eliminating Hill from the claim of precedence.

Linnaeus's plant taxonomy (omitting his animal and mineral classifications because they are not part of the argument) was based wholly on the number and arrangement of the reproductive organs; a plant's class was determined by its stamens (male organs), and its order by its pistils (female organs). This classification posed problems and also appeared unnatural to the British botanists of the 1730s and 1740s. Linnaeus himself attached magisterial significance to plant sexual reproduction, which had only recently been rediscovered, and drew rather astonishing parallels between plant sexuality and human love. As early as 1729 he wrote in his Uppsala medical dissertation that "The flowers' leaves . . . serve as bridal beds which the Creator has so gloriously arranged, adorned with such noble bed curtains, and perfumed with so many soft scents that the bridegroom with his bride might there celebrate their nuptials with so much the greater solemnity. . . ."[17] The sexual component of his classification was controversial in its day: easy to learn and apply but clumsy and ambiguous. Critics attacked it for its sexually explicit nature, as when German botanist Johann Siegesbeck called it "loathsome harlotry."[18] La Mettrie, the French materialist philosopher now (in the 1750s) in exile in Berlin for his own transgression, satirized the sexually explicit taxonomy as if it were pornography applied wholesale to nature's kingdom.

Hill's reservations were also sexual rather than taxonomic but the question about the difference of Linnaeus's two works—1735 and 1753—remains to be put. Before 1753 many British botanists continued to follow John Ray's practice of using morphological evidence from different parts of the organism in all stages of its development rather than merely the number and arrangement of the reproductive organs. Linnaeus opposed this practice: he saw the confusion it caused, especially in a milieu of rocketing numbers of new plants being brought back to Europe from Asia, Africa, and the Americas. The genius of his 1753 *Species Plantarum* is the simplification he makes by giving one Latin name to indicate the genus, and another as a shorthand name for the species. As one historian of science has written, "the wide attraction of the Linnaean taxonomy lay, of course, in its relative simplicity and ease of use in an era when taxonomists were drowning in novelties."[19] Hence Linnaeus' limit of two names—and there are only two—make up the binomial ("two names") species name. After 1753 this binomial system rapidly became the standard system for naming species, and other names were wiped away. He was not the first taxonomer to use binomials, but was the first to use them consistently after 1753, and for this reason, Latin names used prior to Linnaeus are not usually considered valid by naturalists under the rules of nomenclature.

This explanation accounts for authoritative botanical historian Blanche Henrey's—just cited—assessment of Hill's precedence. She notes that although he was first to adopt the Linnaean system, "[Hill's] *History of Plants* has no significance for modern nomenclature, being published before Linnaeus' *Species Plantarum* (1753), the starting point of the modern nomenclatural system."[20] In other words, it may possess "no significance" for nomenclature, but was *nevertheless first* to introduce Linnaeus's "system" into England. The substantive difference between a general system and nomenclatural one is difficult to grasp because we are reconstructing backward: that is, from the vantage of post-1753, to the moment of 1753, and then further back. Hill himself applied the Linnaean "system" in 1750–1751 without its clear reduction to binomials. "I have, both in the *History of Plants,* and that of *Animals,*" he wrote, "adopted as much of the method of Linnaeus, as is consistent with observation: and I have, so far as my examinations of the bodies would enable me, filed up the deficiencies. . . ."[21]

Hill continued: "That I chose the method of Linnaeus for the arrangement of these bodies was, in part, because it is nearer a natural system than that of any other. . . ." This may appear to be covert criticism of English classifiers—especially Ray, Dillenius (the Oxford professor of botany), and others who promoted *non*-sexual arrangement—but Hill writes as if he has detected a paradigm shift: "It is with great pleasure that I see a spirit of this part of knowledge raising itself among us. We have the foundation in our hands, and there requires little more than application for the super-structure"—a grandiose declamation punctuated by neologism ("super-structure") and self-congratulation ("with great pleasure"). Was this, as we shall see, John Ellis's forthcoming "mere drug"—the charge that Hill wrote too glibly—or Hill having it both ways about Linnaean taxonomy?

Stripped of its Hillian rhetorical grandeur the preface is the work of an author who has become a Linnaean, and the volume's subsequent organization substantiates the view:

> . . . I have kept up to the arrangement of the plants in the Linnaean system, the author of which deserves infinite praise; and have preserved his classical as well as generical names, his classical characters, and, so far as nature warrants it, have kept up to even his very terms in the generical distinctions. I have always, where it has been possible, examined the plants themselves, in the time of their flowering where they have agreed with his characters, I have never failed to adopt them; and, even where they might have differed from his descriptions, I have given the account, in terms as like his own might be.

By 1751, however, when this preface was printed, the die was cast. And it is not surprising that naturalists commenting on the book then, many of whom were FRS like Arderon, Baker, and Parsons, would dismiss it, but it is more puzzling to understand why modern historians of botany should. Two of the most eminent, W. T. Stearn and F. A. Staffleu, have done so.[22] But Blanche Henrey, who has been equally eminent, has continued to argue for Hill's precedence on grounds of application of a "new system," even if the binomials had not yet been spelled out. And she is right.

Even so, Hill's adoptions of the Linnaean system cannot be understood solely from the angle of precedence. It certainly was not on philosophical principles, nor had he developed critical skills in university allowing it even if his deep reading did; besides, botany in the two English universities was then barely pursued. It was new and attractive; Hill was young—in his thirties—and anxious to make a name for himself.

He sprung for the new method without digesting its complexity, leaving himself vulnerable to the charge that so far as plants were concerned his *General Natural History* was no more than a new rendition of Dillenius's revision of Ray's *Synopsis* according to the Linnaean system. It was untrue: he did not merely regurgitate Dillenius. He aimed to provide genuine innovation, but that would require the whole Linnaean system at once, which Hill could not encompass. Nor could he produce it in so short a time—nor could others; but the larger point was that he was overreaching, again, and his correspondence during these years (1751–1754) offers a glimmer of his contemporaries' response. There was also a flurry of international interest in his *General Natural History* for its adoption of the new method. Botanists Peter Collinson and Peter Ascanius, both FRS, were concerned that Hill was unqualified to assess the new method. Collinson's name had been omitted from Hill's satires; he had met Linnaeus in the 1730s, mentored Hill's employer Lord Petre to plant the forty thousand American trees at Thorndon, and was widely known to botanists, but he *himself* had reservations about Linnaeus' new method on grounds it would eliminate older gardeners unfamiliar with it. And Peter Ascanius was also dubious about the Swede's method.

Hill's adoption has a more intriguing profile in the sexual realm. Linnaeus recognized twenty-four different classes of plants: "Monandria," or one husband in a marriage, and "Polyandria," twenty males or more in bed with a female. These classes were further based on the arrangement of the sex organs of their flowers. Twenty-three of the classes were identified according to the length and number of a plant's sexual organs, or stamens, while the last class was reserved for non-flowering plants (mosses, ferns, and the like). The classes were then further divided according to the number of its pistons or female sexual organs. Linnaeus endowed them with penises and vaginas, no different from humans, and gave them Greek names: husbands were "*andria*," wives "*gynia*," their power relations based on "*dynamis*," their marriage as "*gamos*," their home within the flower bed an "*oikos*" or, in Greek, house.[23]

These arrangements, Linnaeus asserted in his "loves of the plants," mirrored the marital coupling up of humans: "the singular structure and remarkable office of the stamens and pistil [*sic*] enticed my mind, to inquire what Nature had concealed in them." The method thrived on functionalism: specific functions the sexual organs of plants performed in reproduction. A generation before Erasmus Darwin versified these arrangements Linnaeus's *Preludes to the Betrothels of Plants* (1729) verbalized them as sexually explicit:

> Words cannot express the joy that the sun brings to all living things. Now the black-cock and the capercailzie begin to frolic, the fish to sport. Every animal feels the sexual urge. Yes, Love comes even to the plants. Males and females . . . hold their nuptials, showing by their sexual organs which are males, which females. . . .[24]

Linnaeus struggles to tease out the "frolic" but elsewhere his rhetoric traded on innuendo and metaphor, even if not yet so richly woven as in Erasmus Darwin's later conjugation of flowers and "loves of the plants" in *Zoonomia*. The Swede transformed passive sexual organs in 1729 into the principal actors of matrimonial consummation and then analogized nocturnal activities to those of ordinary men and women; describing a kingdom based on sexual attraction between different sexes, including hermaphroditical ones, and described betrothal and conjugation in the "wedding bed" as commentaries on the so-called lofty "human condition." Historians have demonstrated how women had been prevented from entering the botanical world of Ray and Dillenius, but also how Linnaeus' system—transgressive at the time—paved the way for them as future botanists, even if amateur.[25] Once the vegetable kingdom was revealed as sexually arranged it was a small step to recognition of the importance of female life as half the part of this natural kingdom. Hill minimally participated in this gender transformation more sympathetically than has been acknowledged by touting the cause of an upcoming Swedish naturalist whose classification was still resisted in Britain on grounds of moral propriety.

These views of "Hill's Linnaeus," and the uses to which he put the already great taxonomer, accumulated until c. 1753. Then, in 1754, William Watson's (1715–1787) widely read synopsis of Linnaean classification appeared in the *GM*.[26] Watson was a well-placed London physician and natural philosopher with no checkered past or colorful history of notoriety, and he held that Linnaeus "has perhaps taken too great liberties" but balances his view: "If these are imperfections, they are by no means equal to the excellencies of the work, which . . . will be thankfully received by the botanists as the masterpiece of the most compleat naturalist the world has seen."[27] Early high praise from a "gentleman of science" endorsing the view that Linnaeus was becoming a one-man botanical show at mid-century. After Newton's death in 1727, no other scientist filled the void in England so securely. Linnaeus was popularized and mythologized as the "great man"; the new guru seeking to unlock nature's secrets. The *Annual Register* of 1761 ran an anonymous "Linnaeus Dream" column, imagining him wandering the globe wondering how he should live and speculating about his intimations of mortality. When the narrator wakes up, he bemoans that his ruminations have occurred in a nightmare. Closer to earth and in reality, the English botanical scene held up many other competent figures but Linnaeus was gradually coming to dominate the center stage.

This positioning intensified after his student Daniel Solander arrived in London in 1760, taken under his wing by John Ellis (1715–1787), a zoologist who became one of Solander's confidants. Ellis was no friend of Hill—few of the English botanists in 1757 were except Bute—and addressed the "Master" this way when Linnaeus sought an explanation of Bute's reasons for not appointing Solander to the future Kew Gardens. Bute was Hill's protector, Ellis wrote, and would not hear of replacing Hill with anyone else, to such fervid degree that Bute even prevented George III from full knowledge about Solander's abilities. Ellis spilled the beans:

> The reason he [Solander] was not introduced to the King was owing to Dr. Hill's being so great a favourite with Lord Bute: for if Sollander's [sic] merit had been known to the King, Dr. Hill must have sunk in the opinion of all persons that attend the court, as much as he is fallen in the opinion of all lovers of Botany and Natural History, on account of the little credit that is to be given to what he advances; for though he certainly has great abilities, the want of that fairness and exactness makes the world suspect him; and his writings are a mere drug.[28]

These were old, if incontestably valid accusations, only Ellis hammered them out with renewed vigor. The "mere drug" sneer was new, quipping and punning to cast its own spell. Ellis might as well have charged, "his writings are mere alchemy" for their hypnotic, mesmeric effect. He had hit upon something vital by aligning Hill with hypnotic stylists; "drugging" his readers no better than alchemists did. The latter would have brought to mind Hill-the-itinerant-charlatan too. But the shaft about Hill's books "as drugs" was not directed at his often commented-upon prose flair and fluency, predictable but menacing, but something else: the sense that his fluency was so *potent*; like his panaceas, it was persuasive, even mesmerizing. You believed it, you could not put it down—and Hill could administer his "medicine" so rapidly, could produce copy so quickly, that his readers swooned, fainted, or were moved to altered states. This was the real rebuff—the insult that somehow he wrote *too well*.

It was not, of course, true. Ellis's pronouncement amounted to a huge compliment, but neither his present reader, Linnaeus, nor others, to whom he later vomited his scorn, saw it that way. Hill's ability, however, now rarely went unnoticed, even by harsh assessors like Ellis. Richard Pulteney, less strident and the most authoritative "historian of botany" of the generation succeeding Hill's, glanced back in the 1790s at the botany of his youth and paused over Hill's *Flora Britannica* (according to Staffleu the so-called first Linnaean flora of England) as a "pioneering work."[29] A few pages earlier Pulteney admires Hill for "promoting the science of botany in general" but diminishes him for insufficient application of "the *Linnaean* modification in particular."[30] Pulteney was puzzled, specifically, by Hill's alternating praise and blame: why Hill's vacillation?

Pulteney found no answer to the question but knew where he stood on precedence: Hill *was first* to apply Linnaean binomial method but he "executed [Linnaeanism] in a manner so unworthy of his abilities that his work can have no claim to the merit of having answered the occasion." It is tantamount for a historian of psychiatry claiming that a hypothetical John Doe was the first man to apply Freud's theory to psychiatry but applied it so defectively that his application does not count; in which case the further matter is whether John Doe's application has been fairly appraised? After the FRS debacle and subsequent paper wars, Hill could not get a neutral or objective appraisal of his work—it was impossible. He was irrevocably tarnished after two fatal strikes out.

So the assessments decrying incompetence continued: James Smith after Pulteney, followed by others. Pulteney died in 1801 and his botanical colleague James Smith, an editor of Linnaeus's correspondence translated into English, sustained Pulteney's view: "sometimes, as Linnaeus would say, a blind hen comes across a grain of corn."[31] It was the same argument—lucky priority invalidated by incompetence—repeated to the present day in the assessment of W. T. Stearn, a much-respected historian of botany who understood Hill only as botanist and applier of Linnaeus but without any feel for the whole man in his time.

The charge of incompetence depended on two aspects: hasty application and inaccuracy, the latter more consequential as it claimed that Hill misunderstood Linnaeus's system. After Patrick Browne returned to Jamaica in 1756–1757, William Hudson (1730–1793) posed a more devastating hurdle. He, like Hill, had been apprenticed to a London apothecary and won the prize for botany given by the Apothecaries' Company, a copy of Ray's *Synopsis*; from which moment his pathway as a botanist was ensured, especially when the new librarians at the British Museum picked him to assist cataloguing the vast Sloane herbarium in 1757, just as *The Sleep of Plants* was appearing. Hudson then became resident sub-librarian there, and he was soon elected FRS.

Hudson's criticism surpassed others' and was grounded in Hill's inaccuracy. Hudson's *Flora Anglica*,[32] which—according to Pulteney and Sir J. E. Smith, the editor of Linnaeus's letters in English[33]—marked the establishment of Linnaean principles of botany in England. In awarding the palm to Hudson a challenge was made to Browne as well: not Hill in 1751, not Watson in 1754, not Browne in 1756, but now Hudson in 1762. "Precedence" clearly was a matter of whom you asked, not a fact cut in granite. Set the dials to any year then—from 1757 to 1762—and everyone had a different theory about who arrived first, and more were coming, so by the time Pulteney and Smith wrote a generation later, no one agreed.

In 1762 Hudson was practicing as an apothecary in Panton Street, off the Haymarket. Dig deeper into the new West End just as George III was getting ready to ascend the throne and you find others too, such as Hudson's neighbor, Benjamin Stillingfleet (1702–1771). He was a breed slowly dying out: at home reading the ancient Greeks or editing John Milton, then traveling in the Alps of Switzerland or France, and when he moved to Herefordshire in the 1750s to "botanize" he landed upon Linnaeus's *Species* and—in 1759—published translations of selected essays.[34] His *Tracts* provide a lucid account of the "Linnaean system" as well as an impassioned plea for the study of natural science. He had become mesmerized by Linnaeus's new taxonomy and introduced his neighbor Hudson to the Linnaean system around 1760 and may even have helped him to write the preface to *Flora Anglica*. Here, then, was another figure in the lineage of precedence from Hill and Browne through Watson and Hudson.

The introduction of a new methodology in the history of knowledge is a slippery concept that may or may not include "application." Even the term "introduction" is elusive. Hill, Browne, and Hudson "applied" the Linnaean system in their works; Watson and Stillingfleet "described" it. Hill had been chronologically first but was said to have applied it erratically, haphazardly, and inaccurately. One reason given was his lack of travel. He had never voyaged anywhere, let alone north to Labrador, as Joseph Banks soon would in 1766, or even across the English Channel beyond the peripheries of his island nation. Even as a young man Linnaeus had tasted the advantages of far-flung travel in Lapland, and more locally in Holland and England, which he commented upon as invaluable for a systematic botanist, but Hill—so far as I know—never left his island with the possible exception of one trip to Ireland, never had the means or leisure to do so. If, by the time in the mid-1760s Banks set out for Labrador, the "traveling botanist" became a stereotype as curious, courageous, self-sufficient, imaginative, intent on discovery in the service of his own pocket or country, Hill cannot have been one.

So criticism of him endured and when he published his own *Flora Britannica* in the autumn of 1760, two years before Hudson, his work was met with the customary refrain about inaccuracy.[35] Pulteney, whose first history of "the progress of botany in England" professed to deal systematically with this topic, commented on Linnaeus's status in this very year:

> . . . the learned were prepared to see the English botany modeled according to the rules of the Linnaean school. Dr. Hill seized the *first* opportunity of attempting it, in his *Flora Britannica*, of 1760; but it was executed in a manner so unworthy of his abilities, that his work can have no claim to the merit of having answered the occasion: and thus the credit of the achievement fell to the lot of Mr. William Hudson, FRS.[36]

Not Browne in 1756? Pulteney knew little nothing about Browne's precedence and nothing about Hill's tentacles elsewhere in Georgian culture—and earlier, in 1760, this myopia among some classes of botanists who knew Hill only as one of themselves was the rub, and how much more definitively the moderate Pulteney would have assessed the disparity between ability and accuracy if he had known.

Pulteney was at least prepared to include Hill in 1790; in 1760 others leveled the old saws and begged for respite, as did Stanesby Alchorne, a London botanist in Solander's circle, when writing to botanic savant John Ellis, mentioned above, that Hill's *Flora Angelica* was a failure: "Really, 'tis pity that so pompous a work, which, properly executed, might have been extremely useful, should, for want of care, be thus rendered of no great value."[37] Others merely satirized it, as did the *MR*'s reviewer who may have been reading the first volume of Sterne's *Tristram Shandy*, which had appeared a few weeks earlier, when he opened his lampoon this way:

> A truce for goodness' sake, dear doctor, a truce with your eternal Natural History. So much of it is really enough to turn one's stomach. Natural History roasted, Natural History boiled, Natural History baked, Natural History stewed, Natural History hashed, Natural History fricasseed indeed, indeed, Dr. Hill this is too much.[38]

NOTES

1. LPH, 75. Missing from the record are Linnaeus's responses.
2. LPH, 76.
3. JH (1751b).
4. Durris; Staffleu, 291–336.
5. See Rom Harré, "Knowledge," in G. S. Rousseau and Roy Porter (1980), 47–50.
6. The classic study is Staffleu (1971).
7. *GM* 23 (1753): 592.
8. Koerner, passim.
9. Staffleu recognizes JH for this precedence.
10. Patrick Browne (1756), 12–35.
11. E. C. Nelson (1995): 2.
12. Staffleu, 76 and 197 for the two passages.
13. Blanche Henrey (1975), vol. 2, 92.
14. Some of Browne's manuscripts survive in the Linnaean Society, including *Fa[s]ciculus plantarum Hiberniae* and correspondence with Linnaeus over the years 1756–1771.
15. Carolus Linnaeus (1735).
16. Staffleu, passim.
17. Carolus Linnaeus (1729), 4.
18. Cited in Blanche Henrey (1975), vol. 2, 95, n. 2.
19. Miller and Reill (1996), 8.
20. Blanche Henrey (1975), vol. 2, 92.
21. JH (1751b), preface; all passages in this section are found in the preface.
22. Stearn; Staffleu.
23. Schiebinger (1996a), 167, and Schiebinger (2004), who comments on these arrangements and Linnaeus's metaphorical usages.
24. Cited in Blunt, 34.
25. Schiebinger (2004), 122–25; Shteir, 15–20; Jordanova; more generally see Laqueur (1990), 171; Golinski.
26. William Watson (1754), passim.
27. Watson (1754), 558.
28. LPH, 151.
29. Pulteney (1790), vol. 2, 351; see also his retrospective estimate in Pulteney (1805).
30. Pulteney (1790), vol. 2, 293–94.
31. Pulteney (1790), vol. 2, 194.
32. William Hudson (1762).
33. J. E. Smith (1821).
34. Stillingfleet, passim.
35. *GM* 30 (October 1760): 491; *MR* 23 (1760): 407.
36. Pulteney (1790): vol. 2, 351, italics mine.
37. Cited in LPH, 124–25.
38. *MR* 23 (1760): 407.

V

15

The Theater Too?

Why was Hill "applying" Linnaeus so defectively? Or was he? Had he devoted himself primarily to botany he may not, but despite paper wars and severe writer's fatigue he had continued to toil away intermittently in Grub Street down through the 1750s, until Bute—as we saw—offered him sponsorship, which had a bizarre consequence: it made him want to return to the stage.

Instead of racing ahead with garden designs in 1758 to prove himself to his new patron, and focusing his energy there, he began to write a farce called *The Rout*, a play in two acts, and had it printed in time for Christmas.[1] The galling fact is that he plagiarized some of the plot from Arthur Murphy, the note-maker of Smart's coalition. He pilfered it almost habitually—he had loosely plagiarized all along as part of his method of composition—and probably not to avenge himself for *The Hilliad* or irritate Murphy further.

But what did Hill think he was doing: squandering his talent in this dissipated way and reverting to old habits that had landed him in such trouble? The second and third rate plagiarized and imitated others throughout the eighteenth century but only the front rank did so with impunity; classical composers like Mozart and polymaths like Coleridge brought it off with compliments from the originator but common hacks pelted each other when they detected it. Hack pelting was the order of the day now and Murphy, who perceived himself victimized, was peeved. He marched straight to his theater colleague David Garrick and complained.

The sequence of events was typically Hillian. First Hill sent Garrick, whom he had met at Goodwood almost twenty years earlier, unsolicited correspondence about its possible performance, and—Garrick needing material—agreed it could be performed for the Christmas charity at the General Lying-In Hospital. But when Garrick requested the script Hill demurred and added provisos, especially the condition that certain actors would take specific parts and that Garrick himself would act in it. Garrick generously acceded to many of the conditions and Hill eventually sent in his script. After the first or second rehearsal Murphy got wind of the plagiarisms and moaned to Garrick, by which time it was so close to Christmas as to be too late to cancel the performances to pacify Murphy.

It flopped after two nights and was pulled out of repertory by the hospital's governors at considerable loss of charity revenue. Hill was, of course, disappointed but did not stop here. He demanded payment for the loss he had sustained with Mary Cooper, his printer-publisher. But there had been no agreement to pay him anything—this was a charity. He had indeed paid Cooper to print it but knew that it could flop at any time. The upshot was confusion and the leveling of accusations on all sides, leaving Garrick in the middle of a mess that alienated all those involved: Murphy for having been duped, the governors for loss of revenues, Garrick for not having anticipated the results, and Hill most of all.

Hill had demanded handouts before—this was not new. The sequence is more pertinent for demonstrating how Hill worked, and continued to operate even when things went well as they did now under the promise of Bute's sponsorship. Still worse, such audacious tactics were transparent. Did he think his cohorts were fools? He could not if he had seen the dig in the *LM* around that time. Using the scatological analogy it warned readers that "if wading through dunghills, &c. the impropriety of wading thro' an HILL may be forgiven."[2] The hack writer does not pin his stars to a particular work but refers to Hill-the-phenomenon. Hill's stock that autumn was still high; the *MR* referred to him in November (1758), when rehearsals of *The Rout* had commenced, as "the prince of compilers,"[3] one whose advantages at least equaled his defects. To clinch the claim he and Henrietta moved that autumn from elegant Arlington Street to even finer quarters in St. James's Street; not any distance but a move to prove they were still upward bound.

Garrick was a giant in the eighteenth-century theater, Hill a dwarf, if that, yet they had dealings of a sort even before they fell out over *The Rout*. Earlier, they had grown cool to each other over Peg Woffington, down at Richmond's country house, after which they had no further contact. Not that

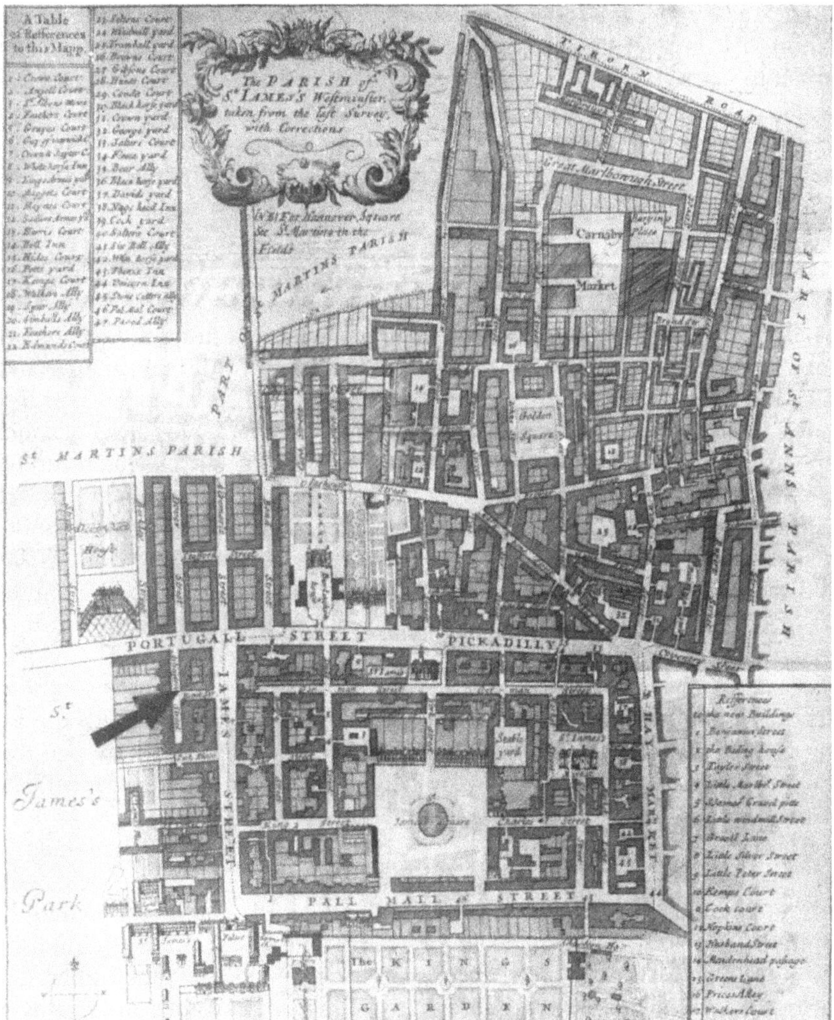

Figure 15.1. St. James Square, London, c. 1760.
Reproduced by kind permission of Professor George Rousseau.

Garrick was in love with Woffington: MacSwiny was, but Garrick supported the Irishman to the end.

Flash forward fifteen years to around 1755, and Hill sends Garrick a farce called *The Maiden Whim; or, the Critical Minute,* a play in two acts about fools in romantic entanglements and stratagems calculated to dupe each other.[4] John Rich, Hill's other dramatic enemy, had rejected it for production at Covent Garden, but Garrick read it for the following season. Hill sent it to

Garrick as by "Dr. Heffinal," perhaps a fantasy on his own shorter name, although it is tempting to see the joke in "Hill-final." Or Hill may have sent it to Garrick himself as the work of this fictitious doctor; which could explain Garrick's interest and subsequent production on April 24, 1756. But it lasted for just one night and quickly fell out of repertoire for lack of sales. Now—two years later, in the autumn of 1758—Hill again approached Garrick, this time in his own name and having already transformed *The Maiden Whim* into *The Rout*.

He was spurred to contact Garrick by Bute's wife, Mary Wortley Montagu (1718–1794), the only daughter of Lady Mary Wortley Montagu, who was Garrick's friend. But the tangle of relations was complicated. Garrick and Lord Bute were on good terms, who so far had no conflict of interest over Hill. But now, by the autumn 1758, Hill was on familiar terms with *both* Butes, husband and wife, and Mary Montagu complemented her husband's largesse by paving the way for Hill with Garrick. So Garrick was receptive, and Hill showed *The Rout* to Garrick in manuscript (it was not yet printed), with its characters Feeble, Felix, Rhodamintha, Lady Never Settle, Blunderbuss, Balloon, and others, and read parts of the farce aloud to him, as well as discussed its strengths and weaknesses.[5] Garrick claimed to like the first act, even agreed to perform in it himself, but judged the second unfit for production in its current state. Hill revised the second act to fit Garrick's suggestions and resubmitted it to him, only to find that Garrick remained steadfast in his earlier negative appraisal. The more Hill nudged, the less Garrick bit, and the likelihood is that Garrick was being polite when they first read the play aloud. Once again, Hill had misunderstood the most basic of social codes, modest interest as polite rejection.

A long extant letter from Garrick to Hill provides the further details. At this first approach Hill read the relevant parts of the farce so quickly—his common daily talk was also presto—that Garrick could not gather his thoughts until he saw the text before him. When he did, he decided that the debauched "Feeble" was inconsistent; impeded the plot rather than furthered it. Worse yet, "Weedle" was entirely implausible, his stratagem to win the girl unsuitable for the stage. Garrick opined that if "Balloon and Blunderbuss"—two other fops—could assume the characters of noblemen and impose on "Feeble" unaware, the plot might work and "the Rout," however mock this would-be rout, could pass muster.

Garrick held out hope, perhaps wishing to please Mary Montagu: your new "Comic Situations," he wrote to Hill, "will mend the plan greatly."[6] And he further described how Hill should revise the plot:

> . . . the Son I think, in the Character of the Fortune teller, should have a tete a tete with the Bawd, & should confess to her, that she is a unhappy Young Woman who was debauch"d, & forsaken & that She follow-d fortune telling for her Livelyhood, and upon Which the Bawd brings him naturally & with

more force into the Plot upon Feeble—this I think would make a comic Scene & Inrich the Piece.

He also forewarned Hill: "without some such alteration, I must repeat what I said Yesterday that there would be danger in it." He also offered his note-jottings if Hill would collect them—"I have many more hints to give; if they are worth Yr Notice, which I have set down in my Memorandum Book"—and offered to meet Hill that very same evening back stage at Drury Lane if Hill would come there. But he could not call on him at his lodgings in St. James's because he was going to retreat to Hampton Court "for my headach [*sic*] which is Still obstinate."

Hill was absent. He requested a private audience with Garrick because he did not wish to be seen backstage "in public." He insisted that if they met in Garrick's apartment near Drury Lane no one else could be present: "what we have to speak concerning the alteration of the farce I think should not be before a person unacquainted with those matters." His reason for demanding a private meeting was financial but nonetheless galling: he pleaded that he was still broke and in failing health and would rather not negotiate a fee in the presence of others. Garrick may have taken pity and eventually agreed, although he must have been puzzled by the extent of Hill's dire financial quandary.

Was he being polite when he wrote to Hill? "I am not well & am oblig'd to go into the Country till Tuesday."[7] Garrick's recuperation at Hampton Court did not serve its purpose; he claimed to be retreating further afield. Hill took umbrage, thought he was being messed about, and pleaded again. Garrick—to his credit and perhaps with a further eye on the Butes—replied with tact and candor, explaining that he had dealt fairly with Hill at every turn, had honestly assessed the farce, and repeated his offer to produce *The Rout* the following season if Hill would revise it.

When Hill became abusive, Garrick kept his cool: "If I could not have Acted your Farce this Winter, I should have said so & my desiring to see it, implied that If I thought any advantage could be reap'd from it, that it should be done. . . ." He urged Hill again not to take offense and revise the farce: "I think it is more *Idle* to lose time about Words & neglect the End of your writing." He invited Hill to send him the revisions as soon as they were ready, indicating he was prepared to slate it for production at the Christmas charity at the Lying-In Hospital in York Road in Lambeth: "If you chuse to trust me with the Perusal of your Farce, I will send You my opinion of it as soon as possible, & if I think yr End of Writing it can be answer'd I will certainly do it—Perform it this Winter."

Coming from Garrick this was genuine promise but Hill's antics stymied him: "There is a certain Air of incivility in yr last Letter which I think is the Idlest thing of all—I Use Every Gentleman with Justice & Good Manners, & Expect from Dr. Hill a return in Kind."[8] The "good Doctor's" letter is lost but he cannot have moaned about Garrick's civility and encouragement, which had been exemplary for someone whose alarm bells about Hill extended back two decades. Garrick held steady, not wanting to lose favor with the Butes and well aware of Hill's new patronage, but also resigned that he stood to make no profit by producing *The Rout* as a charity. It was overreacher Hill—the still thin and overworked Hill forever trying to rise above his talent—who demanded he needed the money.

Hill complied: he took Garrick's suggestions on board, satisfied Garrick and the hospital governors. The December dates of their Christmas play were fixed—until theater manager and actor Arthur Murphy entered the fray. He wrote to Garrick saying that Hill had plagiarized the farce from *him*, and further intimating that if Hill had not stolen it, Garrick had plagiarized it, or would appear to have done so if he produced it. So now Hill was back in the thickets of scandal, as he had been for so much of his public life.

Garrick was stunned: the first performance was in just fourteen days from the time he received Murphy's letter, tickets were being sold, they had arrived at a point of no return. But Garrick was bewildered by the "theft." Had Hill stolen from an as yet *unpublished* farce? Or pilfered from an old farce of Murphy's already printed? What was the truth? Garrick knew well how common charges of plagiarism were on the stage, and pleaded with Murphy to calm down: "I am as ignorant of It's being a Piracy from You, as I am surpriz'd that you shou'd imagine that I would be Either base enough to steal it from You or Malevolent enough to give the hint of it to anyone Else."[9]

Garrick provided Murphy with his reasons: "As to Dr. Hill . . . I have not had the least intimacy with him for some Years." This was true, but even Garrick took offense at Murphy's behavior, claiming that he himself, Garrick, had been the most bruised of all: "But is it not somewhat Extraordinary that You should send Us such a Letter when You gave your Honour to Dr. Macdonaugh (as he told me) that You would Suspend Your Opinion till the Farce was Acted, and that . . . You were quite Satisfy'd about it."[10] In other words, Murphy should "apply" to the hospital governors if he wished to gain compensation from the hospital for performing a play originally his.

Murphy retracted, tickets continued to be sold, the charity produced Hill's *Rout* with Garrick, and perhaps Murphy, too acting in it, but after two nights of boos the managers closed it down for lack of further sales.[11] Hill sat it out, but after Christmas he wrote to the managers demanding the full amount of their agreed sum. No contract has been found, but if they signed one—a big if—it may have provided Hill with royalties whether or not the *Rout* ran its full course; and Hill claimed the managers had no one to blame but themselves for its defective production and ticket sales and therefore they must pay up. When they fell silent he threatened legal action; in return, the managers ran advertisements in London newspapers exposing Hill's extortion. The old-style gossip about Hill began to swell anew—excessive and frantic—and John Hawkesworth, Johnson's early biographer, published his own "Observations" of the growing fracas in the *GM* in January 1759, decrying Hill's pecuniary motives:

> Who now, after all this [fracas], would imagine, that the *veritable* author of the *Rout* is no other than Dr. *Hill*; that it was written and offered for representation *before* the public charity was in view; that the representation of it was *not* interrupted by the indisposition of a performer, but by the distaste of the public; that the primary view of it was *profit to the author*; that the managers, who, in the advertisement, are said to be *welcome* to any advantage that might result from it, have been solicited for a pecuniary gratification, even after the piece was set aside.

Hawkesworth raised everyone's temperature by this revelation that an ailing performer was a cover-up; the real reason for cancellation, he wrote, was "the distaste of the public." The managers, armed with this back-up and ammunition—the honest reason—hardened their reserve not to pay up; and when they continued not to in February Hill retaliated in a vituperative pamphlet claiming it was Garrick's flawed pronunciation that caused cancellation, not some indisposed player.

This new reason was wilder than Garrick could have imagined and went beyond the managers' alibi—at least their cover-up was polite; Hill's was grotesque. Framed as a letter addressed *To David Garrick, Esq; The Petition of I. In Behalf of Herself and her Sisters,*[12] it was written as a woman in first-person narrative, a female actress who had been robbed of fees and alleging that the cancellation was caused by Garrick's funny pronunciation of the letter *i*: *furm* for firm, *vurtue* for virtue, and so forth. Foolishly Hill also sent Garrick advance warning of the pamphlet in the form of manuscript leaves before it was printed in March, again by his old standby Mary Cooper. And Hill also sent similar leaves to two of Garrick's friends: Edmund Burke, recently having finished *Essay on the Sublime*, and Garrick's youthful friend Thomas Gataker, now in the 1750s producing his own herbals and medicinal tracts.[13]

Infuriated, Garrick drafted a severe reply he apparently never sent but which he showed to Burke and Gataker, who urged him not to inflame the debacle further as Hill liked "fights." Garrick took their advice and wrote philosophically to Hawkesworth, in fits and starts, wondering how the world produces "Hills": "could you have imagin'd that there could Exist such a Being as Hill?—Matters very low with him & he wants to make a printed Quarrel of it."[14] Then Garrick, having decided that Hill merited more pity than fury, bit his lip and calmed down, vowing he would say no more to Hill.

Hill's printed *Petition* rolled off Mary Cooper's press by March 20, 1758. He wondered why there was no response from Garrick, who privately confided to Hawkesworth that Hill was seeking to discredit him with the Duke of Devonshire, his friend and moneylender. Perhaps Hill teased this information out of Bute, as it is unlikely Garrick had been foolish enough to divulge it himself. "The virtuous Dr. Hill," a stunned Garrick wrote, "has petition'd ye Duke of Devonshire against me, but that won't do—his Grace knows ye Whole—such a villain never existed! His scheme now is abuse—& he talks of a paper call'd ye *Theatre* in which his Pen will be as free as my Crabstick whenever I meet his Worship—I have prov'd Every assertion in his Petition to be Lyes from his own Letters—I am almost kill'd with my fatigues-dead! dead— . . ."[15]

By the winter of 1759 Hill had played Harlequin, Oroonoko, Blandford, Constant, Lothario, and the apothecary in *Romeo and Juliet*—and disappointed most viewers in all except the last role on grounds that here he could just be himself, an apothecary. He could "act" in daily life but not on the stage; perhaps proving the truism that those uncertain of who they are cannot portray others. Meanwhile it was still winter in 1759 and folk were waking up to the boiling fracas, some wondering how the persistent "Inspector" had risen yet again, like the phoenix, in public awareness, others questioning how he had coerced Garrick to produce his farce. "There is a current question about town," one pamphleteer trumpeted, "notwithstanding all the excellencies of the *Rout*, which few people can resolve. It is how the Doctor has been so far able to recommend himself, and his work. . . ."[16] The anonymous journalist has no solution but continues to wonder how one man can "produce above three eighteen penny pamphlets a week."[17] He could because print turnaround was so swift, as historians of print culture have demonstrated. If weeks, or months, were needed such fracases could not have occurred along these lines and all may have been placated.

Something else momentous also occurred that winter. Robert Thyer, the Oxford educated scholar who became Chetham's Librarian in Manchester, finally brought out his long awaited edition of Restoration satirist Samuel Butler's works.[18] It included Butler's portrait of the "Mountebank," a "character" especially given to selling potions on the street-stage, vivifying their efficacy there, and then puffing them again in cheap penny pamphlets. Garrick was a subscriber. When he received his copy, around at this time, he must have been impressed to read Butler's account of how the charlatan "administers Physick with a Farce," just as Hill had done all his life. He dramatized the medicine's magic and acted out the cure. Butler's point was that the "character of the mountebank" extended back to Paracelsus in a pseudo *traditio studii* that encouraged him to fertilize his profits with effluvia streaming from Grub Street.[19]

Garrick remembered Butler's incisive line, "administers Physick with a Farce." It did not quell his fury over *Hill's* farce but tempered it. He told Hawkesworth that spring, if he ever came upon Hill in the square, "conveniently, I could not help throwing a few pounds upon his bones," and then recounted how he was "with some gentlemen the other day" when one of them produced for his eyes the new mezzotint of Hill by Richard Houston that endowed its subject with a fully rounded face and made him look ruddy and plump.[20] So impecunious Hill was eating after all. And Garrick's narrative evoked such merriment in the company that "it was propos'd Each of us shd try to make a Motto for it Extempore." When the company heard Garrick's Butlerian couplet, they clapped and judged it best of the lot:

> For Physick & Farces, his Equal there scarce is,
> His Farces are Physick, his Physick a Farce is.[21]

Nothing more pithily summed up Hill's multifaceted career. From "Physick" to "Farce" indeed.

NOTES

1. JH (1758l).
2. *LM* (February 1757): 10.
3. *MR* 19 (1758): 508.
4. LPH, xxix; no copy appears to have survived.
5. LPH, 99–113 for the details.
6. LPH, 99 for all quotations in this paragraph.
7. LPH, 101.
8. LPH, 101; see also Little and Kahrl (1963) 1: 293.
9. LPH, 103.
10. LPH, 103–4 for Macdonaugh.
11. The evidence is insufficient to ascertain whether or not Murphy did act in it.
12. JH, 1759f.
13. Little and Kahrl, vol. 1, 303 and LPH, 110; JH was aware of Gataker's botanical books but they seem never to have met.
14. LPH, 110.
15. LPH, 112.
16. Anonymous, *A Letter to the Author of . . . the Rout* (1759), 26.
17. Anonymous, *A Letter*, 26–27.
18. Butler (1759).
19. And also looking forward to Mesmer in France.
20. For the painting and its complicated background see LPH, 108 and Figure 18.1.
21. LPH, 107–8.

16

Annus Mirabilis 1758–1759

Garrick's ditty soared to fame—a type of epigrammatic monument commemorating Hill's folly for eternity. It continued to be an oft-quoted chestnut, toasting Hill and much reprinted in the nineteenth century. Now, as the 1750s drew to a close, the weeklies and monthlies ran their own versions, and anonymous scribblers joined in the litany too, as in this silly ditty imitating Garrick's voice:

> If 'tis true, as you say, that I've injur'd a letter,
> I'll change my notes soon, and I hope for the better:
> May the just right of letters, as well as of men,
> Hereafter be fix'd by the tongue and the pen;
> Most devoutly I wish that they both have their due,
> And that *I* may never be mistaken for *U*.[1]

But these heaps of accumulating verbiage disguise the matter: Bute had held out his palm to Hill but placed little money in it and—more pressingly—he had not yet asked Hill to perform many tasks in Augusta's gardens. This is why the Hills were starving and Hill in such pecuniary straights. They still had young mouths to feed and high rates to pay for their new accommodations in St. James, into which they had moved around 1757–1758.

The gardening component of his arrangement with Bute was fundamental: Hill thought he had been invited to supervise the expanding site, in just a few years to become the vast gardens at Kew, but Bute suddenly selected William Aiton (1731–1793), who was already caring for Augusta's small "physic garden" in Kensington, to be head gardener and charged him with establishing the herbaceous plant garden on the Linnaean system. Perhaps Hill did something to exclude himself; or the squabble with Bute's friend

Garrick may have opened his eyes, or his wife's, to another side of Hill; or Bute may just have preferred his much younger fellow Scot—it is impossible to know. Either way Bute coordinated operations with Aiton rather than Hill, as well as procured trees and plants through his contacts from around the world, creating the foundation on which his successor, Sir Joseph Banks, would subsequently build.

Hill was marginalized—but not entirely. He still rode horse out to Kensington Gardens a few times a week, leaving the children with Henrietta, and worked in various gardening capacities assisting Bute, his main task to increase the number of species at Kew. He did this with ferocious industry, and by 1768 their number reached 3,400.[2] Poetaster Henry Jones prefaced his poem, *Kew Gardens: A Poem in Two Cantos*, with a footnote stating that any verses about that place must mention Hill too.[3] Kew and Sion House, Northumberland's Middlesex seat, were then often yoked in popular sentiment, their adjoining land contiguous; Hill sometimes pictured, or confused, as head gardener of both places. He was not, but what did he do with his time if not garden for Bute to ameliorate his, and Henrietta's, parlous financial condition?

He was churning out herbals whose overall production, including the use of amanuenses, paper, copyright fee paid to the publisher, printing, engravings with the occasional use of the very expensive Ehret, cost him as much as his living expenses. Usually having arriving first, now he tapped into the herbal market: printing pamphlets about them, selling herbs in a stall in Kensington Gardens, and touting their medicinal value.[4] So far the herbal cause found no other major champion at mid-century and Hill sensed the gap, which took time and at first produced few revenues.

In 1758–1759 he also continued to produce potboilers at record speed, at least one a month: *An Idea of a Botanical Garden in England, The Gardener's New Kalendar, The Book of Nature; or, The History of Insects, Outlines of a System of Vegetable Generation, The Conduct of a Noble Commander in America, The Construction of the Nerves and Causes of Nervous Disorders, The Virtues of Wild Valerian in Nervous Disorders*, and many others, many heralding the coming tide of nervous diseases.[5] *Wild Valerian* puffed the valerian cure Hill hoped would take off and it did, for by the end of the summer the monthlies were widely advertising *Wild Valerian* for all conditions of (what we call) stress, not merely an antidote to the use of opiates for nervous folk. This tract brought him credit and profit, as well as the endorsement of others—Wesley and Buchan—who agreed with him.

Hill timed *Valerian*'s appearance perfectly. Nervous afflictions were rarely fatal but they were overtaking others for over a decade: the new, common syndrome medical men—physicians to apothecaries—reporting having heard from their patients. In one post-Cheynean generation nerves had

Figure 16.1A. Water Valerian, 1750.
Reproduced by kind permission of the Wellcome Library, London.

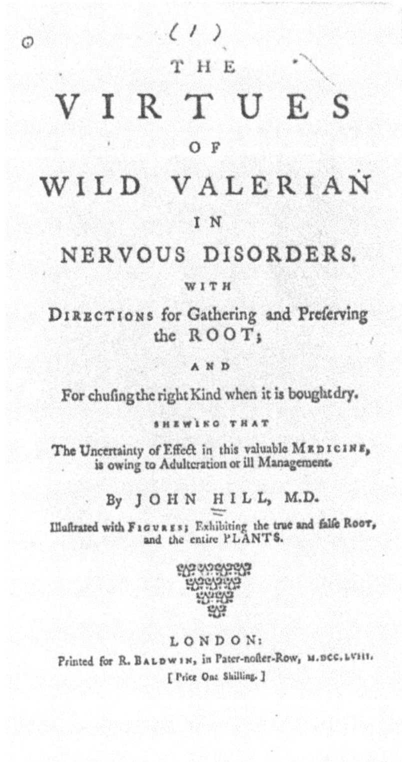
(1)

THE

VIRTUES

OF

WILD VALERIAN

IN

NERVOUS DISORDERS.

WITH

DIRECTIONS for Gathering and Preſerving the ROOT;

AND

For chuſing the right Kind when it is bought dry.

SHEWING THAT

The Uncertainty of Effect in this valuable MEDICINE, is owing to Adulteration or ill Management.

By JOHN HILL, M.D.

Illuſtrated with FIGURES; Exhibiting the true and falſe ROOT, and the entire PLANTS.

LONDON:

Printed for R. BALDWIN, in Pater-noſter-Row, M.DCC.LVIII.

[Price One Shilling.]

Figure 16.1B. Title page of John Hill, *The Virtues of Wild Valerian.*
Reproduced by kind permission of the Wellcome Library, London.

grown from an arcane sphere of human anatomy to one of the most popular sources of patient indisposition. Hill touted his herbs as panaceas, especially the calming and appeasing valerian that, he claimed, was so much more than a sedative.

At Kensington he also began to raise bees, and wrote a tract about the "virtues of honey in preventing many of the worst disorders."[6] More and more of his activity was evolving around Kensington Gardens, and now, in 1758–1759, Henrietta also joined him occasionally with a daughter or two and they gathered honey in jars for sale. He could imagine himself relocating to this area of fields and gardens, so similar to the rural Rothwell of his boyhood.

He went to length to promote his honey remedy, especially as beneficial for weak lungs. By mid-century the dominant view about asthma had changed from just a generation earlier. Now the talk was of asthma's nervous genesis; the position that irritated, trapped, or even damaged nerves,

Figure 16.2. Satire on an Empiric, 1759, showing John Hill with his honey balsam.
Reproduced by kind permission of the Trustees of the British Museum.

especially in the chest, had caused it. Hill subscribed to this view and would soon amplify it for hypochondriacal complaints, which included wheezing and coughing.[7] Now he promoted the ingestion of honey as the best panacea, and advised his contemporaries to renounce exotic remedies from Africa and the East. They should not import Africa's "nauseous Ammoniacum to give breath" for this "worst condition," nor raid the Orient for Gin-seng, Fou tse, Su meon, and other equally exotic cures.[8] Local English honey was more effective but not for "convulsive Asthma," which he considered a "different distemper" altogether from ordinary asthma. While contemporary English physicians such as Philip Stern and John Mudge were patenting inhalers beginning in the 1760s to help asthmatics breathe, herbal Hill believed "Nature will heal directly by ingestion."

He had generated current reasons to think the medicinal virtue of herbs would make him a living after the herbal movement crested in the 1740s.[9] His approach was not entirely focused on herbs as counteragents for modern storm and stress. He also kept a keen ear attuned to the new medical needs of *women*, their birthing and reproductive ordeals; not merely the anxieties attached to menstruation and pregnancy but to emmenagogues, medicines to promote menstrual discharge and necessary to stimulate missed periods in non-pregnant uteruses. Herbs taken to restore the menses had a long history before his era, but most of their wisdom amounted to mumbo-jumbo propagated by charlatans to turn a quick penny. Hill's new remedies were less dishonorable than previous ones, and he also emphasized their *herbal*—their natural—utility, hence their natural efficacy, above artificial chemical preparation.

Hill had been invested, as we saw, in uterine folklore for a long time, at least since the days of his masterful *Lucina* (1750). Since then he had not thrown himself into the production of uteronic drugs, but now he was becoming an academic herbalist, quoting Hippocrates and Soranus in his texts and explicating how herbal emmenagogues could reestablish monthly evacuations and effect other salubrious menstrual conditions. He noted that ordinary maladies—chlorosis, jaundice, fever, colics—suppress the menses, but his individual take on the female predicament around 1759 was that the ever-increasing migraine was taking a toll too, especially during pregnancy. So he peddled the idea that headache complaints must be construed more seriously than they were because there was no way of knowing before the fourth month whether a woman really was pregnant.

All types of quacks and empirics had touted laxatives to induce menstruation, and bona fide doctors prescribed them as well.[10] Hill's ploy was *herbal*: to introduce a whole series of herbal remedies that both helped the openly pregnant woman overcome her tribulations and, alternatively, assist women secretly hoping to abort. But he did not neglect the other gender in its major, non-fatal affliction: gout, the so-called "comic disease" of the century but one that caused as much pain as gain for its sufferers.

During the spring of 1758, just as Smollett reissued his edition of *Peregrine Pickle* in a new, revised edition in which Hill had originally played such a destructive role, announcements rolled forth about a tract entitled *The Management of the Gout*, by "George Crine MD"—alias Hill—the first major statement since George Cheyne's influential work of the 1720s.[11] "Crine's" main reason for writing was to puff his favorite "Burdock root," which, he admitted, was not a "cure" for gout itself but would ease the symptoms and make the condition tolerable. Crine's theoretical foundation, beyond recommending burdock root, was gout's hereditary entitlement:

> Will any conduct, any application of the powers of the mind, or any regimen of life and diet, keep the man always sober, in whose family there is *hereditary madness*? Has any one seen *hereditary Leprosies* kept from appearing to the latest generations? Men therefore smiled with equal reason at the venerable and honest ancient, who thought the Gout was not hereditary; and thought it could be cured.[12]

Hereditary illness was a fraught topic among the Georgians, even if gout in 1758 had not yet provoked the controversies it would soon stir. The reviewers praised "Crine" without appearing to know it was by Hill, and passed it off as another tract. But Hill was also now no longer strenuously gardening at Kensington because pain—the pain of gout—was afflicting him. His condition progressed slowly and one wonders whether he had written, this time, about *The Management of the Gout* because he was simultaneously "managing" his own.

Yet if he was in physical distress it did not slow down his production or fluency. The 556-page book subtitled *The History of Insects* and purportedly "translated from the Dutch and Latin Original Edition, by Thomas Floyd [with] revised and improved by notes from Réaumur and others, by John Hill, M.D." abounds with curiously vivified passages about natural creatures such as "the Cuttle-Fish."

Hill claimed he had first seen it with his microscope, "and many other curious particulars too." In his preface he writes, anticipating Erasmus Darwin's sexual loves of the plants, that his purpose has been "to present a study of the *nymph* as the original ground of all the transformation of insects, or exanguious [minute] Animals." He vivifies how a nymphet drives the insect world, and loads his "revised text" with references to Linnaeus. His gloss on the spider reminds the reader that "the generical characters of the Spider kind, as established by Linnaeus, are that they have eight legs, and the same number of eyes, placed on the back part of the thorax. . . ."[13] Within months word was out that "Crine" was "Hill" and this further appraisal of the book set in:

> Hill once contracted to translate Swammerdam's work on insects for fifty guineas. After the agreement with the bookseller [Baldwin], he recollected that he did not understand a word of the Dutch language! Nor did there exist a French translation. The work, however, was not the less done for this small obstacle. Sir John bargained with another translator for twenty-five guineas. The second translator was precisely in the same situation as the first; as ignorant, though not so well paid as the knight. He rebargained with a third, who perfectly understood his original, for twenty guineas! So that the translator, who could not translate, feasted on venison and turtle, while the modest drudge, whose name never appeared to the world, broke in patience his daily bread![14]

Stories like these proliferated throughout the metropolis. Although it is difficult at this removal of time to separate fact from fiction, Hill did make some beneficial choices about topic. For example, his book about the nerves was timely in 1758: recent debates in Edinburgh, hub of the new Enlightenment medicine, between Doctors Robert Whytt and Albrecht von Haller, the Swiss physician so eager to possess every new book by Hill, were widely reported. Patients were attributing many symptoms, including wasted lungs and dissolving interiors, to its afflictions, and apothecaries who could develop panaceas for nervous ailments stood to become rich. Hill's remedies were herbal—like valerian—and in this work he explained to "nervous patients themselves" why their nervous disorders were genuine.[15] Posing as "Dr. Uvedale Price" from his broad repertoire of sobriquets, he was intuitive: most men, women, and even children, knew their bodies were bundles of nerves but did not know as how to slow them down when excited or distressed. Hill's slender tract explained how nerves were anatomically distributed throughout the body and recommended making them more "flaccid"; in other words, slowing them down; a position "nerve doctors" such as William Cullen, Thomas Beddoes, and Thomas Trotter would also advocate in the next generation.

Having grown interested in anatomical and physiological topics he also wrote a little book about the eye: *The Fabrick of the Eye and the several Disorders Which injure or destroy the Sight*, a work of fifty-six pages explaining what sight is and how to preserve it, didactically setting what to expect when wearing spectacles—a sort of *vade mecum* for the educated—and the maladies affecting the eyes.[16] He provides concise summaries for cataracts and detached retinas, and is keen to establish that "nervous conditions" give rise to these ophthalmologic ailments. But its reception was bland, unsurprising in light of its errors—so many that one wonders whether Hill lost control or was ill. "It is vain to think of assisting the sight with glasses," he notes, "they represent the objects plainer, but they commit a kind of violence upon the Eye, and always hurt weak ones."[17] And he touts his herbal remedies, especially broth of "the leaves of *vervain*" to dissolve the fluid that "fastens the Eyelids together in the morning," so transparently as to be shameless.[18] Hill also consulted standard treatises on the subject, and medical students may have learned what they knew about human sight from it.[19] Not least about the "venereal disorders of the eye," which gets a whole chapter, in an era when other writers were silent about the matter.

How was 1759 an *annus mirabilis* for Hill? For once he felt himself succeeding within a milieu that has been labeled, with some justification, the year Britain ruled the world for its expansion, dominion, and cultural achievements at home. In 1758 he published everything he could think of to bring in the guineas; the new year brought more of the same—tracts botanical, herbal, medicinal, but not literary or offensive except for the one contra Garrick—plus the fillip of Bute's patronage. A column in the *Critical Review*, perhaps penned by the magazine's founding editor—Smollett—captured the essence of Hill: "born a naturalist . . . [but such was] the trifling spirit of the age that he was compelled to become a hack . . . an universal scholar, politician, essayist, poet, novelist, and astronomer, degenerating from, perhaps, the best botanist Britain ever saw to one of the worst of her writers."[20]

Still a compliment from the man whose reputation as a novelist you have ruined, if it was Smollett. Even if not, all readers would have noticed "the best botanist Britain ever saw."

Yet Hill had not been admitted—in Goldsmith's memorable phrase—to the "Fame Machine,"[21] whereas Johnson and Hume had. Goldsmith knew whereof he pronounced, and his essays demonstrate how vigilant he was to the public repercussions of learning or "polite knowledge." Bute's encouragement could seem to have changed the equation, except that Hill was still waiting for the cash as proof. It came in 1759, as we shall see, but not before Hill wore himself out while waiting by writing another dozen books with his team of amanuenses, engravers, and printers.[22] In March *Observations on the Account Given of the Catalogue of the Royal and Noble Authors of England* and *A New Method of propagating fruit-trees, and flowering shrubs*,[23] in April *The Origin and Production of Proliferous Flowers* appeared also in foreign editions, in May *A Method of Producing Double Flowers from Single by a Regular Course of Culture*. Smollett, ensconced in fashionable accommodations on Cheyne Walk, across from the Chelsea Physic Garden and editing the *CR* for three years, wondered what to make of the rush of energy. Although medically trained Smollett was no botanist, so he asked his neighbor Philip Miller, the aging distinguished botanist and keeper of the Physic Garden across the road, to review the book; Miller must have replied negatively if the review Smollett ran indicates anything.[24] Whether Miller or Smollett wrote it is unknown but their correspondence makes plain that Miller was as antagonistic to Hill as ever. *Exotick Botany Illustrated* also appeared and works about gardening, the knowledge of plants, and the value of the microscope for naturalists. When gardener Thomas Perfect, inventor of the new Chinese parterres becoming fashionable among English landscape designers, published a handbook called *The Practice of Gardening* in June, he described himself on the title page as: "By T. Perfect, a pupil of Dr. Hill."

During that summer Hill was often with the Butes, and when Lady Mary Wortley Montagu wrote to her daughter, Lady Bute, on June 24, 1759, she inquired whether Hill would be a member of their botanizing party: "I suppose you are now at Kew, with all your rising Family about you."[25] That summer Prince George moved into the house on Kew Green that Bute had been leasing and Hill was in his company too.

The momentous event of the summer was the announcement in July that the first volume of Hill's much awaited *Vegetable System* was soon forthcoming.[26] Bute was funding it, everyone was discussing it at Kew, and Hill's spirits were high for good reason. It appeared in December and was to become, in time, the pivotal production of his botanical career, philosophical as well as illustrative, the single work to decide what his niche as a naturalist should be.

The other notable event—for English botany at large—was Daniel Solander's arrival in London. Once arrived he was astonished to discover how few English botanists were invoking the new Linnaean binomial classification and set out to convert them. Within months he realized that conversion was no easy task, that he could succeed more assuredly with institutional support; and when the governors of the new British Museum that had opened on January 15 (1759) sought a full-time naturalist Solander was selected. His friends, including Watson, Ellis, Collinson, and Miller, paved the way, Collinson, his sponsor, privately writing to Lord Bute to petition him to have a word with the future king.

Collinson's move was ambitious. His group was certain Solander would be preferred to Hill, and the Swedish Solander's "English capability," as one member put it, was becoming acceptable. Bute was partial to Hill, who had been bucking for years to get a toehold into the British Museum; but, skeptical after the notorious row in the Royal Society and more recently with Garrick, found himself agreeing about Solander as the natural choice. He was happy to continue to sponsor Hill and fund his magnum opus, the *Vegetable System*, but not endorse him for the post to Prince George. Hill knew nothing of Bute's deliberations, lingered in the dark as much as he had when competitors such as da Costa slid away from him. Naïve and possibly altogether deluded about his chances, he continued to hope Bute would endorse him while Bute was secretly promoting Solander. He had other matters on his mind too during that spring as the British tried to protect their troops in Canada.

Hill remained foolishly optimistic this season, even while waiting to hear the outcome. He may have felt differently if he could have known what t'Town was saying. In May Horace Walpole wrote to his constant confidant Henry Zouch that he was "tired of reading foolish criticisms" of himself.[27] A few weeks earlier he emptied his heart about the post to his boyhood friend Thomas Gray, his quondam intimate, explaining how "that puppy Dr. Hill had taken up his cause with the *Critical Review*" and defended him in a full-length pamphlet.

Hill had come to Walpole's defense after the *CR* savaged his publication about England's "noble authors." "Now to my distress," Walpole whined to Gray, "I have been childishly unhappy about it"—about Hill's defense; so miserable that Walpole took out an affidavit against Hill that his cautious friends would not let him sign or send. What disturbed Walpole most was Hill's "affected intimacy"—no wonder he was fed up with "authors" and the sense that Hill could "speak of him in that [familiar] style." There was nothing in this episode beyond Walpole's bruised sense of his own elevated station. He had never met Hill, and if Walpole had not tasted Hill's sycophancy now it was time he did.

The wart crusted and dried, but not without Walpole's eyes and ears open for further Hillian antics. And when the new administration of George III was installed, in just a few months he was shocked to find Hill "preferred" in the equivalent of our New Years Honors List. Simmering, he wrote again to Zouch:

> I am sorry to say this journeyman [Hill] is one of the first men preferred in the new reign: he is made gardener of Kensington, a place worth £2000 a year. The King and Lord Bute have certainly both of them great propensity to the arts—but Dr. Hill, though undoubtedly not deficient in parts has as little title to favour in this reign, as [Samson] Gideon the stockjobber in the last; both engrossers without merit.[28]

Walpole's outrage must be understood in relation to Goldsmith's developing "fame machine" as well as to his specific resistance to Hill, whom he had never met. Today, our "star celebrities" earn fantastic sums for their possessions: wardrobes, wigs, bras, cars, even photographs of their children. Recently, in Britain, a celebrity was paid more than $10,000,000 for permission to publish photographs of her newborn twins. This frenetic pitch had just begun in Georgian England, its signs slowly emerging, and Hill's high pay as journalist and gardener owed more to his celebrity status than any objective measure of his excellence. This is, in part, what Walpole carps against.

Walpole also denounced both Hill and Samson as courting excess—"engrossing"; consuming, amassing, buying up everything, respectively copies of publications to sell (Hill) and stocks to trade (Gideon). Walpole's did so hypocritically, considering that he himself was the most prolific "engrosser"—producer—of letters of his century. As depreciatory was his indictment of Hill as "journeyman": the hireling who drudged away for others and could never be master of his own business. Walpole's blatant hypocrisy apart, Zouch was astonished by the sum of £2000, told Gray how shocked he was, and, presto, now the hard-up Gray too began to follow Hill's career avidly. Within weeks Gray was writing to his own constant correspondent, Thomas Wharton, to confirm Walpole's report about the £2000, and by a process of exponential exchange Hill again became the talk of t'Town in 1759.

What did Walpole know of Hill's past? Was he *au fait* was the scandals in the Royal Society and Hill's paper wars? It is impossible to know, but he had certainly been chasing Hill closely for some time. In 1751 he noted that at £1500 Hill was the highest paid journalist in the realm; not a preposterous sum when one recalls that Robert Baldwin, Hill's most lucrative printer-publisher, paid him almost £500 for a single title, but Walpole's figure was still probably exaggerated. Bute never paid Hill a fee close to £2000 nor bestowed on him the title of "head gardener." Whatever their arrangement, it was less formal than Walpole gave out; and "one of the first men preferred in the new reign" overdoes the reality. The point is rather Hill's public image and Walpole's consequential amazement: what was England coming to if "journeymen" hirelings were earning these amounts? Translate the amounts into contemporary buying power and it is not far from bankers' six-figure bonuses.

Something else occurred to energize Hill as the clock turned to 1760. Despite severe exhaustion his gouty health held up, his children were growing up, and occasionally he and Henrietta entertained in St. James—when they could afford it—sometimes local residents. One was Messenger Monsey (1694–1788), an eccentric physician who moved there in 1751 and liked to boast about *Tristram Shandy*—it had appeared a few months earlier—as the work of "his friend," the curate of Coxwold, silly bravado that riled egoists among their neighbors who wished they had been acquainted with the most talked-up novelist that season.

Figure 16.3. Dr. Messenger Monsey.
Reproduced by kind permission of Professor George Rousseau.

In March someone published *Remarks on Sterne's Tristram Shandy*, glossing Sterne's bawdy allusions and making his innuendoes explicit, as well as imitating his style, including the odd dialects and use of dashes. Hill also exploited the current "Shandy mania" by compiling a first biography of Sterne in the *Royal Female Magazine*.[29] Within days readers detected Hill's hand in it—no other likely author was suggested. It was remarkably well informed for a first life, and named names and exposed confidences despite its genial tone. But where did Hill get all his information? Especially, how did he discover the story about the ecclesiastical quarrel underlying Sterne's *Political Romance*?[30]

Hill's approach is anecdotal and dwells on Sterne's bawdry. He hones in on Yorick, the lascivious parson who may be Tristram's father in Sterne's convoluted plot, having conducted a secret dalliance with Elizabeth Shandy, Tristram's mother, and weaves a web around Yorick's carnal affliction. Then Hill contends that the original of the irreverent "Kunastrokius" was Dr. Richard Mead, the deceased noteworthy London physician, and divulges: "I am afraid Mr. Yorick [read Sterne] has indeed been merry with the respectable character of Dr. Mead under a name—'Kunastrokius'—which I don't know how to write to a lady."[31] Hill was as aware of Mead's "voluptuous foibles," as he was of Sterne's theological disputes. He had referred to Mead's frailty in that department in his letters. But Mead died six years earlier, in 1754,[32] and what had been an open secret about Mead when Hill penned *Lucina* at mid-century now became the topic of public innuendo in Sterne's best-selling novel. Hence Hill seized on this ribald invention of *Tristram Shandy* to vivify his own "little life."

Sterne was not amused, nor was Monsey. They had never met, but Sterne was certain he had been given a licking at Monsey's expense. Within days Sterne dashed off an enraged letter to his friend Stephen Croft in York:

> I this moment received the favour of your kind letter.—The letter in the Ladies Magazine about me, was wrote by the noted Dr. H[ill], who wrote the Inspector, and undertakes that magazine—the people of York are very uncharitable to suppose any man so gross a beast as to pen such a character of himself.—In this great town no soul ever suspected it, for a thousand reasons—[33]

Sterne then embroiders the animosity between Hill and Monsey:

> You must know there is a quarrel between Dr. H[ill] and Dr. M[onse]y, who was the physician meant at Mr. C[harles] S[tanhope]'s, and Dr. H[ill] has changed the place on purpose to give M[onse]y a lick.—Now that conversation, (tho' perhaps true) yet happen'd at another place, and with another physician; which I have contradicted in this city for the honour of my friend M[onse]y, all which shews the absurdity of York credulity, and nonsense. Besides the account is full of falsehoods . . . —and indeed there are so many other things so untrue, and unlikely to come from me, that the worst enemy I have here never had a suspicion—and to end all Dr. H[ill] owns the paper.[34]

Hill may have "owned it" but this was just the commencement of further fracas that spring. Garrick assured Sterne that Hill was its author, further vexing the abused parson. By the end of April the *London Chronicle* was serializing Hill's "life." It appeared in its issues of May 3–6, and soon other newspapers were also reprinting it. Hill no longer needed to puff himself: the weeklies performed that stock-in-trade trick for him. On June 19th Sterne, still fuming, complained to Warburton that Hill's life was "the most inimicitous' [*sic*] thing ever written about him [Sterne] . . . a contexture of Lies."[35] Warburton was then at Prior Park, near Bath, and replied hastily to Sterne: ". . . for dulness, who often has as great a hand as the devil, in deforming God's works of the creation has made them, it seems, *male* and *female*."[36] But Warburton wrote sloppily: the referents of his genders are unclear. Is this ambiguous gender the *Royal Female Magazine* or Hill or both?

Either way, the scuttlebutt continued into the summer without any light breaking on the underlying source of irritation between Hill and Monsey.[37] After all, that had been the *fons et origens*. Hill never met Monsey, despite their being neighbors in St. James, nor corresponded with him. They shared nothing in common. Monsey had been coarse mannered from youth, it is true, but this, in itself, was insufficient for Hill to turn on him. But Monsey had brushed others than Hill the wrong way. Johnson loathed him and Garrick had sparred publicly with him. His loose and debased conversation was couched in a rough sort of charm that pricked Hill, who spoke affectedly himself. Perhaps Hill tapped into something Monsey had done now lost to time. What stands out more than these petty perturbations are the extensive quarrels of the age, many of which have been suppressed by modern scholars to portray an eighteenth century transformed without them. This is the greater point rather than the petty tiff. Did ever authors and physicians quarrel more continuously? What would it even mean to our generation to intimate that authors and physicians "quarrel" to this extent?

Sterne may have thought he had trounced Hill, at least to Stephen Croft and Warburton, but he was further embarrassed the following June (1761) by the reprint of Hill's narrative, together with other scurrilous anecdotes about him, in a pamphlet of seventy-two pages entitled *Tristram Shandy's Bon Mots, Repartees, odd Adventures, And Humourous Stories*.[38] Hill played no part in this pastiche compilation beyond being named, but the knowledge about his authorship of the "little life" was now indelible fact. Christopher Flagellan, a hack's alias, rub-a-dubbed Hill in this parody as: "Hillius Anatomico-Herbario-Ethico-dramatico-philologico-theologico-Chymicus."[39]

Hill was not listening—he was too busy ghosting further pro-Bute pamphlets in his never flagging determination to please his patron and, upon occasion, resorting to old habits, as when he paid the publisher William

Stevens to publish his spoof on the Society for the Encouragement of Arts, Manufactures and Commerce, which Richmond had founded before his death.[40] Hill signed it "Your most Obedient (tho' rejected) Humble Servant, THE INSPECTOR"—reminding them that a decade later he was still remembered in this way—and billed it as a "Second Edition," as he did so many of his first editions; framing it as a "Letter to the Secretary," with asides to "the Leather-Dressers, Tanners and Book-Binders" and inscribing it to "the Inspector's Hide." The Society had rejected him and he reminded them that he was tough; he had been repelled before and was now offering prizes to members who invented "useful" projects such as "To the first Officer that shall wear a pair of Jack-boots made from the hide of a French Trooper, which the Officer has slain, A Gold Medal."[41] The Society never replied.

As the new decade of the 1760s opened Hill's spirit was still intact, although he remained frightfully fatigued and occasionally gouty, and increasingly rode out to Kensington Gardens for "the pure air to relax his nerves." The 1750s had exhausted him; what would the 1760s bring? He published a little tract early in 1760 about Jacob Theodor Klein's (1685–1759) microscopic research into marine plants.[42] Klein was a German naturalist who had read about Hill in the works of European scientists and construed his botany seriously. But marine plants were small feed compared to the fate of one of Hill's next works: *Cautions against the immoderate use of snuff. Founded on the known qualities of the tobacco plant; And the Effects it must produce when this Way taken into the Body: and enforced by instances of persons who have perished miserably of diseases, occasioned, or rendered incurable by its use.*[43] This fifty-eight-page tract argued that chewing tobacco was dangerous and gave rise to different cancers.

In 1970 Dr. Donald Eugene Redmond, an American research physician at the Illinois State Psychiatric Institute, published a learned article in the most prestigious of medical journals—the *New England Journal of Medicine*—claiming he, Redmond, had made a startling discovery: nothing less than that John Hill was the first man to link smoking and cancer.[44] Hill's *Cautions against the immoderate use of snuff* had shown that the excessive use of snuff and tobacco caused ulcerations of the mouth leading to cancer, and that chewing tobacco or smoking it is even more fatal.[45] Hill's hunch was based on anecdotal evidence and the observation of a few dozen cases. Years later he returned to cancer and restated his claim about tobacco's pernicious effects, for which Griffiths ran a long review citing this as one of Hill's more significant medical works but remaining silent about any "discovery."[46]

Dr. Redmond thought he knew better but his history of medicine was defective. A debate had brewed for over a century weighing the virtues of taking tobacco against its vices, the main controversy between tobacco's reparative effects and its injury to health. Simon Paulli (1603–1680), a Dane who became a professor of medicine at the University of Copenhagen, had warned against its excessive abuse; his treatise about it was translated into English as recently as 1746,[47] which Hill may have seen. Doctor Cheyne, on the other hand, considered tobacco a wonderful "Hobby Horse" to those it could divert, as did Dr. Thomas Short, a Bath physician who imported it in quantities from the New World.[48] But as mid-century loomed, concerns about its increased use grew and apothecaries and physicians began to campaign against its excessive use.[49] Even Fielding had recently referred to "the Demon of tobacco" in *Jonathan Wild*, but no one in his generation except Hill had decreed it caused ulcerations and cancer of the mouth.

On what authority? Hill's *Cautions* are concise; his tobacco-loving contemporaries would have done well to follow his advice. But no one can claim, as Dr. Redmond has, that Hill was "the first physician" to associate tobacco with cancer, sensationally positive as it may be for Hill's modern profile. Flash back to Hill in 1760–1761 and he has his eye on his pen and purse: the former churning out pro-Bute pamphlets for which he was paid but not to design gardens. These championed Bute's political savvy and denounced his enemies (there was no shortage) and dripped off the press anonymously. Charles Johnstone, an Irishman turned London author, identified their author source in *Chrysal; or, The Adventures of a Guinea*, the experimental novel he was writing during a visit to the seat in Devon of the Earl of Mount-Edgecumbe.[50] He was no friend of Bute or Bute's anti-war Tory party opposing Pitt.

An aside about *Chrysal* also relates to Hill: Samuel Johnson had been recruited to endorse *Chrysal*, which he decided to puff; an accurate sense as it proved a marketing success. Narrated by an omniscient, non-human, animal figure, it observes the follies of humankind from another worldly perspective. *Chrysal*'s strategy is mainly satiric: to describe comic scenes permitting its author simultaneously to expose and flay. One is Hill, who appears with other notables of the day in an extended scene, following the *topos* of the "lusus naturae"—as in the famous caricature shown on pages 153–54—where Hill figured prominently.

If 1759 was beneficent to Hill, subsequent years were less so. His exhaustion continued, his gout flared; Bute paid for ghostwriting but not gardening; and Hill's finances disintegrated—so calamitously in relation to the expenditures needed to produce his voluminous writing that he began to peddle seeds and plants across the ocean. His resettlement, just a few hundred yards from Kensington Gardens where he had been working for Bute, was costly and added to the burden of paying his rates in St. James.

His and Henrietta's relocation takes some understanding, not merely for the two sets of rent rates he paid but to understand his general finances. Without locating Hill's bank accounts the precise scope of his debt cannot be ascertained but his letters at this time make clear that the burden was swelling. Hill never names his creditors or cites exact figures in his correspondence but his language is expressive: "I!" He may have bleated out to play on his correspondent's (usually a potential patron) sympathy, but external sources confirm how often he exceeded his means one week only to find himself a debtor the next.

He also discovered how he could conduct business through far-flung correspondence from Bayswater, even when gouty in bed. He coordinated his North American exports and imports and increasingly corresponded with American botanists, exchanging information, buying and selling plants and specimens. In December 1766 he wrote to botanist John Bartram, father of William and founder of America's first botanical garden in Philadelphia, to order "Four Pounds of Lobelia syphilitica or the Blue Cardinal."[51] They had not been in contact before: "I believe the name of Doctor Hill is known to you tho we never corresponded: I allways have, and allways shall Espouse your Interests." Bartram was an associate of Benjamin Franklin and, like him, an original founding member of the Philadelphia Philosophical Society—based on British antecedents such as the one in Spalding near Hill's birth.[52]

Hill had followed John Bartram's botanical career in America ever since he heard about him when working for Lords Petre and Richmond, sometimes wondering why he had (Hill) not crossed the ocean too. As early as 1736 those Whig lords commissioned Bartram to travel through North America and collect its plants, and they subsidized him to print his *Observations*.[53] Hill heard much about Bartram's expeditions in Pennsylvania from Richmond and longed to meet him. When Peter Kalm, Linnaeus' disciple, stopped at Richmond's Goodwood en route to America, Hill came as close as he himself would: Kalm was going to the colonies to find Bartram.[54] By the time Hill wrote his *Inspector* columns a few years later he considered Bartram "a genius" and declared so.[55] In awe he wondered how someone so uneducated could become such a proficient naturalist; reciprocally Bartram heard about Hill and encouraged Americans coming to study botany in England to consult Hill.

For instance, William Young (1725–1788), who had been born in the West Indies and craved the English botanical experience.[56] Young set out just before war broke out in 1756 between the British and the French, making it treacherous afterward to cross the Atlantic. Once in London, Young floundered until he met Hill, and then progressed his studies. When John Bartram heard about Young's supervision he wrote to his son—William—that if Young "is put under Doctor Hill's care, he will make a botanist, as he is very industrious and hath a good share of ingenuity."[57] Young remained an assistant of Hill's for about two years, thereafter sailing back to the colonies and noting in his diary: "August 21, 1766, William Young, Jr. left London where he had been a pupil of the entrepreneur, John Hill, to return to Philadelphia."[58]

More than this exists to Young's discipleship. Among the specimens and living plants he brought with him from the colonies was the Venus flytrap, which interested Hill who included discussion of it in various books, especially in a little tract about "Curious Insects, Elegant Trees, and Plants."[59] Hill wrote that his former "pupil" Young—Hill calls him "student"—was responsible for introducing live specimens of the Venus flytrap into England.[60] Young certainly showed Hill *Dionaea muscipula*, which Bartram's son William had given him to convey to England, but Hill makes no mention of William Bartram as the crucial discoverer in this entry. Others later would around 1768.[61] But at this moment in 1766 Hill was focused on insects rather than the carnivorous plants that capture them, the contents of his work a plan to cover nature's whole kingdom.[62]

The two botanists exchanged information and Young also introduced Hill to his father by correspondence; within months the elder Young was advertising Hill's preparations in Pennsylvania.[63] These were especially his "big five": "essence of water dock" for consumptions, valerian for stressed nerves (a medication still used today), pectoral balsam for spasms, elixir bardana for melancholic conditions, and sage for long life. His sales were slow until 1763, but after the war finished and the seas became safer they perked. The English had won the long war with France, and the New World contained the economic engine of the future. Hill thought he could improve his dire condition there if sufficient quantities could be sold; so he balanced the profits with the cost of advertising, shipping the goods, and then collecting on them. David Hall, his old contact from Savoy days, was one vital American link. Hill had encouraged him to go out to the "New World" two decades earlier: Hall did and became successful, joining up with Franklin and Bartram and forming the partnership of "Franklin and Hall" that published—among other newspapers—the influential *Pennsylvania Gazette*.

Hall advertised Hill's panaceas and probably charged him little for the service. He then distributed Hill's seeds far afield from Philadelphia to the rest of the mid-Atlantic colonies from the Maryland shores to the Carolina coves. In February 1767 his newspaper announced that a chemist named "John Boyd" had just received a large shipment and placed "on sale in his shop at Baltimore Town, Maryland, Drugs of all Kinds, carefully chosen . . . Dr. Hill's medicines, so universally famed for curing consumptions, rheumatisms, gout, stone, and gravel."[64] Merchants who saw them advertised there bought them and had them shipped up and down the colonial Eastern seaboard. The letter books of David Hall in the American Philosophical Society in Philadelphia abound with these notes of shipping records and the profits made. One shipment, dated October 19, 1767, netted Hill a profit of £50 and 2 shillings. Hill also had other agents distributing for him in the Carolinas and further north in Massachusetts. Hill may have amassed significant income but he quickly spent it paying rent in Bayswater and funding his *Vegetable System*.

Closer to home his panaceas were ubiquitous, his sales campaign constructed on the belief that success depends on being seen everywhere. In London, John Ridley continued to advertise and sell his remedies, especially the "big five" including valerian for nerves and tincture of centaury, "the great stomachic bitter."[65] A correspondent of Horace Walpole took Hill's *Virtues of Sage in Lengthening Life* with him to read in Holland, as well as sage folded into his pocket, and wrote back to his friend in Strawberry Hill that Hill's text persuaded him that "to live at ease is the sure method to live long."[66]

Hill also warned his London clientele that fake medicines lurked; he cautioned them to certify they had purchased the "authentic product" by consulting "the Bottom of each Bottle, in his own Hand-writing . . . their Success having induced several Persons to imitate them under different Names."[67] The size of his commercial enterprise is understood by looking at his activities in Bath: The *Bath Chronicle* ran advertisements throughout 1767 for his most popular medicines indicating who his agents were.[68] Cornelius Pope distributed them among two dozen shops in the Bath area and announced discounts to those "Merchants & Captains of Shops, and others, who buy a Quantity for Exportation." Hill made similar arrangements in other cities and between 1760 and the time of his death the *Scots Magazine* ran advertisements of his medicines, including "Dr. Hill's Cure for the scurvy."[69] Some commentators reported him to be earning a small fortune, but even if he did he parlayed these profits to fund for the "machine" of assistants producing his publications.

Subsequent years were dismal. Da Costa was apprehended for embezzling the Royal Society for sums more than thirty times his annual salary of £50 and compelled by law to sell his library and collections. John Ellis, the botanist responsible in large part for luring Solander to remain in England, went bankrupt in the immediate aftermath of his wife's death and could not pull himself together. While caring for gardens in Surrey he corresponded with Solander and often brought him down to see his works. "Pray tell me," he begged of Solander on November 22nd, "is Mr. D'Acosta quite ruined so that he is obliged to sell his collection or does he do it for profit?"[70] Another botanist wrote to Ellis: "Dr. Solander tells me you have desired some account of Dr. Hill's new work; but not having seen it himself, the Doctor asked me to send you my opinion of it; which I shall do with pleasure."[71] This was Hill's *Vegetable System*—about which more soon—but the botanist condemns the first installation ruthlessly: ". . . [the pictures] are more like patterns for ladies to work by, than figures to inform a botanist"; it is a "pompous" work which "will grant him no great applause or encouragement, for which I am, very sorry." Ellis concludes ironically and pathetically: "Sir, you would have no difficulty to fix upon the author of it at first sight, though his name were not in the title-page; for really it is worthy only of the great Dr. Hill."[72]

Nonetheless, these botanists kept their eyes affixed to Hill, and Bute's sponsorship kept them all the more blinking; so when Solander complained about the recently dead James Mynde's (fl.1720–1760) botanical illustrations of sponges, Ellis consoled him by referring to Hill and even harped back to the days of *Lucina*:

> There is not a man in England, that will teize you so much, as that impertinent Fellow, Mynde; a man who through consummate assurance, has made himself the Engraver to the Royal Society in the Administration of Dr. Mortimer, when Dr. Hill very properly libelled them [in *Lucina*]. This Fellow through the ignorance or passive temper of the Gentlemen of the Society is continued as a plague & ignominy to them. . . .[73]

That was long ago: since then Henrietta's loyalty counted for more, even when his gout racked him. The years were flying and he continued to think—foolishly—that some post in the British Museum would be made available to him. Just one day after Thomas Birch died on January 9, 1766, Hill launched an inquiry about the disposition of his post. In May he was well enough to travel up to the Strand, where Northumberland had offices, to make the same petition in person. He dramatized his condition as precarious, which it may not have been, and was emboldened to plead: "Dr. Hill begs a thousand Pardons for presuming to name the hour; but his indifferent Health does not permit him to be out earlier."[74] It may have been compromised but visitors—especially botanical visitors—still streamed to him in Bayswater to see his setup and understand his new scheme: he would exchange trees and shrubs from his gardens for their foreign ones.[75] He continued his correspondence with Haller, each keeping the other up to date about the newly evolving *Vegetable System* as well as their respective gouts. When John Pringle, the distinguished military physician long since having set up in London practice and been appointed to all the important societies there, told Hill that Haller's gout had benefited from "Essential Absynthia"—a nervously calming medicinal essence containing *Artemisia absinthium*—Hill asked for the recipe for himself.[76]

His condition worsened. He was fifty-two, a time of life when many parading gentlemen still caroused around Ranelagh and Vauxhall as if young bucks, yet he ailed, periodically in retirement in placid Bayswater with his devoted wife and growing—and dying—children.[77] Perhaps it was death's melancholy that spurred him to write a small treatise on hypochondriasis: not yet the sentimental or romantic malady it would become within a generation but the ancient malady localized in the spleen and containing a venerable pedigree. Hypochondria had been called "Death's Hobby-Horse" many times: by Lesage, by Sterne who was intrigued also by its riddles, by all those preoccupied with their health. Now it was compounded by child-bereavement too.

Hill began the tract by remembering the diagnosis of a young hypochondriac in Leicestershire when he was a youth;[78] this he prefaced with the admission that the little book serves as a personal record of his credo that as our health improves we become more hypochondriacal rather than less.[79] Submerged in the confession is (what we would call) the intensity of depression, from which he was probably also suffering:

> To call the hypochondriasis a fanciful malady, is ignorant and cruel. It is a real, and a sad disease: an obstruction of the spleen by thickened and distempered blood; extending itself often to the liver, and other parts; and unhappily is in England very frequent: physick scarce knows one more fertile in ill; or more difficult of cure.

Hill's contemporaries wanted to hear that "the hyp's" dominant etiology was physical rather than psychological—so obsessed were they becoming with their physical health. Everywhere—in newspapers, books, in markets and squares—they heard much more about their bodies and the need to preserve it than they had when they were children; bombarded, they asked more questions about the proper and rational degree of concern for personal health. Diverse authors flocked to give them assurances that many types of "overwork" could cause it. Hill developed this approach, cautioning them to heed the teachings of the "venerable Ancients," especially that "fatigue of mind," and "great exertion of its powers" often give birth to this disease. The finer "animal spirits" are wasted by the labor of the brain; Hill's example is "the Philosopher [who] rises from his study more exhausted than the Peasant leaves his drudgery; without the benefit that he has from exercise."[80] It was unsurprising that most writers of the epoch had not managed to escape its clutches.

Hill's medical brethren had neglected hypochondriasis before 1766, and in forty pages he claims nothing original about the condition, but his timing was, again, prescient: to revisit hypochondria in 1766 just when Edward Young, the celebrated poet of *Night Thoughts*, had just died, and when its diagnosis was increasingly being made. The "hyp" was also spreading, if such a condition can be configured as contagious, and—more significantly—being viewed as incurable. Hill's eight chapters cover the full physical and psychological range: its mixture of physical and psychological modes of presentation, as well as the types prone to it, its causes, symptoms, and cures; its remedies, especially through diet and exercise but also pharmacologically and predictably his own herbal "spleen-wort" (which is given extended discussion); and—most prophetically—its "danger to life."[81]

He sought therapies that keep the gut calm. This was why "raw vegetables are all bad."[82] He reports that an hypochondriac "nobleman the other day died paralytic: dissection showed him like a learned gentleman whose autopsy revealed a galloping consumption"; that is, a chronic tuberculosis that has irreparably damaged the lungs. Nor, to his discredit, did Hill distinguish hypochondriasis from hysteria: a word he never invokes. But old Stukeley reappears in his text, himself "late" in death, having died a few weeks earlier at seventy-eight, followed by a flashback to Newton's hypochondriasis, and suggesting how prone the studious and religious were deemed. Hill blamed its intensification on physicians who reinforced the patient's sense of dependence on the doctor. His main point augured the future: "Though the physician can do something toward the cure, much more depends upon the patient," a position anticipating the modern self-management by patients themselves.[83] He never suggests the elimination of medical consultation for "nervous disorders," but seeks to sharpen the doctor's scrupulosity, and his assumption in 1766 is that many patients amuse themselves through this ailment and—in a kind of Catch-22—the "ensuing melancholy thrown off by their hypochondria" further energizes them. The point needed formalization, and it is no wonder that Hill's little tract was often cited as the culture of sensibility matured at the end of the century.

As the 1760s ebbed Hill's gout intensified. He fought on and the new decade involved him in a clash that exacerbated it. This was a small skirmish, compared to the gigantic ones, with William Cadogan, a Fellow of the College of Physicians and much respected, although his niche as a practicing physician was his forte so far rather than originality in medical ideas. This changed when Cadogan published a *Dissertation on the Gout,* claiming that gout was *not* hereditary, a view contradicting Cheyne, Hill, and almost everyone else before Cadogan wrote.[84]

Cadogan assaulted the notion of "the privilege of gout" in what seemed to some Georgian readers an anti-hereditary tirade, substituting lifestyle in its place: high living, rich diet, excess in consuming goods, indolence, irregularity, frayed nerves, intemperance, and especially venereal carnality. His English critics viewed this as Welsh censoriousness, and Hill answered him in a revised edition of his earlier treatise on gout, taking this opportunity to exonerate erotic permissiveness.[85] For a long time Hill had believed that moderate carnal license was conducive to relaxation of the nerves, which restored equilibrium, although little was necessary to tip him over the brink of erotic decency.

But Hill invested little energy in the anti-Cadogan campaign—he had more important work in his time left, especially catering to Baldwin's enthusiasm to print more "medical" tracts and to write about geological topics. Since 1758 Hill had subsidized the printing of all his books, which amounted to a large bouquet of works, and received no subsidy for publication apart from ghostwriting political tracts for Bute. Now Baldwin encouraged him to bring out "new editions" of earlier herbal and medicinal pamphlets pertaining to valerian, bardana, burdock root, sage, water dock, and "centaury, the great stomachic"[86]—all of which remedies became best sellers. He also had not pursued geology since da Costa days in the late 1740s, when as collaborators they became the preeminent twin figures in geology before the Vulcanists and Neptunists (those claiming that fire and water, respectively, had been the main elements shaping the history of the earth) began their controversy. Sometime in 1760 Hill arranged Bute's "cabinet of fossils," which rekindled his interest further, and he reminisced that his edition of Theophrastus had been his very first publication, so he returned to that terrain again, particularly to "the origin of spar."[87]

In geology, Hill was a popularizer rather than original researcher or thinker. He identified and classified minerals according to external characteristics visible to the naked eye, and—as he claims in the various treatises—did so in the hope of reaching those with little scientific training. His tract on fossils is undeniably learned and clearly presented, as lucid as George Edwards's *Elements of Fossils* that also appeared at this time; the same "ornithological Edwards" Hill had met at Goodwood and for whom he named his novel of 1750.[88]

But he was not an original observer of stones or tireless field worker. For precedence in collecting and classifying, the myrtle must go to British forebears John Woodward and da Costa.[89] Hill's strength was that he knew how to cash in on the commercial side of geological popularization. Viewed in context, he was making the sciences available to general readers, and as late British historian Roy Porter has written of this decade, Hill's role within it was noteworthy. For example, Hill's generation debated whether stones were "germs growing in the earth" or—by analogy with the panspermist theory—"seeds . . . planted at the time of the creation of the world," or, again, whether minerals were God-given assets implanted at the time of creation from time immemorial. Hill lived through the tense airing of these debates; now, revisiting the geological assumptions almost thirty years later, in Bayswater, was something of a homecoming and we see how he proceeded in *Sparogenesia*.

He chose "spar" because it demonstrated the confluence of microscopic advancement (i. e., the compound microscope revealing its structure) and Linnaean theory about the classification of minerals. Having studied the tradition from Boyle to Buffon on spar Hill was aware that salt is the form-giving property of most minerals; with the aid of his compound microscope he saw that wherever he chipped spar a common geometrical form was plain—this specifically intrigued him. But spar is just "one rock" among many no matter how many crystallines a chip of it contains, and Hill wanted to fathom what spar's ultimate irreducible form was.

Every work he consulted claimed that spar's smallest atoms were polyhedrally shaped but he desired to see for himself. The French naturalists concurred.[90] But Linnaeus compounded the puzzle by announcing a correspondence between the chemical composition of minerals and their crystalline forms; that is, Linnaeus affirmed that a stone's crystalline form offered the surest clue to its chemical composition rather than the other way around. This was the result of Linnaeus's argument favoring an artificial method of classification of minerals according to the stone's essential qualities, rather than a natural method classifying minerals according to the traditional tripartite division of animal, mineral, and vegetable.

Hill's tract explores whether the spar's rhomboid plates he saw through his microscope related to its chemical composition. Buffon had recently noted that chemical attraction amounts to universal gravitation.[91] Developing this thread, Hill wondered whether spar's rhomboid plates could provide the key to their chemistry; he also pursued a connection between geological crystal rhombs and the rhomboidal forms occurring physiologically in muscular action. Thomas Percival earlier posited that "muscular motion could be accounted for by an effervescence and explosion in the imaginary rhomboidal receptacles."[92] Hill went further: he grappled to understand the unitary basis of rhomboidal action even if he made no original discovery in the field.

He must have held da Costa close to the tip of his imagination when writing. He had reconnected with his former friend through correspondence a few years earlier while da Costa was in prison for the *second* time.[93] This was after April 1763—after da Costa was elected Clerk of the Royal Society, a post that gave him perks and a paid housekeeper, including a post as the Society's Librarian and Keeper of its Repository. Hill had also attended his wedding in 1766. However, within five years, da Costa was accused of having defrauded the Society for a *second* time and dismissed in December 1767, his family evicted from Crane Court, their possessions sold at auction. The next May (1768) the Society took him to court and in November he was committed to the King's Bench Prison, his belongings confiscated, everything he owned sold at auction. All was dismal for him. The accumulation of these vast collections had landed him in debt and now he was stripped of everything he owned. While incarcerated, Hill sent him his recently published *Construction of Timber*.[94]

A decade earlier Hill had published a tract about marine flora but it was not clear which microscope he used: his single, compound, or other.[95] Now, in 1770, his treatise on timber was favorably noticed,[96] reviewed as one of the few inquiries executed with the aid of instrument maker George Adams's new compound microscope.[97] Those years working with Lord Petre in his marvelous arboretum now paid off. Adams himself was appointed to the highest honors open to his trade: the king's personal instrument maker, and Hill was thrilled when he had one of Adams's instruments as a gift from Bute.[98] Hill learned that the core impediment to studying the different qualities of pulp, which existed in hundreds of gradations, had been the destructive cutting of the lumber's thin sections. Wood slithers had to be slit so finely that light could pass through them. Adams's new microscope was designed not to injure the fragile threadlike sections, and—furthermore—caused no injury to the pulp's soft tissue at the moment the sections were cut, an advance over prior methods of cutting. The breakthrough was important for enhancing the quality of lumber used to build seagoing vessels in the next generation.

Da Costa read Hill's *Timber* in prison. He verified Hill's tables, and wrote to him confirming Hill's arithmetic used to calculate the wood's growth; Hill in turn wished him good luck in obtaining release.[99] He was not freed for another two years, until late 1772, earning a few guineas here and there by writing the odd piece. But the record breaks off after this exchange and the two men may never again have corresponded. Hill meanwhile was amused to discover that his now antiquated antagonist, Henry Baker, soon to be dead, had savaged George Adams's earlier publication, *Micrographia illustrata* (1746), as a plagiarism. Baker was a considerable microscopist himself but his territoriality colored his interactions with others and, moreover, he disliked compound microscopes and denounced them throughout his life.[100] The catcall of plagiarism was an easy one to hurl in these days before tough libel laws. Yet Haller and Gesner, still corresponding after three decades, read it at once; Haller impressed at Hill's choice of topic, summarizing it to Gesner as "important" and "useful": ". . . Many singular items [are] here. He [Hill] filled vases everywhere. He described the wood at the crown and in the pith from which the branches emerge; and the pith formed after the branches sprout. An exceptional work, if one can trust it."[101]

But Hill was not so intuitive elsewhere. Perhaps he was deflected by the constant rumors still circulating about him despite his having retreated almost a decade earlier from the nerve center of St. James. One was that he was the author of Hannah Glasse's cookbook published as long ago as 1747: *The Art of Cookery Made Plain and Easy.*[102] Glasse died that summer (1770) and speculation arose about her life and mysterious book that became a minor best seller in an age when cookery was taking off. Speculation arose about the book's origins, especially how someone with so little education could write a book that made her rich, and the editions subsequent to 1747 continued to be published anonymously as "By a lady," until a rumor started—in the immediate aftermath of Glasse's recent death—that Hill was the author. The route to attribution seemed direct: via the anonymous author of *The Younger Brother*, a popular romance whose unknown writer inserts a discussion of *Hill's authorship* in relation to Martha Bradley, then a respected cookbook writer.[103] "Type" and "Smutt," the main antagonists, scramble the various cookery writers, reflecting knowledge then common about them:

> Descending into the kitchen! (cry'd TYPE), staring me [SMUTT] full in the face, why [*sic*], you fancy scoundrel, you give yourself fine airs! What the devil's the matter that you can't condescend to write a Cookery-Book, when my friend Dr. J—N H-LL did not disdain the task, but kindly obligd the world with three large octavo volumes, under the title of the British Housewife, and under the fictitious name of Mrs. Martha Bradley.

When Samuel Johnson was asked to give his opinion at a supper party at Dilly's, on an occasion where British cookery was the topic of the chitchat, he resisted Hill's authorship; his reason empirical: "I doubt if the Book be written by Dr. Hill; for, in Mrs. Glasse's 'Cookery,' which I have looked into, salt-petre and sal prunella are spoken of as different substances, whereas sal-prunella is only salt-petre burnt of charcoal; and Hill could not be ignorant of this."[104] Hill was too fine a botanist. Score a point for Johnson's willingness to endorse Hill's knowledge of the natural world.

And Bute's patronage and promised support? It had evaporated by 1764, but not without tribulation for the Hills. By 1773, only two years before Hill's death, his perennial peril reappeared—the curse of poverty—and Hill could not pay his creditors. This was the first time it seemed he would actually go to debtor's prison despite Henrietta's strokes of comfort. To deaf ears he badgered Northumberland yet again about public posts, like the new one opening up in the old Lock Hospital. He was even rebuffed to supervise the cleanup of the clogged canals around Kensington Palace, and Bute was no longer around to plead his cause. Had the "doctor" progressed from the regal "Inspector" to linkboy vile?

NOTES

1. LPH, 111 for sample titles; M. E. Knapp, 153–218 passim.
2. JH documented some in JH (1768a).
3. Henry Jones (1767), 1.
4. For JH as herbalist in 1758–1759 see Janet Wright.
5. Respectively, JH (1758g), JH (1758f), JH (1758b), JH (1758d), and JH (1758m); for the others see LPH, 120–22.
6. JH (1759h).
7. JH (1766a).
8. JH (1759i), 4, 26–31 for these citations.
9. Stearn; Stannard, part 4.
10. Blackwell, passim.
11. JH (1758h); JH (1758n) is the same work touting Burdock root for gout.
12. JH (1758n), 6.
13. JH (1758b), 20.

14. Cited in Blanche Henrey (1975), vol. 2, 94.
15. JH (1758d), 19. JH had already invoked these ideas of nervous sensibility in *The Actor* (1750).
16. JH (1758e); *GM* 28 (November 1758): 542.
17. JH (1758e), 18.
18. JH (1758e), p. 31.
19. His reading was spotty but wide, and he obtained books wherever he could find them: in libraries and shops, on book stalls, from Stukeley and other men of science.
20. *CR* 8 (1759): 272.
21. Friedman, vol. 1, 449, *The Bee*, 4: 149–50.
22. For the list see LPH, 123–25.
23. JH (1759b) and JH (1759c).
24. *TLS* 24 (June 1944): 312; Lewis Knapp (1974), 74.
25. Halsband, vol. 3, 214.
26. JH (1759g).
27. *HWC*, vol. 16, 29, May 14, 1759.
28. *HWC*, vol. 16, 29, May 14, 1759.
29. JH (1760c); see also New and de Voogd, vol. 7, 148–51.
30. Sterne's most learned editors, Melvyn New and Peter de Voogd, also raise the question without supplying an answer; see New and de Voogd, vol. 7, 150.
31. Wilbur Cross (1904), vol. 1, 42; New and de Voogd, vol. 7, 151–52.
32. Sterne, 91.
33. Sterne, 110.
34. Sterne, 110. It is often stated that JH was then editing the *Royal Female Magazine* but I know of no external evidence proving it, and those alleging it in this fracas did so to suit their purpose.
35. New and de Voogd, vol. 7, 154.
36. New and de Voogd, vol. 8, 686–87.
37. Two generations later John Taylor, a miscellaneous hack addicted to the gossip he heard in the Turk's Head coffeehouse, and to whom William Wordsworth often sent his poems, thought he had discovered the source of the conflict—in Monsey's rough speech—but there is no reason to think it true; see Taylor (1833), vol. 1, 46–61.
38. *PA* (June 12, 1760).
39. Flagellan, 6.
40. JH (1761b).
41. JH (1761b), 4.
42. JH (1760b).
43. JH (1761a).
44. D. E. Redmond, 18.
45. JH (1773b).
46. *MR* 25 (August 1761): 127–30.
47. Paulli, passim.
48. Short, 232.
49. Anon, *Two Letters from a Physician in London, to A Gentleman at Bath . . . with some Observations on the Present Use of Tobacco* (1749); Simon Mason (1757).
50. Johnstone, 117–34.
51. LPH, 147.
52. William Darlington, 442, for JH's correspondence with John Bartram.
53. John Bartram, passim.
54. John Bartram, passim.
55. *Inspector* 17 (March 30, 1751), where JH comments on Bartram as a natural "genius."
56. For Young and JH see Kinch.

57. Darlington, 267, 449.
58. Darlington, 36.
59. JH (1773a).
60. Ewan (1973), 178; Kinch, 386.
61. See chapter 18.
62. JH (1773a).
63. Kinch,17–22, for the American newspapers and agents involved.
64. LPH, 148–49.
65. *London Chronicle* (January 2, 1766).
66. *HWC*, vol. 30, 90–91.
67. *Lloyd's Evening Post* (March 28, 1766).
68. JH appointed "Mr. Cornelius Pope, Printer, in Bath, my agent for the Sale of my Medicines . . . All Persons may be supplied by him on advantageous Terms"; *Bath Chronicle* (January 19, 1767).
69. *Scots Magazine* 22 (February 1760): 88.
70. Duyker (1995), 193.
71. LPH, 124.
72. LPH, 125.
73. Duyker (1995), 221.
74. LPH, 144.
75. JH (1766b).
76. LPH, 145.
77. Three of their girls died during these years; see 177.
78. JH (1766a): 14.
79. JH (1766a): 26.
80. JH (1766a): 6.
81. JH (1766a): 16–19.
82. JH 1766a, 32.
83. JH (1766a): 24.
84. Cadogan, passim; Kevin Fraser (1982) admirably summarizes the controversy; see also Rendle-Short; Porter and Rousseau (1998), 109–19.
85. JH (1758h).
86. JH (1765a).
87. JH (1772).
88. JH (1771b) and George Edwards (1773).
89. John Woodward (1728) and da Costa (1757).
90. L'isle de Rome.
91. Buffon.
92. Percival, 29.
93. LPH, 128–30 .
94. JH (1770a); G. B. Thomas for a modern treatment.
95. JH (1760b).
96. *GM* 40 (1770): 626; *MR* (1770) 43: 210–12.
97. Bridges, 248.
98. LPH, 165–66.
99. LPH, 160–64.
100. Henry Baker (1742); Henry Baker (1753).
101. Cited in LPH, 165.
102. Glasse.
103. Anon, *The Younger Brother, a Tale* (1770–1772), 160–63.
104. G. B. Hill, vol. 3, 285.

17

The Final Blow

1758–1759 had been remarkable years for Hill but were also permeated with pangs of disappointment. That autumn (1759) Oliver Goldsmith, now coming into his own as a "polite author," turned his thoughts to the state of "knowledge and learning" in Georgian society, especially to celebrity culture in *The Bee,* which he called "Essays on the Most Interesting Subjects." He ruminated on greatness and mediocrity, lamenting that every generation forgets the "greats" of prior eras. He listed acknowledged celebrities—the triumphant monarch Charles XII of Sweden, the polymathic Spanish friar Father Feijoo of Spain, radical philosopher Voltaire in France, and several brand-name European scientists. Goldsmith lamented that some were on their way out, and that huge acclaim in one's lifetime was no more a guarantee of enduring fame than the number of copies of books sold by contemporary Georgian authors. Time has proved his precept true.

In one essay, "A Reverie," Goldsmith imagined the "greats" boarding "a small carriage, Berlin fashion" that would convey a select band to the Temple of Fame.[1] The coach was labeled "The fame machine." Two celebrity *aspirantes,* Hill and Arthur Murphy, tried to board, but the driver refused them entrance. Johnson, Hume, and Smollett got on, but when Goldsmith tried to enter the driver showed him a copy of *The Bee* and swiftly denied him entrance too. Then Goldsmith turns to "Proteus Hill":

> . . . a most whimsical figure indeed. He was hung round with papers of his own composing, not unlike those who sing ballads in the streets, and came dancing up to the door with all the confidence of instant admittance. The volubility of his motion and address prevented my being able to read more of his cargo than the word Inspector, which was written in great letters at the top of

> some of the papers. He opened the coach door himself without any ceremony, and was just slipping in when the coachman, with as little ceremony, pulled him back. Our figure seemed perfectly angry at this repulse, and demanded gentleman's satisfaction.[2]

Altercation ensues, tempers flare, while Proteus's papers "flutter in the wind." Yet Hill, true to character, changes form and returns refashioned as this "harlequin upon the stage, and with the same confidence again made his approaches, dressed in lace, and carrying nothing but a nosegay."[3] And "upon coming near he thrust the nosegay to the coachman's nose, grasped the brass, and seemed now to resolve to enter by violence." Then the narrator, who is not Goldsmith but who will watch Goldsmith be ejected too, enters the fray and pitches in to assist the coachman: ". . . I stept in to his [the coachman's] assistance, and our united efforts sent our literary Proteus, though worsted, unconquered still, clear off, dancing a rigadoon, and smelling to his own nosegay."

But Hill, naively assuming he was *in*, discovered himself to be *out*. Inclusion into the "fame machine" then was as fraught a business as it is today, and whole libraries have been created since then chronicling the disappointed forgotten who have been first put in, then put out. In some senses Goldsmith's reverie was a replay of "Lusus Naturae" six years earlier, which had included Hill among those guaranteed celebrity only to discover he was simultaneously ejected—or soon would be. It was one reason why after 1760 he turned so fanatically to botany and continued to remind the Wits that his genuine acclaim was as a botanist. He was not alone. Shortly thereafter, his patron—the fallen Bute—asked "why am I doomed to climb ambition's steep and rocky height who early in life, had the meanest opinion of politicians?" Ambition had been the crux for both men.

This lament about "ambition's steep height" was passed from Bute to courtier Baron Mure just before he, Bute, fell from grace with his former ward, now the king, George III.[4] Bute too discovered he was out almost as quickly as he had been in. His story has often been told: how Prince George favored him throughout his youth and made him prime minister in 1762, and then, once in office, how George—now king—fell out with him many times, not merely over his unpopular Cider Tax, causing his resignation only a year later. Much less well understood are Bute's years after stepping down as a patron—the "Maecenas of Botany"; his self-imposed exile as a gardener at Luton Hoo, his large estate built by architect Richard Adam, and, afterward, aimlessly traversing Europe as a rejected and forlorn wanderer.

To understand their relation further, we must flash back to their meeting and the terms of Bute's patronage. Bute, having been impressed with Hill's botany at least since 1757, brought him to Kensington Gardens; but he soon recognized that Hill was the not the man to renovate them or Kew and, more consequentially, that Hill was more useful to him as a ghostwriter. Hill preferred gardening to ghostwriting but did not have the option of declining Bute's support, so he wrote to please. The bone of contention, however, was not gardening versus ghostwriting but the funding of the twenty-six-volume *Vegetable System*, Hill's opus magnum.[5]

About this enormous work many facts are known: that Baldwin printed only the first volume and that Hill changed his publisher frequently for the other volumes; that all twenty-six volumes eventually appeared (the last in the year of his death in 1775); the date of publication of each volume; that Bute helped Hill write the text which uses Linnaean nomenclature throughout; that the Hills did not own the copyright; that the composite volumes contained 1541 copperplates; what the cost of the colored and non-colored volumes amounted to; and the verdict of Britain's most authoritative recent historian of botany on the set: "it must be pointed out that this great undertaking, which occupied more than fifteen years of its author's life, has considerable nomenclatural importance."[6] But it is far from clear how Hill came to write it or who subsidized its formidable cost over that decade and a half. That Hill died leaving huge debts related to its preparation and publication is not in doubt, and no letter survives, from any party, glossing the unknown facets. The only extant source is Henrietta's very short *Address to the Public*, published thirteen years after her husband's death, which is useful but not entirely reliable.[7]

Baldwin did not balk or blink at the prospect of printing twenty-six folio volumes, with hundreds of plates, and despite his contract with Hill and Bute not having survived he must have forked over a pretty pound in advances to them for the copyright—so eager was he to have it. He signed a contract with *both* men: the legal basis for Hill's widow's attempt to compel Bute to fork over his half of the bill, especially for the very last volumes. The plan was to issue two volumes per year, containing a total of approximately 1600 copperplates and 26,000 figures. Subscriptions would be solicited from the great and the good, who would doubtlessly be willing to sponsor a project on this scale manned by two such botanical eminences as Hill and Bute, especially in 1759 when Bute's cache, both politically and botanically, was high.

With fanfare the monthlies announced the plan in large font, advertising it as the "good Doctor's" *piece de resistance*. Baldwin and associates talked up the volumes, as did Hill-Bute, puffing them to such swollen skies that a sense developed during these first few years that all naturalists *had* to own copies. Hill gifted the first three volumes to Haller in Göttingen, who nervously awaited them, to see for himself whether England had finally caught up with "Linnaean Sweden." Once he assessed his "gift" Haller wrote enthusiastically to his faithful Gesner on June 19, 1763:

> Vols. II, III, & IV of Hill have arrived. It is a sound system, the reproductive system is contained in these four volumes, with nearly all new orders, many

> illustrations, and if all species are not included, there are however many rare species. I will read it with more care. There are twenty-seven books in the folio in which the whole system is contained. . . . There are innumerable new orders. He uses only the common name, which is certainly troublesome. The engravings for his plants are neither very good nor very bad. . . . You definitely cannot afford to be without the Hill work. For he includes many engravings, all new, numerous orders, which one ought to compare, and few common plants. . . .[8]

A few days later Haller wrote again, reassuring Gesner of Hill's achievement: "I read the Hill. *Because of the very large number of engravings done from nature, no one should be without it.*"[9] High praise indeed accompanied by reservations such as this: "The rest of his philosophy of plant reproduction does not yet hold accuracy."[10] Haller also wrote to Hill that summer, thanking him profusely for the gift, but without noting that he and Gesner simultaneously and frantically exchanged notes attempting to distinguish which parts Hill wrote and which Bute—so far had the rumor about dual authorship traveled. Bute for his part also sent copies far and wide, as well as locally to the president of the Royal College of Physicians in Edinburgh, Robert Whytt of reflex nerve fame, who thanked him politely, and when he did Whytt made perfectly clear he knew it was "Dr. Hills *Vegetable System*" and no one else's.

Oddly, neither Bute nor Hill seem to have sent copies to Linnaeus, who had to obtain it elsewhere. Hill's reason is transparent and absurdly grandiose: to persuade the Europeans that the English now had their own Linnaeus. It seems impossible to believe that Hill can have thought so well of himself, but he did, and this was his motive for excluding Linnaeus: a few years earlier, when writing the *Flora Britannica,* he reiterated that he had been the first Englishman to introduce Linnaean classification to England, and now he enlarged the claim to embrace a type of "English Linnaeus." But subsequent volumes lowered his esteem in the eyes of Haller and Gesner, who—like others—continued to dwell on the defect of the engravings. When Bute withdrew financial support Hill managed for a while; but eventually he depleted his savings and had to draw the illustrations himself, which the English reviewers lamented.[11]

Henrietta describes the Hills as domestically settled in 1757–1758, the period when her husband was first introduced to Lord Bute and the *Vegetable System* initiated; indeed "rich and happy, [Hill] pursuing his favorite . . . study, botany; and making a rapid fortune by his medicines."[12] Settled perhaps, but they were far from financially comfortable, which casts doubt on the accuracy of her memory thirteen years after the fact. She claims that soon after the two men became friends, Bute suggested the idea of publishing a magisterial magnum opus to be titled the *Vegetable System* in "twenty-six volumes folio, containing sixteen-hundred copper plates . . . the paper was of the most expensive kind, the drawings by the first hands, the printing was also a very weighty concern."[13]

Hill's correspondence demonstrates that Bute's overture occurred around 1758 and Henrietta recounts how her husband weighed the benefits and eventually declined. But Bute reassured him in no uncertain terms, saying "that the expense had been considered, and that Sir John Hill [after her husband's death always 'Sir John' to her] might rest assured, his circumstances should not be injured by the undertaking."[14] Convinced that Bute meant what he said, Hill finally succumbed, and her husband "entered upon and finished his destruction: for what he received from my Lord Bute for three books, for the King, the Princess of Wales (Augusta) and himself, three times a year, which were the periods of its publication, together with all that were sold, bore no proportion to the expense; so he became overwhelmed in debt."

Yet not before he and Bute embarked on other experiments in natural history. When, for example, George Edwards shocked the community of scientists—the same Edwards on whom Hill had earlier based his novel—Hill quickly enlisted Bute and entered the fray. Edwards had stumbled upon so-called "vegetating insects," which die and grow into plants. He did not read Spanish but came upon Jose Torrubias's intriguing book describing these insects and extracted Torrubias's pith about their transformation into plants.[15] Edwards then sent his observations to the FRS, which if accepted as valid science, would have disturbed the order of nature by permitting previously unknown transformations in the animal-vegetable-mineral kingdom. Hill alerted Bute to Edwards's maneuvers, and Bute "put into his [Hill's] hands some of the insects to examine."[16] After doing his experiments Hill reported to Bute that Edwards's was the "*Tettigometra*, which buries itself in the ground to rest until the Cicada bursts from it," and that their plant was the "Clavaria," a type of fungus.

Characteristically, Hill harshly disparaged the three naturalists' conclusions, which he communicated to John Hope, the professor of botany at the University of Edinburgh, as well as Bute, resisting the theory that some insects grow into trees, as well as debunking such absurd "miracles" as the remnants of dead insects sprouting plants. Bute encouraged him to do so. "I hope Mr. Edwards will retract his error," Hill carped, "his book is not yet published, and I have given him notice of it." Edwards overlooked the advice and incorporated the descriptions anyway.[17] He too sought Bute's patronage and was probably unaware of Hill's experiments with Bute. But the criticism scored points for Hill, who used it, as we shall see in the next chapter, in productive ways.

Meanwhile, the two men drifted apart owing to Bute's constant demands—Henrietta calls them "trifles," even if they were not always, such as inventing a microscope under a new construction.[18] This was George Adams's new compound instrument that Bute indeed gave to Hill as a gift. Bute's "distractions" were calls for ghostwriting more than "toys" such as Adams's new compound microscopes and the experiments they could enhance, and Hill was even more distressed that this was the only form of payment he was receiving. But what was he writing for Bute?

We cannot be certain. In 1761 Hill's health turned for the worse again. Henrietta began her second round of childbearing: she would replace the losses of three daughters in the 1750s. Hill was still overworked, and continued so into 1762. The reissue of *Lucina sine concubitu* perhaps momentarily buoyed him that spring,[19] but he seems to have been working on little other than the *Vegetable System* that year. Bute defended himself robustly during the months in late 1762, when the Whig opposition was attacking him vigorously. His short columns appeared in Tory biased newspapers such as the *North Briton*, often with pieces ghostwritten by Hill.

But Bute's political woes were curiously mute in the Hills' household. Even Henrietta makes no mention in her *Address to the Public* of Bute's political difficulties, his removal from office and retirement to Hertfordshire, and then his far-flung travels. Instead she leaps from Bute's "coolness" toward her husband to the last year of Hill's life (1774–1775): "After the *Vegetable System* was completely finished [in 1774], Lord Bute proposed another volume to be added, which Sir John strenuously opposed, as he said it would only load the work both in matter and expense." This was a volume of corrections, of "Errata," for which Bute pressed him and Hill eventually complied, "because he would not," according to Henrietta, "throw water upon his cooling friendship . . . He therefore made the necessary preparations; such as drawings, engravings, paper, and other materials, too numerous to mention." Hill did not dissemble now, nor had he earlier, in the enterprise of this vast publishing venture. Deceit had ruled earlier in his life but now he dealt honestly—at least in relation to the *Vegetable System*—with those involved: his assistants, the illustrators while he could afford them, his printer Robert Baldwin, the many others now lost to time whom he paid out of his own pocket, and Bute himself.

The "recollection of what follows," Henrietta continues, "makes my heart tremble, and my whole frame suffers an agitation, too great to be described; this was the crisis of my fate!" What was it? An "exorted task" that directly led to her husband's death "before he produced a line" of the added volume.[20] In death Hill became "a victim to the greatest tyrant that ever disgraced humanity," leaving his widow in tears with "children looking up to her for protection" in her penurious condition.

Figure 17.1. Matthew Darly Print, "A Polite Artist on St. Luke's day, 18 October 1773 . . . under the patronage of Dr. Bardana 1773."

Grief followed grief: a physician was called to calm Henrietta, too smitten to search for a last will and testament herself. He found one naming Henrietta and Bute as joint executors. This was conveyed to Bute at Luton Hoo, who claimed he was too "infirm" to serve as executor and offered Henrietta a pension as recompense.[21] "Six weeks later"—some time early in 1776—Bute sent a note "in such a stile as would disgrace the meanest person," indicating he wished nothing more to do with Henrietta because she had not encouraged her late husband to produce the last volume. "A dead weight," she writes, "for its costs,"[22] and she sent Hill's notes for the last volume together with debtor receipts to Bute for "between two and three hundred pounds" requesting he pay them. Bute replied by sending "two Germans" to her house in Bayswater to inspect the notes and complete the volume themselves, which they claimed they could not.[23] Bute then instructed Henrietta to donate Hill's botanical books to Scottish universities, as well as send a copy of the last, but unwritten, volume to William Watson, the botanist earlier discussed who described Linnaeus's binomials in 1754.

The remainder of Henrietta's *Address* consists of a dialogue between herself and the lawyer Bute sent to examine her.[24] By the end confusion sets in and Henrietta grows too emotional to continue, narrating only that "her late friend the Duchess of Northumberland . . . pressed me to make immediate application for a pension" and the Duchess of Argyll "did me the honor of presenting me to the Queen," Charlotte, wife of George III.[25] She closes her appeal plaintively, saying she has written to advise the public that her "husband's memory has been injured by his dying so deep in debt" and that Bute has "heaped oppression . . . on a WIDOW."[26]

However melodramatic her tract—"Fatal Acquaintance" to characterize Bute and similarly hyperbolic expressions demonstrating she has been reading gothic novels—Henrietta's *Address* "trembles to name" the *Vegetable System* or recount how Bute encouraged her husband to produce "the most voluminous, magnificent, and costly work that ever man attempted."[27] Not quite: doubtlessly she lived in terror but its production over fifteen years, she avers, with good reason, "killed him."

Her *Address* contains invaluable, if partial, biographical information nowhere else available. She records how Bute entrusted Hill with overseeing the blueprints for colonial planting in the Caribbean to make these "colonies profitable . . . under [governors] Melville, Johnstone, Stewart."[28] How Bute compelled Hill to conduct "experiments" with the microscope injurious to his health, such as "pouring over crucibles and poisonous vapours," and how Bute "threw out hints" pressing Hill to write tracts "in favor of the American War," which Hill refused, his own judgment and politics running contrary to this position.

All this must be taken with a grain of salt but not entirely dismissed; its details should be assessed in light of the ravages of Henrietta's grief and memory but not the drift of its main message: that the men fell out, that an already exhausted and gouty Hill disintegrated to a point of no return, and—most unknown until her revelation—the story of the *Vegetable System*'s "unwritten volume." Some details Henrietta doubtlessly embroidered or possibly invented but probably not this one. Her disappointment at never receiving a pension is predictable yet not the size of the family's debts—her crucial detail that her "debts . . . exceeded all the property" she owned, including the royalties for Hill's medicines[29]—or the delay of thirteen years before writing to the public. So passionate was her hope that Bute, still alive for another four years after 1788, would recompense her.

This final blow was the bottom line: not Bute's withdrawal (he had not been paying up for years) but his request for a *twenty-seventh* volume. The public could have imagined that when the patron (Bute) fell from political favor he abandoned the patronized (Hill). Henrietta's narrative is more poignant; it amounted to the belief that Hill had struck out thrice before: once in his election as FRS, a second time as first applicator of Linnaean nomenclature, and a third time when Bute changed the terms of his sponsorship. In each case Hill emerged the loser. Now, in 1774–1775, for the dying Hill to confront a fourth and final assault—Bute's request of a twenty-seventh volume Hill could neither produce in illness nor afford—was more than he, or Henrietta, could bear. Husband and wife and their small team of paid amanuenses and assistants had produced an average of two volumes a years since the mid-1760s that exhausted them and depleted their funds (see appendix B).[30]

Bute's new request was more than Hill could ponder—instead he died. Furthermore, the reception of the *Vegetable System* was far worse than it merited—after three decades of feuding in public Hill could not hope to find sympathy for its production despite its subscriptions. Both colored and non-colored plates are defective, and the botanical circle gathered around John Ellis, which included Solander, Pulteney, and other "Linnaeans" in London, were swift to condemn them. Ellis had his own agenda: he was also studying vegetating insects, especially the *Dionaea muscipula,* and was not about to be beaten to solving their mystery by Hill. Linnaeus had awaited the volumes of the *Vegetable System* for a long time and claimed to be disappointed: "I fainted at the sight of Hill's great work . . . with the most beautiful plates of plants on each alternate page, but I could weep when I saw such a costly work without botanical science."[31] Linnaeus's main objection was the lack of systematic use of his own binomial classification, yet here we see him extolling the illustrations. William Rose, an English journalist jealous of Hill's attainments, found the volumes wildly conjectural, dismally flawed, and was silent about the illustrations, even if he himself could produce nothing remotely comparable.

Henrietta's *Address* curiously omits mention of Bute's fall from power and subsequent departure from London, a lacuna raising questions through omission about the Hills' parlous financial situation after the autumn of 1763. That was when Bute left London, resigned his last post as keeper of the Privy Purse, and withdrew to Luton Hoo, his large country estate in Hertfordshire. Charles Churchill, the shrill satirist, portrayed him, and Hill too, this way after his fall in *The Prophecy of Famine*:

> Presumptuous wretch! and shall a *Muse* like thine,
> An *English Muse*, the meanest of the nine,
> Attempt a theme like this? Can her weak strain
> Expect indulgence from the mighty THANE?
> Should he from toils of government retire,
> And for a moment fan the poet's fire,
> Should he, of sciences the moral friend,
> Each *curious*, each *important* search suspend,
> Leave *unassisted* HILL of herbs to tell,
> And *all the wonders of a Cockle-shell.*

"Unassisted," botanically and financially, Hill may have been in 1764, but he continued to fly high the Bute flag, well after Bute's fall in 1763. He wrote to Haller after the Swiss naturalist thanked him for sending volume six of the *Vegetable System* as a gift that both *Bute* and the king had never been more supportive of him.[32] Nor could he resist laying on characteristic unction when telling Haller that "all Europe except the cubs of Linnaeus Schools consider [you] as the first Botanist of the world." He ends noting: "The Expense of a few volumes [of the *Vegetable System*] is trifling when I print great numbers." In fact the "expense" was onerous: he could not afford to be generous. And the sets were not printed in "great numbers" (master of innuendo that he was), which was precisely the reason Lady Hill would bring suit so assiduously against Bute. Hill concludes by thanking God for being well off: "I thank God and my great Patrons"—Bute and the king—"as not to make a greater thing of any moment to me."

Similar exchanges contradicting the known facts demonstrate the difficulty of chronicling the Hills' daily life during his last decade. Others promoted half-truths about him and his *Vegetable System*. Poet-naturalist Thomas Gray, now resident in London, informed his constant correspondent Dr. Thomas Wharton, his former Cambridge University chum with whom he never lost epistolary contact, that "Lord Bute . . . himself a botanist, and having now in the press a new system of botany of his own writing, in several volumes; the profits of which he gives to Dr. Hill."[33] Gray's account is garbled. The "new System" was *Hill's* "System" with *new* nomenclature, and Bute *never* gave "the profits" to him, nor was it of Bute's "own writing."

Even if defective, all twenty-six volumes of the *Vegetable System* contained Hill's own text.[34] But after 1764 Bute, now at Luton Hoo, dropped Hill, and as the years passed—1765, 1766, 1767—Hill gave up hope of hearing from him. His last known letter to Bute, commenting on the forthcoming fifth volume of the *Vegetable System*, was written just before Bute left office in September 1763 and while Bute continued to be widely ridiculed in the press, as in this quip:

> My Body would do if my Mind was but well,
> But that has more Torments to plague me than Hell.

Hill for his part was wary, but not too tired occasionally to please Henrietta who liked to attend lavish town parties given by her two aristocratic friends, the Duchesses of Northumberland and Argyll. Horace Walpole eyed Hill at the former, at Sion House, with Henrietta on June 8, 1764, among 1500 guests: "Besides the sumptuous liveries, the illuminations in the garden, the pages, the two chaplains in waiting and their gowns and scarves, *à l'irlandiase*, and Dr. Hill and his wife, there was a most delightful Countess. . . ."[35] Walpole calls Henrietta "junketaceous," perhaps indicating her degree of making merry, and further suggesting how far he retained Hill on the tip of his imagination if he could single him out in a crowd this size.[36]

However wary, Hill remained the "*lusus naturae*" par excellence, as in the engraving of 1753 (figure 10.1), and continued to be imagined together with the *illustrati* of the age. A pamphlet of 1772, entitled *The Last Masquerade at Mrs. C——ys*, places him there early in the 1760s, together with Johnson, Burke, Savage, Sterne, and other notables and captures him in this hypochondriacal pose, forever ailing or whining:[37]

> Dr. H—came up boldly with towel and soap;
> He started, he trembled, he made for the door;
> He had seen, but not taken, such physic before.

She was, of course, the charismatic inamorata Teresa Cornelys, "the Heidegger of the age," named for the Swiss count, Johann Jacob Heidegger, who had introduced masked balls in London earlier in the century. Cornelys threw huge parties at her magnificent residence at Carlisle House in Soho Square, which no one rivaled.[38] A woman with a checkered past and in dubious financial circumstances, she sold subscriptions to her masked balls to all who could afford them. She added new, marble-inlay doors to admit the crowds to above four hundred. Her festive attendees included members of the Royal Family, the Prince of Monaco, the King of Denmark, and his entourage and half the peerage. To be glimpsed there was itself the mark of celebrity. A few years after Hill was seen there, Parliament adjourned early to enable members to attend her masquerade. His vital spirits must have rallied if he could endure an evening in Cornelys's riotous company.

In October 1760 the king died and his grandson, the future George III, was swiftly crowned. As the year evolved the Hills suffered further financial reversal and Hill's health again deteriorated. Henrietta glossed over the reality when she recalled in her *Address* that they had then been "happy and rich." A major change they had made, at her prompting, was their translation from Westminster to Bayswater—from Hill's many, and often multiple, residences in the West End in what he now viewed in his exhausted mind as its urban menace, to the pastoral rusticity he associated with his childhood. Nostalgia for the fields of his youth crops up in his writing during this period, as well as in his fortitude to endure illness physical and mental.

Bayswater in 1760 still consisted of green fields dotted with cowsheds and a few houses. Even a generation later, when the composer Josef Haydn retreated there in 1791, he called it "rural Paddington." Its fields dipped and rose and were prone to flooding, as the Hills discovered; provided its inhabitants could endure wet cellars and rooms, it seemed a small paradise. During the 1760s market gardeners and nurserymen found it pastorally seductive because they could plant and grow surrounded by plenty of space and pure air. The land was cheap to buy as well as rent, and the Hills let a large field from the Godfreys.[39] Godfrey had rented several fields to one John Frine in the 1740s for which he was levied £65 a year in two installments. Hill's name first appears in the rate book in 1760 on the same line as Frine's, each paying approximately half the £65. These rates continued with only slight fluctuation for the next fifteen years until Hill's death, except that beginning in 1762 Hill seems to have rented part of Frine's "Farm" as well, as the rate book describes it.[40]

Ambrose Godfrey, a German by birth, had been one of Robert Boyle's chemical technicians, charged with isolating white phosphorus, a newly discovered substance that attracted great attention early in the century. Its preparation in large quantities was a closely guarded secret, and Godfrey held the monopoly on its lucrative trade for over forty years. He made a fortune this way and a second one before the South Sea Bubble burst, using his funds to scoop up much of the land in the current Bayswater, but the estate and grounds remained in the hands of his sons who sold it off in parcels after his death.[41] Lord Craven, for whom the current Craven Hill in Bayswater is named, bought one large parcel at mid-century and by the 1790s it had become such a fashionable place that Paul Sandby, the prolific artist who intensely dispraised Hogarth, sold numerous copies of both Hill's tea-gardens and the Bayswater fields to gentry such as Lady Townsend, who lived next door to Hill.

Hill had constructed sheds there to store his plants and seeds even before he relocated. Just before Christmas 1759 he wrote to Bute that he would seek the desired seeds "first in my own Store at Bayswater" but he was not yet living there.[42] When his gout flared around 1760 he and Henrietta decided to make the move. Bayswater seemed the perfect place for them, a view confirmed three decades later by one of London's first synoptic historians, Daniel Lysons, who described what the Hills constructed there:

> Bayswater tea-gardens were some years ago the gardens of Sir John Hill, who cultivated there his medicinal plants. . . . The springs at this place lie near the surface, and the water. . . . is very fine. The reservoir at Bayswater was intended for the supply of Kensington-Palace, and the property was granted to the company who the Chelsea water-works, upon their engaging to keep the basin before the palace full. . . .[43]

Lysons might have added that the Hills' house stood at the corner of the present Bayswater Road and Leinster Gardens, today boasting a blue London County Council plaque for "John Loudon," the eminent landscape gardener and horticultural writer who bought it from Henrietta, when she was old and in need to be cared for by her daughter Juliana. Loudon tore down Hill's house to build his own; yet forty years earlier, at the start of the 1760s, Henrietta had fixed up a pretty house with a sunny kitchen garden next to the large stores Hill kept for his business.

Their children grew up here, in pastoral if partial retreat, while their father, Hill, corresponded with botanists and composed pro-Bute political pamphlets as relief. John Symonds, one of Bute's agents, visited him around this time and found the "house elegant & his garden pleasant as well as useful."[44] When Bute, now wandering across Europe's girth like some agonizing romantic Werther in search of a purpose, inquired about Hill, Symonds sent him this reply:

> I called on Dr. Hill at Bayswater, who has fitted up House elegantly, & his Garden pleasant as well as useful. He is in most perfect Health, & I think, in great Spirit, tho' the British Herbal has sold but ill—His little English Tract on the Virtues of Plants has had a most amazing Run—He promises in five or six weeks to publish another volume of the Vegetable System—I have given him Directions about Count Firmian's Copy, & on my Return hither [to Bayswater] shall settle with him how he shall manage about those to Fassetti, & Pasquali.[45]

Symonds tactfully omitted the floods the Hills endured and the cost of repair, but included mention of Fassetti, Pasquali, and company: Venetians Bute introduced to Hill's botanical works, using the alias "Sir John Stuart" for himself to avoid detection. Symonds' appraisal of Hill's mood is curious: "in great Spirit" and "perfect Health." Hill and Henrietta had picked Bayswater for its proximity to Bute and Kensington Gardens, but within a couple of years after Symonds visited them their rent begins to show as "in Arrears." The dagger of debt had again struck.

Hill continued to rent Frine's Farm until 1766 when the rate book notes that "it is empty" and Hill is now charged "for House and Land" at a semi-annual amount of £28 and eleven pence, which continued until 1772, during which year Frine is described as "the late Frine" and Hill appears to have added more land to his lease for which he was levied semi-annual amounts varying between £40 and £45. In 1774 the rate book lists him, for the first time, as "Sir John Hill" and his semi-annual amounts revert to £28. Next year, 1775, he appears as the "Late Dr. Hill." Lady Hill's name is substituted, and Henrietta continues to be levied about £28 until she departs around 1790 to reside with Juliana. The "poverty" described in her *Address* is well founded. She was broke.

NOTES

1. Friedman, vol. 1, 444.
2. Friedman, vol. 1, 445.
3. Friedman, vol. 1, 446.
4. Cited in Lovat-Fraser, 60.
5. See Lemay and Rousseau, 124, for the bibliographical details, early reviews, and cost of the plates.
6. Blanche Henrey (1975), vol. 2, 107.
7. Henrietta Hill (1788).
8. LPH, 137.
9. LPH, 137.
10. LPH, 137.
11. *CR* 3 (July 1758): 80.
12. Henrietta Hill (1788), 6.
13. Henrietta Hill (1788),10.
14. Henrietta Hill (1788), 10–11.
15. See Torrubias.
16. LPH, 131–32, for this and the other citations in this section.
17. George Edwards (1758–1764), vol. 3, 262–65.
18. Henrietta Hill (1788), 11.
19. Published in [Anonymous], *Fugitive Pieces on Various Subjects* . . . 1761. It was reprinted again in 1762. These were probably large compilations by the Dodsley brothers.
20. Henrietta Hill (1788), 14.
21. Henrietta Hill (1788), 23.
22. Henrietta Hill (1788), 17.
23. Henrietta Hill (1788), 18.
24. Henrietta Hill (1788), 19–21.
25. Henrietta Hill (1788), 24.
26. Henrietta Hill (1788), 24 and 27.
27. Henrietta Hill (1788), 9.
28. Henrietta Hill (1788), 8.
29. Henrietta Hill (1788), 16.
30. No letters have been found between husband and wife or from either parent to their children or vice versa; JH's letters to others are the only source.
31. Cited with sources in Blanche Henrey (1975), vol. 2, 108.
32. LPH, 137–38.
33. Toynbee and Whibley, vol. 2, 91.
34. LPH 133–34; reviewed in *LM* 14 (July 1763): 396.

35. W S Lewis, vol. 38, 401.
36. W S Lewis, vol. 38, 59.
37. Anonymous (1772).
38. *Notes and Queries* 2nd Series 23 (June 11, 1861): 30; for the balls Hill attended see Summers, chapter 4.
39. Paddington Parish Rate Book tells the story and survives in two volumes for the period 1755–1775.
40. JH's name shows up in a separate entry.
41. Lysons, vol. 4, 331.
42. LPH, 119.
43. Lysons, vol. 3, 331.
44. LPH, 161.
45. LPH, 161, Symonds to Bute, September 1, 1770; the English tract is *Virtues of British Herbs* which had just appeared in September.

VI

18

Knighthood and Death

Henrietta's husband was now "Sir John": the rate books, visitors, Henrietta in her *Address* of 1788—all refer to him this way. Hill himself entered his name in the Westminster Parish rate books of 1774 as "Sir John" and was decorated by the Swedish government that year; an honor that mollified disappointment and illness, and prepared him to die.

The story of his knighthood is never told in detail and requires a context for the use of titles and public decorations then. By the 1770s men of educational distinction used two types of titles in England, other than aristocratic: locally academic—including the professions of law, medicine, and the church—and foreign academic. You could sign yourself "master of arts" or "bachelor of divinity"; alternatively FRS or as a member of foreign societies. Denied all membership in England, Hill was relegated to the latter camp. In his early days he signed himself a member of the Academy of Bordeaux, having been elected, but latterly it was the Academy of St. Petersburg, which elevated him to their ranks by virtue of his reputation, gave him a small pension, requiring in return only copies of his books sent to them in Russia.[1] A few dozen Anglo-American scientists had been elected in Hill's decades—including Benjamin Franklin, Joseph Priestley, and Charles Morton with whom Hill had competed for the British Museum post—and Russia's ambassador made these appointments while in England. But Hill could not have known in 1772 when the Russians elected him that something grander was on the way.

During the late 1760s Hill continued to jockey to get himself elected to the librarianship of the British Museum, two decades after his vengeful bombshell hurled at the Royal Society. Each attempt backfired—the politically minded have long memories—and by the decade's end Hill was no closer to being elected FRS than he had been twenty years earlier. Worse yet, on the day of his election—November 17, 1768—da Costa's embezzlement was also discussed. A vote was taken that boded menacingly for Hill, yielding "14 friends, 82 against him."[2]

But the fates spoke. Never again would he propose himself despite increasing worry over money and his growing brood in the nursery: at least four children growing up, and three new daughters born since 1761. His patron Bute was fallen from favor—all influence gone there. Newcastle had just died—not that he had ever proved useful. Da Costa was thrown into the King's Bench, as we noted, coincidentally on the same day as Northumberland's local election in Middlesex. The phalanx of FRS naturalists—the Collinsons, Watsons, and Mortons, et al.—was incapable of swaying others, let alone implacable antagonists like Baker and Ellis; the same Ellis who continued to exclaim that ". . . though he [Hill] certainly has great abilities, the want of that fairness and exactness makes the world suspect him; and his writings are a mere drug. . . ."[3] At long last, some literary acknowledgment, for Ellis meant hypnotic, mesmeric rhetorical power rather than sedative potion; in any case, writing as medicament rather than vehicle to convey truth. No wonder the vote was a landslide against Hill. But a survivor to the finish, Proteus-Hill turned away from them and intensified his efforts abroad.

For years he had been sending his books to naturalists in Europe, the aggregate of whose effect was considerable: they returned Hill's gift with their works, often addressed to him "c/o the Royal Society," and before long it was assumed he was a leading member there. He also cultivated foreign ambassadors in London, like Baron Praun from Germany, who would return home and suggest Hill's elevation to their leading academies. Often Hill's mail arrived with theirs, having been directed to "Dr. Hill in the care of Baron Praun," as in this case. The strategy paid off: having corresponded and sent his books to A. E. Buchner, president of the Academia Leopoldina, the leading scientific society in Germany, Hill was elected in 1763; but not without marking the occasion by noting he had prevented an international error from being promoted about "vegetating flies." These were the flies caught—hardly vegetating—in *Dionaea muscipula* that Hill had heard about early in the 1760s from William Bartram via his student Thomas Young. Hill was also careful to report that the Royal Society had thanked him for the correction—which it did—and that owing to his efforts Edwards's publication did not appear in the *PT*.

Hill engaged more with Middle Europe, especially with Germans, than this. Through da Costa he had made German contacts in London, men such as Ehret the botanical illustrator, Jacob Trew, and Jacob Schaeffer. He had been corresponding with Gesner in Zürich and Haller in Göttingen for two decades; with A. E. Büchner in Nürnberg for a decade and befriended

German ambassadors posted to London. By 1763 his correspondence with Büchner had paid off. Büchner was now president of the oldest scientific academy in Germany, the impressively titled Academia Sacri Romani Imperii Leopoldini-Carolina Naturae Curiosorum, and paved the way for Hill's election. He had no objection to Hill's promoting himself among its members, indeed he encouraged him to do so. Members of the Leopoldina followed the ancient custom of using the aliases of notable worthies of the distant past. Linnaeus was *Dioscorides secundus*, Hill became *Dioscorides quartus*, and there were other Dioscorides too.

Not even foreign decorations, however, appeased the English naturalists, nor was Hill shy about trumpeting his honors: the more he referred to distant memberships on his title pages, the more he raised the temperature of hostility among those opponents—the Bakers and company—who had done what they could to block his advancement. After his final blow in 1768 Hill had a new idea: to form his *own* Royal Society, which he called "a Royal Academy of Sciences in Britain" established along the lines of the existing one, except that he was to be the "perpetual president" and George III its patron. Kevin Fraser, an Australian physician, discovered a copy of Hill's plan in German libraries and identical letters Hill sent to German naturalists.[4] Hill proceeded as if he were a modern photocopy operation, first printing a single sheet announcing the Academy, with himself as its perpetual "Conductor" (on the model of his former incarnation as "Inspector"?) and then posting identical letters to dozens of European scientists together with the printed sheet. A trawl through Continental libraries might well yield many more copies.

Fraser acknowledges Hill's phantasmagoric life: "While it is clear that Hill believed the Academy was the sort of body that should be promoting scientific endeavor in Britain, it is by no means certain that it ever existed outside his imagination." None indeed—not even when Hill wrote that "the Academy has just been established in Great Britain" or that he had named himself as its "President for life." Worse yet, as "Conductor," he would "establish all its bye-laws and regulations," no less autocratically than Pekuah in Samuel Johnson's *Rasselas* imagines her own "Academy" for women over which she shall perennially preside.

Hill worked in 1769 to establish his "Academy," puffing it as he had puffed himself and his books throughout his life. At home he may have succeeded in corralling a few English scientists who—like him—had also never been elected FRS, but beyond this the Academy existed, as Fraser observes, only in his mind. Then to make it more credible he ran an advertisement claiming that the Academy already boasted "107 corresponding members," and that its purpose was the free exchange of information, just as in the old Republic of Letters.[5]

But Hill inadvertently revealed his ulterior motive. He claimed that the Academy's main focus of research was twofold: on "a species of small animal," which he called "funguses" identical inside and out, and—among plants—on the *Dionaea muscipula*, if not the Venus flytrap itself then a close relative. Hill doubted they were "vegetative insects" and corrected those believing they fermented inside the plant leaves.

Even in 1766, when in discussions with William Young, he had been attentive to the then new sexualization of plants and recognized how disturbing the idea could be to his contemporaries. This was two full decades before Erasmus Darwin poeticized, and further sexualized, the "loves of the plants" in his poetry. Gender disruption was not new to Hill, and he had ruthlessly invented aliases of both genders to his own gain when publishers in the 1750s refused to publish books under his given name. It would be intriguing to know precisely how Hill entered the discussions of the Venus flytrap but the record is silent beyond the fact of his declared interest. By 1768, however, when the English botanists recognized the sexual implications of William Bartram's plant, Bartram himself was still geographically based in the colonies, even if he had left the Carolina bogs—where he had originally found *Dionaea muscipula*—for Pennsylvania. He would not become famous for his mysterious "Venus Flytrap" for another century—until Victorian times—and for now only heard about the discussions occurring in London.

Hill for his part set himself up as an authority on both the "small animal" (fungus) and the "Venus Flytrap," intimating he understood the operations of each. He had collected dozens of the funguses, and was quick to note that Bartram, acting through William Young, had presented him with the *first* Venus flytrap. The London botanical men countered his claims. Arguments ensued and Hill, never far from the imagination of many naturalists in the late 1760s, again became a focus of controversy, debate, and gossip. One imagines what foreigners arriving at the Royal Society in London thought: they knew Hill's name, many had read his books, and wondered why on his own native ground he provoked such animosity—this while many had been duped into thinking the king his patron. George III knew something, of course, about the confusion over patronage through Bute and the workers at Kew. And the conflicting views constitute the main reason—controversy—why he asked Johnson what he thought of Hill in the famous interview of 1767.

Despite the occasional gouty infirmity, Hill plowed on. With France, Germany, and Russia in his pocket, what remained was the land of Linnaeus—Sweden. Hill and the Swede had been in communication for decades, but it is unlikely that Linnaeus would have proposed him, not after the letters he had received over the years from John Ellis discrediting Hill.[6] This is a fine point: Ellis conceded Hill's great ability but found fault in every botanical work he produced. Nor was Linnaeus pleased in 1770–1773 by his protégé's—Solander's—lack of advancement: all Solander's attempts came to nothing and Ellis assured Linnaeus it was owing to Hill's connections who continued to block Solander. Ellis put it bluntly: ". . . The reason he [Solander] was not introduced to the King was owing to Dr. Hill's being so great a favorite with Lord Bute."[7]

But Hill thought Linnaeus esteemed him, and from this perspective wrote to him in unctuous tropes, such as "nothing can be a greater Pride or Pleasure to me than seeing any work on mine quoted in your immortal writings," and "there has not arisen in the philosophic World, nor I think ever will arise your equal."[8] The great man was not invulnerable to such adulation, not even from an Englishman, but in reality the best Hill could expect in Uppsala was a nod from the eminent Swede who was by now the most celebrated naturalist in Europe.

No, the enabler of his knighthood was a less visible figure—the Swedish ambassador in London, Gustaf Adam Baron von Nolcken, Envoy Extraordinary to Great Britain (1764–1793).[9] He was posted to London as a young man, and Hill used his ties to Bute to cultivate him, often visiting him at his house in Richmond. Nolcken was his conduit to Linnaeus, especially for the shipment of the weighty volumes of his folio *Vegetable System.* Throughout 1771–1773 Hill sent Linnaeus dozens of books via the baron, including an entire set of the twenty-four volumes of the *Vegetable System,* the last two volumes not yet published. A final touch may have softened the Swede when Hill told him that he was sending his "Pupils . . . to different Parts of the world" and that he wished to arm them with all ten volumes of Linnaeus's *Amoenitas Academiae,* the master's collected wisdom about natural science. It was untrue—if he had students they have disappeared—but a masterful stroke that may have persuaded Linnaeus, when consulted in Sweden, to accede to Hill's decoration.

No records survive of the deliberations in Uppsala and Stockholm, and it cannot be known what was said about Hill there. Anglo-Swedish correspondence remains, such as Ellis to Linnaeus, Solander to Linnaeus, Hill to Linnaeus, and in the opposite direction, all of which offer different points of view. But if results count rather than processes, King Gustavus III's decree to Hill, written in French, dated April 29, 1774, and still extant in the Kunglingen Bibliothek in Stockholm, pronounces the last word about Swedish intentions:

> The King, knowing your zeal for society's well-being, and the useful works by which you approach the crossroads of human knowledge, has decided to bestow upon you, Sir, a public stamp of approval by naming you as a Cavalier of the Order of Wasa [*sic*]. By order of his Majesty I have the honor of apprising you today of this appointment, and of telling you that the tokens of the Order shall be sent to the Baron Nolcken, special envoy of his Majesty to his Majesty of Britain who shall be authorized to qualify you are Cavalier and to invest you with the title. You cannot imagine, Sir, the pleasure I feel on my account in announcing to you so distinguished a favor . . . Please accept my sincerest compliments and the assurance of the regard with which I have the honor, Dr. Hill. . . .[10]

Nolcken performed the investiture in London on June 17, 1774, most likely in the Swedish Embassy then in Portland Square. The king's letter makes clear that Hill has been decorated for "useful works" that advance "human knowledge," not for one book or contribution to the discipline like botany.[11] Two days later Hill wrote to Haller on a medical topic and concluded his letter by noting that "the king of Sweden has honourd me with the order of Vasa Established by himself for literary merit. . . ." A week later the *GM* reported that ". . . Dr. Hill, having been invested with the order of knighthood by the Swedish Ambassador [Nolcken], appeared at court for the first time with the proper ensigns."[12]

Just as Nolcken had shipped Hill's botanical books with official post in Swedish ships, he also received the gold medals with Vasa engraved from Stockholm and passed them on to Hill. One would give a lot to see a painting, or even engraving, of Hill at court donned in his badge and necklet, with his gold collar consisting of four sheaves and a star in the middle, Henrietta dressed in finery at his side, and propping him up if he happened to be gouty on that June day.

Guesses can be made about the identity of Hill's sponsors in Sweden but they remain conjectures. Linnaeus would have had weighty input, as would his associates, especially the botanists among them who had been writing home about Hill for years. They must have known something about Hill's scandalous side: if not King Gustavus III himself, then his courtly scientists. But what?—this too remains mere surmise, yet what is clear is that the knighthood was awarded for the *Vegetable System*. The Swedes were well aware of Hill's prolific publications over three decades and his contributions to natural history, but the twenty-six volumes of *Vegetable System* constituted another order of achievement. Had Hill been healthier Gustavus may have summoned him to Stockholm as he did French chemist Lavoisier in 1777, barely two years after Hill's death, for the same award. Back in London no doubt existed: Hill's decoration was the Swedish Order of Vasa, founded two years earlier in 1772 for service to state and society, especially in the fields of agriculture, mining, and commerce, to which Linnaeus had been the first scientist elevated.

In London, Hill was entitled to use his new title—"Sir John"—by proclamation of the king and "was received and recognized, at the levee of his own Sovereign, as a Knight of that Order [Vasa]."[13] No wonder Hill was signing rate books after June as "Sir John" and Henrietta referring to him in this style. A decade after Hill's death the Marquess of Carmarthen petitioned George III for a similar acceptance of a foreign title for one of his friends, referring in his letter to "former knights" such as Sir William Chambers (knight of the Swedish Order of the Polar Star) and Sir John Hill (of the Order of Vasa), both decorated abroad. The right was granted.

Figure 18.1. Engraving of John Hill after receiving his knighthood, by Giovanni Vendramini (1769–1839), from a painting by Francis Coates, a Royal Academician, ca. 1757. Reproduced by kind permission of Professor George Rousseau.

The foreign honor buoyed his self-esteem, and lifted him as nothing earlier had. Within bounds: he was ailing, aging, almost burned out. His elation was curbed when the sharks returned to devour their prey. They raised the old caveats about lack of scientific veracity and spread new rumors about moral imperfection; for example, the sexual gossip promoted by two friends, the satiric poet Charles Churchill and political figure John Wilkes, who were themselves hardly morally perfect. The duo portrayed Hill as a profligate and womanizer, imagining him still strutting with "Diamond" and other whores despite his incapacitating gout. Hill took little solace that they had also "bitten" Hogarth; and if Hill reflected that he had survived the strictures of his *bete noire* Christopher Smart two decades earlier, now he had an equal menace to contend with in *The Rosciad*:

> With sleek appearance, and with ambling pace,
> And, type of vacant head, with vacant face,
> Then Proteus Hill put in his *modest* plea,—
> "Let Favour speak for others, Worth for me."—
> For who, like him, his various powers could call
> Into so many shapes, and shine in all?
> Who could so nobly grace the motley list,
> Actor, Inspector, Doctor, Botanist?[14]

Figure 18.2. Eighteenth-Century Proteus, photographed by Remi Jouan and released under a Creative Commons Attribution Share Alike license.

"Proteus" in Churchill's *Rosciad* may not be Richmond's Goodwood "puppy" of two decades earlier. But he would have remembered Pope's pithy linkage of the two—puppy and Proteus—in *The Dunciad*: "So Proteus, when hunted in a nobler shape, / Became, when seiz'd, a puppy, or an ape." Churchill's "Hill" has hardened into "Proteus," who is anything but a flexible "puppy" in Churchill's fierce reduction. Furthermore, Churchill's "protean" character in the mock-epic poem is crafted as if a cliché known to every reader; as if "Proteus" had been Hill's unique Georgian moniker without the need for any gloss. But the sobriquet was not new: Defoe was described this way for arguing all positions and, more recently, Bolingbroke in the 1740s, but here it is used by Churchill to cast opprobrium on Hill as a monstrous writing-machine *ne plus ultra*.

The Greek god had changed shape as a protective measure: to prevent others from profiting from his gift of prophecy. He had a plain purpose. He altered his bodily form to *avoid* having to, and only complied with the requests of those capable of capturing him. In contrast, Churchill's target in *The Rosciad* is presented as someone whose basic character is "protean," including his versatility, mutability, flexibility, and adaptability.

Churchill was not alone. *The Adventures of an Author* also invokes Hill by this moniker: "Like another Proteus, thou takest every shape—thou art indiscriminately concealed under every form."[15] Other ephemera then also invoked this designation, making it apparent that Proteus was not merely a convenient sobriquet but a Georgian biographical frame for our provocateur. The heart of this protean designation may lie in unrelenting change but, more specifically, in endless *professional* transformation—this is what makes it so intriguing. Personal Hill is not "protean," however given to wives or women, lavish living, or vulgar display. Nor is his degree of biographical energy: the frantic Hill in combat, always restlessly in motion, expending so much energy to extricate himself from feud and fracas. Far more vexatious is his *professional* proteanism, and the voracious, almost self-destructive, ambition underpinning it. Yet even this biographical frame—the Protean one—is delimiting for its difference to "Notorious Hill." The Greek god was protectively protean, for survival, but hardly notorious.

It is hard to believe that the figure described in Churchill's *Rosciad* is of a man who has been elevated to knighthood by the Swedish monarch:

> Knows any one so well—sure no one knows—
> At once to play, prescribe, compound, compose?
> Who can—but WOODWARD came,—HILL slipp'd away,
> Melting, like ghosts, before the rising day.
> With that low CUNNING, which in fools supplies,
> And amply too, the place of being wise,
> Which Nature, kind, indulgent parent, gave
> To qualify the Blockhead for a Knave;[16]

Churchill situates Hill in a theatrical rather than botanical context. The wide world of Linnaeus is absent despite Hill being so well known within it—all of which demonstrates that potshots at "versatile Hill" could be taken in any field. It was the price of his adaptability. When Churchill published his portrait of Hill based on *The Actor* (1760), a verse satire by Robert Lloyd, he struck out at the malice and cunning of Hill's dissembling far more than his diverse occupations:

> With that low CUNNING, which in fools supplies,
> And amply too, the place of being wise,
> Which Nature, kind, indulgent parent, gave
> To qualify the Blockhead for a Knave;
> With that *smooth* FALSEHOOD, whose appearance charms,
> And Reason of each wholesome doubt disarms,
> Which to the lowest depths of guile descends. . . .[17]

Churchill's charge is premeditated deceit—never spontaneous or impromptu, as in the theater, but calculatingly "cold":

> With the *cold* CAUTION of a coward's spleen,
> Which fears not guilt, but always seeks a screen,
> Which keeps this maxim ever in her view—
> *What's basely done, should be done safely too;*[18]

Churchill could have added unction to his attack on cowardice even if he (Churchill) had not teamed up with Wilkes; and he further lumped Hill in *The Ghost* (Book IV) among the "COXCOMBS" and "*grave* Fops" together with Joshua Ward, the quack doctor of "pill and drop" fame. But Hill and Churchill never met—there was no known personal animus between them; Churchill was making his name by lashing Bute and those surrounding him. By the time Bute's patronage of Hill was widely known and his Swedish knighthood reported, Hill had been mythologized in ways Churchill capitalized on. He could be all things negative, as Churchill writes, in addition to representing some rare "disease" of pride prompting ridicule even in far removed strangers: third-handers, who were repeating what they had heard from the second-handers.

Not everyone in 1774 was so disparaging. The response to his knighthood traveled swiftly. Once reported, it was jabbered about; printed digs, demonstrating that despite his last decade spent in near seclusion compared to his earlier "inspectatorial" gadding about, speculated about why he was still a household name. The London literary scene was small, but Hill's medicaments ensured that he continued to be widely known; so routinely discussed as a household name that his decoration figures in many places as a toss-away, as in this *Poetical Epistle from a Gentleman to his Son*—a satire on Chesterfield's *Letters to his Son*—printed a few months after Hill's elevation:

> Once more, my Child! adieu! Remember me,
> And ne'er, O ne'er forget the Graces Three!
> Hug 'em as Close, as, when he goes to rest,
> Hill hugs his graceful Order to his breast.[19]

Some aspersions were more benign. While the colonials in Massachusetts were dumping India tea into their bay in Boston, Hill published a new edition of *Eden*, several botanical compilations,[20] and yet another tract about those vegetating insects.[21] All but one appeared before his knighthood, and all were restatements; perhaps the semi-favorable review of his two-year-old *Fossils Arranged According to their Obvious Characters* that gave him the spur to edit another version of his *Plain and Useful Directions for those who are Afflicted with Cancers*.[22]

In the lead-up to his honors, the printer Darly in the Strand was selling engravings of an impoverished "Polite Artist on St. Luke's day, Under the Patronage of Dr. Bardana"—none other than "Dr. Hill" with "patronage" the fitting key word, showing Hill wearing superannuated frippery and torn stockings, and donning a short wig failing to conceal his own hair.

Even Samuel Derrick, his old standby who had offered his aid when the paper war with Smart and Fielding was brewing, and who had since relocated from London to Bath as Master of Ceremonies there, included jibes just before his own death in 1769:

> Thou essence of Dock, of Valerian, and Sage,
> At once the disgrace and the pest of the age,
> The worst we can wish thee for all thy damn'd crimes,
> Is to take thy own physic, and read thy own rhymes.[23]

Forever the figure of ridicule—the nuisance as rhyming pest: the scribbling doctor reduced to his "big five" panaceas, leading to Derrick's even terser phrase cribbed from Garrick's more cited one: "His physic a farce is." After Derrick's death the Bath papers were filled with anecdotes about Hill's quasi-comical life. The darts suggested his concoctions had finished off Derrick too: ". . . all my untaken nostrums of his [Hill's] composition, as I shall soon find, by woeful experience, that his *Guide to Health and Longer Life*, cannot protract even the fate of a king one single moment."[24] One could think Hill a modern hedge-fund criminal or political traitor—eighteenth-century blame and censure had hardly run its course.

After his knighthood Hill lived on for just one more year, permeated by gouty moments and related ailments. There was little time to make use of his recent decoration, although the life left in him must have imagined how he had persisted and prevailed. But now he was fatally tired too. This man who from youth lived on the verge of recasting himself had run out of tricks, however well intentioned his desire to reform science in an era when it was badly in need of it. Having been honored by Sweden, the land of Linnaeus, and—in Hill's mind—probably by dint of Linnaeus's intervention, it was time to die.

He had been declining for years but despite being in straits still gave charity. Eight years earlier, in the severely cold winter of 1767–1768, when the poor suffered appallingly, there is record of his doing deeds of good: ". . . During the severity of the winter . . . a great deal was done for the relief of the poor, particularly in the following instances . . . besides these generous acts, large sums were collected in various parishes, and the Queen [Charlotte] gave 500l under a feigned name, through the hands of Dr. Hill."[25] Hill's final letters suggest he was in such desperate arthritic pain death would be a blissful release.

But further reversals arose. On Friday night, January 29, 1770, he was physically assaulted: "On Tuesday as Dr. Hill was returning in his Chariot from Ranelagh to Bayswater, he was stopt by two Highwaymen in Tyburn-Lane, who robbed him of his Watch and Money."[26] He was not hurt but the incident disturbed him and aggravated his gout. He could rest that he had made final preparations. His last will and testament was signed and sealed, leaving everything to Henrietta, especially the patents on his potions. But most of his remains were debts. Debt above all else.

If the myth of gout as protective shield rang true to its universal victims, it acutely resonated with Hill. The refuge in illness gave him time to make preparations for death: to process the lull of ambition now that he had been recognized, arrange his affairs, make his will, provide for his family, reconsider his life, especially the range of activity he had undertaken.[27] Ambition was quelled: a shadow of its former self. More essentially, he was deeply in debt no matter how much activity he had enacted in sixty years—and in his mind his knighthood was proof. He recognized that his last decade was the calmest of his life, and that Henrietta had remained the loyalist of wives. His greatest wish, to see all twenty-six volumes of the *Vegetable System* published, was granted. Some of his enemies were now dead; he had fewer now than at any time in his memory. He was slowly disintegrating, surrounded by his family, wife, children, and occasionally sister Anne. Perhaps he died with all at his side.

The official cause of death was cardiac failure, a common effect of the chronic gout and the arthritic afflictions he had endured for over a decade. It occurred on Friday November 24 at a house, according to the newspapers, on Golden Square behind Piccadilly.[28] No record exists of his having bought

Figure 18.3. Portrait of John Hill by Giovanni Vendramini (1769–1839) linking him to Kew Gardens.

Reproduced by kind permission of the Wellcome Library, London.

or rented a house here, and one can only assume it is a mistake; if not, that his failing health brought him to town from Bayswater, to a house just behind the present Upper Regent Street, to be close to physicians, or he may have happened to be visiting one there and unexpectedly died. He was still signing his letters as from "his residence" in "St. James's" in 1774, which he may not have actually retained. But whether his lodging or someone else's, he died in Golden Square.

Nothing suggests that on November 24 anyone other than his family was present. No accounts survive of his last few hours and dying words—this detail, like so much of his life, is lost. It is unclear whether Henrietta and the second brood of young children were at his bedside, let alone their four older siblings. In her *Address* of 1788 Henrietta remembered that "his decease was not known abroad for some time" but was silent about his final hours.[29] No last dying words or circumstances were recorded, nor the details of the funeral, perhaps suggesting that the Hills' debts were greater than the public knew. The newspapers reported his death early the following week but omitted the place of burial.[30] The *Gazeteer* used his title, "Sir John Hill" and called him "one of the most distinguished botanists of the age."[31]

Henrietta had lived with her husband's debts, weaknesses, and strengths as the most loyal of wives and saw his vast alterations: from the proud puffer and promiscuous rake of the early 1750s to the serious botanist and hack in search of patronage through the rest of that decade; and finally to the responsible but indebted father of about ten children (all totaled), husband, and gardener in semi-retreat. Firsthand she had witnessed the antipathy to him, and saw how the die against him was cast. She knew how indefatigably he worked and believed in him; his staunchest advocate while piercing through to his panoply of faults. Her assessment, captured in her pathos-driven defense thirteen years later, was that he should be seen as a figure tragically deceived by his patron rather than demonized, or ridiculed, by Grub Street.[32]

Da Costa was crestfallen. He had not seen Hill since his own release from the King's Bench Prison in October 1772, but wrote an account to his old friend Thomas Knowlton, the antiquarian and botanist with whom he had been corresponding for half a century. "Sir John Hill died poor and in debt."[33] Octogenarian Knowlton was now almost blind; the long letter was read to him. Hill's "books," da Costa curiously continued, "will be sold and his villa at Bayswater." Then he lamented that Hill "vanishd [sic] like smoak and his name is now is hardly ever mentioned." Someone with so many enemies could "vanish"—disappear—like that. But da Costa knew better. The exotic creature, who had risen from unknown itinerant charlatan-quack vending his potions, to become the highest-paid journalist of his era, as Horace Walpole affirmed, and considerable botanist too, was no more.

NOTES

1. Several were sent there but I have found no Russian translations; English traveler John Bell described the Imperial Academy in 1763; see Bell, 2, 14–15. By 1766–1767 the *AR* was describing its experiments for English readers; see *AR* 9 (1767): 94–95. English scientist Joseph Priestley (1733–1804) was also a member.
2. Royal Society Certificates III, f 45.
3. See above, chapter 14, 223–24.
4. Fraser (1994), 57–59; Fraser reprints the proposal including the printed sheet; citations in this paragraph are from Fraser to whom the credit must be given for the discovery of JH's plan.
5. *PA* (September 13, 1770).
6. See above 258–59, 277.
7. LPH, 151.
8. LPH, 173; JH sent this letter of March 2, 1772, several times to Linnaeus in both English and French.
9. His life spanned the whole course of Linnaeus's.
10. LPH, 180–81; the French original is printed in Blanche Henrey (1975), vol. 2, 108–9.
11. Blanche Henrey (1975), vol. 2, 109 reiterates the point.
12. *GM*, 44 (June 1774): 282. This was Gustavus III who established the Order of Vasa on May 29, 1772; it was discontinued in 1974.
13. See Blanche Henrey (1975), vol. 2, 108, for misinformation circulated in JH's time about the veracity of the knighthood; Henrey notes: it "was received and recognized, at the levee of his own Sovereign, as a Knight of that Order; for the Order see Francis Townsend 1828: x."
14. Grant (1956), 6, lines 105–112.
15. Anonymous, *The Adventures of an Author* (1767), 18.
16. Grant (1956), 6, lines 113–120.
17. Grant (1956), 6, lines 117–23.
18. Grant (1956), 7, lines 131–34.
19. Anonymous, *The Graces* (1774).
20. JH (1773a); JH (1773c).
21. JH (1773a).
22. JH (1773b).
23. Derrick (1769), 72.
24. *Town and Country Magazine* 1 (1769): 180.
25. *DA* 26 (February 1768).
26. *DA* 29 (January 1770).
27. LPH, 185–90.
28. Records of Burial in the Parish of St. James, Piccadilly, Westminster, 1775.
29. Henrietta Hill (1788), 16.
30. He was not buried with the Hill family in Denham Churchyard; I found no grave of him there when I searched in 1982.
31. I. e., November 24, 1775.
32. Henrietta Hill (1788).
33. BL MSS 28539, f 90, May 2, 1776.

19

Lady Hill Persists

Notices appeared in 1776 to mark his death yet nothing observed it so well as his wife. The obituaries politely praised where they could but Hill's afterlife, as it were, was not celebratory, and nothing he might have done while alive could have made a difference now. He had no funds while dying to hire a biographer, nor would further reissues of his works have changed anything. Short of Henrietta's having whispered Hail Marys for his reputation while she prayed for his soul, nothing was to be done. There were no memorials or monuments; no posthumous markers to commemorate any of his accomplishments. Wife and family remembered him, and it would be worth much to know how his children fared later in life in the household of such a hyperactively compulsive father.[1] Henrietta's much later *Address* is terse but even then—in 1788, thirteen years after her husband's death—its pathos trumpets loss rather than denial to the fame machine. She must have mourned plentifully when the sting of death bit, but once recovered, she took charge to preserve not only his collections and copyrights but also her financial self.

Hill would have been a fool not to recognize how she had sustained him over the twenty-two years they were married. Her loyalty was remarkable: not merely to accommodate his unflagging compulsions and multiple refashionings but in the light of his tenacity—as da Costa earlier described Hill—"to keep scribbling," and if she demonstrated her mettle during his life she did so even more so after his death. Judging by the obituaries she remained a shadowy creature throughout the years of marriage, and few of them mentioned her as a new widow. It was only after she began her legal challenges to her husband's creditors and competitors, and to Bute himself, that she gained public visibility. One scrap of evidence offers comic relief.

The *Morning Post* of April 23, 1777, carried notice of a treaty of marriage "between Governor Pownal [*sic*] and Lady Hill, dowager of the late Sir John Hill." This was Thomas Pownall (1722–1805), the British colonial statesman and soldier who went to America at the time Hill was feuding with the Fielding "coalition," met Benjamin Franklin with whom he established a long friendship, and occupied colonial posts. But in 1760 he returned to England, was soon afterward posted to command the British troops in Germany, and on his return became an MP in the West of England. It is possible he met Henrietta soon after her husband's death, but Pownall's biographer says nothing about their liaison—if it was that—and Henrietta never referred to it, unless it is the reason she possibly moved out of Bayswater in 1777.[2] Perhaps they made a "treaty" only to break it. Besides, why would a widow who had married in 1777 wait eleven years to pursue Bute?

The widow Henrietta had more pressing work. Her hands were full with two lots of children: four entering their twenties, and three girls in adolescence.[3] After closing down the estate, a delicate task in light of the secret medical recipes she took care to preserve, her creditors began to clamor, with the upshot that she could no longer afford to pay the rates in Bayswater. Estate agents were hired to sell the place: the house, garden and storage spaces "in lots till the Sale."[4] The children must have pitched in. By the next spring (1776) she had not sold, but an advertisement dated May 1776 explains that:

> . . . Sir John Hill, deceased, situate at Bayswater, near Kensington, consisting of a Messuage [a dwelling house together with its outbuildings and the adjacent land assigned to its use] and Garden, lett to Mr. Bowles, at £20 per Ann. and also a capital new-built House, the Apartments of which are spacious, and elegantly furnished; the Garden is embellished with a Greenhouse, Storehouses, a fine sheet of Water, and a Lawn enameled with the choicest Plants. The situation of this Villa is perfectly retired, the most beauteous Meadows are its Environs, and the richest Views are commanded from the principal Floor. The said Estate may be viewed.[5]

The house was sold in 1777 and it is unclear where Henrietta went (off with Pownall?). Whatever profit she took must have been used partially to pay off huge debts. Hill's library was also sold, in two lots, by Abraham Langford, the auctioneers, during the previous spring (1776) and following winter (1777).[6] Once sold, the house could be emptied of its furniture and vacated. No Sales Catalogue survives but it was a large collection of perhaps two or three thousand volumes to extend to two days. The auctioneers attended less out of deference to a former celebrity who had been deprecated in the press than as money-grubbers eager to turn a quick shilling on expensive books. Langford also ran further adverts for the sale of the house, making plain that the place was not sold by May 1776.

The first few years of widowhood were the most difficult for Henrietta and impossible to document with certainty. She still had at least three adolescent daughters at home. The debts Hill left meant she could not afford to run their compound in Bayswater. The place's transformations after 1777 are unclear, but by 1790 it had been turned into a small amusement park—"Bayswater Tea Gardens"—where the denizens of Oxford Street and the current Mayfair retreated for food, drink, and summer sunsets.[7]

Henrietta understood that Hill's financial legacy, despite his debts, was founded on pills and potions far more than books—with few exceptions they were encumbrances rather than profit makers. Even today, after so much print has appeared about Enlightenment quackery, we underestimate how widely the Georgians medicated themselves—deadening their bodies through (what we call) analgesics, narcotics, sedatives, stimulants, and outright poisons, everything the "old quacks" sold them under the ruse of hard names.[8] They were the first modern society to douse themselves in these often-expensive panaceas and could do so because England had never before grown so rich. The common man had more disposable wealth to hand than ever before and spent it. Earlier periods had indulged themselves too but not to this degree, and Hill's "famous five" remedies fit squarely into this category of analgesics and sedatives. Bardana and valerian alone made plenty of profit.

Hill's "famous five" took off and occasionally earned sums funding his lavish style of living and the publishing projects he desperately pursued to the end of his life, especially the *Vegetable System* and the exorbitant cost of producing its hand-colored plates. Had he not been such a high-liver, his debt would have been much less despite the *Vegetable System*. As Tobias Smollett commented at the opening of *The Adventures of Humphry Clinker*, Hill's "five" were hugely successful because they tapped into bewildering conditions afflicting the public: nervous disorders, sleepless nights, bilious afflictions from late night suppers and heavy drink—the new maladies of Georgian stress and excessive indulgence familiar to us more than two centuries later. Hill had kept plugging the new *nervous* maladies. All was nervous, as he had emphasized in his tracts on hypochondriasis, the management of children, and the construction of our nervous physiology.

Edmund Burke, the political thinker and orator, is a good example of someone prominent in Georgian society who could have told you a great deal about the notorious "Inspector." When just twenty-one he wrote "A Mock Funeral Oration on Dr. Hill" to be "Pronounced in the Bedford Coffee house by Mr. [Charles] Macklin" the actor.[9] Macklin may or may not have recited it, but Burke's parody speaks for itself. Two years later, he penned a "Satire of 1753, declaiming against the Knavery and Dupery of the Town, Elizabeth Canning, Dr. Hill & c."[10] By the time Burke was thirty he was stressed over his father's death and the knowledge of his Irish-Catholic past, as well as his new high-powered job as assistant to the Chief Secretary for Ireland. He sought personal relief in Hill's "famous five"—valerian, bardana, essence of water dock, balsam of honey, and sage—which apparently provided temporary respite. "I am much better," he wrote confidentially to Charles O'Hara on July 10, 1761, "since I came into the Country, though by [no] means free from pain."[11] The "pain" arose from gout he thought also afflicted him; so he took more and more of Hill's panaceas. Others less illustrious than Burke became addicted to these new strains of modern nervous life, as P. G. Wodehouse might call them in the 1930s, but in the second half of the eighteenth century Hill's "famous five" had made the Hills rich—if only he could have curbed his excesses. His famous five may not have made as much profit as Joshua Ward's "pill and drop" or, earlier in the century, Bishop Berkeley's "Tar-water," but was nevertheless close to the top of the pharmacological pack.

Henrietta had observed her husband patent his "famous five," and recognized—in widowhood—that they were her sole reliable source of income. Accordingly, she followed Hill's habit of advertising and selling them, while continuing to grow the herbs and plants in their compound in Bayswater and also supplying apothecaries and booksellers; claiming that "none are genuine, but what are sold at her house . . . and by her appointment at the following places. Mr. Joliff . . . Mr. Newberry . . . Mr. Baldwin. . . ."[12] Hill had copied his secrets, given the recipes to Henrietta, who stored them, and patented several, especially the herbal remedies for sleep and nervous disorders. In an era when nervous complaints were growing, the profits involved, if claimed, could amount to significant income. But the piracy of potions was in constant crescendo, if the suits brought against the popular Ward's "pill and drop" were any indication. Henrietta had a litigious side too, and when she detected infringement on the recipes she proceeded to her solicitors and into the courts, as she did against the distributor John Horden in 1779 in a case typical of others she also pursued.

Horden had been purchasing his medicines from the druggist William Brook of the wonderfully titled "Savage Garden" near Kensington Fields and selling them in his shop. Brook somehow obtained Hill's "Balsam of Honey" without paying their authorized dealer, Benjamin Shaw, a major patent holder located in St. Paul's Churchyard.[13] Hill's will left everything to Henrietta but its terms also authorized several distributors to sell his patented preparations, of which Shaw was one. When Henrietta appealed to Shaw about his having defrauded her, Shaw took action through the Lord Chancellor who granted an injunction to apprehend the offenders, labeling Brook's bottles frauds, which, in turn, released Horden from guilt as the defrauder. The Lord Chancellor's published appeal is more important for describing Henrietta's parlous state than for warning Brook to cease and desist:

> . . . The following acknowledgement of deliberate fraud, attended with consequences nearly fatal to an amiable Lady, speaks too forcibly to need any com-

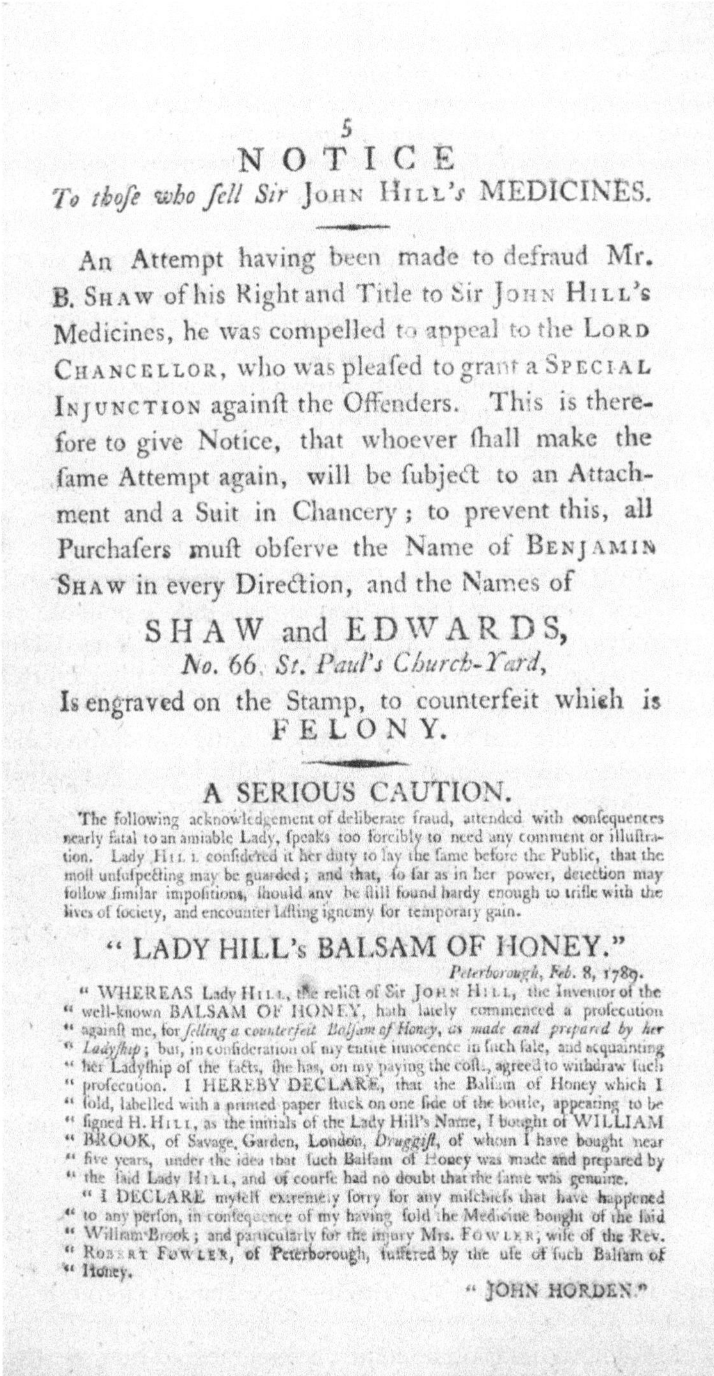

5

NOTICE

To thoſe who ſell Sir JOHN HILL's MEDICINES.

An Attempt having been made to defraud Mr. B. SHAW of his Right and Title to Sir JOHN HILL's Medicines, he was compelled to appeal to the LORD CHANCELLOR, who was pleaſed to grant a SPECIAL INJUNCTION againſt the Offenders. This is therefore to give Notice, that whoever ſhall make the ſame Attempt again, will be ſubject to an Attachment and a Suit in Chancery; to prevent this, all Purchaſers muſt obſerve the Name of BENJAMIN SHAW in every Direction, and the Names of

SHAW and EDWARDS,
No. 66, St. Paul's Church-Yard,
Is engraved on the Stamp, to counterfeit which is
FELONY.

A SERIOUS CAUTION.

The following acknowledgement of deliberate fraud, attended with conſequences nearly fatal to an amiable Lady, ſpeaks too forcibly to need any comment or illuſtration. Lady HILL conſidered it her duty to lay the ſame before the Public, that the moſt unſuſpecting may be guarded; and that, ſo far as in her power, detection may follow ſimilar impoſitions, ſhould any be ſtill found hardy enough to trifle with the lives of ſociety, and encounter laſting ignomy for temporary gain.

"LADY HILL's BALSAM OF HONEY."

Peterborough, Feb. 8, 1789.

"WHEREAS Lady HILL, the reliſt of Sir JOHN HILL, the Inventor of the "well-known BALSAM OF HONEY, hath lately commenced a proſecution "againſt me, for *ſelling a counterfeit Balſam of Honey, as made and prepared by her "Ladyſhip*; but, in conſideration of my entire innocence in ſuch ſale, and acquainting "her Ladyſhip of the facts, ſhe has, on my paying the coſts, agreed to withdraw ſuch "proſecution. I HEREBY DECLARE, that the Balſam of Honey which I "ſold, labelled with a printed paper ſtuck on one ſide of the bottle, appearing to be "ſigned H. HILL, as the initials of the Lady Hill's Name, I bought of WILLIAM "BROOK, of Savage, Garden, London, *Druggiſt*, of whom I have bought near "five years, under the idea that ſuch Balſam of Honey was made and prepared by "the ſaid Lady HILL, and of courſe had no doubt that the ſame was genuine.

"I DECLARE myſelf extremely ſorry for any miſchiefs that have happened "to any perſon, in conſequence of my having ſold the Medicine bought of the ſaid "William Brook; and particularly for the injury Mrs. FOWLER, wife of the Rev. "ROBERT FOWLER, of Peterborough, ſuffered by the uſe of ſuch Balſam of "Honey.

"JOHN HORDEN."

Figure 19.1. "Notice to those who sell John Hill's Medicines."
Reproduced by kind permission of Professor George Rousseau.

> ment or illustration. Lady Hill considered it her duty to lay the same before the Public, that the most unsuspecting may be guarded; and she, so far as is in her power, detection may follow similar impositions, should any be still found hardy enough to trifle with the lives of society, and encounter lasting ignominy for temporary gain.[14]

There were probably cases similar to Shaw's while Henrietta's plea to Bute continued. In law there were precedents for widows seeking to recover the profits of their late husbands' patents. In 1759 Lady Mansell, relict of Sir Edward Mansell, brought a case against her husband's heir, and subsequent decades increased the numbers. But Henrietta had no response from Bute, who was now ensconced at Christchurch, Hampshire, in the villa he called Highcliffe, overlooking the Needles and the Isle of Wight. Here he still pursued his lifelong botanical study, collected prints, books, and scientific instruments, and devoted himself to the patronage of literature, science, and the arts.[15] He had become immensely rich, having acquired a fortune upon the death of his father-in-law, Edward Wortley Montagu, Lady Mary's husband.[16] This inheritance had helped propel Bute's political cache in 1759–1760, and now—since his fall from political office—he used it for other purposes. Lady Bute had been the sole inheritor of her father's fortune and was left a life interest in the Wortley estates worth £17,000 per annum, her personal fortune estimated at over £1 million. Little wonder that Henrietta raved in sleepless nights, hoping to recoup Hill's losses in producing the twenty-six folio volumes of the *Vegetable System*.

Bute and his lawyers had other designs for promoting the scientific and intellectual life of Scotland. Bute's gifts were deployed almost entirely to Scottish people and places, his botanical largesse to the establishment of botanical gardens in old universities in Edinburgh, Glasgow, and Aberdeen. He was not about to fork out to Hill's widow, no matter how hard up. Despondent, she pursued those who infringed on her late husband's secret recipes. Until the new century's turn, advertisements about violations by Hill's patent holders continued to appear in newspapers.[17] It was a far cry from the spotlight her "celebrated" husband had held during the good years. Yet Henrietta coordinated the effort as long as she could and reaped the profits until she became too frail.

Meanwhile, Hill's reputation was sinking fast. The old charge of "Vanity, pure Vanity" surfaced posthumously, as if he had been an Event in the History of Pride. An occasional memento remembered him, as when Jeremiah Whitaker Newman (1759–1839), a London surgeon and commentator on the medical scene who had been friendly with Dr. Messenger Monsey, noted that Hill's disputes and tactics broke all the norms of his age. But gone was his presence in the media and Hill was certainly not collectable in the way so many icons of his generation became.[18] The newspapers too were silent. Newman remembered the firsthand sight of Hill around 1774—"if my memory is correct" he admits—decked out in "ribbons . . . and the finest equipage" after he received the Order of Vasa. Two decades later, when succumbing to the tendency of the eighteenth-century *fin de siècle* to reconstruct the temper of the preceding generation, Newman pieced together the main lines of Hill's biography. As he did, he found himself increasingly attracted to the man.

Newman's categories suggest he spoke to people who remembered Hill, not long since dead. He calls him a "literary drawcansir" and the "AT ALL of his day; players, poets, philosophers, physicians, antiquarians, commentators, critics, free-thinkers, and divines" were all abused by his fluent pen. His chief sin was "preposterous affectation" and Newman revives all the old words to describe Hill's productions: "pert," "vane," "self-sufficient," declaiming that "the sin of Dr. Hill . . . was insufferable vanity." But he concedes that the public "swallowed his preparations with avidity" and made him a fortune, and that he pulled himself up from "obscurity, poverty, and insignificance" to effect "that purpose for which millions are daily toiling in vain." The line is rags-to-riches-Hill who has cashed in on the celebrity culture of the age. Newman's personal intellectual interest when he was not "compiling" was the medical profession, specifically whether "merit or manners" led to medical success.[19] But he could not omit Hill from his anecdotes about the most curious characters of the prior age.

Henrietta may not have listened but would have heard about such abuses of her husband's memory. She still pursued Bute, and while Newman was compiling she continued to go after Bute down through the 1780s. The chase exhausted her, especially its legal challenges for someone without high-end resources. Without the assistance of her dowager friends perhaps she would have given up long ago. After publishing her *Address* in 1788 to expose Bute publicly, she conceded defeat and became invisible. Bute died in 1792, and Bute's widow two years later. A few months later, in March 1793, Hill's only surviving brother, Theophilus Jr., died at almost eighty in Lincoln.[20] Henrietta's only brother, in Ireland, was also dead. No avenue of recourse remained.

Henrietta died quietly in the winter of 1802, aged about seventy-five, in the house of her daughter Juliana, in Surrey, and was buried in the local churchyard there in accordance with her wishes.[21] A year later spinster Juliana sold her recipe-rights to the firm of Benjamin Shaw, and then she too disappeared from public record.[22]

Dr. Newman's synopsis of the 1790s prognosticated what was coming as the century ground to a close. He emphasized Hill's victimization of *others*; this is what Newman's oral sources told him, those who knew and remembered Hill, perhaps including Dr. Monsey. Pride and vanity drove Hill, they assured him, but Newman had no feel for what it was like *to be* Hill himself: the man who already became a legend during his lifetime. Historically his profile demonstrates the power of reputation in an era that appears to resemble ours far more than his own. Without the new periodical press and media (especially the plentiful caricatures and broadsides), the myth of Hill could not have rooted itself so swiftly or widely. His typology struck his contemporaries not only as ignominious but novel in its ability to deceive.

Nothing in Newman's vignette acknowledges Hill's disappointment at being second rate, not even genius manqué. The truth was that nothing Hill touched could soar to the first class. In polite literature he was no Fielding or Richardson, not even a Smollett or Sterne; in botany he had corresponded with the greatest pioneer, Linnaeus, but did nothing himself that could be compared with the Swede's contributions to general science, not merely to natural classification and taxonomy. Hill stood for experimental approaches to science, which many others in his era did not, but he made no major discoveries.

His most lasting contribution was doubtlessly reform, for if he had not acted so rashly the Royal Society would have been slower to change itself. Where did reform land him? In the state of a self-deluded outcast more than he realized; and as a reformer he never understood that the securest reforms are those achieved from within—instead he attacked from without and then struck with his fluent pen or acerbic tongue, and the tragedy of his career was that he could not stop writing or quit the compulsion. Ellis's "drug" describing the effect of his writing was misplaced: Hill *himself* was addicted to scribosis, and when he no longer could scribble he died.

His best literary vocation had been gardening: there he could have gone on producing competent books, which sold well and imparted new information, and collecting for the great Whig lords of his day, but was he was hardly satisfied with that niche. Had he been less unctuous—the sickening "puppy," as Richmond quipped—he would have been elected to all societies, for he was gifted beyond most men of his generation. Instead he flattered or railed, never proceeding in the neutral middle. He lashed out, claiming that he must respond or be roasted, and believed that attack was the first principle of public relations. If only Jonathan Swift were composing his *Tale of a Tub* with its deluded knaves now, in the 1770s, rather than two generations earlier.

NOTES

1. No primary documents of any type have been found between the members.
2. See Schutz, passim.
3. For the names and ages of the children now, see p. 177.

4. *DA*, May 21, 1776.
5. *DA*, May 21, 1776.
6. Nichols, vol. 6, 89; it consisted of expensive botanical books, works the auctioneers wanted; these fetched large sums in London auction houses given the half century of the cult of botanizing. Botanical books authored by JH also fetched large sums and continue to do so to the present day, his first editions now commanding four-figure sums.
7. Wroth, 116–22.
8. As the surgeon Daniel Turner charged in 1718; see Roy Porter (2000), 15–17, 97–101.
9. Burke, I, 140.
10. Quoted in Burke, vol. 1, 140.
11. Burke, vol. 1, 140.
12. Henrietta Hill (1788), 2.
13. A court case ensued by 1792 naming "William Bacon of Paddington in the County of Middlesex" as complainant and Henrietta as defendant. But in 1794 Bacon assigned all his rights over to Benjamin C. Collens of Salisbury, Wiltshire. Benjamin Shaw then entered the fray, claiming that Lady Hill had assigned the whole royalties to him. The entire case is found in Middlesex County Archives, C12/244/23 and C12/2166/10, dated June 29, 1798.
14. Anonymous, *Notice to Those Who Sell Sir John Hill's Medicines* (1779).
15. D. P. Miller (1988), 214–22.
16. Schweizer, passim; Montagu died in 1761 having lived to an old age.
17. Wellcome Library, London, MSS 76213 for the year 1796.
18. Newman (1799), vol. 4, 173–79 for the passages cited. Although Newman knew Monsey he played no role in the fracas involving Sterne and Monsey.
19. Newman (1783).
20. See *The Genealogist* new series 15 (1922): 229.
21. Surrey Probate Records 11/1368/35/279, Surrey County Archives.
22. Henrietta's will was drawn on October 28, 1801, a few months before her death; she named Juliana as the sole beneficiary of her mother's will, which also entitled her to the complete remaining profits from her father's medicinal patents.

20

Forgotten Hill

"Sir John Hill, this despised man, after all the fertile absurdities of his literary life, performed more for the improvement of the *Philosophical Transactions* [of the Royal Society], and was the cause of diffusing a more general taste for the science of botany, than any other contemporary."[1] So astonishingly declaimed Isaac D'Israeli (1766–1848), father of the future prime minister, Benjamin D'Israeli, in his multi-volume *Calamities of Authors*, shortly after Newman pronounced, as we saw in the last chapter. It was not merely the deference Hill had sought all his life but—finally—respect and reverence.

D'Israeli could have pronounced of Hill, with his predecessors, "Vanity, pure vanity." He did not, and his approach differed from Newman's. He read widely rather than summoned oral reports, and decided to cast Hill as a mainstay of his best-selling *Calamities of Authors*. D'Israeli knew that Hill had been "written out" of the fame machine, but his deference nevertheless resounds and tells much about Hill's afterlife at the turn of the nineteenth century. His revaluation is brief—a packed dozen pages—but sympathetic, and imposes broad historical contexts Newman never knew existed. His plea for revaluation reduces to the pathos over someone eminent who has been strangely forgotten and will never have lasting renown. In addition, D'Israeli seems to have been imagining himself as he wrote.

He admires Hill from afar while piercing to the core of his frailties. He removes the feral aspect—the wild Hill who cannot be tamed—and replaces it with a brave, even heroic, Hill who had been in the line of fire in the wrong place at the wrong time. He sees Hill as someone willing to sacrifice himself on the altar of envy—especially envy for his unusual ability. He concedes that Hill deserved much of what he reaped and had been a prime target: a naïve sheep waiting to be destroyed. But D'Israeli also gazes deeply into Hill's contradictions and cuts through them, seeking to understand why he possessed a deviant type of ambition coupled to indefatigable industry and an unquenchable instinct to survive. When all is tolled, he cannot help esteeming him for these divergent, if also disturbing, qualities and judges him one of his notable "worthies": a new type of "literary character" who had been in advance of mid-century Georgian intellectual climate.[2]

D'Israeli's brief life of Hill was no nostalgic elegy, but the product of an erudite mind better informed than most of his contemporaries who were academics in British universities, where he himself would probably have been installed had he not been—like da Costa—a Jew. Henrietta Hill would have rejoiced if she could have read what he eventually wrote (no evidence exists that she did). D'Israeli understood Hill's predicament because it was parallel to, if also different from, to his own. For years D'Israeli had buried himself in English libraries, filling vast notebooks with "facts," and he was astonished at the frequency with which Hill's name recurred. How could this be? He set out to excavate the reasons. His conclusion was that Newman merely repeated what he heard at face value. When Newman, for example, had watched Hill ride by in 1774, decked out in his Swedish paraphernalia of medals, he had already bought into the Hill legend. No scope for exploration existed.

D'Israeli sympathized with the Hill of humble origins and poverty; the Hill who had no formal education. He observed profound divergence in two directions: first, astonishment at how much Hill-the-*wunderkindt* had actually written and published, and, second, his belief that Hill, more than any other post-1750 "gentleman of the age," epitomized the realities and values, the cutthroat competition and man-eat-man proclivity of the Age of Duncery: its economic realities, the new Grub-Street rivalry, and the hacks' instinct for survival at any cost.

The thick detail—minutiae of every type—D'Israeli incorporated into his books on "Quarrels" and "Calamities" still astonishes us two centuries later, as it did early nineteenth-century authors and publishers, especially Byron.[3] There had been earlier accumulations—for example, by John Nichols—of all sorts of remarkable anecdotes; but they were based on diaries, memoirs, and memory, and—most of all—on rumor, memory, and oral testimony. D'Israeli swept away that line and based his "quarrels" and "curiosities" on vast reading and note taking and thereby introduced a new threshold for the literary history of the Georgians. It is the reason he has suddenly turned into a canonical figure of such interest to academic Romantic scholars.[4]

D'Israeli read every analysis of the Georgian profession of authors he could find; tracts such as James Ralph's on what it meant to be an author during the 1750s. They informed his sense of the despised "professional writer."[5] This wide reading instilled in him an acute sense of the role played by the patron in shaping both the author's "life" and "works" of the author, not merely one. Indeed D'Israeli saw the two as integral. The difference endowed him with a securer sense of the past when gleaned from diverse printed sources rather than the single point of view: Newman's view, for example, that Hill was a one-dimensional scoundrel. D'Israeli was also eclectic and made choices about the "parts of lives"—and the "specific quarrels"—he would revive. Rather than produce a miscellany of everything he found, competing with dictionary entries, or synopses like Newman's regurgitating the gossip of his sources, D'Israeli's chapters sought to produce a compelling narrative for each author's particular plight. Each of his "calamities" has the imprint of a story relating an idiosyncratic development based on causes and effects, circumstances and consequences.

D'Israeli's main point was that Hill's reforms had been both misunderstood and neglected, and that his writing about scientific topics achieved a level of fluency rarely seen at mid-century. He thought he stood for the all-around-polymathic-man, one of its last survivors.[6] Uniquely, he yoked Hill to "Orator Henley" (1691–1756),[7] claiming that both men suffered similar fates at having been "written out," although D'Israeli was vigilant to their differences. Henley was born more than two decades before Hill. He was Cambridge educated, became a dissenting minister, was genuinely eccentric, whereas Hill was undeniably notorious—a celebrity vulture. But no one before D'Israeli had thought of yoking them.

D'Israeli's reasons, based on reading rather than gossip or oral interview, are compelling. The two men had briefly corresponded after Hill abused Henley in the "Inspector," but this was not D'Israeli's main reason. It is that they both were *rebels*, both charted their own course apart from the norm and without patronage, both defied the Establishment by initiating rival institutions, both struggled economically and were often within sight of the debtor's jail, and both ended their lives in desperate circumstances, although Henley started life more comfortably than Hill and suffered a worse ending, hardly knighted by anyone. Having fallen out with both church and state, Henley started his own "religion," founded the periodical *Oratory*, his own chapel, and assumed the enduring sobriquet the "Orator," in parallel to Hill's inimitable "Inspector."

Both men also lived to be about sixty (Hill had died at sixty-one), and both endured fierce attacks and abuses. Henley, like Hill, advertised his "Gentlemen's Own University," offering lectures and private tutorials in so many subjects that the plan exposed him to the fiercest ridicule and slander. No less than Hill he puffed his claims to confirm that he was serious about initiating a new type of education, which further exasperated the press and the satirists. The similarities, D'Israeli thought, were too numerous to neglect. Henley was a compulsive scribbler, and when his publications were rejected, as they often were, he began his own weekly newspaper, the *Hyp Doctor*, to respond to the tirade of satirical attacks on him in the *Grub Street Journal*. We glimpse him toiling hard in the *Calamities of Authors* to penetrate to the heart of mid–Georgian Grub Street culture through the lens of these two figures—specifically the two "H's."

D'Israeli sought to understand fracas and furore above all, as the title of his book reflects, as well as the underpinnings of authorial feud in the new craze for publication and celebrity, and, specifically, the relation of fracas to the fraught economic survival of professional writers.[8] D'Israeli possessed no vocabulary capable of coping with the new interior life of selfhood advanced by the late eighteenth-century novelists.[9] Nevertheless, he sought to understand how the post-Popean hack is not merely a compulsive scribbler but a complicated psychological creature in need of wider contexts for the comprehension of his character.

D'Israeli was the only penetrating and impartial assessor of Hill's Georgian niche. Not even Samuel Johnson had been. Had D'Israeli written a full-length life it would have been insightful and still consulted. But he neglected one-half of Hill's activity: his natural history, primarily because he could not easily retrieve it. Furthermore, he was not confident he could understand the "quarrels of authors" of scientific works. Literature and religion he could include, as well as history and politics, but science and medicine appeared beyond his reach. It is almost as if the "two-culture" rift between the arts and sciences has already displayed small cracks in his sensibility.

But D'Israeli was not alone in excavating Hill as a man too facilely dismissed. Charles Burney, the acclaimed music critic and father of novelist Fanny, wrote a judicious précis of the paper wars of the 1750s that aimed to illuminate them to his generation; his tack was contrast between Hill's and Smart's positions.[10] Burney offered a resolution: if Hill was incapable of understanding Smart's poetic talent he was nevertheless "an able botanist" who made a long-lasting contribution to natural history; Smart, for his part, was clearly a gifted poet but blind to Hill's merits, and could only see him "as a quack and a coxcomb." Time, moralist Burney decreed, assigns every man his proper niche, and "though [Hill's] nostrums and panaceas are now exploded, his voluminous works in natural history have advanced toward fame, with nearly as much rapidity as his empirical productions have descended toward oblivion."[11] Burney's "explosion" contradicts Newman's sense of Hill's pharmacological success and D'Israeli's claim that the Georgians consumed Hill's panaceas as fast they could obtain them. Did Burney know something now lost about rival medicines bumping Hill's out of the market by 1792?

We doubt it. Hill's legacy in the practical and theoretical botanical sphere was more straightforward, divided between those who remembered him as one of the most capable Georgian botanists and—on the American side of the ocean—those who used his medicines daily. During Hill's lifetime, Hill's agents sold more of his preparations in the colonies than in England. Samuel Thompson (1769–1843) was one of dozens of colonial apothecaries stocking Hill's medicines. He grew up in colonial Pennsylvania during the peak of Hill's popularity. When he himself set up as an apothecary and herbalist after the American Revolution, Hill's potions—especially the big five, including "Essence of Water Dock"—were at the top of his sales and remained so to the end of his selling days.

Despite the robust North American sales of Hill's medicaments, musicologist Charles Burney's 1792 estimate that Hill's "natural history [has] advanced toward fame" since his death, was controversial at home. The caveat depends on the view taken of his various activities: put otherwise, Hill's reception must be defined in relation to his various fields rather than as a composite whole—botany, literary and scientific writing, and the pills and herbal preparations. For example, James Edward Smith, already mentioned as the founder of the Linnaean Society in England, had been born in the year we call Hill's *annus mirabilis*, 1758–1759. He was a lifelong devotee of Linnaeus's theories, and did everything possible to elevate Linnaeus's legacy in England after Hill's death.[12]

When, for example, Joseph Banks declined the purchase of Linnaeus's unrivaled botanical library and collection of manuscript letters in 1783, Linnaeus's son Carl offered it to Smith. Privately wealthy Smith brought it to England, had its Swedish and Latin translated into English, and from its contents extracted a two-volume collection of *The Correspondence of Linnaeus and Other Naturalists*.[13] Shrewdly, Smith also seized this opportunity to "write out Hill" in the notes to these volumes. He was too young to have met Hill, which did not deter his dislike. His main point was that Hill's botany is flawed and overstated—anything but Burney's incremental "advance" of his botanical reputation. Burney's précis looks to time as the rightful arbiter: ". . . even some of the decisions of Boileau and Pope have been reprehended and reversed by posterity." So hope was on the horizon for much-maligned Hill, according to Burney, and "eventually the world will see that Hill was a better botanist . . . than has been thought."[14]

Small homage arose later, in 1799, from Robert Bonnell Thornton (1768–1837), like Hill a medical man and botanist. By this time botany had risen beyond other sciences to assume universal human and religious functions.[15] Decades earlier in the 1750s Hill had dealings with his father, the actor Bonnell Thornton, but this is not the reason for the younger Thornton's accolade. While a student at Cambridge, Thornton became deeply engrossed in botany—especially botanical history—but by 1798 he thought he discovered biographical parallels between himself and Hill, vocationally in their double allegiance to botany and medicine, and in the massive publishing enterprise on which he had embarked to print in unparalleled magnificence illustrated folio volumes of a history of British botany. A confirmed Linnaean,[16] he called it the *New Illustration of the Sexual System of Linnaeus* (better known under its 1804 title of *The Temple of Flora*), and included Giovanni Vendramini's portrait of Hill, to which he also affixed an engraving of Kew Gardens. He placed Hill's portrait near the more famous one of Linnaeus in Lapp (Sami) dress, the first time Hill's portrait had appeared in such grand company. The huge cost of botanical illustration eventually ruined Thornton, as it had Hill earlier, and Thornton had no Bute to subsidize him or Henrietta to plead his cause. Yet he enlisted the finest engravers of his generation, including Francesco Bartolozzi, Vendramini's drawing master in London and Hill's portrait painter, to produce his colored illustrations.

Only D'Israeli sought to rescue the *whole* of Hill, despite his (D'Israeli's) sense of inadequacy in treating Hill's controversies—his "calamities and quarrels"—among the *naturalists*. Here, in natural science, D'Israeli was out of his depth. While Hill's reputation consolidated during this eighteenth-century fin de siècle, not a year elapsed without some commentator noting the retribution Hill had paid for his excesses through illness; if not detriment to his whole body, then to particular body parts. The *European Magazine* recounted, in August 1793, how "Dr. Hill was in one of his illnesses . . . attended by a celebrated Physician of London, who asked him if he could really continue to permit such harm to be done to his body. . . ."[17] The "famous doctor" is unnamed, as is the specific injury, but the sacrifice is clear.

The same was true of his legacy in botanical nomenclature. This is not the place to enumerate the list of species named after him or assess the taxonomic validity of attribution since his death, but its number has augmented, now bringing the total currently to over fifty.[18] Even in the eighteenth century, the list was long; lengthiest when read in foreign countries. Leyden botanist Nicolas-Joseph Jacquin (1727–1817), whose career peaked around the time of Hill's death, named *Hillia parasitica* for him, and in our time the number has increased. Hill's activity in nomenclature ran parallel to the translation of his works into foreign languages: in the last two decades of the eighteenth century his main writings, in literature as well as botany, appeared in several Western languages: French, German, Italian, Danish, and Spanish.

The French were particularly industrious because their translations of *Lucina sine concubitu* reinterpreted it as a political allegory prognosticating nothing less radical than the French Revolution.[19] A brave Lucina, as we recall,[20] gives birth without impregnation; in this allegorical reading, Lucina births the new, liberated French nation without male seed, which will topple the corrupt *ancien regime*.[21] French readers were never apprised that Hill was the author; those who read *Lucina* allegorically in the 1790s would have viewed him as prophetic had they known. For historians of revolutionary France, the *Lucina* tract alone would place Hill on the eighteenth-century map.

Marc Eidous, a French compiler and translator, was unaware of this future when he began to translate Hill's works in the 1750s.[22] Nor did the first European translators in the 1760s of *Lucina,* whom the late Lynn Sbiroli has studied in depth.[23] As time marched, *Lucina* was the one English work readily lending itself to political, allegorical interpretation, rather than the biological satire Hill intended in 1750. By 1800, almost a dozen of Hill's works could be read in French, but *Lucina* remained the one with political clout. D'Israeli, reviving Hill's reputation in the 1790s, had no inkling of the French translations of Hill's works. Had he, they would further have heightened his sense of Hill's achievement.

> Three great wise men in the same era born,
> Britannia's happy island did adorn:
> Henley in cure of souls displayed his skill,
> Rock shone in physic, and in both John Hill;
> The force of nature could no farther go.
> To make a third she joined the other two.

This is not D'Israeli or Burney but ephemera cited in a Victorian work about the caricature of the Georgians.[24] The three "wise doctors" are Henley, discussed above, Dr. Rock,[25] a quack mentioned earlier with a vast reputation for dispensing hermetic potions, and Hill himself.[26] Hill had commented on Henley as a rebel, as we saw: this disaffection causing alienation.

But Hill was a psychological type rather than modern eccentric. By the Regency "excentricity" (with an x), both in English and French contexts denoted, according to *saloniste* Madame de Staël, "a wholly original way of behaving which pays no heed to the opinions of others." Staël thought "eccentrics" were plentiful but nowhere more so than in England. When amateur historian Thomas Wright revalued Hill in the mid-nineteenth century, incorporating the ditty just cited, a European genealogy about eccentrics had begun to accumulate, ranging from the original, if solitary, intellectuals whose domestic habits were odd, to the certifiably insane who were desperately in need of medical attention. Hill lived at neither extremity of the scale, but his behavior could appear wild to those looking back after 1850 because they were reconfiguring their—particularly English—heritage along these lines. Small wonder that American sociologist Lewis Mumford has written: "every generation rebels against its fathers but makes friends with its grandfathers."

Stories of extraordinary behavior were marketable as species of the monstrous tale: so decreed the *Eccentric Magazine* in 1821 when printing its first *"collection of anecdotes."* Charles Dibdin, writing his *Complete History of the Stage* as the new nineteenth century commenced, nailed Hill's eccentricity to *galloping scribosis* while omitting feud and fracas.[27] He labeled it "excentricity," as if *scribosis* were some newly discovered insanity. Dibdin later revised the appellation to a rare form of "voluminosity" of "a kind that nothing came to him amiss," and a type that "beat out any author that had ever existed in point of quantity." It was false: others in his time had written more words but Dibdin viewed scribosis apart from the contexts of Hill's creations and captured him as a grotesque writing machine living in dread of looming menace if he stopped scribbling. This was no different than if Hill strolled with a lobster on a pink ribbon.

Dibdin's "excentricity" departs from D'Israeli's broad canvas and depiction of character, which matter-of-factly documents Hill's life and works without the fanfare of monstrosity or malady. What D'Israeli saw as achievement (especially Hill's breadth and daring across the two-cultures divide), Dibdin construed as marketable monstrosity, proceeding as if the aberration itself constituted its commercial merchandise. It is not clear why Dibdin sought to include Hill among noteworthies of the stage—he was not that. But Dibdin still ranked Hill among the "inferior writers of the eighteenth century stage," locating his Achilles' heel in ranging too far: promiscuous, far-reaching, fluency; "nothing came to him amiss"; "he could write about anything."[28] This "*generalism*," Dibdin suggests, was a vendible curiosity. But whereas collectors in the milieu of Parsons and da Costa were "respectable naturalists," according to Dibdin, the new antiquaries were degenerate eccentrics, abnormally focused on themselves.

Richard Cumberland (1732–1811), the stage figure and man of letters, cheerfully remembered that Hill's fortunes took a turn for the better when "by a happy transformation into Hannah Glass he turned himself into a cook, and sold receipts for made-dishes to all the savoury readers in the kingdom."[29] Cumberland probably never met Hill, yet assumed, like many others, that Hill wrote these cookbooks around 1747. The value of Cumberland's memory is that he remembered how food recipes in his formative years (what we would call *fast-food recipes*) were taking off. Cumberland had enjoyed a privileged life: his grandfather was Richard Bentley, the great classicist, and he was born in the Master's Lodge of Trinity College Cambridge. He was in his twenties when Hill "transformed" himself into Hannah Glasse and the news obviously impressed him. So vivid that he recollected it when composing the memoirs forming part of the social history of England during the Age of Hill, including its view about original characters: "I perceive that I had fallen upon a time when great eccentricity of character was pretty nearly gone by. . . ." For Cumberland, Hill was the exception.

It is no exaggeration to claim that hundreds of Victorians would have read D'Israeli's chapter about Hill—so popular were his *Quarrels of Authors*. Its picture of weakness coupled to strength—these two forces—is the one they remembered rather than D'Israeli's deference or reverence, but by the 1860s, on the anniversary of George III's 1767 interview with Samuel Johnson, D'Israeli's vignette appeared outdated when the historian-antiquary Thomas Wright recolored it. Writing with D'Israeli's book at his side, Wright visualized a Hill located at the epicenter of taste's transformation from duncery to "Pertness." His stunning chapter on "The Reign of Pertness"—the strange word we have fleshed out in this book—ends in this way:

> . . . Dr. Hill has deserved our notice, as a somewhat exaggerated type of the fashionable literary men of the latter half of the reign of George II. Dulness, the goddess [*sic*] who presided over Grub Street in the days of Pope, was resigning her scepter to another goddess not less fatal to good taste, Pertness, who was removing the seat of power further west. It was a sovereignty, which had risen up with the critics and feuilletonists.[30]

If duncery arose as a collective "Anti-Christ" in the ascendancy of taste, it succumbed when manners overruled its edicts; that is, when behavior counted for more than verbal production. What is "pertness" if not a public show of brazenness; an "acting out" of impertinence and impudence; a raw parade of personal temerity about one's presumed abilities? Pertness is activated when public behavior is elevated above other forms of self-identity; when one's smallest actions are scrutinized under the lens of a magnifying glass. This, *au fond*, was what the paper wars of the 1750s had aimed to defuse—the subtle shift from artifact to behavior—and what author William Kenrick had unpacked in *Pasquinade*.[31] If his couplets limped less their content might be remembered, for it lodges a fortissimo note about Georgian social history: the new rule of action over motive.

A century later, in the 1860s, Wright was intrigued by the concept of "pertness," and wrote as if he had stumbled upon something entirely new in Georgian social history. It is only when he situates the "pert class" firmly in the camp of quacks that one wonders about his drift. His alliance of the sister goddesses—Dulness and Pertness—is straightforward and reasonable: Pope's "Reign of Dulness" yielding after 1740 to "Pertness's Rule." But if Pope had allied duncery and antiquarianism, as he does in the *New Dunciad* (1742) among the collectors of butterflies and fossils, Wright grounds it in "medical quackery" deeply tied to literary fakery:

> Dr. Hill stands forth as a type not only of *literary* but also of *medical* quackery, the wide prevalence of which was among the distinguishing characteristics of the period. . . . Amid the general venality, degrees and honours were not always a proof of merit in the individual upon whom they were bestowed; and from this cause, or from the wide-spread spirit of credulity, people sought with more eagerness the nostrum of the quack, than the experience of the proficient.[32]

Pertness's frauds in deception and incompetence take center stage; they even resonate in our own time despite the different vocabulary. The specific charge leveled at Hill is that his writings are as "fraudulent" as his nostrums—the hack as "literary quack." How did Wright know? His knowledge of medicine, especially its past, was limited and he probably read very little, if anything, Hill had written. He knew even less about Hill's botany, certainly not a deceptive or fraudulent zone as Wright gives out. Wright, writing for the Victorians as Newman did for the Georgians, relied on opinion, especially his reading of D'Israeli—except that he did not scan D'Israeli's chapter closely enough. Instead he tapped into the Victorian craze to detect Georgian imposition. Imposters in history,[33] who drove him to despair more than original research he had performed about Hill, besieged his imagination.

After Wright, Hill more or less disappears from the radar except for histories of the stage that view him nostalgically. As theater historian Percy Fitzgerald wrote: ". . . a most remarkable character . . . a detailed account of his career would be most entertaining." But no one undertook it, and when Leslie Stephens assigned his life in the 1882 *Dictionary of National Biography* he gave it to Norman Moore (1847–1922), a Cambridge trained medical doctor interested in diseases of the chest who was not at all nostalgic. Moore worked in a London hospital for his entire career and was an amateur, if nevertheless industrious, medical historian. He delivered a Linacre Lecture in Oxford that surveyed the "English physician in history," and petitioned for the serious study of medical history when there was no institutional place for this subject. Consistent with his belief he accepted Leslie Stephens' assignment and wrote several medical lives for the (then) new *DNB*, including one about Hill. It contains not new ideas. He regurgitates dates and titles and takes no account of D'Israeli's far more cogent view. He has not even digested D'Israeli's position.

Of what value a life of Hill? In another mode, how will John Hill be remembered? Surely within the contexts of Georgian fracas and scandal, as well as its burgeoning botanical cultures and expansion of Grub Street. The question *how would Hill himself want to be remembered* is less pressing: history does not resurrect the dead as they would have wished, let alone the notorious dead who have even less say. D'Israeli's response arose from an impulse to indulge curiosity—itself an old Enlightenment category even if it loomed large in D'Israeli's own psychological mind-set; specifically, from his intuition that Hill had been one of the most "curious characters" of his era. And D'Israeli construed his essayistic task, when writing about Hill, as unpacking and unraveling this nagging element of "curiosity" within the developing threads of Georgian culture and society, as this chapter has attempted to demonstrate.[34]

The naked facts about Hill are, like all facts, given to slippage but nevertheless speak plainly, in his era as now. He lived at the intersection of several developing "cultures." His gaze never arose from within one culture, as if he had been an insider, but at distant points of their intersection; yet he rarely connected the various cultures in which he was implanted. He must be remembered for his prodigious output in many disciplines and swaggering rhetorical style, as well as for his flamboyant lifestyle and chronic debt: the upstart who moved from watery fens to posh pads in Westminster and St. James, and who was an insufferable nuisance to his contemporaries as self-appointed "Inspector" rambling t'Town. Also remembered for the sheer variety of itinerant poses and authorial aliases and multiplicity of roles he could assume. Georgian society threw up few Proteuses like him. A man apart, he had few rivals in the extent to which he was willing to thrust himself as a pest into the public domain—all for the sake of asserting his indomitable personality. He left no followers or disciples, just biological children who amounted to little themselves; was incapable of engendering disciples or heirs apparent. He could write better than anyone who could write faster than he could, and faster than anyone who could write better. His Georgian epoch had far more consummate writers and scientists, but few, doubtlessly, who could write more fluently and pronounce on such a wide range of subjects. His confidence was overweening, even exasperating, and he must have been impossibly tiresome in the flesh.

Memorials can also be less sanguine than these judgments, founded on familiarity with the subject and his psychological mind-set. Nothing of Hill survives except his writing, caricatures of him in prose, poetry, and the visual arts, and a few front-face engravings: no memorabilia or monuments, no museums or shrines, no library intact, not even the desk on which he wrote. More villain and fake than his contemporaries ever knew, and coward to boot, he was one of the saddest examples among the Georgians of what it means to be *driven to succeed;* of permitting society to tempt you into pseudo-celebrity from such inauspicious origin and at such high cost.

The price he paid was staggering, as were the sacrifices he made to his family, finances, and personal health. What did he want? He would not have known how to answer the question except to say "more." In this sense, excess was his nemesis. His life was not joyless but engined by a combination, rare among the Georgians, of sustained high anxiety, hyperactive energy, and studied notoriety.

If biography can be a call to think compassionately about the human condition, then this multi-talented creature should be a candidate, especially for his brief moment in the sun when he rose to notoriety. Had he placed more weight on the *way* we are remembered, he may have behaved differently. When self-reflecting, perhaps he thought that by manipulating his terrestrial existence he could ensure the eternal one. But he banked little on the intimations of mortality that would follow him beyond the grave. And after the early nineteenth century he fast faded, as we have seen, into an oblivion from which he has never awakened. The wasted ability, the surfeit of nervous energy, the protean self-reinventions and transformations, the forgotten hours when the "Inspector" pounded the pavements of t'Town in search of news—all to what end?

A biographer also wants to put certain questions to the subject himself; to interrogate him directly or in imaginary conversations. Given the chance, I would ask the dead Hill three questions, resembling George III inquiring of Samuel Johnson about Hill in the interview with which this book started. Did you ever pause to reflect? Was the remove to Bayswater your first genuine opportunity to flee the rat race, when your health was already compromised and your finances ruined? If you could look back with self-awareness, would you have lived in the same frantic way? These questions, in hindsight, are futile—impossible to answer.

Biographers also learn that we—the biographers—live twice: once during our lifetime (while writing the biography), again afterward (the book that remains after our death). In some ways the second life—the book we leave behind for posterity—is the more intriguing for the way it focuses our images of ourselves through our reflections on the deceased. During a first life, we forge the image we wish to leave, and allow others to adumbrate it. One thinks of Charles Dickens in this year of his bicentenary: which of Dickens's two lives is the more authentic? The one he actually lived, with its sharp edges and contradictions, or the sweet nostalgic one his biographers have deposited for those in love with Victorian England? Perhaps *both*. One is hard put to say that the image we want to leave is any less valid than the one posterity judges us to have left.

This book has centered on the *first full life* of a doomed subject: the protagonist struggling to survive in a fiercely competitive and combative milieu where he is reviled; self-chasing every form of notoriety, winning and losing, straying more than succeeding, and dying in desperate circumstances just when he acquires a foreign knighthood, the only unequivocal public recognition he ever received. Future studies may inquire how his society acted collectively to propel him to covet such excess.

But not even D'Israeli's deferential panegyric could restore Hill from the dead: he was not the sort of figure the Romantics or Victorians cared to revive. Ultimately, the subject's survival after death depends on *others*: those who personally knew him, as well as all those who, like D'Israeli, never met him yet had formed a lasting image—an unquenchable curiosity; had heard something, had imagined him, especially when he had been—as had Hill—for three decades a household name in the public domain.

In every phase of life Hill struggled with stratospheric goals prevented from attainment by inner demons often more comic than tragic. Yet even when riding high during the pivotal years clustered around 1751–1753 and 1758–1760, he rarely felt secure. He was too restless to be anchored, despite the interludes when his contemporaries allowed him to be. The ways he has survived after death are both more and less fragile than his first, terrestrial, life. Less fragile because he quickly sank into oblivion, to the chagrin of Henrietta who loved and admired her husband more than anyone else in the world and did everything possible to restore his former worth. More fragile because Hill's denigrators hounded him after death; desecrated his memory in the generation after 1775 by deprecating his achievements and further demonizing his defects. After their deaths, clustered around the turn of the nineteenth century, this harsh storm of commentary subsided. The chorus of abuse ceased. Only D'Israeli spoke benignly. Then there was silence.

NOTES

1. D'Israeli (1859; 1812), vol. 2, 179–98; these volumes continued to be reprinted in the first half of the nineteenth century and their pagination will vary with each edition; the reader must attempt to see D'Israeli's layout on the page, with only a few lines of text on each page and massive footnotes occupying the rest. It is remarkable how many of D'Israeli's "facts" have stood the test of time; many of his sources may have been oral rather than printed. For further analysis of D'Israeli on JH also Rousseau (2006), 247–53.
2. Midgley, 84–86.
3. Mole, introduction.
4. For example, Nigel Leask.
5. Ralph; Kenny; Dibble.
6. For a modern take see D. P. Miller (2000).
7. Midgley, passim; Pope had lampooned Henley abundantly in *The New Dunciad.*
8. A main concern of one of Grub Street's modern students: see Gross, passim.
9. Rousseau (2006), 213–54.
10. *MR* 7 (1792), 38.
11. *MR* 7 (1792), 39; D'Israeli (1859; 1812) was unaware of Burney's judgment.
12. Walker, 1–9.
13. J. E. Smith (1821).
14. *MR* 7 (1792), 38.
15. Samantha George; Miller and Reill (1996); Londa Schiebinger (2004).
16. By then it was almost impossible *not* to be a confirmed Linnaean.
17. *European Magazine* (1793), 121–22.
18. This is a contested area; the number differs with each botanist. For an authoritative view in our time see Reveal, as well as the works listed by Henrey, Staffleu, and Stearn.
19. Sbiroli has admirably written about this aspect of Hill's afterlife.
20. See chapter 5.
21. See Cody for discussion of this biological-political analogy.
22. He was also the first French translator of *The Adventures of Loveill,* which appeared in French for a second time in 1765.
23. Sbiroli, 141–52.
24. Thomas Wright, 219.
25. See p. 26 above.
26. *Inspector* 533, *LDA* November 24, 1752.
27. Dibdin, vol. 5, 182–83.
28. Dibdin, vol. 5, 183.
29. See Cumberland, 259, for the passages in this paragraph.
30. Thomas Wright, 225.
31. Kenrick (1753).
32. Thomas Wright, 228, italics mine.
33. The phrase and concept are glossed by Clance, introduction and passim.
34. For further amplification of D'Israeli's "curiosity" in relation to JH see Rousseau (2006), 248–56.

Afterword

On the Trail of John Hill

Sometime in the 1980s I copied a line about Hill from a dusty Victorian volume of ephemera in the British Library: "In short, the history of this singular being would form one of the most extraordinary stories to illustrate an adventurer's course." I paused over the bit about the "adventurer's course," wondering whether I understood how "adventurer" resonated in the mid-eighteenth century. Our equivalents today—bounder, charlatan, opportunist, scoundrel, villain—are approximations that make us uneasy. We have no exact equivalent; the reason we cannot quickly situate Hill or understand where he fits.

He was an *adventurer*; a shady adventurer, among other types, but that niche confused his story for prospective biographers and deterred them. Harold Nicolson, author of a classic study of biography, quipped that it is a mistake to embark on the biography of a man one neither likes nor respects.[1] He later recanted from the position, for if we only wrote the biographies of those we "liked" what would we know about Stalin, Mao, Hitler, Franco, Mussolini, the African dictators, and dozens of other repellent *non*-political figures? Should we be silent because we abjure their politics, morals, or character? Write no biographies of Shostakovich, Stockhausen, or Philip Glass because some of us dislike their music? No biographies of painters and writers we loathe? Few of us approve the way Mata Hari (1876–1917) lived her life as a double agent: the exotic Frisian dancer and treacherous courtesan executed by firing squad for espionage during World War I, but biographers have continued to be intrigued by her story to compile multiple biographies.[2] Recently, O. J. Simpson and Michael Jackson have had few rivals among "notorious Americans," yet their numerous biographers have been unable to restrain readerly curiosity. The lists are long and continue to swell: history is indeed littered with figures whose lives have been anything but exemplary yet who ensnare biographers as well as readers. Increasingly we lust to excavate the source and sediment of notoriety.

In the 1970s I began to collect any fact I could discover about Hill, yet his riddles continued to perplex me. By 1980 I located over two hundred titles attributed to him, assembled 220 letters scattered on several continents, and supplemented them with another dozen found during the 1980s,[3] two portraits, dozens of caricatures and engravings, the record of baptism verifying his date of birth as 1714 rather than the older and erroneous 1707, the baptismal records of at least six children, the family grave in Denham, Buckinghamshire, his marriage certificate to Henrietta, the rate books showing Hill's dates of occupancy and rates paid in Westminster and Bayswater, the name of the London bank with which he was associated (but not Hill's ledgers), his last will and testament, the names of druggists and patent holders who battled with Henrietta after her husband's demise, and Hill's looming presence in the vast manuscript archive of Emanuel da Costa[4]—but no memoirs or autobiographical self-reflections.

The absence of bank ledgers was significant. Without them I could never ascertain the highs and lows of Hill's finances; his often-lavish earnings as well as more frequent debts. It also became clear that the ephemera of his era—especially the anonymous tracts in the British Library listed in the bibliography—were key sources for understanding the man. That is why they loom so prevalently in my narrative: a now neglected mid-century subgenre amounting to more than one hundred titles dealing with Hill. Another fifty tracts, also used, have attributed authors. Without these combined ephemera this biography could not have been written.

Hill's public and private life also had to be reconstructed from his own writings and from the extant commentary about him not contained in those anonymous tracts. Everything I found suggested that the English milieu of his maturity commencing during 1740–1744—watershed dates for so many pursuits and professions—was altering, particularly its print culture.[5] The new modes would carry on into the 1750s. Competition to break into print, as distinct from the paid political hack writing with which it is often confused, had become significantly fiercer. The technology had also changed, enabling writers to break more quickly into print. Much also had changed vis-à-vis the author's expected code of conduct, comportment, manners, and even conversation—the whole sphere of an "author's life."

My "take" on Hill also wavered. Eventually I recognized I was searching for a social anthropology of competition that did not exist.[6] In the 1970s the historiography of marketplace competition was principally sociological;[7] it aimed to explain how groups function under specific conditions and how peer culture is structured in ways that render its arrangements predictable, but it was not historicized nor took account of the competitive aspects of particular professions, least of all the rise of professional authorship.[8] The analysis omitted persons who might make a difference to particular sociological paradigms, and announced results from modern perspectives, whether capitalistic, Marxist, or from other predilections.[9] I soon became aware how his contemporaries' extreme notions of approbation and condemnation refracted Hill, but I could not explain *which cultural buttons* he pressed to activate these responses, nor why similar behavior a generation earlier would have produced different results.

Two components specifically—feud and quarrel—were daunting in the public sphere. Historians took them for granted as intrinsic to Grub Street,[10] but rarely unpacked them at deep layer. James Ralph's *Case of Authors by Profession*, published in 1758, just as Hill was reaching the pinnacle of his celebrity, sheds light on each component when suggesting that authors quarreled profusely because their status was so low: rudely paid and residing at the bottom of the social scale. His argument was that low stakes produce high consequences.

Small wonder that "Estimate Browne," named for his *Estimate of the Manners and Principles of the Times* (1757), slashed his own throat at fifty in his bed. His versatility propelled him to the center of Grub Street but he was attacked nevertheless from all sides: by his patrons for his neglect of his clerical duties, by his enemies because they could brand him as mad as he was jealous, and by fellow writers for giving out that he was an all-around, know-it-all, polymathic thinker. "That mountebank," Horace Walpole wailed, "who for a little time made as much noise by his *Estimate*, as ever quack did by nostrum," was persuaded Browne was an insane creature to be pitied and despised. Perhaps he was, but Walpole's ears quivered in partial envy, aware that in 1757 Browne had lucidly argued that hacks were a despicable lot because driven by penury to materiality. Browne and Ralph, insightful about the despised tribe, never enlarged their argument beyond Mammon and Venality—put simply: reward authors more handsomely and the figures they cut would change. Three centuries later it has not, except for those fortunate few admitted to the "Fame Machine."

What, I kept asking myself, was an anthropology of feuding in non-primitive societies and why has the function of attack and quarrel been taken for granted? The obvious answer is that this behavior is perennially latent in human nature and therefore requires no comment, or that these antics were sensational and sold print copies just as extraordinary news does today. But fracas and feud intrinsically differ from the vicarious thrill of crime and punishment, especially when carried out routinely *ad hominem*. Today, weekly and monthly reviews encourage mild attack on the grounds that they pique curiosity and sell print copies, but our culture has simultaneously generated codes and protocols—some based in law—to prevent the eruption of fracas solely for the sake of fracas. In Hill's era, by contrast, fracas and paper warfare paved the way to "puffery" and the securement of patronage—indeed, they were its prerequisites, except that codes to diminish its excesses slowly evolved after the 1740s.[11]

I also searched for a social anthropology of puffery—the personal domain of self-promotion—rather than merely its socioeconomics or commercialization.[12] "Puffery" had existed before the mid-Georgians, but became crucial to a commercial society quickly expanding after 1760 into a global empire; and it is no surprise to scholars of sentiment and sensibility that it should have appeared in both approved and nefarious forms simultaneously—genteel, polite, mendacious, ostentatious—according to the class and rank targeted in the puff. Some of Hill's contemporaries recognized that puffery was traceable to the invention of printing and that its more recent version was owing to a fast-moving consuming society.[13] What had started in the early eighteenth century as "puffing" for commerce, goods, and objects, was transferred laterally to writers. Hill intuitively understood its mechanisms, even if he was blind to the proximity of his tactics to the epicenter of this development. *Au fond* the irony of his life was that he spent years dreaming of being "puffed," of finding himself at the nerve center of the action, and when he discovered himself there through a series of partial bungles and cock-ups—mercilessly attacked and badgered even when innocent—he yearned for puffery's opposite. Quiet—the illusion of being sequestered in rustic Bayswater.

Hill's public milieu could appear refined but was also rawer and more brutal than ours, far less polite and lacking our legal checks and balances: you as easily sneered at someone in a lampoon as knocked him down with a folio book.[14] British print historian Henry Plomer credibly recounts that Pope did exactly "that" in *The Dunciad* to Thomas Osborne, the printer who published many of Hill's works, and Samuel Johnson too, who literally knocked down Osborne with a folio. Georgian hacks in the age of Pope and his dunciads wrote to eat, not to quarrel, but by the next generation (1740–1770) fracas and feud became a way of life as well.[15] Paradoxically seen as fashionable, they permeated the literary sphere of the Republic of Letters more than has been acknowledged; not fracas as fun and prank for the sake of it but as territorial *ad hominem* warfare intended to injure.

It is difficult to explain this paradoxical quality of Hill's contentious contemporaries but it proved essential to understand it for the writing of this biography: the available, mainly socioeconomic, models are inadequate and our historiography remains largely silent, perhaps because present-day parallels are so disarming. The past's "noble learning" and "diligent application" have commanded more attention, especially among scholars prone to idealizing the eighteenth century; yet even contention's opposites in modesty and self-effacement have been reassessed in our time. Sir Hans Sloane, perhaps the most distinguished physician-collector of Hill's era, springs to mind. Hill, by contrast, needs to be situated in this landscape of jagged claws and competitive teeth despite our inadequate explanations for his society's penchant for fracas and contention. His industry was as legendary as it was uncanny. But he lacked modesty and veracity—as Johnson tried to tell George III—more than most of his contemporaries. He was a talent being burned alive by his combined ambition and drive. My task was to unify these incommensurabilities and inconsistencies, oddities and paradoxes, into a biographical narrative.

Hill impressed his contemporaries as a phenomenon in the history of efficiency, and his machine-like diligence bruised and offended them. He was not the only "writing machine" of his generation—others wrote more words. Yet he continued to amaze observers like Horace Walpole, who was dazzled to hear that Hill was "at once employed on six voluminous works of botany, husbandry, &c., published weekly."[16] Such a surfeit of activity and speed was suspicious, "ungentlemanly" as well, and destined to breed jealousy and contempt; yet calculate the numerical years of canonical prose writers—Defoe to Richardson, Fielding, and Scott—in relation to their total number of published words, and it is clear that they scribbled far more than Hill did.

Why the smears? Hill's verbal production was not the only source of bruising: his dissembling and deceit struck them as equally monstrous, as sly as his never failing record of having *got there first*, an infantile sense that you beat the competition by arriving early. His deceptions proved galling because often credible. His alibis for his behavior were rarely drawn in black and white, so to speak, but limped in a gray cumulus between them; and he worked his intuition overtime to "psyche out" the next fad, the new wave, and the incontestable fact that he could do so in many different fields further shocked them. Today natural history, tomorrow a novel, the next day a play: unflinchingly he gadded from one to the other to survive, even if his published works marked a moment in the history of mediocrity gone amok. He was indefatigable and remained so to the end, even when writing with gouty fingers. He turned to imaginative literature early on because he believed it could transform him into a "personality"; when that failed, he sought the thrill of celebrity in natural history, especially in botany, with more promising results, all without concern for the Stoic virtue and humility his father Theophilus Sr. had instilled—indeed, celebrity was his antidote to religion. I came to see it *was* his religion, and construed my task as portraying him against this backdrop even if this book is not per se a general study of Georgian celebrity culture. Had he succeeded in literature, he would have penned few further herbals and the botanical market spared his "famous five" panaceas that made him rich. But he could neither manage money nor curb his excesses and extravagances.

Hill was also a filter, a siphon for transmitting some of the beliefs and values of his contemporaries; and through his persona I wanted to revise our sense that mid-eighteenth-century science can only be understood through the eyes of its major figures—its illustrious Newtons and Linnaeuses. To explain how he filtered its values I had to recognize that in this book my métier is the *second* rank—as the list of *dramatis personae* at the end demonstrates—and occasionally even the *third*, precisely because they too were becoming preoccupied with celebrity in ways anticipating our contemporary craze. Despite Hill's idiosyncrasies he refracts the wider political, economic, and social changes of his lifetime clustered around the transforming networks of patronage, publishing, and puffery (the old word for "PR"). His startling career (if it can be labeled by this modern word) is a beacon shining light on what those institutions had been, and where they were headed, in each of these complex "P" categories.

The pre-Georgian model of literary patronage was built on a premise of comfort—the sense that once secured it offered sinecure;[17] the newer one forming in Hill's maturity was less predictable because it thrust authors into the commercial marketplace without guarantees of any type. The older, safer version was marginally tinged by politics insofar as it leaned to the Tory mind-set; the newer to Whig commercialism and entrepreneurship as proof of success; but there were exceptions to these views and some authors steered a middle course despite leaning to one view or the other.[18] The patronized were, of course, ostensibly of the patron's party. But beyond that, the old Tory values and new commercial mind-sets could not be bedfellows. Moreover, during the 1750s indications arose that the old model—secure patronage—was diminishing if not altogether becoming moribund; that writers, if clever and governed by right manners and fitting morals, could succeed by their own wits. Hill never became "political Hill," nor could he decide which system of patronage—old or new—he preferred: he craved the guarantees of sponsorship while gesturing he would lurch out on his own but he never took the leap.

Sociologist Jürgen Habermas might have considered his ingenuity to survive a laboratory specimen for the developing eighteenth-century "public sphere": when one avenue failed, Hill tried another with the sharpened sense of a "second son" who knows that he must fend for himself. Booksellers (who in many capacities were similar to our contemporary publishers) then exerted huge influence on their authors: often dictating what they wrote, when their works appeared, taking fewer risks than subsidized presses do today, and behaving as combined literary agents, editors, arbiters of taste, and printers. Hill was in bed with all, and because he had purchased shares could exert more pressure on them than impoverished hacks. As James Raven has put it, "[the 1740s] was the threshold decade for the great take-off in book trade productivity in the eighteenth century."[19] And if you substitute our new operative words—advertising, marketing, promotion, publicity, and PR—it becomes paramount that Hill anticipated the future too, operating on an unstated principle that he had to promote himself to survive.[20] This meant: be seen everywhere, regularly appear in print, become a household name—combined, the three would ensure visibility. "Careerist" words were not in his vocabulary: in the 1740s "career" meant the "racetrack" on which horses ran, as at Richmond's Goodwood where the young Hill once lived, and would not assume its modern meaning about "the public track of someone's life" until the nineteenth century. Hill intuited it nonetheless.

Visibility rather than fame was his grail, and to his dying day Hill, to his mortal shame, never forgot (or was not permitted to forget) that he was not a university graduate. His contemporaries considered a university education the first requirement par excellence, even antecedent to the ownership of land, for entry to the virtuous Republic of Letters: that borderless network of scholars and scientists communicating with each other across national boundaries about which so much has been written and disputed in our generation.[21] Entry in the 1740s was gained principally by the writing of letters within a code of gentlemanly behavior, but epistolography was not its only activity.[22] The Republic itself was "virtual"—it had no fixed address, location, or even nationality—and its members emphasized different elements at different times despite its exchange of information through correspondence. Hill's extant correspondence numbers no more than three hundred letters at the outer limit, at least half of which deal with the securing of patronage rather than the exchanging of information. His correspondents' letters have been kept intact and it is unlikely that swaths of Hill letters have been lost. Some correspondence with Lord Bute has probably disappeared,[23] but I think little else. Biographically, he was interested in the growth of knowledge only when the demons of self-advancement receded. When they did, they revealed a Hill of immense capability. As Charles Burney, the famous musicologist who was his contemporary, noted: Hill was a much better botanist than he has been credited with being.[24]

For these reasons an approach to Hill's life organized around subjects or topics—Hill the apothecary, Hill the botanist, Hill the geologist, Hill the journalist, Hill the novelist—rather than evolving chronology would be confusing to the reader. His life was guided by the moment, not abstract principles or academic disciplines; compelling circumstance rather than religious belief or polymathic affiliation determined his mind-set and daily mood. He responded to the strains and stresses his overreaching ambition dictated, as well as the cries of hungry young mouths. His story—especially in a *first* life—begs for an evolving, chronological approach.

One early avenue I took was misguided: the polymathic route. In the 1970s, when I knew less about Hill's frailties than I do now, I was dazzled by his diversity. He seemed to embody the "Renaissance Man" residual in the Enlightenment in the aftermath of such figures as Athanasius Kircher and Leibniz.[25] Placing him in the context of Franklin and Jefferson, I published a short monograph entitled "Sir John Hill: Renaissance Man or Genius *Manquè*?"[26] He was no genius in the classical sense, or the newer one emerging in the second half of the eighteenth century as someone inspired, intuitive, unpredictable, and mad. But he had sufficient affinities with the type to build a case for a genius *manquè*. I answered the rhetorical question in the negative for both types; yet in 1978 the reader of my essay could come away thinking my attraction to Hill was based on some type of genius.

It was difficult to resist that approach for a number of reasons. First and foremost, the 1970s in America was a decade celebrating diversity, when "theory" came into its own and interdisciplinary methods were being extolled in American universities. The latter thrived on polymathy and the historicization of interdisciplinarity was a valuable approach for demonstrating that much Enlightenment culture depended on it. Hill could seem to embody these trends, working in so many different fields and proficient in several. In two—literature and botany—a case for eminence could be made: among the first journalists of his era and, as he was often referred to, "the English Linnaeus." He appeared to be the silhouette of a polymath of interest to the forming interdisciplinary culture of modern American research universities.

The image of a "remarkable Hill" was also encouraged abroad: in England especially at "Hillia," the Sussex residence of Dr. Arthur Morris (1889–1979), an English physician who dabbled in the history of medicine.[27] Morris and his wife were keen on Hill's polymathy and collected every scrap about it, naming their house after him. Further afield, in Gloucestershire, Sir Victor Eyles, an eminent historical geologist, considered Hill seminal to the formation of a science of geology,[28] and so did the late eminent historian Roy Porter by the end of the decade.[29] In London, Hill's presence figured in the historical remains at Kew Gardens, especially among proficient historians of botany such as the late Ray Desmond, and Hill's name was familiar to the Linnaean Society's archivists, where many of his manuscript letters were housed. This was just his niche in medicine, geology, and botany. Other disciplines remained, so why not advocate "remarkable Hill"?

Internationally, Hill cut a figure that also surprised me in those early days. He had made contacts in Denmark and Germany, and even aroused the curiosity of the learned gentlemen of Nuremberg to join forces with him to establish a "new Royal Society" after his native country's would not have him. The late Dr. Lynn Sbiroli discovered French and Italian translations of *Lucina sine concubitu* (1750), interpreting this intriguing work allegorically to prognosticate the French Revolution. An Australian historian of medicine, Dr. Kevin Fraser, was writing a dissertation about Hill's role in the history of gout and arthritic diseases. A vice president at the United Nations, Helmut Watzlawick, found Danish translations of *Lucina* unknown to me while traveling in Scandinavia. Every year produced new developments in far-flung places. Missing, however, was the man: the essential protagonist behind this curious beehive.

Eventually I faced the fact that I was writing "a life," not compiling the history of several "sciences" or polymathic contexts; and nothing would answer the quandaries about the man—essential Hill—except the drudgery of year-by-year analysis: what every thorough biographer does despite the inevitable dead spots. The hurdles of retrieval were compounded by the disappearance of traces after circa 1800, when Hill began to fall into oblivion. I could have answered most of my own questions if I were living in 1780 or 1790, around the time when Boswell was consulting everyone who had known Johnson, but those oral accounts have disappeared for Hill. One thing alone was clear: Hill himself, as well as his contemporaries, ensured his fall, not merely during his lifetime but after his death. Set the dials to 1805, exactly three decades after his death, and this once-a-household-name is fast fading from memory.

My narrative about his rise and fall set me on a journey that has lasted for four decades, longer than I dreamed it would. I could not have known what I would find in the 1960s when I started out, and the surprises have been both intriguing and disappointing: for example, the Hill-Linnaeus correspondence. Hill wrote many letters in English to the Swedish scientist. Why were no replies from Linnaeus to Hill found when it is all but certain that Linnaeus answered many? Language was no obstacle: Linnaeus had a far-flung correspondence in Latin with Englishmen and employed translators to whom he dictated replies and amanuenses who copied them out. Besides, Hill's Latin was excellent.

Hill corresponded prolifically to secure patronage, but could also retreat into a self-absorbing loneliness breeding silence. In these periods he wrote no letters, nor left intimate diaries or letters written to his wife or children. The husband, lover, father, brother, cousin, and so forth, are reinvented in this biography rather than reconstructed from existing documents. The same cannot be said for "public Hill": Hill the author; Hill the naturalist; Hill the botanist; Hill the provocateur, scandalist, self-puffer, and so forth. Here the evidence is abundant.

His lifelong friend, William Stukeley, the amiable and loyal naturalist, kept detailed diaries that are as informative as they are narratively drab;[30] yet they provide information, which, if it were available for Hill, would have permitted more pronouncements about the personal realm than this life can evince. Stukeley listed every person he himself met, lists of stocks and bonds he purchased, lunch menus and the bodily aches endured—manna for a biographer. Instead, Hill's biographer struggles to discover "truest Hill" and wrestles for a "frame"—a persuasive grid—through which to present him. My colleagues in California and Oxford quipped when replying to their questions by claiming I was "framing Hill." The double entendre was more literal than I knew.

During the 1970s and 1980s I also wondered whether a biography of Hill was worth the effort. The topic intrigued me, especially its Enlightenment conjunction of cultures, but I disliked the man. I had stumbled upon him by accident—as recounted in the *Anticipations*—but could not become sufficiently attached to him to write a praising biography. I assembled his papers and manuscripts, letters and documents, and published them with annotations as preparation;[31] to see whether a biography was feasible, and then, whether I could locate the man behind the words. The overriding historical question was how he behaved and appeared in his era.

It was tempting to vindicate or, alternatively, discredit him, but eventually I narrowed my focus to one question: how someone could become so notorious in Georgian England. He was a post-Popean dunce of sorts, and his niche would have differed if Pope had still been alive to flay him in dunciadic couplets; but comparisons with Theobald, Cibber, Curll, and their tribe broke down, for Hill was also a remarkably talented naturalist and—without his character defects—might have become the leading English botanist of the century. But all roads led to the same place: Hill outrageously courted notoriety, almost involuntarily, and chased it more than fame; nothing in the notoriety he achieved was ersatz. Yet the more genuine it became, the further he was spurred to multiple refashionings, through his protean ability to start over each time—never to quit until illness finally dug him into the ground.

The *adventurer* inside him, who lived by his wits, was sufficiently plain: he belongs to the world of rogue adventure and survival instinct as securely as the history of literature and science and medicine;[32] a cater-cousin to Smollett's fictional adventurer-hero "Count Fathom"—written in the year when Hill himself became the hero of the most widely discussed mock-epic poem *The Hilliad*. And how ironic that Smollett should have been writing his third novel just as the "Inspector's" fame was peaking in 1752–1753.[33] By the time Hill parted company with the Royal Society and began to "rule with his Lion" at the Bedford, he was already reinvented; delighting in everything hybrid, fluid, and unpoliced—like himself. Refashioning one's self at mid-century, as Smollett's Fathom learns, did not depend on professional loyalty or disciplinary savvy. Psychologically, Hill's root cause may have been a perpetual adolescent still craving to be a "stage player," and as he aged he grew increasingly confused about his direction—"borderline identity" in our sense—but nonetheless adept in remaking himself. If refashioning lives suggests modernity, Hill anticipates the activity as a major player long before its advent. This may be his superlative legacy: surpassing his botany, topping the mountains of publication his contemporaries called "a drug," and even exceeding his obsession with "puffing" himself.

I spent two years reading the *Inspector* columns, classifying their contents, and eventually persuaded myself that the *Inspector* was the clue to his biographical figure, especially his sense of himself as a man of letters within the good Republic despite his having broken its protocols. Indeed, he was never more focused than while writing those editorials. This Hill between *Lucina* and the *Inspector* was *echt* Hill, and the dilemma in labeling him, or defining his niche, arises from our lack of suitable categories to fit the model. He exceeded dunciadic arrogance and was a phenomenon in the history of vanity. He was, as a famous cartoon of 1753 presented him, "*Lusus Naturae,*" a wonder *sui generis* and entirely of his own making.

Hill's politics was a politics of survival; one temperamentally conservative in its views of church, state, and the place of mankind in the cosmic order. But he was less hypocritical than "survivalist," and survival for him included notoriety predicated on vanity in his unreflectively homespun recipe: the brazen gesture, the get-there-first mentality, the competitive edge. I wondered how neurobiologists would explain him but never pursued them. Construed as survivor, he embodied some of the worst facets of his already competitive era (here again, specifically as Hill-the-filter of his print culture), and the most difficult aspect of reconstructing him has been deciding what role his society played in the shaping of the man.

His public behavior and conversation, his antics, the figure he cut, his positioning of himself, his sense of timing and his obsession with not being slighted or duped—these mattered to him. But too often his responsive ploy resulted in a quirk of the moment: the brash or prideful reply (as in *Lucina*), his bravura in launching the *Inspector* when competition among new periodical magazines was already keen—these were the intuitive moves that backfired. Whatever he attained he fought for hard—too hard—and was usually savaged. Yet to look back and imagine he was monolithically loathed falsifies the evidence: he was awed and feared as well, and was, besides, too ribald a figure of fun for such any mono-dimensional view. His life from 1753 forward amounted to comedy or tragedy, depending on your perspective, but never a hagiography.

The search for "traces" included modern approaches, especially methods of "framing." Much, for example, has been made of "imposter fraud syndrome" in our time—the common denominator of the successful among celebrities and those who have "just made it."[34] The idea is that *all* acclaimed people experience anxieties about not deserving their success. Experiments about the syndrome have been substantiated, tested, and verified by psychologists and celebrants, and the latter concede that at major points in their life they believed they were frauds. Psychologists consider this sense of fakery and imposition protective, that the perpetually confident who do *not* "make it" are the *imposters*. Hill belonged to the latter group, having persuaded himself he was an "outsider" destined for "insiderdom," that his innate gifts and hard-earned attainments should have initiated him; that the only reason he failed for so long was bad luck, and that when he finally found a patron (Bute) he was doubly unlucky in his protector's fall.

The famous cartoon of him as "Lusus Naturae" presents Hill as a self-made wonder of the world.[35] Chevalier Taylor, the so-called "Inoculator," allegedly had "two sexes," and Charlotte Charke dressed and passed herself off as a man, but these figures were imagined as aberrations of monstrosity rather than of character or temperament. Cibber and Theobald, previous generation "dunces," were lambasted by Pope and other detractors as frauds, but they had more *ex cathedra* qualifications than Hill and have found contemporary biographers. Hill has been altogether forgotten—written out—because he was far more outrageous and fits no facile categories. Answers to the question what it is about notoriety that makes people opprobrious, answers do not rush forward. Perhaps the annals of notoriety have been dispersed to the winds.

Georgian iconoclasm proved a dead end. Iconoclasm inevitably presents an aesthetic or ideological edge and functions other than disruptively, but notoriety breaks the back of continuity. Notoriety, on the other hand, exists at the extremities of behavior, and usually exposes lives lived on the fringes of social norms. Combined, iconoclasm and notoriety disturb established protocols, puncture hierarchies, and force ruptures where none were intended. Historically, progress and improvement depend on these "breaks"; without them there would be less—just the dull rule of repetition and the status quo. But notoriety boldly asserts itself—Hill's contemporaries would have said "pertly"—especially in Hill's variety, without the leisure to take stock of the notorious object itself. Notoriety is an odd sociocultural niche, problematic to situate. It has appeared contiguous to fame but is hardly identical with it: the notorious are necessarily "famous," or infamous, as the case may be, but the famous are hardly notorious. *Au fond* notoriety shuns fame because it thrives on the edge of unpopularity.[36] Negativity—negative actions, negative words, negative relationships—is notoriety's chief attribute and accompanies it everywhere by leading to its closure: the notorious, like Hill, fall into disgrace through heinous acts.

Here then, it seemed, were competing frames for Hill: Notorious Hill, Celebrity Hill, Proteus Hill, all courting fame historicized yet themselves in need of framing. Without becoming obsessed by framing, I found the act crucial to my presentation of Hill, as every biographer eventually learns. Historians of Georgian culture also know that all three categories were being born during the same generations when Hill was living them.[37] And all three involve image making, whether or not the celebrity is conscious of so doing and whether actively engaging in the process. But notoriety is more vexing, as I have tried to demonstrate in this book; however much the Georgians chased it, it was publicly loathed, often in the rhetoric of defamation deployed against Hill. The Georgian metropolis thrived on assumptions about notoriety, in every profession, yet public manners and decorum were already idealized to such levels by the late eighteenth century that even the notorious had to pretend to be modest. Hill fits into this cultural map as a naïf rarely reflecting on his image. It is as if he could not view his framed portrait for what it was. If he succeeded in many ventures, this owed more to native ability and sheer luck than to any conscious plan to position himself to his advantage.

These frames—celebrity, notoriety, vanity, proteanism—were also fueled by terrific personal rage ever since his debacle with the Royal Society. Was that rejection a sufficient cause? The concept of "outrage" developed from its lexical root in "rage": to eject and expel rage, and no student of Hill's life need be a psychoanalyst to see that his internalized rage—introjected to form the basis for chronic depression—was expressed as *out*rage in perpetually *out*rageous acts, as if (what we would call) his "inner child" was forever acting out its torment. Pope had yoked the two emotions in his pugnacious satire on education in *The New Dunciad* when distinguishing between personal and poetic outrage.[38] A decade later, in the 1750s, Hill courted notoriety so assiduously, it seems he lived to elicit its responses from his contemporaries.

I also came to appreciate the toll taken by Hill's contentious era despite its accompanying cults of politeness and denials of outrage; for example and to take someone central to Hill's mid-Georgian botanical culture, why those who avoided contention at all cost, like Hans Sloane, president of the Royal Society when Hill was still in his twenties, stood apart. In this context the tag "hegemonic masculinity" (in sociologist R. W. Connell's phrase) is useful but ultimately limited to describe Hill's case even if Connell historically schematizes it according to period norms: "anxious, patriarchal, godly masculinity" (mid-seventeenth century); "libertine" and "foppish" masculinity (the late-seventeenth century); most significantly, "polite" or "civil" masculinity (c. 1720–1780) for the decades of Hill's lifetime.[39] The contemporaries with whom Hill crossed swords (sometimes literally) were anything but polite and civil. Their versions of masculinity enacted raw forms of feud as ordinary conditions of life, as becomes evident in almost every chapter of this book. Norms of masculine self-control and urban(e) civility also describe some members of Hill's society but he himself, and many of those with whom he feuded, defy these tags. Ironically, they were birds of a feather.

Fame in our time brings wealth, sex, and a glamorous lifestyle. Hill enjoyed none: the first fleetingly, the second never, and the third when he could afford it. Despite periods of extravagant earnings he was constantly in debt, could not pay his creditors and for a while was also fugitive and kept a low profile. He courted "sex" for a brief period in an era when it was almost unheard of not to, but biographically appears to have been monogamous after he married Henrietta. His glittering high living was self-generated and self-supported, nothing celebrity bestowed on him.

My early dislike later turned compassionate, and the more I learned the more I began to understand why he behaved as he did. If you had to sum up Hill in a word, it must be "ambition," yet the striking feature is that future reversals produced more striving in an unending, upward spiral. His was not appetite for monetary gain or fame but the hunger to become a celebrity in an epoch when it was becoming coveted even if those craving it had far less sense of its blessings than we do. He craved to become a "notable person"—a "personage"—more than to find stardom or heroic grandeur.

Anyone who gave himself the airs Hill did was bound to elicit dislike, and one is hard put to name another figure of his era, apart from criminals or disgraced politicians, which Hill never was, who courted enmity so routinely. Besides, as Australian historian D. P. Miller has argued, no one likes a know-it-all.[40] Hill's forms of self-aggrandizement can beggar belief: he could not forgo the coach and six, the elegant gloves and cape, the late nights and silver service, none of which he could afford. These traits tempted me to reconstruct my protagonist only to destroy him—to sacrifice him on the altar of modesty—and for years I thought this approach prudent by imagining how readers of this book would find themselves enthralled by a hatchet job as *tour de force*. Presentation of a so-called "neutral Hill" was unthinkable, but readers would pulsate at a biographer's scorn in ways impossible when judgment and prudence are courteously balanced. Yet a hatchet job would have served up a fiction. In the end I could not savage Hill in a *first* biography: revisionary works intent on balancing out opposing views—Anne Hathaway the good wife of Shakespeare, Hathaway the inept wife, and so forth—can do so but a *first* biography poses different challenges, other hurdles, including the establishment of facts and a modicum of neutral interpretation.

I also searched for a victimized Hill who could be shown to have acted in self-defense to circumstances beyond his control. Pope expurgated his poems and cheated his amanuenses, Jean-Jacques Rousseau was a crybaby who whined and wailed his way to posterity, and Beethoven—to call a spade a spade—was a nasty genius who enjoyed perpetrating wicked actions despite being the great of musical composers. No one sensible would give up their poetry, philosophy, or music but the dilemma with the second rank, in contrast, or even third, is that their works are insufficient to speak for themselves. We are likelier to dismiss a second-rate philosopher or composer than hold up their works as deserving merit. If the figure is also personally troubled, as was Hill, we sympathize even less.

During phases when my sympathy for Hill was aroused, a psychoanalytic perspective, even psychosexual approach, tempted me for several reasons. First, for Hill's biographical courting of pornography by skirting it. He internalized his temperamental promiscuity—the native and habitual desire to scatter seed widely—by repeatedly refashioning himself. And when he recognized how useful his medical knowledge could be in the service of this innate promiscuity, he applied that knowledge in his behavior and writing, nowhere more deftly than in *Lucina*. Medicine and pornography in the eighteenth century often danced together—as in the career of early eighteenth-century English surgeon John Marten, author of pornographic medical romances—yet Hill's intention was less the sexual arousal of his readers, as was Marten's, than the sublimation of his native promiscuity.[41] This dynamic cannot be proved, nor its component parts demonstrated to be anything more than conjecture; and only those already holding a psychohistorical perspective on reality capable of application to past figures would be persuaded anyway—so I abandoned the approach.

Second is the incontestable biographical fact that Hill was an unusual type of hypomaniac: hyperactive to the degree that his health was compromised, and in this sense he augurs the stress of the workplace in recent modernity. His hyperactivity bore on his temperamental promiscuity: each fed the other almost vertiginously. And his troubled life can appear to be a parable of crazed ambition riddled with cowardice and narcissism. My interest in his hyperactivity was ancillary to the organic sense of his whole life, but it has always seemed one of my tasks as a first biographer to describe this hypomania as *Hill* lived and experienced it. The omission would be unforgivable, but as I strived to, I found myself increasingly frustrated: was it a trait capable of presenting in anyone in any century—a psychotemperamental characteristic unrelated to historical context—or did particular socioeconomic conditions induce it? I came to believe that a combination had been the reality—that one fed the other in an organic whole, as it were: the more Hill craved patrons the harder he strove, and the more intensely he burned himself out the more strangely promiscuous and hypomanic he grew—as if once hypomanic one became incrementally more so by mere dint of having acceded to the final prong of its intensity.

Why tell Hill's story at all? Perhaps to fix his niche in the growth of botany: a worthwhile cause, but not mine. For me it has been more important to understand the overlap of the "gentlemanly" pursuit of botany in relation to one man's notoriety: how the two became entangled, or, put otherwise, to explain how an extraordinarily talented Georgian exploited botany's upsurge for his own aggrandizement. Botany was then still a "pursuit" rather than a professionalized part of organized science, and it was fast growing into a widespread fashionable activity among several social classes—not merely the upper crust—soon to be sweeping up almost everyone in its tide. Its status as a "science" in transformation is pertinent to my narrative about Hill: when fields and professions settle down, as it were, into accepted practices they are less capable of exploitation. Yet Hill would probably have turned notorious in *any* field, and it is imprudent to read too deeply into his vocations as apothecary and botanist as avenues *specifically leading him* to the notoriety he courted. He spent years during middle life chasing *other* fields than botany and only returned to natural history in his last fifteen years (1760–1775) when it was evident that botany could pay his rent.

I would not have written solely to situate Hill's niche in the development of eighteenth-century natural history: a worthwhile task but not mine. Within the history of Enlightenment sciences botany has only recently been recognized as a crucial activity.[42] Yet botany both reflected and refracted Georgian social patterns, cultures of sensibility, and the contours of patronage defining this moment approaching the pinnacle of Whig life. Yet this odd creature—Hill, who was by turns outrageous and ridiculous, ambitious and over-reaching—was wedded to it.

Botany's history qua history, *apart* from the man, would have been an insufficient reason to probe interior Hill's life to this extent. Nor is biography an adequate route to understand the whole man: ever since Robert Merton's pioneering study about the development of seventeenth-century English science, the social milieu in which a figure worked and the structure of scientific communities in his era have been equally important.[43] No single label suffices to describe the life of someone so contradictory as Hill—he was too versatile to be pigeonholed, and his versatility prevented commitment and loyalty to any one group. It remains to assess him biographically, completely, almost as a "diagnostic exercise" held up to the practices of authorship as well as scientific endeavor in Georgian England, rather than as merely "representative" or "unrepresentative" of a single calling—botany.

Some figures intrigue posterity without divulging anything significant about themselves or writing a page. This cannot be true for Hill, who in that state would merely have been a colorful anomaly. The narrative about him is one of uncanny ability wrecked by little loyalty to any professional group compounded by disturbed personality, and for long periods I asked myself how natively attuned he was to the contradiction. Innate ability is not tantamount to sheer industry or Herculean persistence: the obstacle in his ordeal is that the two overlapped so seamlessly that a first biographer struggles to separate them, probing the rest of Hill's personality for answers and then exploring whether his behavior arose from, or followed as a consequence of, his compulsive hypomania.

Whether primarily compulsive or hypomanic Hill was clearly a borderline psychological type. All would have been different if he had displayed chronic illness from birth; then he could be assessed for its psychological effects. But Hill was physically healthy, even strangely robust until his forties, when, having run himself ragged by overwork and overachieving, his body gave up. The evidence that he wrecked his health by overwork, or "over strife," is abundant, yet in purely physical terms only the gout hounded him other than the cardiac arrest that killed him at sixty-one. Furthermore, this is a biographical study rather than medical analysis, but his hypomania could not be so entirely overlooked that readers wonder what made the protagonist tick. In sixty short years Hill's energy rarely flagged, even when he was in pain, broken and bitter, and close to death, nor did he surrender the naïve optimistic hope that tomorrow would bring something better.

A more promising approach than the psychoanalytic was through Hill's self-reinventions. In an era when the strategies of those in search of patronage resembled each other far more than they (the strategies) differed, it was not outrageous to change vocation, but the tactics Hill used amounted to more than an ingenious approach. The hack and apothecary, the musician and actor, the journalist and connoisseur: all strove to climb the ladder of success by finding persons of rank and wealth capable of lending credibility to their ventures. Hill refashioned himself so compulsively that one wonders who, or what, his model was, if it was not some intuitive survival mechanism.

This is a life assembled primarily from middle age onward. The young Hill remains partly hidden and unknown, and even if our shadowy "Proteus" began to change his shapes in adolescence, moving in different circles, little is known in depth about him then. More consequential than the time of onset was the jealousy his frequent adult reinventions instilled in others, principally because modesty was foreign to his disposition. This was not envy lodged in a few figures or groups but a widespread, almost universal, dislike, and it turned him into a figure of fun and perpetual gossip. The more such notoriety attached to him the more rumor spread; one feeding the other so continually, like sparks from flame, that it is often impossible to distinguish fact from fiction.

Hill's ambition aroused an uncanny type of envy in other males. Having no close female friends, or female correspondents, it is hard to know what the other sex thought of him; but men, in droves it seems, disliked him instantly, so much so that they responded to his escapades with aversion. The process combined antipathy and grudge, and it is not difficult to see why: he boasted and puffed and pranced and strutted. His height, lanky thin torso, and inimitably affected speech, were constantly greeted with repugnance. He dressed ostentatiously and walked with an affected gait. His conversation bristled with condescension and breathed superiority. The mature Hill of the 1750s was a "celebrity" projecting an image of wealth, footmen and livery, a carriage and six, and—most galling of all in an era when publication was starting to count for so much—torrential publication.

Hill chose the "old way" of success through conventional patronage in his early decades; by his last in the 1770s he was merchandising his goods—botanical, medicinal, geological, verbal—according to the laws of a different model. In this context he is, above all, a transitional figure. His niche shows him existing on both sides of the divide: among the old "patronized gentlemen" who survived by reliance on their networks of friendship and chains of correspondence, versus the new "self-made gentlemen" who replaced privilege with discipline, talent, and the shrewd management of resource. For this ambivalence he was unrepresentative of the virtuous Republic and instead typifies the struggling, self-made man when that new niche was *arriviste.* If only he had been cleverer he may have succeeded. But he was neither of the first water of merit nor lucky. So it is little surprise he failed; elicited fierce *schadenfreude* from contemporaries as they pelted him with catcalls of "upstart" and stigmatized him as "Proteus the parvenu." Had Pope been alive and watching from afar he might have captured Hill, as he had Newton, in a ready-made couplet; not as a dunce who was, in Pope's words, the "Anti-Christ of Wit" but—as some rhyming poetaster might have claimed—the "Cain of rising stars."

But time marches, and my concerns in the 1970s (to discover anything I could), were not those of the 1980s (to explore how I could classify and frame this material), or those of the 1990s (when I debated for years whether any other form of narrative than a biography could capture the essence of the man). And then, when I decided *au fin* on biography, I spent more years debating what *type* of biography. Since the turn of the century my focus shifted yet again. It seemed far less pressing in the last decade to martial every fact and get those facts right than to locate Hill within the flow of early modern celebrity culture. A thin and thoroughly factual life might have sufficed, even without biographical slant or historical focus, in 1980. In the first decade of the twenty-first century it lacks significance—seems the nostalgic gesture and effete throwback to the world we have lost since then.

Early modern celebrity culture is Hill's final resting place: his fittest niche and the one in which he had few rivals in Georgian England. His importance for eighteenth-century print culture and developing botany pales in comparison. If Hill is to endure at all in our contemporary sensibility it is as someone who wanted to be a "celebrity" far more than "an author" or "botanical authority" and he forged a way, however maddening, to become one.

NOTES

1. Nicolson, 15.
2. Shipman, 2007.
3. Rousseau (1984); Rousseau (1986a).
4. See *DAC*.
5. James Raven (2007).
6. Giddens and Turner address some of the issues.
7. Eisenstadt and Roniger.
8. Gross (1991) is an exception.
9. Eisenstadt (1968).

10. Pat Rogers, the first scholar to open our eyes to the psychology of authors in Grub Street.
11. McKendrick, Brewer and Plumb, 148–49.
12. I would have understood more if I could have read James Raven's marvelous book around 1980; see Raven (2007).
13. Brewer and Porter.
14. Plomer, 185.
15. James Raven (2007); Gross (1991).
16. Toynbee and Whibley, vol. 3, 15–16.
17. Lytle and Orgel, passim.
18. Scriblerian writer John Gay is exemplary here.
19. Raven (2007), 130.
20. Raven (2007), 130.
21. Fumaroli; Goldgar; Brockliss; Grafton.
22. Grafton, chap. 1; Brockliss, passim.
23. According to Catherine Armet, archivist of the Bute Archives, they were shelved as U45-56; see also Schweizer.
24. See below.
25. Findlen (2004)
26. Lemay and Rousseau.
27. A. D. Morris during the decades 1930–1970.
28. Eyles (1969).
29. Roy Porter and Kate Poulton (1977).
30. Stukeley: Stukeley Papers in the Bodleian Library, Oxford.
31. The book LPH.
32. Suzanne Roth; Rousseau (1998b).
33. As angry with JH as Smollett was, no evidence exists to suggest Smollett had JH in mind as the original for his protagonist in *The Adventures of Count Fathom* (1753).
34. Clance; Graden.
35. See illustration 10.1 above in chapter 10.
36. Braudy.
37. The fundamental secondary work remains by Braudy; more recently, see the important studies on the birth of celebrity by McDayter, Kahan, and Engel. The enduring philosophical question is whether notoriety is a function of inherent personality or something else and—if the former—to what degree predetermined. The concept itself has a low profile apart from its occasional figuration in biographies: think of the American "Biggie Smalls," known as "the Notorious B.I.G.," perhaps the most discussed rapper of our time who was murdered in Los Angeles in 1997 for similar reasons that "did in" Hill.
38. Rousseau 1988, especially the section "Pope and outrage."
39. Connell, 28.
40. D. P. Miller (2000).
41. Marten.
42. Especially in a spate of books all appearing in 1996: see Jardine; Miller and Reill (1996); Shteir (1996).
43. Merton.

Dramatis Personae

ARDERON, William (1702/3–1767), naturalist based in Norwich who assisted Henry Baker in his campaign against Hill.

BAKER, Henry (1698-1774), natural philosopher, microscopist, teacher of deaf people, who fell out with Hill after Hill brutally satirized him in his prose works.

BALDWIN, Robert (unknown), London bookseller who printed the largest number of Hill's works, especially the scientific titles.

BARTRAM, John (1699–1777), American medical botanist and explorer born in Pennsylvania, father of William (see below), and constant correspondent of Peter Collinson, whom he never met.

BARTRAM, William (1739–1823), uneducated son of naturalist John Bartram, yet distinguished American botanist and ornithologist in his own right who sent several students to Hill and had discovered the Venus flytrap in the South Carolina marshlands.

BOYCE, Samuel (?–1775), playwright, poet, and member of Hill's cabal from the early days at the Bedford coffeehouse.

BOYLE, John (1707–1762), fifth Earl of Cork and fifth Earl of Orrery, biographer of Swift whom Hill courted as a patron during the *Inspector* years, 1751–1753.

BROWNE, Patrick (c.1720–1790), physician and botanist, whose reputation as a botanist stems from his claim to having been the first English-speaking author to use Linnaeus's system of classifying plants in print.

CANNING, Elizabeth (1734–1773), convicted perjurer who claimed she had been kidnapped by the gypsy Mary Squires; was found to have been lying and imprisoned.

CHURCHILL, Charles (1732–1764), satiric poet who collaborated with John Wilkes to attack Bute and his ministry in the anti-ministerial periodical the *North Briton.*

COLLINSON, Peter (1694–1768), botanist, most powerful London broker among natural historians of the early Georgian period.

COOPER, Mary (unknown), bookseller who sold Hill her copyrights and helped him to establish himself as an author in the early part of his career.

DA COSTA, Emanuel Mendes (1717–1791), Jewish naturalist of Portuguese descent who distinguished himself in the fields of natural history, conchology, and mineralogy.

DERRICK, Samuel (?–1775), Irish playwright and poet who migrated to London and assisted Hill in his paper wars contra Fielding, Smart, Kenrick, and their cabal.

D'ISRAELI, Isaac (1766–1848), writer and father of the future prime minister Benjamin, who made the first attempt to resuscitate Hill's life and works.

EDWARDS, George (1694–1773), ornithologist and artist Hill made the protagonist of his satirical anti-novel *The Adventures of Mr. George Edwards, a Creole.*

EHRET, George Dionysius (1708–1770), German botanical artist who migrated to London and became successful there.

FIELDING, Henry (1707–1754), novelist and magistrate with whom Hill feuded at the end of the novelist's life, especially over the testimony of Elizabeth Canning.

FOLKES, Martin (1690–1754), antiquary and natural philosopher who served as president of the Royal Society during the years (1741–1753) when Hill sought election.

FOOTE, Samuel (1721–1777), actor and playwright, controversialist who joined the Hill faction after 1750 through their mutual attacks on Henry Fielding.

GARRICK, David (1717–1779), actor, playwright, and most distinguished theater manager of the mid-Georgian period whom Hill tried to persuade to hire him.

GESNER, Johannes (1709–1790), professor at the University of Zurich, typical man of the Enlightenment Republic of Letters; actively cultivated botany and geology.

GRIFFITHS, Ralph (1720?–1803), journal editor and prosperous bookseller with whom Hill often collaborated; in trouble with the law on many occasions.

HALLER (1708–1777), Swiss scientist and poet interested in all forms of natural history whose theory of irritability/sensibility caused widespread Enlightenment debate.

HILL, Henrietta Wilhelmina Jones (?–1802), sister of fourth Viscount Ranelagh and Hill's second wife who was loyal to him from their marriage in 1753 until his death.

JOHNSON, Samuel (1709–1784), moralist, man of letters, compiler of *An English Dictionary*, who gave King George III his candid view of John Hill.

KENRICK, William (1729/30–1779), writer and translator who sought patronage as fervently as Hill and joined the Fielding-Smart cabal against Hill.

KNIGHT, Gowin (1713–1772), physician, inventor of geomagnetic instruments, and first librarian of the British Museum from 1756 to the time of his death.

KNOWLTON, Thomas (1691–1781), gardener and botanist, antiquarian, and longtime correspondent of Hill's friend Emmanuel da Costa.

LINNAEUS, Carl [later Carl von Linne] (1707–1778), the great Swedish naturalist and taxonomist who became one of the Enlightenment's most famous scientists.

MACSWINY, Owen (?–1754), Irish actor who managed the Queen's Theatre in the Haymarket, friend of Colley Cibber, and lover of Peg Woffington to whom he willed his fortune.

MARTYN, John (1699–1768), botanist and physician who corresponded with Linnaeus and fell out with Cambridge University when he failed to perform as their professor of botany.

MILLER, Philip (1691–1771), horticulturist and writer, often said to have been the most influential British gardener of the eighteenth century; consulted by Petre and Richmond.

MORTON, Charles (1716–1799), FRS, physician, one of three librarians after 1756 to the new British Museum, who remained opposed to Hill's election to the Society.

MURPHY, Arthur (1727–1805), actor and writer, one of Hill's betes noires who feuded with him throughout 1752–1753 as part of the coalition of Fielding and Smart.

NEEDHAM, John Turberville (1713–1781), Roman Catholic priest and natural scientist, FRS, whose microscopy significantly influenced Hill.

NEWCASTLE, Thomas Pelham-Holles (1693–1768), Duke of Newcastle, prime minister whose patronage Hill sought for more than a decade.

NORTHUMBERLAND, Hugh Percy (formerly Smithson) (1712–1786), first Duke of Northumberland, politician who gave Hill hope he might sponsor him.

OSBORNE, Thomas (1704–1767), bookseller who printed almost a dozen of Hill's books and pamphlets.

PARSONS, James (1705–1770), physician and antiquary, who took Hill under his wing and invited him to his weekly scientific meetings in his house.

PETRE, Robert James (1713–1742), eighth Baron Petre, patron of botany and garden designer, employer of the young Hill.

PULTENEY, Richard (1730–1801), botanist and physician, remembered as a zealous promoter of the methods and nomenclature of Linnaeus who wrote the English biography of him.

RAY, John (1627–1705), most influential naturalist in England before the advent of Linnaeus, whose naturalism and theology had been the greatest influence on Theophilus Hill Sr.

RICH, John (1692–1761), pantomimist and theater manager of Drury Lane with whom Hill quarreled in 1739–1740 over the authorship and production of *The Rout*.

RICHMOND, Charles Lennox (1701–1750), second Duke of Richmond, second Duke of Lennox, and Duke of Aubigny, politician and sportsman, first patron of Hill.

SLOANE, Sir Hans (1660–1753), physician and collector who became president of the Royal Society and whose bequest of his vast collections formed the basis of the first British Museum.

SMART, Christopher (1722–1771), poet and journalist with whom Hill feuded; his mock-epic poem *The Hilliad* was the most extended attack on Hill of the 1750s.

SMITH, Sir James Edward (1759–1828), English botanist and founder of the Linnaean Society responsible for bringing Linnaeus's manuscripts to England.

SMOLLETT, Tobias (1721–1771), writer and physician whose novel *The Adventures of Peregrine Pickle* (1751) Hill tried to sabotage.

SOLANDER, Daniel (1733–1782), Swedish botanist and disciple of Linnaeus who became Linnaeus' representative in England and presented Linnaeus's natural history to the English.

STERNE, Laurence (1713–1768), writer, clergyman, and author of *Tristram Shandy* about whom Hill penned the first life to appear in any English publication.

STUART, John (1713–1792), third Earl of Bute, prime minister also known as "the Maecenas of Botany" who was Hill's most enduring patron.

STUKELEY, William (1687–1765), antiquary and natural philosopher, father of British field archaeology, friend of Hill's father and John Hill throughout his lifetime.

WATSON, Sir William (1715–1787), apothecary, physician, advocate of Linnaeus, Trustee of the British Museum upon its opening in 1753, experimenter in electricity.

WOFFINGTON, Margaret [Peg] (1720?–1760), actress, famous on the London stage; rebuffed Hill's advances while they were together at Goodwood.

WOODWARD, Henry (1714–1777), actor and pantomimist who attacked Hill as a defective actor and journalist in the *Inspector*.

WOODWARD, John (1665/1668–1728), polymathic physician, natural historian, and antiquary in whose footsteps Hill sometimes tried to follow.

Appendix A

Booksellers and Printers with Whom Hill Entered into Publishing Contracts

Bookseller—Printer	*Number of separate titles written by Hill*
Robert Baldwin	36
Mary Cooper	14
Thomas Osborne	9
Ralph Griffiths	6
J. Whiston	3
T. Gardner	2
T. Robinson	2
John Clarke	2
W. Owen	2
C. Corbet	1
C. Davis	1
R. Davis	1
J. Doughty	1
T. Longman	1
H. Woodgate	1
J. Waugh	1
E. and C. Dilly	1
P. Elmsly	2
J. Nourse	1
T. Evans	1
T. Trueman	1
Total	89

Note: The eighty-nine works in this list are works by Hill in which his name appears on the title page. Hill had his hand in another fifty to one hundred titles that do not bear his name on their title page. The list aims to provide a sense of the printers and publishers with whom he entered agreements rather than serve as a count of any type. R. Baldwin published by far the largest number of his titles (thirty-six); the first work—*The Conduct of a Married Life*—appeared in 1753 and Baldwin continued to publish didactic rather than literary titles. Mary Cooper published the second largest number and should be considered Hill's other primary printer-publisher, even when she appears in the company of other printers; in those instances Hill cut deals with her despite their contracts reflecting the names of others, e.g., John Hill 1751c. Thomas Osborne printed the third largest number of titles and is the only bookseller for whom contracts with Hill have been found. Ralph Griffiths printed the fourth largest number, beginning with *The Actor* in 1750 (John Hill 1750a), and Griffiths reissued it in 1755. Although fourth in the number of titles by Hill he printed, Griffiths was important for Hill's dealings with the trade, especially for producing the *London Daily Advertiser* containing Hill's biweekly *Inspector* columns.

Appendix B

Publication details of THE VEGETABLE SYSTEM

Volume	*Date of Publication*	*Price*	*Printer*
I	1759	£1, 11shillings, 6 pence	"For the author" and Baldwin
II	1761	£2, 12 shillings, 6 pence	"For the author" and Baldwin
III	1761	£2, 06 shillings	"For the author" and Baldwin
IV	1762	£1, 11 shillings, 6 pence	"For the author" and Baldwin
V	1763	£1, 11 shillings, 6 pence	"For the author" and Baldwin
VI	1764	£2, 10 shillings, 6 pence	"For the author" and Baldwin
VII	1764	£1, 10 shillings, 6 pence	"For the author" and Baldwin
VIII	1765	£1, 12 shillings, 6 pence	"For the author" and Baldwin, J. Ridley
IX	1765	£1, 10 shillings, 6 pence	"For the author" and Baldwin, J. Ridley
X	1765	£1, 10 shillings, 6 pence	"For the author" and Baldwin, J. Ridley
XI	1767	£1, 12 shillings, 6 pence	"For the author" and Baldwin, J. Ridley
XII	1767	£1, 10 shillings, 6 pence	"For the author" and Baldwin, J. Ridley

Volume	*Date of Publication*	*Price*	*Printer*
XIII	1768	£1, 10 shillings, 6 pence	"For the author" and Baldwin, J. Ridley
XIV	1769	£1, 10 shillings, 6 pence	"For the author" and Baldwin, J. Ridley
XV	1769	£1, 10 shillings, 6 pence	"For the author" and Baldwin, J. Ridley
XVI	1770	£1, 10 shillings, 6 pence	"For the author" and Baldwin, J. Ridley et al.
XVII	1770	£2, 06 shillings, 6 pence	"For the author" and Baldwin, J. Ridley et al.
XVIII	1771	£2, 06 shillings, 6 pence	"For the author" and Baldwin, J. Ridley et al.
XIX	1771	£2, 06 shillings, 6 pence	"For the author" and Baldwin, J. Ridley et al.
XX	1772	£2, 06 shillings, 6 pence	"For the author" and Baldwin, J. Ridley et al.
XXI	1772	£2, 06 shillings, 6 pence	"For the author" and Baldwin, J. Ridley et al.
XXII	1773	£2, 11 shillings, 6 pence	"For the author" and Baldwin, J. Ridley et al.
XXIII	1773	£2, 11 shillings, 6 pence	"For the author" and Baldwin, J. Ridley et al.
XXIV	1774	£2, 06 shillings, 6 pence	"For the author" and Baldwin, J. Ridley et al.
XXV	1774	£2, 06 shillings, 6 pence	"For the author" and Baldwin, J. Ridley et al.
XXVI	1775	£2, 06 shillings, 6 pence	"For the author" and T. Trueman

Comment: Hill published without subscription at least one volume each year from 1759 until his death in 1775 except during the years 1760 and 1766. All title pages read "Printed at the EXPENCE of the AUTHOR." R. Baldwin in Paternoster-Row sold all the volumes, except for the last, and other printers and booksellers were added after 1765, especially J. Ridley in St.

James Street where Hill rented accommodations. The volumes average 100–170 pages; only vol. 2 containing 226 pages is significantly longer. The first volume commences with a history of botany discussing John Ray and referring to Carl Linnaeus as the primary classifier of the age. Beginning with vol. 16 Hill arranged for the volumes to be sold more widely than hitherto, adding to Baldwin and Ridley the booksellers J. Nourse in the Strand, L. Davis in Holborn, and T. Becket, P. Elmsly, and J. Campbell also in the Strand. In 1772, vol. 20, he also added Balfour in Edinburgh; this is also the first volume that identifies Hill as a "Member of the Imperial Academy in St. Petersburg." In 1773 Hill further added the booksellers B. White in Fleet Street and L. Davis in Bond Street, suggesting that sales of the set was growing. Vol. 24 added J. Robson in Bond Street. No contracts with any of these publisher-booksellers survive. Vol. 26 deletes the names of all former booksellers, replaces it with "sold by T. Trueman at No. 394 in the Strand," and includes an index to all twenty-six volumes. No consistent pattern exists for the pricing of volumes. Nothing in the above publishing history permits secure speculation about Bute's financing of the volumes, and the fact that Hill included on the title page of every volume, from first to last, "Printed at the EXPENCE of the AUTHOR" further discourages conjecture.

Abbreviations of Frequently Cited Works

Note: Unless indicated otherwise, the place of publication of all works is London.

AR: *The Annual Register . . . for the years [1758–1800]*
Baker Corr: Correspondence of Henry Baker, Beinecke Library, Yale University, Osborn fc. 109.2, 1749–1770
BL: British Library, London
BLB: Bute letter-books, BL, Add. MS 36797
BM: British Museum, London
Bod MS Eng Misc.: Bodleian Library Oxford English Manuscripts
Bute MSS: Manuscripts of John Stuart, 3rd Earl of Bute, Mount Stuart, Rothesay, Isle of Bute, Scotland and Mount Stuart Trust, Isle of Bute
CR: *The Critical Review*. London, 1756–1812
DAC: 2,487 autograph letters in eleven volumes of letters to and from Emanuel Mendes da Costa, 1737–1787, at BL Add MSS 28534-44
DAC Archives: "The Da Costa Archives," in G. S. Rousseau and David Haycock, *History of Science* 38 (2): 160–61, describing the extant manuscripts
Darlington: William Darlington, *Memorials of John Bartram and Humphrey Marshall*, Philadelphia, 1849
DNB: *Dictionary of National Biography*, Oxford: Oxford University Press, 2004–
Dodsley: Robert Dodsley, *London and its Environs Described*, 1761, 6 vols.
Fitzgerald: Percy Fitzgerald, *The Life of David Garrick: From Original Family Papers, and Numerous Published and Unpublished Sources*, 1868, 2 vols.
FRS: Fellows of the Royal Society of London
GM: *The Gentleman's Magazine*

Goodwood MS: Goodwood Archives, West Sussex Record Office, Chichester, England

HWC: *Horace Walpole's Correspondence*, ed. Wilmarth S. Lewis, et al., New Haven, 1937–1984

JH: John Hill

LDA: *London Daily Advertiser*. London, 1751–1753. This abbreviation is for the newspaper and includes the Inspector columns in its references

LM: *London Magazine*

LPH: G. S. Rousseau, *The Letters and Papers of Sir John Hill 1714–1775*, New York, AMS Press, 1982.

McCann: Timothy J. McCann. *The Correspondence of the Dukes of Richmond and Newcastle 1724–1750*. Chichester: The Sussex Record Society, 1984.

Morris MSS: Manuscript Notebooks of Arthur Morris 1930–1970 (unpublished)

MR: *Monthly Review*

Nichols: John Nichols, *Literary Anecdotes of the Eighteenth Century*, 1812, 6 vols.

N&RRS: *Notes and Records of the Royal Society*

PA: *Public Advertiser*. London 1751–1775

Phillips: Hugh Phillips, *Mid-Georgian London: A Topographical and Social Survey of Central and Western London about 1750*. Collins, 1964.

PT: *Philosophical Transactions of the Royal Society of London*, 1662–1820

Renaissance Man: J. A. Leo Lemay and G. S. Rousseau, *The Renaissance Man in the Eighteenth Century*. Los Angeles: Williams Andrew Clark Memorial Library, 1978

RG: Manuscripts of Ralph Griffiths containing his correspondence, Miscellaneous Manuscripts 28460–61; Montagu MSS 25433, Bodleian Library, Oxford

RS MSS: Minute Books of the Royal Society

Smith: *Memoir and Correspondence of the Late Sir James Edward Smith, M.D.*, ed. Lady Smith, 1832, 2 vols.

SP: Stukeley Papers in the Bodleian Library, Oxford, Stukeley MSS Eng. Misc. e. 131

Spalding Gents. Soc.: Maurice Johnson's MSS, Drawer 1, in the Spalding Gentleman's Society, Spalding, Lincolnshire

Stephens: *Satirical Prints: Catalogue of Prints and Drawings in the British Museum, Division I. Political and Personal Satires*, ed. F. G. Stephens and M. D. George, vol. 3, 2 parts. Printed for the British Museum, 1877

TLS: Times Literary Supplement (London)

Bibliography

Note on the Bibliography: Unless otherwise indicated the place of publication of all works is London. Anonymous works are listed alphabetically rather than chronologically, and form a crucial component of this book's content. References in the notes are often to primary sources rather than to individual pages within that source, in which case only the work is listed, e.g., Woodward 1728, a reference indicating that the material discussed in the text originated in this source. Notes provide the author's first name *only* when more than one author of the same name appears; e.g., Henry Baker because there are several Bakers. And the same rule applies to dates, i. e., when the bibliography contains more than one item by the same author; e.g., J. E. Smith 1832 because more than one of J. E. Smith's works is listed. Works by authors with multiple entries are listed chronologically. The place of publication is not provided for works published prior to 1850, except for Hill's primary works. Those listings intentionally cite the printer as a convenience to readers, and unless there is a further specific reason, i. e., to call attention to a specific work by an author other than Hill that was printed by one of his rogue publishers, such as Mary Cooper. All Hill's works were published in London.

Adair, James Makktrick. *Essays on Fashionable Diseases*. 1786a.

Adair, James Makktrick. *Medical Cautions for the Consideration of Invalids. . . .* 1786b.

Adanson, Michel. *A Voyage to Senegal, the Isle of Goree, and the River Gambia*. 1759.

Addison, Joseph. *Tatler*. In James Ferguson, ed., *The British Essayists*. 1823 [1709].

Aikin, John. *An Essay on the Application of Natural History to Poetry*. 1777.

Albin, E. *A Natural History of Birds*. 1738.

[Aldrovandus]. "Account of Aldrovandus." *Universal Magazine*. 1752.

Allen, D. E. *The Naturalist in Britain: A Social History*. Allen Lane, 1976.

[Almon, John]. *Political Register*. 1767.

Alston, C. *A Dissertation on the Sexes of Plants in Essays and Observations, Physical and Literary*. 1756.

Altick, R. *The Shows of London*. Cambridge, MA: Harvard University Press, 1978.

Alton, William. *Hortus Kewensis; or, a Catalogue of the Plants Cultivated in the Royal Garden at Kew*. 3 vols. 1789.

[The] Annual Register. 1756–1776.

[Anonymous]. *An account of the birth, education, life and conversation of that notorious and bold scribbler the Observator* . . . 1705.

[Anonymous]. "An Account of the Life and Writings of Dr. John Shebbeare." *European Magazine* 14 (1788): 23–28.

[Anonymous]. *The Adventures of an Author. Written by himself and a friend.* 1767.

[Anonymous]. *An Apology for the Conduct of a Lady of Quality, lately traduc'd under the Name of Lady Frail.* 1751.

[Anonymous]. *The Authors of the Town: A Satire.* 1725.

[Anonymous]. *The Character of the Times Delineated . . . Containing a description of the most flagrant enormities. . . .* 1732.

[Anonymous]. *Codgill and Mango, An Essay on the Rationality of Brutes.* 1752.

[Anonymous]. *A Complete Guide to Arlington Street London.* 1749–1758.

[Anonymous]. *A Description of the Gardens and Buildings at Kew, at Surrey . . . To which is added, a Short Account about Richmond and Kew.* [1760].

[Anonymous]. *The Devil of Delphos, or, the prophets of Baal: containing an account of a notorious impostor, call'd Sabatai Sevi. . . .* [1708].

[Anonymous]. *Dr. Bodadil's Monody.* 1752.

[Anonymous]. *An Essay on the Antiquity, Dignity, and Advantages of Living in a Garret.* 1751

[Anonymous]. *The Eventful life, and wonderful history of that most notorious character, swindler, and forger, Charles Price . . . commonly called Old Patch.* 1800.

[Anonymous]. *Friendship, A Satire.* 1763.

[Anonymous]. *Fugitive Pieces on various Subjects* . . . 2 vols. 1761.

[Anonymous]. *The Geese Stript of their Quills: Or, Proposals for Depluming and Rusticating the Rival Literati.* 1753.

[Anonymous]. *George's Coffee-house: A Satire.* 1763.

[Anonymous]. *The Graces: A Poetical Epistle from a Gentleman to his Son.* 1774.

[Anonymous]. *The History of the Human Heart: Or the Adventures of a Young Gentleman.* 1749.

[Anonymous]. *The Humbug. The Town Whim, Being a Collection of the most comical and merry Songs.* 1753.

[Anonymous]. *The Ill State of Physick in Great Britain.* 1727.

[Anonymous]. *The Inspector in the Shades. A New Dialogue in the Manner of Lucian. . . .* 1752.

[Anonymous]. *The Inspector's Rhapsody or Soliloquy, . . . at Ranelagh.* 1752.

[Anonymous]. *The Judicious Midwife: Or, All Safely Delivered. Being an Answer to Wit flying at St. J——'s [James's].* 1751.

[Anonymous]. *The Last Masquerade at Mrs. C——s.* 1772.

[Anonymous]. *The Laurel Containing Various Branches of Poetry.* 1747.

[Anonymous]. *A Letter from a Physician in Town to his Friend in the Country.* 1753.

[Anonymous]. *A Letter from Henry Woodward, Comedian, The Meanest of all Characters . . . to Dr. John Hill, Inspector-General of Great Britain, the Greatest of all characters.* 1752.

[Anonymous]. *A Letter to the author of . . . the Rout. To which is subjoined, An Epistle to Mr. G——k.* 1759.

[Anonymous]. *Libertina Sine Conflictus; Or, A True Narrative of the Untimely Death of Dr. Atoll . . . and a Faithful Copy of his will, etc.* 1752.

[Anonymous]. *A Lick at 'em All; Or the Moderator: . . . Between the Inspector and his Opposers.* 1753.

[Anonymous]. *Low Life; Or One Half of the World . . . With an Address to . . . Mr. Hogarth.* 1764.

[Anonymous]. *The March of the Lion, Or the Conclusion of the War Between Dunce and the Dunces. Written with all . . . the Politeness of the Inspector—The Progress of the Golden Savage from the Bedford coffee-house.* 1752.

[Anonymous]. *Memoirs of the Bedford Coffee House. By a Genius.* 1763.

[Anonymous]. "Memoirs of the Late John Hill." *Walker's Hibernian Magazine Dublin* (1775): 799–801.

[Anonymous]. *Modern Characters.* 1753.

[Anonymous]. *A Narrative of the Affair Between Mr. Brown and the Inspector . . . With . . . The Inspector's Own Account of it*. 1752.

[Anonymous]. *Notice to those who sell Sir John Hill's Medicines*. 1779. [broadside]

[Anonymous]. *Now You have all settled it . . . The March of the Lion, or the Conclusion of the War between Dunce and the Dunces* . . . 1752.

[Anonymous]. *A Parallel between the Characters of Lady Frail, and the Lady of Quality in Peregrine Pickle* . . . 1751.

[Anonymous]. *A Particular Account of the Noble Large House, Gardens . . . of the Late Duke of Argyll, Situate at Whitton, near Hounslow in Middlesex*. n.d.

[Anonymous]. *A Particular Description of a Certain Lady at Present Conceal'd. Her Person, Dress, Temper, and Dispositions . . . Also a Slight Sketch of her Niece the Fair Incognita* . . . 1752.

[Anonymous]. 1753. *Philologus: The Inspector Inspected: Or, Dr. Hill's Story of Elizabeth Canning Examined.*

[Anonymous]. *The Present State of the Literati: A Satire*. 1752.

[Anonymous]. *The Prophetic Physician*. [1751].

[Anonymous]. *The Quack Doctors. A satire . . . in hudibrastic stile*. C. Moran. 1762.

[Anonymous]. *Rules for Being a Wit*. 1753.

[Anonymous]. *A Short Account of the Life, Writing, and Character of the Late Sir John Hill*. 1779.

[Anonymous]. *A Sketch of the Spring-Gardens, Vaux-hall*. 1751.

[Anonymous]. *Some Observations on the Writers of the Present Age*. [1751].

[Anonymous]. *Some Remarks on the Life and Writings of Dr. J—H—, Inspector General of Great Britain, in a Series of Letters . . . with Occasional Hints Relative to . . . a Certain Noble Earl*. 1752.

[Anonymous]. *A Treatise on the Passions, so far as they Regard the Stage. With a Critical Enquiry into the Theatrical Merit of Mr. G——k, Mr. Q—n, and Mr. B——y*. 1747.

[Anonymous]. *A Trip Through the Town*. 1735.

[Anonymous]. *Two Letters from a Physician in London, to A Gentleman at Bath . . . with some Observations on the Present Use of Tobacco*. 1749.

[Anonymous]. *Universal Visitor, and Monthly Memorialist*. 1756.

[Anonymous]. *A View of London and Westminster: Or, the Town Spy*. 1725.

[Anonymous]. *A Vindication of an Innocent Lady from the Cruel and Unjust Aspersions of a Certain News-Writer* [*The Inspector*]. 1751.

[Anonymous]. *The Younger Brother, a tale*. 1770–72.

Arber, Agnes. *Herbals: Their Origin and Evolution, A Chapter in the History of Botany, 1470–1670*. Cambridge: Cambridge University Press, 1938.

Aspinall, A. *The Later Correspondence of George III*. Cambridge: Cambridge University Press, 5 vols. 1962–1970.

Atkinson, A. D. "Dr. Johnson and the Royal Society." *N&RRS* 10 (1952): 131–38.

Babbage, Charles. *Reflections on the Decline of Science in England*. 1830.

Baker, E. A. *Biographia Dramatica*. 1782.

Baker, Henry. *The Microscope made Easy*. 1742.

Baker, Henry. *Employment for the Microscope, in Two Parts*. . . .1753 [1764].

Baker, John R. *Abraham Trembley of Geneva: Scientist and Philosopher 1710–1784*. Edward Arnold, 1952.

Baker, Robin. *Sperm Wars: The Science of Sex*. New York: Basic Books, 1996.

Barriére, Pierre. *L'Academie de Bordeaux, Centre de Culture Internationale aux XVIII Siecle 1712–1792*. 1792.

Barton, Richard. *Lectures in Natural Philosophy, Designed to be a Foundation*. . . .1751.

Bartram, John. *Observations on the Inhabitants . . . made by Mr. John Bartram, in his travels from Pensilvania* [sic] *to Onondago, Oswego and the Lake Ontario, in Canada. To which is annex'd, a curious account . . . By Mr. Peter Kalm, a Swedish gentleman who travelled there*. 1751.

Bartram, William. *Botanical and Zoological Drawings, 1756–1788*. 1788.

Battestin, M. C. *Henry Fielding: A Life*. Routledge, 1989.

Beasley, J. C. *Novels of the 1740s*. Athens: University of Georgia Press, 1982.

Beddoes, Thomas. *Manual of Health*. 1806.

Bell, John. *Travels from St. Petersburg*. 2 vols. 1763.

Bickham, George. *A Description of the Most Noble Houses and Gardens . . . at Stowe, in Buckinghamshire*. 1756.

Birch, Thomas. *The History of the Royal Society of London*. 1756–1757.

Birt, Samuel. *Micrographia Illustrata: or, the knowledge of the microscope explain'd: together with an account of a new invented universal, single or double, microscope* . . . 1746.

Birt, Samuel. *The wonders of nature and art: being an account of whatever is most curious and remarkable throughout the world* . . . 1750.

Blackwell, Elizabeth. *A Curious Herbal, Containing 500 cuts of the Most Useful Plants* . . . 2 vols. 1737.

Bloom, Edward A. *Samuel Johnson in Grub Street*. Providence: Brown University Press, 1957.

Blunt, Wilfrid. *The Art of Botanical Illustration*. Collins, 1950.

Bonnet, Charles, R. G. Mazzolini, S. A. Roe, and Joseph Turberville Needham. *Science against the Unbelievers: The Correspondence of Bonnet and Needham, 1760–1780*. Oxford: Voltaire Foundation at the Taylor Institution, 1986.

Bonney, George. *Goodwood: An Illustrated Survey of the Dukes of Richmond and Gordon*. Derby: English Life Publications, 1951.

Boyce, Samuel. *Lyra Britannica: being a collection of songs, duets, and cantatas, on various subjects*. 1747.

Boyce, Samuel. *Poems on Several Occasions*. 1757.

Boyce, Samuel. *The Rover; Or, Happiness, at Last: A Pastoral Drama*. 1751b.

Boyle, Emily Charlotte, ed. *The Orrery Papers*. 2 vols. Duckworth and Co., 1903.

Boyle, John, Earl of Cork and Orrery. *Letters from Italy in the Years 1754 & 1755*. 1774.

Boyle, John, Earl of Cork and Orrery. *The Life and Writings of Dean Swift*. 1751a.

Bradbury, Simon. *The Evolution of the Microscope*. Oxford: Pergamon Press, 1967.

Bradley, Martha. *The British Housewife*. 1756–1758.

Braudy, Leo. *The Frenzy of Renown: Fame and its History*. Oxford: Oxford University Press, 1986.

Brett-James, Norman George. *The Life of Peter Collinson*. E. G. Dunstern and Co., 1929.

Brewer, John, and Roy Porter. *Consumption and the World of Goods*. Routledge, 1993.

Bridges, John. *The History and Antiquities of Northamptonshire*. Oxford, 1791.

Brockliss, Laurence. *Calvet's Web: Enlightenment and the Republic of Letters in Eighteenth-Century France*. Oxford: Oxford University Press, 2003.

Brooke, Henry. *Gustavus Vasa*. 1739.

Browne, Patrick. *The Civil and Natural History of Jamaica*. 1756.

Buck, J. D. C. "The Motives of Puffing: Newberry's Advertisements 1742–1767." *Studies in Bibliography*, 30 (1977): 196–210.

Buckinghamshire Record Office. *Papers of the Way Family of Denham Place*. BRO D/W.

Buckinghamshire Record Office. *Vestry Papers of Denham Parish*. BRO PR 61.

[Buffon]. *Buffon's Natural history . . . From the French with notes by the translator, ed. J. S. Barr*. [privately printed], 1807–12.

Bullion, John L. "The Origins and significance of gossip about Princess Augusta and Lord Bute, 1755–1756." *Studies in Eighteenth-Century Culture* 21 (1991): 245–65.

Burke, Edmund. *The Correspondence of Edmund Burke*. Edited by Thomas W. Copeland. 10 vols. Cambridge: Cambridge University Press, 1958–1978.

Burnby, J. G. *A Study of the English Apothecary from 1660 to 1760*. Wellcome Institute Publications, 1983.

[Bute] John Stuart. "MSS Travel Book in Italy." Add. Manuscript 8826. Cambridge University Library, c. 1768.

The Butiad . . . a Concise View of the Posture of Political Affairs, During the Remarkable Years 1762 and 1763. 1763.

[Butler, Samuel]. *The Genuine Remains in verse and prose of Mr. Samuel Butler, published by R. Thyer*. 1759.

Bynum, W. F., and Roy Porter, eds. *Medical Fringe and Medical Orthodoxy, 1750–1850*. Croom Helm, 1987.

Byrd, Max. *London in the Eighteenth Century*. New Haven: Yale University Press, 1982.
Cadogan, William. *A Dissertation on the Gout, And All Chronic Diseases*. 1771.
Calmann, Gerta. *Ehret*. Phaidon, 1977.
Cambridge, Richard Owen. *The Scriblerian: An Heroic Poem*, 1751.
[Camlin]. *A Satisfactory Refutation of Sir Hypo Bardana's "Circumstances." Clearly Proving that they were Framed by Him. . . .* [1755].
Campbell, Archibald. *Lexiphanes. . . .* 1767a.
Campbell, Archibald. *The Sale of Authors*. 1767b.
Campbell, Robert. *The London Tradesman*. 1747.
Carter, Elizabeth. *A Series of Letters between . . . Elizabeth Carter and . . . Catherine Talbot from . . . 1741 to 1770*. 2 vols. 1809.
Cash, Arthur H. *Laurence Sterne: The Early and Middle Years*. Methuen, 1975.
Cashmore, Ernest. *Mass Media and Culture Celebrities*. Abingdon: Routledge, 2006.
Catesby, Mark. *The Natural History of Carolina, Florida, and the Bahama Islands*. 2 vols. 1748.
Chamberlayne, John. *The Natural History of Coffee, The* [sic], *Chocolate, Tobacco . . . from the Writings of the Best Physicians and Modern Travelers*. 1682.
Chambers, D. D. C. *The Planters of the English landscape garden: botany, trees, and the Georgics*. New Haven: Yale University Press, 1993.
Chambers, Ephraim. *Cyclopedia: or, An Universal Dictionary. . . .* 2 vols. 1741–1743.
Chambers, William. *Designs of Chinese Buildings, Furniture, Dresses, Machines, and Utensils . . . A Description of Their Temples, Houses, Gardens, etc*. 1757.
Chapman, R. W. *Boswell's Life of Johnson*. Oxford: Oxford University Press. 1953.
Cheyne, George. *An Essay of the True Nature . . . of Treating the Gout*. 1724.
Cheyne, George. *The English Malady*. 1733.
Clance, Pauline. *The Impostor Phenomenon: Overcoming the Fear That Haunts Your Success*. New York: Harcourt, 1985.
Clarke, George Augustine. *Family Instructor in the Knowledge of Medicine . . . by a Physician in London*. 1750.
Clark, J. C. D. *The Dynamics of Change: The Crisis of the 1750s and English Party Systems*. 1982. Cambridge: Cambridge University Press.
Clary, E. J., et al. *Authorship, Commerce and the Public: scenes of writing 1750–1850*. Basingstoke: Palgrave Macmillan, 2000.
Cleland, John. *Memoirs of a Coxcomb*. 1751.
Clifford, J. L. *Dictionary Johnson: Johnson's Middle Years*. New York: McGraw-Hill, 1979.
Coats, Alice M. *Lord Bute. Lifelines 27*, Aylesbury: Shire Publishing, 1975.
Cody, Lisa Forman. *Birthing the Nation: Sex, Science, and the Conception of Eighteenth-Century Britons*. Oxford: Oxford University Press, 2005.
Cokayne, G. E. *Pedigree of the Family of Hill, of Rothwell, Co. Northampton*. MSS notes by Cokayne Family, n.d.
Coke, David, and Alan Borg. *Vauxhall Gardens: A History 1659–1859*. New Haven: Yale University Press, 2011.
Collins, A. S. *The Profession of Letters: A Study of the Relation of Author to Patron, Publisher, and Public, 1780–1832*. Routledge, 1928.
Coltheart, Peter. *The quacks unmask'd . . . their pernicious and destructive practice; with some reasons why it ought to be entirely abolished*. 1737.
Connell, R. W. *Masculinities*. Cambridge: Polity Press, 1995.
Connoisseur. *The Connoisseur, by Mr. Town, critic and censor-general* [G. Colman, B. Thornton and others]. 1755–56.
Cook, Judith. *Dr. Simon Forman: a most notorious physician*. Vintage, 2002.
Cooke, William. *Memoirs of Samuel Foote, Esquire*. 3 vols. 1805.
Copeman, W. S. C. *The Worshipful Society of Apothecaries of London: A History, 1617–1967*. Oxford: Pergamon, 1967.
Corea, Gena. *Man-Made Women: How New Reproductive Technologies Affect Women*. Hutchinson, 1985.

Coxe, Stephen D. *"The Stranger within thee": Concepts of the Self in Late-Eighteenth-Century Literature*. Pittsburgh: University of Pittsburgh Press, 1980.

Craford, Robert. *The Young Traders [sic] vade mecum*. 1732.

Cronstedt, Axel, and G. von Engeström. *An Essay towards a system of mineralogy . . . translated from the original Swedish*. 1788.

Cross, Wilbur, ed. *The Complete Works of Laurence Sterne. Twelve Volumes*. New York: J. F. Taylor, 1904.

Cumberland, Richard. *Memoirs of Richard Cumberland. . . .* 1806–1807.

Curtis, L. P., ed., *Letters of Laurence Sterne*. Oxford: Clarendon Press, 1935.

Dack, C. "The Peterborough Gentleman's Society." *Journal of the British Archaeological Association* 29 (1899): 5–8.

da Costa, Emanuel Mendes. *A Natural History of Fossils*. 1757

da Costa, Emanuel Mendes. *Essay towards a System of Mineralogy*. 1770.

da Costa, Emanuel Mendes. *Elements of Conchology, or, An Introduction to the Knowledge of Shells*. 1776.

Darlington, Cyril. *The Place of Botany in the Life of a University*. Oxford: Clarendon Press, 1954.

Darlington, William. *Memorials of John Bartram and Humphrey Marshall*. 2 vols. New York: Hafner, 1967.

Darwin, Erasmus. *The botanic garden; a poem*. 1789.

Darwin, Erasmus. *Zoonomia; or, the laws of organic life*. 1796.

Davies, Thomas. *Memoirs of the Life of David Garrick, Esq*. 3 vols. 1781.

de Beer, G. R. "Correspondence between Linnaeus and [Johannes] Gesner." *Proceedings of the Linnaean Society* 161.2 (1949): 225–241.

Delpit, Jules. *Le Fils de Montesquieu*. Bordeaux, 1888.

Derrick, Samuel. *Derrick's Jests; or. The Wits Chronicle*. 1769.

Derrick, Samuel. *Fortune, A Rhapsody*. 1751.

Derrick, Samuel. *The Smartiad, a satire. Occasioned by an epic poem, intitled The Hilliad*. 1753.

Desmond, Ray. *Kew: the history of the Royal Botanic Gardens*. Oxford: Oxford University Press, 1995.

Dibble, R. F. "James Ralph, Jack of all Literary Trades." *Nation* 13 (1926): 22–26.

Dibdin, Charles. *A Complete History of the Stage*. 6 vols. 1800.

Dillenius, J. J., and William Sherard. *Hortus Elthamensis, seu Plantarum rariorum. . . .* 1732.

D'Israeli, Isaac. *An Essay on the Manners and Genius of the Literary Character*. 1795.

D'Israeli, Isaac. *Quarrels of Authors . . . memoirs for our literary history*. 1814.

D'Israeli, Isaac. *The Literary Character . . . illustrated by men of genius*. 1818.

D'Israeli, Isaac. *The Calamities and Quarrels of Authors: With Some Inquiries Respecting Their Moral and Literary Characters, and Memoirs for our Literary History*. 2 vols. Routledge, 1859 [1812].

Dodsley, Robert. *London and Its Environs Described*. 6 vols. 1761.

Dodsley, Robert. *The Preceptor*. 1793.

Drury, Dru. *Illustrations of Natural History*. 1770–1782.

Dudden, F. Holmes. *Henry Fielding: His Life and Times*. 2 vols. Oxford: Clarendon Press, 1952.

Duffin, C. J. *Fossils as Drugs: Pharmaceutical Paleontology*. Luxembourg: Ferrantia, 2008.

Dunbar, Howard A. *The Dramatic Career of Arthur Murphy*. New York: Modern Language Association, 1946.

Dunbar, Janet. *Peg Woffington and her World*. Heinemann, 1968.

Dutens, Louis. *Memoirs of a Traveller*. 1806.

Duyker, E. *Daniel Solander: collected correspondence, 1753–1782*. Melbourne: Miegunyah Press, 1995.

Duyker, E. *Nature's argonaut: Daniel Solander 1733–1782: naturalist and voyager with Cook and Banks*. Melbourne: Miegunyah Press, 1998.

Earle, Peter. *The Making of the English Middle Class: Business, Society, and Family Life in London, 1660–1730*. Methuen, 1989.

Eaves, T. C. Duncan, and Ben D. Kimpel. *Samuel Richardson: A Biography*. Oxford: Clarendon Press, 1971.

Edwards, Edward. *Lives of the Founders of the British Museum*. 2 vols. Thoemmes Press, 1996.
Edwards, George. A *Natural History of Uncommon Birds*. Royal College of Physicians, Warwick-Lane. 1743–51.
Edwards, George. *Gleanings of Natural History*. 3 vols. 1758–64.
Edwards, George. *Essays Upon Natural History*. 1770.
Edwards, Sampson [pseudonym]. *A letter to Mr. Woodward, on his triumph over the Inspector. By Sampson Edwards, the merry cobler* [*sic*] *of the Haymarket*. . . . 1752.
Eisenstadt, S. N., and L. Roniger. "Patron-Client Relations as a Model of Structuring Social Change." *Comparative Studies in Society and History* 22 (1980): 42–77.
Eisenstadt, S. N. *The Protestant Ethic and Modernization: A Comparative View*. New York: Basic Books, 1968.
Ellis, John. *Directions for Bringing Over Seeds and Plants from the East Indies . . . a New Sensitive Plant, Called Dionaea Muscipula*. . . . 1770.
Emery, Clark. "Dr. Johnson on Dr. Hill." *Modern Language Notes* 64 (1949): 15–18.
Emery, J. P. *Arthur Murphy*. Philadelphia: University of Pennsylvania Press, 1946a.
Emery, J. P. "Murphy's Authorship of the Notes of Smart's 'Hilliad.'" *Modern Language Notes* 61 (1946): 162–65.
Engel, Laura. *Fashioning Celebrity: Eighteenth-century British Actresses and Strategies for Image Making*. Columbus: Ohio State University Press, 2011.
Erickson, Gunnar. "Linnaeus the Botanist." In *Linnaeus the Man and his Work*, edited by Tore Frängsmyr, 64–96. Berkeley: University of California Press, 1983.
European Magazine. 1782–1825. 87 vols.
Evans, R. J. W., and Alexander Marr, eds. *Curiosity and Wonder from the Renaissance to the Enlightenment*. Aldershot: Ashgate, 2006.
Ewan, Joseph. "Annals of the Most Wonderful Plant in the World." In *Festschrift für Claus Nissen*, edited by E. Geck. 175–84. Wiesbaden: Pressler, 1973.
Eyles, V. A. "John Woodward, FRS, FRCP, MD, 1665–1728." *Journal of the Society for the Bibliography of Natural History* 5 (1968): 399–427.
Eyles, V. A. "The Extent of Geological Knowledge in the Eighteenth Century." In *Towards a Historical Geology*, edited by C. J. Schneer, 159–83. Cambridge: Cambridge University Press, 1969.
Fara, Patricia. *Sympathetic Attractions*. Princeton: Princeton University Press, 1996.
Feingold, Mordechai. "Mathematicians and Naturalists: Sir Isaac Newton and the Royal Society." *Annals of Science* 56 (1999): 271–316.
Fielding, Henry. *The Author's Farce*. 1730.
Fielding, Henry. *The Mock Doctor*. 1732.
Fielding, Henry. *An Enquiry into the Causes of the Late Increase of Robbers*. 1751.
Fielding, Henry. *A Clear State of the case of Elizabeth Canning*. 1753.
Fielding, Sir John. *A Plan to Establish an Universal Register Office*. 1752.
Findlen, Paula. *Possessing Nature: museums, collecting, and scientific culture*. Berkeley: University of California Press, 1994.
Findlen, Paula, ed. *Athanasius Kircher: the last man who knew everything*. Routledge, 2004.
Flagellan, Christopher. *Tristram Shandy's Bon Mots* . . . 1761.
[Foot, Ferdinando, pseud.]. *The Nut-Cracker . . . Collected from the Most Sprightly Wits of the Present Age*. 1751.
Fowler, Thomas. *Medical Reports of the Effects of Tobacco*. 1785.
Frängsmyr, Tore, ed. *Linnaeus: The Man and his Work*. Berkeley: University of California Press, 1983.
Fraser, Kevin. "William Cadogan and the Gout." *Medical History* 36 (1982): 160–86.
Fraser, Kevin. "John Hill and the Royal Society in the Eighteenth Century." *N&RRS* 48 (1994): 43–67.
Freke, William. *An Essay to show the cause of electricity . . . as it may affect the sensitive plant*. 1748.
Friedman, Arthur, ed., *Collected Works of Oliver Goldsmith*. 5 vols. Oxford: Clarendon Press, 1965.
Fuller, Francis. *Medicina gymnastica: or, A treatise concerning the power of exercise*. 1737.

Fumaroli, Marc. "The Republic of Letters." *Diogenes* 36 (1988): 129–52.

Fussell, Paul. "William Kenrick, Eighteenth-Century Scourge and Critic." *Journal of the Rutgers University Library* 20 (1957): 42–59.

Garrick, David. *The Fribbleriad*. 1761.

Gascoigne, John. *Joseph Banks and the English Enlightenment*. Cambridge: Cambridge University Press, 1994.

Gataker, Thomas. *Observations on the Internal Use of . . . Nightshade*. 1757.

The General Advertiser: A Daily Newspaper . . . 1746–1770.

Gentilcore, David. *Medical Charlatanism in Early Modern Italy*. Oxford: Oxford University Press, 2006.

George, Mary Dorothy. *English Political Caricature to 1792; A Study of Opinion and Propaganda*. 2 vols. Oxford: Clarendon Press, 1959.

George, Mary Dorothy. *Hogarth to Cruikshank: Social Change in Graphic Satire*. Allen Lane, 1967.

George, Samantha. *Botany, Sexuality and Women's Writing 1760–1830: From Modest Shoot to Forward Plant*. Manchester: Manchester University Press, 2007.

Gerstner, Patsy. "John Hill." In *Dictionary of Scientific Biography*, edited by Charles C. Gillispie, 16 vols., vol. 6, 400–401. Princeton: Princeton University Press, 1970–1980.

Giddens, Anthony, and Jonathan H. Turner. *Social Theory Today*. Cambridge: Polity, 1988.

Glasse, Hannah. *The Art of Cookery Made Plain and Easy*. 1747.

Goldgar, Anne. *Impolite Learning: Conduct and Community in the Republic of Letters, 1680–1750*. New Haven: Yale University Press, 1995.

Golinski, Jan. *Science as Public Culture: Chemistry and Enlightenment in Britain, 1760–1820*. Cambridge: Cambridge University Press, 1999.

The Goodwood Estate Archives: A Catalogue. 2 vols. Chichester: West Sussex County Council, 1972.

Gordon, Lyndall. *Lives Like Loaded Guns: Emily Dickinson*. Virago, 2010.

Gordon-Lennox, Charles Henry. *A Duke and His Friends: The Life and Letters of the Second Duke of Richmond*. 2 vols. Hutchinson and Co., 1911.

Göttingsche Gelehrte Anzeigen. 49 vols. Göttingen, 1753–1801.

Graden, John. "The Impostor Syndrome: How to Replace Self-Doubt with Self-Confidence and Train Your Brain for Success." Accessed March 2008. http://www.JohnGraden.com.

Grafton, Anthony. *Worlds Made by Words: Scholarship and Community in the Modern West*. Cambridge, MA: Harvard University Press, 2009.

Grant, Douglas, ed. *The Poetical Works of Charles Churchill*. Oxford: Clarendon Press, 1956.

Grays-Inn Journal. 6 vols. 1751–56.

Griffiths, Ralph. *A Charge of Publishing a Palpable Falsity, Exhibited against . . . the Authors of Monthly Review*. 1755.

Griffiths, Ralph. *Ascanius, or, the young adventurer; a true history . . . sold by Ralph Griffiths*. 1756.

Grosley, Pierre Jean. *A Tour to London; or, New Observations on England and its Inhabitants*. 2 vols. 1772.

Gross, John. *The Rise of the Man of Letters*. Harmondsworth: Penguin, 1991.

Gunther, A. E. "The Royal Society and the Foundation of the British Museum, 1753–1781." *N&RRS* 33 (1979): 207–16.

Gunther, A. E. *The Founders of Science at the British Museum: 1753–1900*. Suffolk: The Halesworth Press, 1980.

Gunther, A. E. *Dr. Thomas Birch*. Suffolk: The Halesworth Press, 1984.

Gunther, R. T. *Early British Botanists*. Oxford: Oxford University Press, 1922.

Guthke, Karl S. *Haller und die Literatur*. Göttingen: Vandenhoeck & Ruprecht, 1962.

Habermas, Jürgen. *The Structural Transformation of the Public Sphere: An Inquiry into a Category of Bourgeois Society*. Cambridge: Polity, 1989 [1962].

Haller, Albrecht von. *Albrecht von Haller, 1708–1777*. Basel: Schweizerische Naturforschende Gesellschaft, 1977.

Halsband, Robert, ed. *The Letters of Lady Mary Wortley Montagu*. 3 vols. Oxford: Clarendon Press, 1967.

Hancock, D. *Citizens of the World: London Merchants and the Integration of the British Atlantic Community, 1735–1785.* Cambridge: Cambridge University Press, 1995.
Harris, Moses. *The Aurelian; or, Natural History of English Insects.* 1765.
Haycock, David Boyd. "'The Cabal of a Few Designing Members': The Presidency of Martin Folkes, FRS, and the Society's First Charter." *The Antiquaries Journal* 80 (2000): 273–84.
Haycock, David Boyd. *William Stukeley.* Woodbridge: Boydell, 2002.
Heilbron, J. L. *Electricity in the 17th and 18th Centuries: A Study of Early Modern Physics.* Berkeley: University of California Press, 1979.
Henrey, Blanche. *British Botanical and Horticultural Literature before 1800. . . .* 2 vols. Oxford: Oxford University Press, 1975.
Henrey, Blanche, *No Ordinary Gardener: Thomas Knowlton, 1691–1781.* British Museum for Natural History, 1986.
Henry, David. *An Essay on the Rationality of Brutes. With a Philosophical Comparison Between Dr. Codgill* [*JH*], *Inspector General of Town-Island. And Mango, the Great monkey* [*i.e., Christopher Smart*], *Director General. . . .* 1752.
"Hilario" [pseud]. "Libertine." *Magazine of Magazines.* 1751.
Hill, G. B. *Boswell's Life of Johnson, rev. and enlarged by L. F. Powell . . . in 6 vols.* Oxford: Clarendon Press, 1964. [1934–50].
Hill, Henrietta. *The Following Medicines have some years been in the first estimation for the cure of the several disorders for which they are recommended: they are the result of many years study of that great botanist Sir John Hill, D.M.* [Privately printed 1780].
Hill, Henrietta. *An Address to the Public: by the Hon'ble Lady Hill; Setting Forth the Consequences of the Late Sir John Hill's Acquaintance with the Earl of Bute.* N. p., 1788.
Hill, James. *The Grub-Street Journal.* Durham, NC: Duke University Press, 1928.
Hill, John. *An Answer to the . . . Lyes Advanc'd by Mr. John Rich, Harlequin.* John Clarke, 1740a.
Hill, John. *Orpheus: An English Opera.* John Clarke, 1740b.
Hill, John. *Remarks on Squire Ayre's Memoir of the Life of Mr. Pope.* M. Cooper, 1745.
Hill, John. [*The*] *British Magazine.* Charles Corbet, 1746a.
Hill, John. "A Letter Concerning the Matter of Seeding Mosses." *PT* 44 (1746): 60–66.
Hill, John. *Theophrastus's History of Stones.* C. Davis, 1746b.
Hill, John. "A Letter Concerning Windsor Loam." *PT* 44 (1746–47): 458–63.
Hill, John. *Compleat History of Drugs.* J & J Bonwicke, 1748a.
Hill, John. *A General Natural History. A History of Fossils.* T. Osborne, 1748b.
Hill, John. *The Actor: A Treatise on the Art of Playing.* R. Griffiths, 1750a.
Hill, John. *A Dissertation on Royal Societies.* John Doughty, 1750b.
Hill, John. *The History of Mr. Loveill, A Novel.* M. Cooper, 1750c.
Hill, John. *Lucina sine Concubitu. A Letter Humbly Address'd to the Royal Society.* M. Cooper, 1750d.
Hill, John. *A Treatise on the Plague and Pestilential Fevers.* T. Robinson, 1750e.
Hill, John. *Lucina sine concubitu. Del loix du concours. Lettre addressée a la Société Royale de Londres, . . . Traduite de l'Anglois d'Abraham Johnson.* Paris, 1750f.
Hill, John. *A letter to dr Abraham Johnson, on the subject of his new scheme for the propagation of the human species* [*in Lucina concubitu*]*: in which, the reflections that author has cast upon the Royal society of London, are answered. By a fellow* (*Richard Roe*). 1750g.
Hill, John. *The Adventures of Mr. George Edwards, A Creole. The Second Edition.* T. Osborne, 1751a.
Hill, John. *A General Natural History; Or, New and Accurate Descriptions of the Animals, Vegetables, and Minerals of the Different Parts of the World.* T. Osborne, 1751b.
Hill, John. *The History of a Woman of Quality; Or, The Adventures of Lady Frail.* M. Cooper & G. Woodfall, 1751c.
Hill, John. *A History of the Materia Medica.* T. Longman, 1751d.
Hill, John. *The Inspector . . . A Collection of [Fourteen] Essays.* R. Griffiths, Davis, Baker, Ward, 1751e.
Hill, John. *Memoirs of a Man of Pleasure.* T. Osborne, 1751f.
Hill, John. *The Oeconomy of Human Life. Part the Second.* M. Cooper, 1751g.

Hill, John. *A Review of the Works of the Royal Society of London*. R. Griffiths, 1751h. [2nd ed., Dodsley, 1780.]

Hill, John. *The Adventures of a Valet . . . Two Volumes*. T. Robinson, 1752a.

Hill, John. *Clio; Or a Secret History*. M. Cooper, 1752b.

Hill, John. *Essays in Natural History and Philosophy*. J. Whiston & B. White, P. Vaillant & L. Davis, 1752c.

Hill, John. *An History of Animals*. T. Osborne, 1752d.

Hill, John. *The Inspector's Rhapsody*. M. Cooper, 1752e.

Hill, John. *Letters from the Inspector to a Lady . . . a courtesan known as 'Diamond' . . . with the Genuine Answers*. M. Cooper, 1752f.

Hill, John. *Some Observations on the Writers of the Present Age, and Their Manner of Treating Each Other*. M. Sheepy, M. Cooper, & G. Woodfall, 1752g.

Hill, John. *The Conduct of a Married Life*. R. Baldwin, 1753a.

Hill, John. *The Inspector . . . in Two Volumes*. R. Griffiths, J. Whiston, B. White, S. Baker, W. Shropshire, L. Davis, J. Ward, 1753b.

Hill, John. *Letters from Several Parts of Europe, and the East, Written in the Year 1750*. R. Griffiths, 1753c.

Hill, John. *Observations on the Greek and Roman Classics*. Dan Browne, J. Whiston & B. White, S. Baker, Lockyer Davis, 1753d.

Hill, John. *The Smartiad*. D. Job, 1753e.

Hill, John. *The Story of Elizabeth Canning Considered . . .* M. Cooper, 1753f.

Hill, John. *The Gardener's Pocket-Book; or, Country Gentleman's Recreation*. W. Owen, 1754a.

Hill, John. *The Maiden Whim; Or, The Critical Minute, A Farce*. n. p., 1754b.

Hill, John. *On the Management and Education of Children*. R. Baldwin, 1754c.

Hill, John. *Urania; Or, a Compleat View of the Heavens*. T. Gardner, 1754d.

Hill, John. *The Useful Family Herbal*. W. Owen, 1754e.

Hill, John. *The Actor: A Treatise on the Art of Playing*. R. Griffiths, 1755a.

Hill, John. *Thoughts Concerning God and Nature, in answer to Lord Bolingbroke's philosophy*. "Printed for the Author," 1755b.

Hill, John. *The British Herbal; An History of Plants and Trees, Natives of Britain, Cultivated for Use, or Raised for Beauty*. T. Osborne & J. Shipton, 1756a.

Hill, John. *The Compleat Body of Husbandry*. T. Osborne & J. Shipton, 1756b.

Hill, John. *The Naval History of Britain . . . To the Conclusion of the Year 1756*. T. Osborne & J. Shipton, 1756c.

Hill, John. *Eden, Or a Compleat Body of Gardening*. T. Osborne, T. Trye, S. Crowder, H. Woodgate, 1757a.

Hill, John. *The Sleep of Plants and Cause of Motion in the Sensitive Plant*. R. Baldwin, 1757b.

Hill, John. *An Account of a Stone, in the Possession of the . . . Earl of Stafford, Which on Being Watered Produces Excellent Mushrooms*. R. Baldwin, 1758a.

Hill, John. *The Book of Nature; Or the History of Insects*. R. Baldwin, 1758b.

Hill, John. *The Conduct of a Noble Commander in America*. R. Baldwin, 1758c.

Hill, John. *The Construction of the Nerves and Causes of Nervous Disorders*. R. Baldwin, 1758d.

Hill, John. *The Fabrick of the Eye*. J. Waugh & M. Cooper, 1758e.

Hill, John. *The Gardener's New Kalendar*. T. Osborne, 1758f.

Hill, John. *An Idea of a Botanical Garden in England*. R. Baldwin, 1758g.

Hill, John. *The Management of the Gout by a physician in his own case with the virtues of an English plant, Bardana*. R. Baldwin, 1758h. [reissued in 1771]

Hill, John. *A Method of Producing Double Flowers from Single By a Regular Course of Culture*. R. Baldwin, 1758i.

Hill, John. *The Old Man's Guide to Health and Longer Life*. M. Cooper & J. Jackson, 1758j.

Hill, John. *Outlines of a System of Vegetable Generation*. R. Baldwin, 1758k.

Hill, John. *The Rout; A Farce of Two Acts*. M. Cooper & J. Jackson, 1758l.

Hill, John. *The Virtues of Wild Valerian in Nervous Disorders*. R. Baldwin, 1758m.

Hill, John. *The Management of the Gout with the virtues of the Burdock Root*. 6th ed. R. Baldwin, 1758n.
Hill, John. *Exotic Botany Illustrated*. "For the Author." 1759a.
Hill, John. *Observations on the Account Given of the Catalogue of the Royal and Noble Authors of England*. H. Woodgate & S. Brooks, 1759b.
Hill, John. *Of the Origin and Production of Proliferous Flowers*. R. Baldwin & J. Jackson, 1759c.
Hill, John. *Practice of Gardening, Explained to All Capacities*. R. Baldwin. 1759d.
Hill, John. *To David Garrick, Esq; The Petition of I. In Behalf of Herself and her Sisters*. M. Cooper. 1759e.
Hill, John. *The Usefulness of a Knowledge of Plants*. R. Baldwin & J. Jackson. 1759f.
Hill, John. *The Vegetable System; Or, a series of experiments and observations tending to explain the internal structure, and the life of plants . . . including a new anatomy of plants. in Twenty-Six volumes*. "Printed at the Expence of the Author, and sold by R. Baldwin." 1759g. [1759–1775]
Hill, John. *The Virtues of Honey in Preventing Many of the Worst Disorders*. M. Cooper, 1759h.
Hill, John. *Flora Britannica. Sive Synopsis Methodica Stirpium Britanicarium . . . C. Linnaei Methodum Disposita*. J. Waugh, 1760a.
Hill, John. *Hillii Enucleata Observatio Microscopica Decima et Sexta*. Petrópolis, 1760b.
Hill, John. "Life of Laurence Sterne." *Royal Female Magazine* 2 (April 1760c): 53–60.
Hill, John. *Cautions Against the Immoderate Use of Snuff, Founded on the Known Qualities of the Tobacco Plant*. R. Baldwin & J. Jackson, 1761a.
Hill, John. *Some Projects Recommended to the Society for the Encouragement of Arts, Manufactures, and Commerce . . .* Stevens, 1761b.
Hill, John. *Botanical Tracts. By Dr. Hill*. R. Baldwin, 1762.
Hill, John. *On the Virtues of Sage, in Lengthening Human Life. With Rules to Attain Old Age*. "For the Author & sold by R. Baldwin & J. Ridley," 1764.
Hill, John. *Centaury, The Great Stomachic, in Preference to all other Bitters, in that it gives Appetite and Digestion*. R. Baldwin, 1765a.
Hill, John. *The Power of Water Dock against the Scurvy*. R. Baldwin, 1765b.
Hill, John. *Hypochondriasis. A Practical Treatise on the nature and cure of that disorder*. R. Baldwin, 1766a.
Hill, John. *Trees, Shrubs, and Plants, Cultivated in Britain*. Printed for the Author in Arlington Street, 1766b.
Hill, John. *Hortus Kewensis: . . . Exoticas . . . Rariores . . . Apud Kew Cultas*. R. Baldwin, 1768a.
Hill, John. *A Method of Curing Jaundice*. R. Baldwin, 1768b.
Hill, John. *A New Astronomical Dictionary, Or, A Compleat View of the Heavens . . .* T. Gardner, 1768c.
Hill, John. *Polypody. The Ancient Doctrine of the Virtues of that Herb*. R. Baldwin, 1768d.
Hill, John.. *The Family Practice of Physic*. R. Baldwin, J. Ridley, J. Campbell, J. Tilly, 1769a.
Hill, John. *Herbarium Britannicum Exhibens Plantas Britanniae Indigenas . . . Two Volumes*. R. Baldwin, J. Ridley, Nourse, Becket, Davies, Campbell, Elmsly, 1769b.
Hill, John. *The Construction of Timber, from its Early Growth*. R. Baldwin, 1770a.
Hill, John. *The Twelve Letters of Canana; on the Impropriety of Petitioning the King to Dissolve the Parliament*. R. Davis, 1770b.
Hill, John. *Virtues of British Herbs*. R. Baldwin, 1770c.
Hill, John. *Cautions against the Use of Violent Medicines in Fevers*. E. and C. Dilly, 1771a.
Hill, John. *Fossils Arranged According to their Obvious Characters*. R. Baldwin, 1771b.
Hill, John. *The Management of the Gout. The Eighth Edition*. R. Baldwin, 1771c.
Hill, John. *Sparogenesia: Or the Origin and Nature of Spar*. P. Elmsly, 1772.
Hill, John. *A Decade of Curious Insects . . . Trees and Plants*. B. White, P. Elmsly, Parker, Baldwin, Ridley & J. Balfour, 1773a.
Hill, John. *Plain and Useful Directions for those who are Afflicted with Cancers*. R. Baldwin, 1773b.
Hill, John. *Twenty-Five New Plants, Rais'd in the Royal Garden at Kew: Their History and Figures*. M. Cooper, 1773c.

Hill, John. *Horti Malabaraci Pars Prima . . . Nunc Primum Classicum, Generum, et Speciarum Characteres Linnaeanas, Synonyma Authorum*. J. Nourse, 1774a.

Hill, John. *Observations on the New-discovered Swedish Acid: and on the Stone from which it is Extracted. . . .* R. Baldwin, 1774b.

Hill, John. *Circumstances which Preceded the Letters to the Earl of* [*Mexborough*]; *And May Tend to a Discovery of the Author*. T. Evans, 1775a.

Hill, John. *Enquiries into the Nature of a New Mineral Acid Discovered in Sweden . . . Two Parts*. T. Trueman. 1775b.

Hill, T. G. "John Hill." In *Makers of British Botany*, edited by F. W. Oliver. Cambridge: Cambridge University Press, 1913.

Hill, Theophilus. *Stoic Philosophy; Or, the Praise of Poverty. A Poem*. 1720.

Hill, Theophilus. "Will of Theophilus Hill, Rector of Hedgerley, Buckinghamshire, 1746." Buckinghamshire County Record Office, Aylesbury, 1746. Box DA We 81, no. 68.

Hillhouse, James T. *The Grub-Street Journal*. Durham: Duke University Press, 1928.

Hogarth, William. *Anecdotes of William Hogarth, Written by Himself, with Essays on his Life and Genius*. J. B. Nichols and Son, 1833.

Holbrook, S. H. *The Golden Age of Quackery*. New York: Macmillan, 1959.

Holmes, Su, ed., *Framing Celebrity: New Firections in Celebrity Culture*. Routledge, 2006.

Hudson, William. *Flora Anglica*. 1762.

Hudson, William. *Flora Anglica, Exhibens Plantas per Regnum Angliae Sponte Crescentes* . . . 1798.

Huet, Mari. *Monstrous Imagination*. Cambridge MA: Harvard University Press, 1993.

Hutcheson, Francis. *An Inquiry into the Original of our Ideas of Beauty and Virtue*. 1726.

Jardine, Nicholas, James A. Secord, E. Spary, eds. *Cultures of Natural History*. Cambridge: Cambridge University Press, 1996.

Jeffers, Robert H. "Richard Pulteney, M.D., F.R.S. (1730–1801) and his Correspondents." *Proceedings of the Linnaean Society* 87 (October 1959): 15–26.

Jensen, G. E. *The Covent Garden Journal. By Sir Alexander Drawcansir, Knt. Censor of Great Britain*. Edited by Henry Fielding. 2 vols. New Haven: Yale University Press, 1915.

[Johnson, Samuel]. *Samuel Johnson's Celebrated Letter to the Earl of Chesterfield and his Interview with King George III as published in 1790 by James Boswell*. Buffalo, NY: n. p., 1927.

Johnson, Samuel. *The Yale Edition of the Works of Samuel Johnson. 18 volumes*. New Haven: Yale University Press, 1958–1995.

Johnstone, Charles. *Chrysal, Or the Adventures of a Guinea*. 1760.

Jones, Henry. *An Epistle to the Right Honourable the Earl of Orrery*, 1751.

Jones, Henry. *Kew Garden. A Poem in Two Cantos*. 1767.

Jones, W. P. *Thomas Gray, Scholar: the True Tragedy of an Eighteenth-Century Gentleman*. Cambridge: Harvard University Press, 1937.

Jordanova, Ludmilla. *Nature Displayed: Gender, Science and Medicine, 1760–1820*. Longman, 1999.

Kahan, Jeffrey. *Bettymania and the Birth of Celebrity*. Bethlehem: Lehigh University Press, 2010.

Kennedy, [Dr] John. *Whipping rods, for trifling, scurrhill, scriblers; as Mr. F-t on Taste, Spectorhill his late Pamphlet and Papers: his Theophrastus on Stones or Gems, with other of his principal Performances . . . with Other of his Principal Performances*. Mary Cooper, 1752.

Kenny, Robert W. "James Ralph: An Eighteenth-Century Philadelphian in Grub Street." *Pennsylvania Magazine of History and Biography* 44 (1940): 218–42.

Kenrick, William. *The Grand Question Debated; Or, Being an Essay to Prove that the Soul of Man is Not . . . Immortal*. 1751a.

Kenrick, William. *A Reply to the Grand Question Debated; Fully Proving, that the Soul of Man is, and Must be, Immortal. . . .* 1751b.

Kenrick, William. *Fun: A Parodi-tragi-comical Satire. As it was . . . but Suppressed. . . .* 1752.

Kenrick, William. *The Pasquinade, with Notes Variorum*. 1753.

Kenrick, William. *A Scrutiny; Or the Critics Criticis'd*. 1759.

Kinch, M. P. "The Meteoric Career of William Young, Jr. (1742–1785)." *Pennsylvania Magazine of History and Biography* 110: 3 (1986): 359–388.

Kittredge, Katharine. *Lewd & Notorious: Female Transgression in the Eighteenth Century*. Ann Arbor: University of Michigan Press, 2003.
Knapp, Lewis. "Ralph Griffiths, Author and Publisher, 1746–1750." *The Library* 24 (1939): 197–213.
Knapp, Lewis. *Tobias Smollett*. Princeton: Princeton University Press, 1949.
Knapp, Lewis. *The Letters of Tobias Smollett*. Oxford: Oxford University Press, 1974.
Knapp, Mary E. *Checklist of Verse by David Garrick*. Charlottesville: University of Virginia Press, 1955.
Knight, Gowin. *Two Simple Active Principles, Attraction and Repulsion*, 1748.
Koerner, Lisbet. *Linnaeus*. Cambridge, MA: Harvard University Press, 1999.
Kuhn, Thomas S. *The Structure of Scientific Revolutions*. Chicago: University of Chicago Press. 1970.
[The] Ladies Magazine. 1760–1762.
Lamont, Peter. *The First Psychic: The Peculiar Mystery of a Notorious Victorian Wizard*. Abacus, 2006.
Laqueur, Thomas. "Orgasm, Generation, and the Politics of Reproductive Biology." In *The Making of the Modern Body: Sexuality and Society in the Nineteenth Century*, 1–42, edited by Catherine Gallagher and Thomas Laqueur. Berkeley: University of California Press, 1987.
Laqueur, Thomas. *Making Sex: Body and Gender from the Greeks to Freud*. Cambridge MA: Harvard University Press, 1990.
Larson, James L. *Reason and Experience: The Representation of Natural Order in the World of Carl von Linné*. Berkeley: University of California Press, 1971.
La Solle, Henri Francois de. *Memoirs of a Man of Pleasure, or the Adventures of Versorand*. 2 vols. 1751.
La Solle, Henri Francois de. *Anecdotes de la cour de Bonhommie*. Paris, 1752.
Laudan, Rachel. *From Mineralogy to Geology: The Foundations of a Science*. Chicago: University of Chicago Press, 1987.
Laundon, J. R. "The Date of Birth of Sir John Hill (1714–1775)." *Archives of Natural History* 10 (1981): 65–66.
Leask, Nigel. *Curiosity and the Aesthetics of Travel Writing, 1770–1840: "From an Antique Land."* Oxford: Oxford University Press, 2002.
Lemay, J. A. Leo, and G. S. Rousseau. *The Renaissance Man in the Eighteenth Century*. Los Angeles: Williams Andrew Clark Memorial Library, 1978.
Lennox, Charles H. G. *A Duke and His Friends: The Life and Letters of the Second Duke of Richmond*. Hutchinson, 1911.
Levine, Joseph M. *Dr. Woodward's Shield: History, Science, and Satire in Augustan England*. Berkeley: University of California Press, 1977.
Lewis, W. S., ed., *Correspondence of Horace Walpole*. 50 vols. New Haven: Yale University Press, 1937–1984.
Liguori, Alphonsus de. *The Glories of Mary*. N. p., 1750.
Lillywhite, Brian. *London Coffee Houses: A Reference Book. . . .* G. Allen and Unwin, 1963.
Lind, James. *Essay on the most effectual means of preserving the health of seamen*. 1762.
Linnaeus, Carolus. *Systema Naturae, sive Regna Tria Naturae Systematicae Proposita Per Classes, Ordines, Genera, and Species*. 1735.
Linnaeus, Carolus. *Materia Medica per Regna Tria Naturae . . . Vires usus Composita Digesta*. 1773.
Linnaeus, Carolus. *Praeludia Sponsaliorum Plantarum*. 1729.
Linnaeus, Carolus. *Species Plantarum, A Facsimile of the First Edition 1753. With an introduction by W. T. Stearn*. Dorking: The Ray Society, 1957 [1753].
L'isle de Rome, J. B. L. *Essais de Cristallographie*. Paris, 1772.
Little, D. M., and G. M. Kahrl, eds. *The Letters of David Garrick*. 3 vols. Cambridge, MA: Belknap Press, 1963.
Lloyd, Evan. *The Powers of the Pen, a poem*. 1766.
Lloyd's Evening Post. 1757–1805.
London Evening Post. 1741–1778.
Longden, H. I. *Northamptonshire and Rutland Clergy 1500–1932*. 16 vols. Northampton: Archer, 1938–1952.

Lovat-Fraser, J. A. *John Stuart, Earl of Bute*. Cambridge: Cambridge University Press, 1912.
Lyons, Henry. *The Royal Society, 1660–1940*. Cambridge: Cambridge University Press, 1944.
Lysons, Daniel. *The Environs of London* . . . 4 vols. 1792–1796.
Lytle, Guy F., and Stephen Orgel. *Patronage in the Renaissance*. Princeton: Princeton University Press, 1981.
MacGregor, A. *Sir Hans Sloane: Collector, Scientist, Antiquary, Founding Father of the British Museum*. British Museum Press, 1994.
MacKay, Charles. *Some Extraordinary Popular Delusions*. Harmondsworth: Penguin, 2010.
MacKenzie, James. *History of Health*. 1758.
MacSwiny, Owen. *The Quacks: Or, Love's the Physician. A Farce*. 1745.
Mahony, Robert, and Betty Rizzo, eds. *Christopher Smart: An Annotated Bibliography, 1743–1983*. New York: Garland, 1984.
Mahony, Robert, and Betty Rizzo, eds. *The Annotated Letters of Christopher Smart*. Carbondale, IL: Southern Illinois University Press, 1991.
Mann, Abbé. "The Life of John Turberville Needham." *Mémoires de l'Académie de Bruxelles. Volume 4*. Bruxelles, 1783.
Marten, John. *Gonosologium novum: or, a new system of all the secret infirm and diseases, natural, accidental, and venereal in men and women. . . .*1709.
Martin, Benjamin. *New Elements of Optics; Or, the Theory of the Aberration. . . .* 1759.
Martyn, Thomas. *The Language of Botany*. 1793.
Mason, Simon. *Practical Observations in Physick wherein is exhibited the ætiology, or the rise and nature of the most prevalent distempers, with a plain, rational and concise method of treating them. . . . By the late Simon Mason, apothecary*. 1757.
Mason, William Hayley. *Goodwood; Its House, Park, and Grounds . . . With Six Illustrations*. 1839.
McCann, Timothy J. *The Correspondence of the Dukes of Richmond and Newcastle 1724–1750*. Chichester: The Sussex Record Society, 1984.
McClellan III, James E. *Science Reorganized: Scientific Societies in the Eighteenth Century*. New York: Columbia University Press. 1985.
Mcdayter, Ghislaine. *Byromania and the Birth of Celebrity Culture*. Albany: SUNY Press. 2009.
McDowell, Paula. *The Women of Grub Street*. Oxford: Clarendon Press. 1998.
McKelvey, James Lee. *George III and Lord Bute: The Leicester House Years*. Durham, NC: Duke University Press. 1973.
McKendrick, Neil, John Brewer, and J. H. Plumb, eds. *The Birth of a Consumer Society: The Commercialization of Eighteenth-Century England*. Europa Publishing, 1982.
McLaren, Angus. "The Pleasures of Procreation: Traditional and Biomedical Theories of Conception." In *William Hunter and the Eighteenth-Century Medical World*, edited by W. F. Bynum et al., 127–43. Cambridge: Cambridge University Press, 1985.
McLean, Elizabeth. "A Preliminary Report on the 18th Century Herbarium of Robert James, Eighth Baron Petre." *Bartonia* 50 (1984): 36–39.
Merton, Robert K. *Science, Technology & Society in Seventeenth-Century England*. New York: Harper & Row, 1970.
Midgley, Graham. *Life of Orator Henley*. Oxford: Clarendon Press, 1973.
Milburn, J. R. *Adams of Fleet Street, Instrument Makers to King George III*. Aldershot: Ashgate, 2000.
Miller, D. P. "'My Favourite Studdys [sic]': Lord Bute as Botanist and Scientific Collector." In *Lord Bute: Essays in Reinterpretation*, edited by Karl W. Schweizer, 213–39. Leicester: Leicester University Press, 1988.
Miller, D. P. "'Into the Valley of Darkness': Reflections on the Royal Society in the Eighteenth Century." *History of Science* 27 (1989): 155–166.
Miller, D. P. "The Usefulness of Natural Philosophy: The Royal Society and the Culture of Practical Utility in the Later Eighteenth Century." *British Journal for the History of Science* 32 (1999): 185–201.
Miller, D. P. "Everyone Hates a Know-all" [Review of Andrew Robinson, *The Last Man who Knew Everything*]." *Nature* 441 (2000): 409.

Miller, D. P., and P. H. Reill, eds. *Visions of Empire: Voyages, Botany, and Representations of Nature.* Cambridge: Cambridge University Press, 1996.

Miller, H. K. "Henry Fielding's Satire on the Royal Society." *Studies in Philology* 57 (1960): 72–86.

Miller, Vincent. *The Man-Plant: or, Scheme for increasing and improving the British Breed.* 1752.

Mole, Timothy, ed. *Romanticism and Celebrity Culture, 1750–1850.* Cambridge: Cambridge University Press, 2009.

Monsey, Messenger. *Life and Eccentricities of the late Messenger Monsey FRS.* 1804.

Moore, Judith. *The Appearance of Truth: The Story of Elizabeth Canning and Eighteenth-Century Narrative.* London: Associated University Presses, 1994.

Moore, William. *The Gentleman's Society of Spalding; its Origin and Progress.* Spalding: Spalding Gentleman's Society, 1851.

Moss, Norman. *The Pleasures of Deception.* Chatto & Windus, 1977.

Mounsey, Christopher. *Christopher Smart: Clown of God.* Lewisburg, PA: Bucknell University Press, 2001.

Murphy, Arthur. *Sine conflictu.* 1753.

Murphy, Arthur, ed. *The Gray's Inn Journal.* 1754.

Murphy, Arthur. *The Triple Revenge.* 1756.

Murphy, Arthur. *The Theatre.* 1758.

Murphy, Arthur. *What we Must All Come To.* 1764.

Murray, Frances. *Memoirs of the Celebrated Miss Fanny M[urray].* 2 vols. 1759.

Nangle, Benjamin C. *Monthly Review . . . Indexes of Contributors and Articles.* Oxford: Clarendon Press, 1934.

Needham, John Turberville. "A Summary of Some Late Observations upon the generation, composition, and decomposition of animal and vegetable substances." *PT* 45 (1748): 615–666.

Needham, John Turberville. *Nouvelles observations microscopiques.* Paris, 1750.

Needham, John Turberville. *Observations upon the generation, composition and decomposition of animal and vegetable substances.* 1749.

Nelson, E. C. "Patrick Browne and the Flowers of Mayo: A Biographical Essay." In *The Flowers of Mayo: Dr. Patrick Browne's Fasciculus plantarum Hiberniae, 1788,* edited by E. C. Nelson, 1–27. Dublin, 1995.

Nelson, E. C. "Patrick Browne's *The Civil and Natural History of Jamaica* (1756, 1789)," *Archives of Natural History* 24 (1997): 327–36.

New, Melvyn, and Peter de Voogd, eds. *The Florida Edition of the Works of Laurence Sterne, Volumes 7–8: The Letters.* Gainesville: University of Florida Press, 2009.

Newman, Jeremiah Whitaker. *An Essay on the principles and manners of the medical profession.* 1783.

Newman, Jeremiah Whitaker. *The Lounger's Common-Place Book.* 4 vols. 1799.

Nickelsen, Kären. *Draughtsmen, Botanists and Nature: The Construction of Eighteenth–Century Botanical Illustrations.* Amsterdam: Rodopi, 2006.

Nicolson, Harold. *The Development of English Biography.* Hogarth Press, 1927.

Nussbaum, Felicity. *Rival Queens.* Philadelphia: University of Pennsylvania, 2010.

Oliver, F. W. *Makers of British Botany.* Cambridge: Cambridge University Press, 1913.

Olson, Alison G. *The Radical Duke: Charles Lennox, Third Duke of Richmond.* Oxford: Oxford University Press, 1961.

Orrery, Countess of Cork. *The Orrery Papers.* 2 vols. Duckworth, 1903.

Owen, J. B. *The Rise of the Pelhams.* Methuen, 1957.

Parsons, James. *A Mechanical and Critical Enquiry into the Nature of Hermaphrodites.* 1741.

Parsons, James. *The Microscopical Theatre of Seeds . . .* M. Cooper, 1745.

Parsons, James. *Human physiognomy explained: The Croonian Lectures 1744–1746.* 1747.

Parsons, James. "A Letter to the President Concerning the Hermaphrodite Shewn in London." *PT* 47 (1751–1752): 141–46.

Partridge, Simon [pseudo.]. *A Letter to Henry Woodward . . . Occasioned by his Letter to the Inspector.* Mary Cooper, 1752.

Paulli, Simon. *A Treatise on Tobacco. . . .* 1746.

Paulson, Ronald. *Hogarth's Works*. 2 vols. New Haven: Yale University Press, 1965.

Peltonen, Markku. *The Duel*. Cambridge: Cambridge University Press, 2007.

Percival, Thomas. *Essays medical and experimental*. 1767.

[Peterborough]. "Peterborough Baptisms, Marriages, Burials 1658–1726." MSS in Northampton Record Office.

Phillips, Hugh. *Mid-Georgian London*. Collins, 1964.

Pinkus, Philip. *Grub Street Stripped Bare: The Scandalous Lives . . .* Constable, 1968.

Plomer, Henry. *A Dictionary of the Printers and Booksellers . . . from 1668 to 1725*. Oxford: Oxford University Press, 1922.

Poelnitz, Carl Ludwig von. *The Memoirs of the . . . Baron Poelnitz*. 3rd ed. 5 vols. 1745.

Pomet, Pierre. *A Compleat History of Drugs . . . and Their Use in Physic, Chemistry, Pharmacy*. 1737.

Porter, Roy, and Kate Poulton. "Geology in Britain, 1660–1800." *Journal of the Society for the Bibliography of Natural History* 9 (1978): 74–84.

Porter, Roy. *The Making of Geology: Earth's Science in Britain, 1660–1815*. Cambridge: Cambridge University Press, 1977.

Porter, Roy. "John Woodward: A Droll Sort of Philosopher." *Geological Magazine* 116 (1979): 335–43.

Porter, Roy. *Quacks: Fakers & Charlatans in English Medicine*. Stroud: Tempus, 2000.

Porter, Roy, and Dorothy Porter. *In Sickness and in Health: The English Experience, 1650–1850*. Fourth Estate, 1988.

Porter, Roy and George Rousseau. *Gout: The Patrician Malady*. New Haven: Yale University Press, 1998.

Potter, G. R. "Mr. Hill, Eminent Scientist, and His Theory of Tittlebats." *Philological Quarterly* 2 (1923): 48–54.

Potter, G. R. "John Hill's *'Review.'*" *California University Publications in English* 14 (1943): 157–80.

Pulteney, Richard. *Historical and Biographical Sketches of the Progress of Botany in England*. 2 vols. 1790.

Pulteney, Richard. *A General View of the Writings of Linnaeus* . . . 1805.

Ralph, James. *The Case of Authors by Profession or Trade*. 1758.

Ransom, Harry. "The Rewards of Authorship in the Eighteenth Century." *University of Texas Studies in English* 7 (1938): 47–66.

Rappaport, Rhoda. *When Geologists Were Historians, 1665–1750*. Ithaca: Cornell University Press, 1997.

Ratcliff, Marc. *The Quest for the Invisible: Microscopy in the Enlightenment*. Aldershot: Ashgate, 2009.

Raven, C. E. *English Naturalists from Neckham to Ray*. Cambridge: Cambridge University Press, 1946.

Raven, C. E. *John Ray, Naturalist: His Life and Works*. 2nd ed. Cambridge: Cambridge University Press, 1986.

Raven, James. *The English Novel 1770–1829: A Bibliographical Survey of Prose Fiction Published in the British Isles*. Oxford: Oxford University Press, 2000.

Raven, James. *The Business of Books: Booksellers and the English Booktrade, 1450–1850*. New Haven: Yale University Press, 2007.

Réaumur, Rene Antoine. *Art of Hatching and Bringing up Domestick Fowls. . . .* 1750.

Redmond, D. E. "Tobacco and Cancer: The First Clinical Report [by John Hill], 1761." *New England Journal of Medicine* 282 (1970): 18.

"Register of Burials in Woolen . . . in Northampton Record Office from 1678 to 1726." MSS in Northampton Record Office.

Reveal, J. L. "Two Previously Unnoticed Sources of Generic Names Published by John Hill in 1753 and 1754–1755." *Bulletin of the Museum of Natural History* 4th Series 13 (1991): 197–239.

Rich, John. *Mr. Rich's Answer to the Many Falsities and Calumnies Advanced by Mr. John Hill, Apothecary, and Contained in the Preface to Orpheus, An English Opera*. 1739.

Riskin, Jessica. *Science in the Age of Sensibility: The Sentimental Empiricists of the French Enlightment*. Chicago: University of Chicago Press, 2002.

Rizzo, Betty. "Authorship in Transition: Christopher Smart and the Paper War(s) of 1752–1753." In *Christopher Smart and the Enlightenment*, edited by Clement Hawes, 122–35. New York: St. Martin's Press, 1999.

Roach, Joseph. *The Player's Passion: Studies in the Science of Acting*. Ann Arbor: Michigan University Press, 1993.

Robson, James. *A Catalogue of a very fine collection of Books, containing the elegant and very valuable library of a person of . . . the late George Edwards*. 1773.

Rock, Richard. *Tincture for curing the teeth*. 1740.

Roger, Jacques. *The Life Sciences in Eighteenth-Century French Thought*. Edited by Keith R. Benson. Stanford: Stanford University Press, 1997.

Rogers, Pat. *Grub Street: Studies in a Subculture*. Methuen, 1972.

Rogers, Pat et al., ed. *Edmund Curll, Bookseller*. Oxford: Clarendon Press, 2007.

Rosenfeld, Sybil. *Theatre of the London Fairs*. Cambridge: Cambridge University Press, 1960.

Roth, Cecil. *Essays and Portraits in Anglo-Jewish History*. Philadelphia: Jewish Publication Society of America, 1962.

Roth, Suzanne. *Adventure et adventuriers au dix-huitième siècle*. Lille: Université de Lille, 1980.

Rousseau, G. S. "The London Earthquakes of 1750." *Cahiers de Histoire Mondiale* 11:3 (1968): 436–54.

Rousseau, G. S. "The Much Malign'd Dr. Hill." *Journal of the American Medical Association* 212 (1970): 103–108.

Rousseau, G. S. "Smollett's *Memoirs of Lady Vane* and Hill's *History of a Woman of Quality*." *Notes & Queries* 217 (October 1972): 375–78.

Rousseau, G. S. "A Short Biographical Account of Dr. John Hill." In *Proceedings of the 24th International Congress of the History of Medicine*, 5 vols. II: 367–375. Semmelweis: Budapest, 1974.

Rousseau, G. S. *The Letters and Papers of Sir John Hill*. New York: AMS, 1982a.

Rousseau, G. S. "Science Books and their Readers in the Eighteenth Century." In *Books and their Readers in Eighteenth-Century England*, edited by I. Rivers, 197–255. Leicester: Leicester University Press, 1982b.

Rousseau, G. S. *Tobias Smollett: Essays of Two Decades*. Edinburgh: Clark, 1982c.

Rousseau, G. S. "Six New Hill Letters." *Medical History* 28 (1984): 293–302.

Rousseau, G. S. "Seven New Hill Letters." *Etudes Anglaises* 39 (1986a): 174–87.

Rousseau, G. S. "Madame Chimpanzee." *Papers of the Williams Andrews Clark Library*. Los Angeles: Clark Library Papers, 10 (1986b): 1–7.

Rousseau, G. S. "Pope and the Tradition in Modern Humanistic Education: 'In the Pale of Words till Death.'" In *The Enduring Legacy: Alexander Pope Bicentenary Essays*, edited by G. S. Rousseau and Pat Rogers, 199–240. Cambridge: Cambridge University Press, 1988.

Rousseau, G. S. "'Stung into Action . . . ': Medicine, Professionalism, and the News." *Prose Studies: History, Theory, Criticism, A Special Issue on News, Newspapers and Society in Early Modern Britain* 21:2 (August 1998a): 176–205.

Rousseau, G. S. "War and Peace: Some Representations of Nostalgia and Adventure in the Eighteenth Century." In *Guerres et Paix: La Grande Bretagne au xviiie siecle*, edited by Paul-Gabriel Boucé, 121–40. Paris: Presses de la Sorbonne Nouvelle, 1998b.

Rousseau, G. S. "'While Excoriating Fanaticism and Superstition': An Eighteenth-Century Case in the Law—Henry Fielding and John Hill among the Gypsies." In *Foi, croyances, superstitions dans l'Europe des Lumières: Le Spectateur Européen*, edited by C. Prunier, 161–86. Montpellier: Centre de Recherche sur l'Europe, 2001.

Rousseau, G. S. *Nervous Acts: Essays on Literature, Culture, and Sensibility*. Basingstoke: Palgrave Macmillan, 2004.

Rousseau, G. S. "Curiosity and the *Lusus Naturae*: Proteus Hill." In *Curiosity and Wonder from the Renaissance to the Enlightenment*, edited by Robert Evans and Alex Marr, 213–254. Aldershot: Ashgate, 2006.

Rousseau, G. S. "Panspermist Jokes, Reproductive Technologies, and Virgin Births: *Luciniades* of the Enlightenment." In *A Cultural History of the Human Body in the Enlightenment*, edited by Carol Reeve and Tim Hitchcock, 53–71. Oxford: Berg, 2010.

Rousseau, G. S., and David Haycock. "Voices Calling for Reform: The Royal Society in the Mid-Eighteenth Century—Martin Folkes, John Hill, and William Stukeley." *History of Science* 37 (1999): 1–30.

Rousseau, G. S., and David Haycock. "The Jew of Crane Court: Emanuel Mendes da Costa (1717–1791), Natural History and Natural Excess." *History of Science* 38 (2000): 127–70.

Rousseau, G. S., and Roy Porter, eds. *The Ferment of Knowledge: Studies in the Historiography of Eighteenth-Century Science*. Cambridge: Cambridge University Press, 1980.

Russel, George. *The Adventures of a Goose Quill*. Mary Cooper, 1752.

Saint-Albine, Remono de. *Le Comedien*. Paris, 1747.

St. John, Henry [Lord Bolingbroke]. *Letters on the Study and Use of History*. 2 vols. 1752.

Sbiroli, Lynn. *Libertine O Madre Illibate*. Venice: Marcilio, 1989.

Schiebinger, Londa. "Gender and Natural History." In *Cultures of Natural History*, edited by Nicholas Jardine, 163–77. Cambridge: Cambridge University Press, 1996A.

Schiebinger, Londa. "The Loves of the Plants." *Scientific America* (February 1996b): 100–4.

Schiebinger, Londa. *Plants and Empire: Colonial Bioprospecting in the Atlantic World*. Cambridge: Harvard University Press, 2004.

Schneller, Beverly. "Using Newspaper Advertisement to Study the Book Trade: A Year in the Life of Mary Cooper." In *Writers, Books, and Trade: An Eighteenth-Century English Miscellany*, edited by O. M. Brack, 123–43. New York: AMS, 1994.

Schomberg, Ralph. *Iatrorhapsodia: or, A Physical Rhapsody*. 1751.

Schutz, John A. *Thomas Pownall. British Defender of American Liberty: A Study of Anglo-American Relations in the Eighteenth Century*. Glendale, CA: A. H. Clark Co., 1951.

Scott, William. "Smollett, Dr. John Hill, and the Failure of *Peregrine Pickle*." *Notes & Queries* 200 (1955): 389–92.

Schweizer, K. W., ed. *Lord Bute: Essays in Re-interpretation*. Leicester: Leicester University Press, 1988.

Secondat, Jean-Baptiste de. *Observations sur les Fossiles* . . . Bordeaux, 1745.

Secondat, Jean-Baptiste de. *Observations de Physique et d'Histoire Naturelle*. Bordeaux, 1750.

Sherbo, Arthur. "Survival in Grub-Street: Another Essay in Attribution." *Bulletin of the New York Public Library* 64 (1960): 147–58.

Sherbo, Arthur. *Christopher Smart, Scholar of the University*. Ann Arbor: Michigan State University Press, 1967.

Shipman, Pat. *Femme Fatale: A Biography of Mata Hari*. Weidenfeld & Nicolson, 2007.

Short, Thomas. *Discourses on Tea . . . Tobacco*. 1750.

Shteir, Ann. *Cultivating Women, Cultivating Science: Flora's Daughters and Botany in England, 1760–1860*. Baltimore: Johns Hopkins University Press, 1996.

Siegerist, Henry E. "Albrecht von Haller's Briefe on Johannes Gesner 1728–1777." *Abhandlungen der Koeniglichen Gesellschaft der wissenschaften zu Goettingen* 11 (1923): 1–574.

Silvette, Herbert. *The Doctor on the Stage: Medicine and Medical Men in Seventeenth-Century England*. Knoxville: University of Tennessee Press, 1967.

Smart, Christopher. *Libertina Sine Conflictus* . . . 1752.

Smart, Christopher. *The Hilliad*. 1753.

Smart, Christopher. *Ode to . . . Earl of Northumberland . . . with Some Other Pieces*. 1764.

Smith, J. E. *A Selection of the Correspondence of Linnaeus, and Other Naturalists*. 1821.

Smith, J. E. *Memoir and Correspondence of the Late Sir James Edward Smith, M.D.* . . . 2 vols. 1832.

Sorrenson, Richard. "Towards a History of the Royal Society in the Eighteenth Century." *N&RRS* 50:1 (1996): 29–46.

Sorrenson, Richard. Special Issue of *The British Journal for the History of Science* 32:2 (1999).

Staffleu, F. A. *Linnaeus and the Linnaeans: The Spreading of Their ideas in Systematic Botany, 1735–1789*. Utrecht: Oosthoek, 1971.

Stafford, Barbara Maria. *Good Looking: Essays on the Virtue of Images*. Cambridge, MA: MIT Press, 2002.
Stannard, Jerry. *Herbs and Herbalism in the Middle Ages and Renaissance*. Aldershot: Ashgate, 1999.
Stearn, W. T. "Hill's *'The British Herbal'* (1756–1757)." *Taxon* 16 (1967): 194–98.
Stearns, Raymond P. *Science in the British Colonies of America*. Urbana: University of Illinois Press, 1970.
Stefani, Marta. *Corruzione e generazione: John T. Needham*. Florance: Leo S. Olschi, 2002.
[Sterne, Laurence]. *Letters of Laurence Sterne*. Edited by L. P. Curtis. Oxford: Clarendon Press, 1935.
Stevens, F. G., and M. D. George, eds. *Catalogue of Prints and Drawings in the British Museum. Division I. Political and Personal Satires. Vol. III (2 parts)*. 3 vols. Printed for the British Museum, 1954 [1870–1954].
Stevens, G. A. *The Birth-day of Folly, an Heroi-Comical Poem* . . . M. Cooper, 1755.
Stillingfleet, Benjamin. *Miscellaneous Tracts Relating to Natural History, Husbandry, and Physick*. . . . 1759.
Stirling, A. M. W. *The Ways of Yesterday: Being the Chronicles of the Way Family from 1307 to 1885*. T. Butterworth, 1930.
Stone, George W. *The London Stage: Part. 4. 1747–1776*. 3 vols. Carbondale: Southern Illinois University Press, 1968.
Straub, Kristina. *Domestic Affairs*. Baltimore: Johns Hopkins University, 2009.
Stuart, John. *Botanical Tables, Containing the Different Families of English Plants*. 1785.
[The] Student. 1750–1755.
Stukeley, William. *Itinerarium Curiosum . . . Antiquities and Remarkable Curiositys in Nature and Art* . . . 1724.
Stukeley, William. *Of the Gout*. Dublin, 1735.
Stukeley, William. *The Philosophy of Earthquakes, Natural and Religious*. 1750.
Stukeley, William. *The Family Memoirs*. Edited by W. C. Lukis. 3 vols. Surtees Society, vols. 73, 76, 80, 1880–83.
Stukeley, William. *The Commentarys, Diary, and Common-Place Book and Selected Letters of William Stukeley*. Doppler, 1980.
Summers, Judith. *The Empress of Pleasure: The Life and Adventures of Teresa Cornelys, Queen of Masquerades and Casanova's Lover*. Viking, 2003.
Talbot, Catherine. *The Works of the late Miss Catherine Talbot*. Rivington, 1819.
Taylor, George. "'The Just Delineation of the Passions': Theories of Acting on the Age of Garrick." In *Essays on the Eighteenth-Century English Stage*, edited by K. Richards and P. Thomson, 51–72. Methuen, 1972.
Taylor, John. *Records of My Life*. 2 vols. New York, 1833.
Teigen, P. M. "Dr. Hill and Gracy's 'Mopeing Owl.'" *American Notes and Queries Supplement* 1 (1978): 168–70.
Theorides, John. "Réaumur (1683–1757) et les insectes sociaux." *Janus* 48 (1959): 62–76.
Thomas, G. B. "John Hill and the *Construction of Timber*." *Proceedings of the Royal Microscopical Society* 3:4 (1968): 186–209.
Thomas, Keith. *Man and the Natural World: Changing Attitudes in England, 1500–1800*. Allen Lane, 1983.
Thompson, C. J. S. *The Quacks of Old London*. Brentano, 1928.
Thompson, George. *Against Tobacco-Smoking*, 1672.
Thornton, Bonnell. *The Actor: A Poetical Epistle*. 1760.
Thornton, Robert John. *A New Illustration of the Sexual System of Linnaeus*. T. Bensley, 1799. [Retitled in 1804 *The Temple of Flora*].
Thyer, Robert. [See Samuel Butler].
Tierney, James E. *The Correspondence of Robert Dodsley 1733–1764*. Cambridge: Cambridge University Press, 1988.
Torrubias, Jose. *Aparato para la Historia Natural Espanola*. Madrid, 1754.

Town and Country Magazine. 24 vols. 1769–1792.

Townsend, Francis. *Calendar of Knights . . . containing lists of Knights bachelors . . . from 1760 to the present time*. W. Pickering, 1828.

Toynbee, P., and L. Whibley, eds. *Correspondence of Thomas Gray*. 3 vols. Oxford: Clarendon Press, 1935.

Turner, Daniel. *The Modern Quacks*. 1718.

Turner, G. L'E. "Henry Baker, FRS, Founder of the Bakerian Lecture." *N&RRS* 29 (1975): 53–79.

Turner, G. L'E. *Essays on the History of the Microscope*. Oxford: Oxford University Press, 1981.

Venn, J. A. *Alumni Cantabrigiensis: Part One*. Cambridge: Cambridge University Press, 1922.

The Visitor. 1755–1756.

Walker, M. *Sir Edward James Smith, 1759–1828, First President of the Linnaean Society of London*. Linnaean Society of London, 1988.

Wanley, Nathaniel. *The Wonders of the Little World. . . .* 1678.

Warburton,William. *An Enquiry into the Nature and Origin of Literary Property*. 1762.

Warburton, William. *Letters from a Late Eminent Prelate to . . . one of his Friends* [Richard Hurd]. Kidderminster, 1809.

Warner, Marina. *Alone of All Her sex: The Myth and Cult of the Virgin Mary*. Vintage, 2000.

Watson, William. "An Account of a Treatise in Latin, intitled Caroli Linnaei . . ." *GM* 14 (December 1754): 555–58.

Watt, Ian. "Publishers and Sinners: The Augustan View." *Studies in Bibliography* 12 (1959): 3–20.

Weld, Charles. *A History of the Royal Society*. 2 vols. Parker, 1848.

West, S. "Polemic and Passions: Dr. James Parsons's *Human Physiognomy Explained* and Hogarth's Aspirations for British History Painting." *British Journal for Eighteenth-Century Studies*, 13 (1990): 73–89.

Wheatley, Henry B. *Round about Piccadilly and Pall Mall*. Smith, Elder and Co., 1870.

Wheatley, Henry B. *Hogarth's London*. Smith, Elder and Co., 1909.

Wheatley, Henry, and P. Cunningham. *London, Past and Present*. J. Murray, 1891.

Whitehead, P. J. P. "Emanuel Mendes da Costa (1717–1791) and the 'Conchology, or Natural History of Shells.'" *Bulletin of the British Museum (Natural History), Historical Series* 6 (1977): 1–24.

Wilkes, Benjamin. *One hundred and twenty copper-plates of English moths and butterflies, . . . and the plants, flowers, and fruits, whereon they feed*. 1773.

Wilkes, John. *The Political Controversy: or, Weekly Magazine of Ministerial and Anti-Ministerial Essays . . .* 1762.

Williamson, Raymond. "John Martyn and the *Grub Street Journal*." *Medical History* 5 (1961): 361–74.

Wimsatt, W. K. *Philosophic Words*. New Haven: Yale University Press, 1948.

Winter, Carl. "Francis Cotes." *The Connoisseur* 87–88 (1931): 1–15.

Winter, H. J. "Scientific Associations of the Spalding Gentleman's Society during the Period 1710–1750." *Archives Internationales d'histoire des Sciences* 3 (1950): 73–79.

Wollaston, William. *The Religion of Nature Delineated*. Dublin, 1726.

Woodruff, J. F. "Microscopy before the Nineteenth Century." *The American Naturalist* 73 (1942a): 485–516.

Woodruff, J. F. "The Versatile Sir John Hill, M.D." *The American Naturalist* 60 (1942b): 417–42.

Woodward, Henry. *A Letter from Henry Woodward, Comedian, the Meanest of all Characters; to Dr. John Hill, Inspector-General of Great Britain*. 1752.

Woodward, John. *Natural History of the Earth*. 1719.

Woodward, John. *The Art of Getting into Practice in Physick. . . .* 1722.

Woodward, John. *Fossils of All Kinds Digested into a Method*. 1728.

Woodward, John. *An Attempt Towards a Natural History of the Fossils of England*. 1729.

Wright, Janet. "Sir John Hill." *The Herbalist* 21 (1955): 33–38.

Wright, Thomas. *Caricature History of the Georges*. J. C. Hotten, 1867.

Wroth, Cecil. *The London Pleasure Gardens of the Eighteenth Century*. Macmillan, 1896.

Yogev, Gedalia. *Diamonds and Coral: Anglo-Dutch Jews and Eighteenth-Century Trade*. Leicester: Leicester University Press, 1978.

Index

About the Author

George Rousseau is a fellow of the Royal Historical Society and the recipient of honorary degrees honoris causa. He has been a professor at UCLA, Regius Professor at King's College Aberdeen, and codirector of the Centre for the History of Childhood at Oxford University, where he currently works. His books include (with Marjorie Hope Nicolson) *This Long Disease, My Life: Alexander Pope and the Sciences*; *The Languages of Psyche: Mind and Body in Enlightenment Thought*; a trilogy entitled *Pre- and Post-Modern Discourses: Medical, Scientific, Anthropological*; (with Roy Porter) *Gout: The Patrician Malady*; *Framing and Imagining Disease in Cultural History*; *Nervous Acts: Essays on Literature, Culture, and Sensibility*, and *Children and Sexuality: The Greeks to the Great War*. He is a cultural historian who works in the interface of literature and medicine, and emphasizes the relevance of imaginative materials—literature, especially diaries and biography, art and architecture, music—for the public understanding of medicine, past and present. His academic career was built on interdisciplinary scholarship, and from the 1970s he has participated in many national and international debates about its triumphs and failures.

Milton Keynes UK
Ingram Content Group UK Ltd.
UKHW020644040724
445115UK00006B/39

9 781611 461206